This is the first modern intellectual biography of the Scottish Covenanters' leading theorist Samuel Rutherford (c. 1600–1661). The central focus is on Rutherford's political thought and his major treatise, *Lex, Rex*, written in 1644 as a justification of the Covenanters' resistance to King Charles I. The book demonstrates that while *Lex, Rex* provided a careful synthesis of natural-law theory and biblical politics, Rutherford's Old Testament vision of a purged and covenanted nation ultimately subverted his commitment to the politics of natural reason.

This book also discusses a wide range of other topics, including scholasticism and humanism, Calvinist theology, Presbyterian ecclesiology, Rutherford's close relationships with women and his fervent spirituality. It will therefore be of considerable interest to a range of scholars and students working on Scottish and English history, Calvinism and Puritanism, and early modern political thought.

N 0184507 1

Cambridge Studies in Early Modern British History

POLITICS, RELIGION AND THE BRITISH REVOLUTIONS

Cambridge Studies in Early Modern British History

Series editors

ANTHONY FLETCHER
Professor of History, University of Essex

JOHN GUY
Professor of Modern History, University of St Andrews

and JOHN MORRILL
Reader in Early Modern History, University of Cambridge, and Vice-Master of Selwyn College

This is a series of monographs and studies covering many aspects of the history of the British Isles between the late fifteenth and the early eighteenth century. It includes the work of established scholars and pioneering work by a new generation of scholars. It includes both reviews and revisions of major topics and books, which open up new historical terrain or which reveal startling new perspectives on familiar subjects. All the volumes set detailed research into broader perspectives, and the books are intended for the use of students as well as of their teachers.

For a list of titles in the series, see end of book.

POLITICS, RELIGION AND THE BRITISH REVOLUTIONS

The mind of Samuel Rutherford

JOHN COFFEY

University of Cambridge

CAMBRIDGE
UNIVERSITY PRESS

PUBLISHED BY THE PRESS SYNDICATE OF THE UNIVERSITY OF CAMBRIDGE
The Pitt Building, Trumpington Street, Cambridge, United Kingdom

CAMBRIDGE UNIVERSITY PRESS
The Edinburgh Building, Cambridge CB2 2RU, UK
40 West 20th Street, New York NY 10011–4211, USA
477 Williamstown Road, Port Melbourne, VIC 3207, Australia
Ruiz de Alarcón 13, 28014 Madrid, Spain
Dock House, The Waterfront, Cape Town 8001, South Africa

http://www.cambridge.org

First published 1997
First paperback edition 2002

Typeface Sabon 10/12 pt.

A catalogue record for this book is available from the British Library

Library of Congress Cataloguing in Publication data
Politics, religion, and the British revolutions: the mind of Samuel Rutherford / John Coffey.
p.   cm. – (Cambridge studies in early modern British history)
includes bibliographical references.
ISBN 0 521 58172 9
1. Rutherford, Samuel, 1600?–1661.   2. Presbyterian Church – Scotland – Clergy –
Biography.   I. Title.   II. Series.
BX9225.R94C64   1997
285′092–dc20   96-43925   CIP
[B]

ISBN 0 521 58172 9 hardback
ISBN 0 521 89319 4 paperback

For my parents

CONTENTS

ACKNOWLEDGEMENTS

This book could not have been researched and written without the assistance and encouragement of many people, and it is my pleasure to take this opportunity to acknowledge their help.

I should begin by expressing my thanks to the Scottish Education Department, whose financial support made this research possible, and to the Master and Fellows of Churchill College, Cambridge, who not only provided an ideal environment for my work but also enabled me to complete the book by electing me to a junior research fellowship.

The research on which the book is based was mainly carried out in the Cambridge University Library, and I owe a considerable debt to the staff there – particularly to those in the Rare Books room – for their continual helpfulness and efficiency. In addition, the staff of St Andrews University Library, Edinburgh University Library, the National Library of Scotland, New College Library, and the Hornel Library in Kirkcudbright patiently answered my queries concerning Rutherford and guided me to relevant books and manuscripts.

The idea of researching Rutherford was first suggested to me by Eugenio Biagini, and I am deeply indebted to him for pointing me towards a subject who opened up many areas of seventeenth-century life and thought. Other scholars provided valuable advice along the way. I was very fortunate to have another Rutherford scholar nearby at Gonville and Caius College; John Ford's essays on Covenanter thought have been a stimulating influence on my own work, and his careful and detailed comments on my drafts forced me to think more clearly about my ideas. John Morrill and Roger Mason, the examiners of my doctoral dissertation, offered many useful suggestions on the work as a whole, as did Conal Condren and James Burns. For comments and corrections on theological topics I am grateful to David Como, Mark Dever, Sean Hughes and Jonathan Moore, whilst for stimulating correspondence or conversations I should also thank Keith Brown, Michael Lynch and Allan MacInnes.

Without doubt, however, my greatest intellectual debt is to Mark Goldie.

As my undergraduate Director of Studies and supervisor in the history of political thought, he sparked my interest in intellectual history, and encouraged me to think about research. As a Ph.D. supervisor he was constantly encouraging, ever available to dispense advice and books, and marvellously efficient in providing thoughtful comment on each chapter as it was written. Whatever merits this book possesses inevitably owe much to his teaching and example. The faults and shortcomings that remain are entirely my own responsibility.

Many friends have helped to make life enjoyable over the past few years. In particular, Joong-Lak and Eun-Jung Kim have displayed generous Korean hospitality on numerous occasions, and my parents have shown constant care and concern, providing help whenever it was needed. My father's decision in 1975 to leave the Presbyterian ministry and become a Baptist has undoubtedly shaped the perspective from which this book is written, and I can only hope that my Presbyterian friends do not find this Baptist life of Rutherford too unsympathetic.

Finally, I wish to thank Cate, whom I met at the outset of my research, and who has put up with Rutherford and me ever since with unfailing good humour and commonsense. Without her intelligence, affection, spirituality and good looks this book would have been much harder to write.

ABBREVIATIONS

Christ Dying *Christ Dying and Drawing Sinners to Himself* (1647)
Communion Sermons *Fourteen Communion Sermons by Rev. Samuel Rutherford,* ed. A. Bonar (1877)
Covenant of Life *The Covenant of Life Opened* (1655)
Divine Right *The Divine Right of Church Government and Excommunication* (1646)
Due Right *The Due Right of Presbyteries* (1644)
Free Disputation *A Free Disputation Against Pretended Liberty of Conscience* (1649)
Influences *Influences of the Life of Grace* (1659)
Letters *The Letters of Samuel Rutherford,* ed. A. Bonar (1891 edition)
Lex, Rex *Lex, Rex, or the Law and the Prince* (1644)
Peaceable Plea *A Peaceable Plea for Paul's Presbyterie* (1642)
Quaint Sermons *Quaint Sermons of Samuel Rutherford,* ed. A. Bonar (1885)
Sermon to Commons *A Sermon preached before the honourable House of Commons* (1644)
Sermon to Lords *A Sermon preached before the honourable House of Lords* (1645)
Survey of Antichrist *A Survey of Spiritual Antichrist* (1648)
Survey of Hooker *A Survey of the Survey of that Summe of Church Discipline penned by Mr Thomas Hooker* (1658)
Testimony *A Testimony to the Work of Reformation in Britaine and Ireland* (1719)
Tryal *The Tryal and Triumph of Faith* (1645; quotations in text from 1845 edition)

—————————————————— ⫸ 1 ⫷ ——————————————————

Introduction

On a hilltop above the tiny hamlet of Anwoth in south-west Scotland there stands a fifty-six foot granite obelisk. Erected in the mid-nineteenth century, its inscription praises the parish's former minister, the Covenanter Samuel Rutherford, for his 'distinguished public labours in the cause of civil and religious liberty'.[1] Its presence is indicative of Rutherford's posthumous fame, a fame which rested above all on his political treatise *Lex, Rex*, and on his pious *Letters*. Rutherford was lionised by Victorian Evangelicals as a towering defender of constitutional freedoms and as one of the greatest devotional writers in the history of the church. His *Letters* passed through approximately one hundred editions (including at least twenty in foreign languages), formed the basis for a popular hymn, turned Anwoth into a place of pilgrimage, and made Rutherford the subject of numerous popular essays and biographies. Even in the 1980s, his *Letters* were still in print, and *Lex, Rex* was being cited by the religious right in the United States as an important influence on the US Constitution and a powerful justification for civil disobedience to liberal abortion laws. One American admirer – as unaware as the obelisk-builders of Rutherford's support for persecution – went so far as to establish an international 'Rutherford Institute' to protect religious freedom.

However, Rutherford's Evangelical admirers were not the only ones to stress his historical significance. Historians have also acknowledged his status as 'the Scottish Revolution's most distinguished theorist'.[2] According to W. H. Makey, Rutherford understood better than any of his contemporaries the nature of the revolutionary process; he knew exactly where he was going and why he failed.[3] The book he wrote to justify the Covenanting

[1] See the description in F. H. Groome, ed., *Ordnance Gazetteer of Scotland*, 6 vols. (London, 1894–5), I, pp. 1–10.

[2] A. Williamson, 'The Jewish dimension of the Scottish apocalypse: climate, covenant and world renewal', in Y. Kaplan, H. Mechoulan and R. H. Popkin, eds., *Menasseh Ben Israel and his World* (Leiden, 1989), p. 25. Michael Lynch describes Rutherford as 'the leading theoretician of the Covenanting kirk', *A New History of Scotland* (London, 1991), p. 251.

[3] W. H. Makey, *The Church of the Covenant* (Edinburgh, 1979), p. 91.

1

revolution, *Lex, Rex* (1644), has been called 'the most influential Scottish work on political theory',[4] and 'the classic statement' of Covenanter political thought.[5] His *Free Disputation Against Pretended Liberty of Conscience* (1649), has been described by Owen Chadwick as 'the ablest defence of persecution in the seventeenth century'.[6] In addition, Rutherford was undoubtedly one of the most prominent defenders of Presbyterianism in his day, and a Calvinist theologian with an international readership.[7]

Yet for all this, there has been no modern intellectual biography of Rutherford. This book therefore seeks to provide the first comprehensive study of his life and thought. The Introduction sets the scene by surveying Rutherford's changing reputation from his own lifetime to the present day. It shows how his admirers have focused selectively on particular aspects of his works and missed the whole picture. It also explains why Rutherford and other Scottish Presbyterians have been neglected by academic historians and argues that the time is ripe for a reassessment of their religion and politics.

THE REPUTATIONS OF RUTHERFORD

Rutherford's reputation in his own lifetime

The only surviving portrait of Samuel Rutherford was probably painted while he was at the Westminster Assembly, by the artist Robert Walker.[8] Rutherford is shown in skull cap, gown and clerical bands, his hair tumbling down over his gown in thick curls, his face plump, his features prominent, and his gaze intense but enigmatic. From the early eighteenth-century Presbyterian historian Robert Wodrow we know that Rutherford was 'a little fair man', with 'two quick eyes'. Whether walking or preaching, it was observed that 'he held ay his face upward and heavenward'.[9]

---

[4] D. Stevenson, *Revolution and Counter-Revolution in Scotland, 1644–51* (London, 1977), p. 235.
[5] J. Robertson, *The Scottish Enlightenment and the Militia Issue* (Edinburgh, 1985), p. 57n.
[6] O. Chadwick, *The Reformation* (Harmondsworth, 1964), p. 403.
[7] On his preeminence among the conservative Reformed theologians of Scotland see J. Walker, *The Theology and Theologians of Scotland, 1560–1750* (Edinburgh, 1982 edn), p. 8, and M. C. Bell, *Calvin and Scottish Theology: The Doctrine of Assurance* (Edinburgh, 1985), p. 70.
[8] Robert Gilmour, one of Rutherford's biographers, owned this portrait and describes its history. Apparently it was once owned by a Roman Catholic priest who gave it to a Presbyterian friend after explaining, 'That is the arch-heretic, Samuel Rutherford'. Gilmour thought that Rutherford resembled his mother and her sister, who were rumoured to be descended from a close relative of Rutherford! See *Samuel Rutherford: A Study* (London, 1904), pp. 233–5. The portrait now hangs in St Marys College, St Andrews University, the college where Rutherford was principal.
[9] R. Wodrow, *Analecta, or Materials for a History of Remarkable Providences*, 4 vols. (Edinburgh, 1842–43), II, p. 4; III, pp. 88–9.

We know too that Rutherford was a deeply emotional man, given to fits of depression and moments of ecstatic exaltation. As will become apparent, his friendships – particularly with his female parishioners – were intense, and throughout his life he seems to have struggled with lust. Yet his warmth and energy earned him great respect and love among the godly. Friends and allies were quick to point out that Rutherford 'shined in humility, and thought alwayes meanly of himself and highly of other ministers'. He insisted on calling his friend and colleague, Robert Blair, 'Sir' rather than 'Brother'.[10] He was, moreover, 'extremly, and almost excessively, charitable',[11] especially to the poor.[12]

To those who opposed him, however, Rutherford could turn another face. Wodrow tells us that he was 'naturally hote and fiery'.[13] In a debate with other ministers in the 1650s, he fell on one 'like a falcon', 'with a great warmth, and abused him pretty severely',[14] and on another occasion when a drawing of lots fell out badly he was described as 'extremely stormy'.[15] Wodrow records the Marquis of Argyll as saying that Rutherford 'was a good man, but soon sadled [encumbered], because of his acrimoniouse writing'.[16] Those at the sharp end of Rutherford's bitter attacks failed to see any goodness in him at all. The royalist Sir James Balfour described him as 'a hatter of all men not of his opinion, and one quho if never so lightlie offendit, unreconciliable; voyd of mercy and charity, although a teacher of both to others'.[17]

To the wider reading public who never met him in person, Rutherford was known above all as a controversialist. He wrote for an international audience and commanded international attention. Of the sixteen works published during his lifetime, twelve were printed in London, only three in Edinburgh.[18] His first published work, *Exercitationes pro Divina Gratia* (1636) was printed in the Netherlands, as were his *Letters* (1664), and a book compiled from his lecture notes, *Examen Arminianismi* (1668). The Latin treatises against Arminianism earned him invitations to professorships at Dutch universities in 1649 and 1651, but some Reformed theologians, like John Owen and Richard Baxter, felt that he had taken the orthodox

---

[10] Wodrow, *Analecta*, III, p. 90.   [11] Wodrow, *Analecta*, II, p. 147.
[12] Wodrow, *Analecta*, III, p. 89. Rutherford left some money for the use of the poor of St Andrews in his will. See T. Murray, *Life of Rutherford* (Edinburgh, 1828), p. 360.
[13] Wodrow, *Analecta*, II, p. 147.   [14] Wodrow, *Analecta*, II, p. 118.
[15] Wodrow, *Analecta*, I, p. 140.   [16] Wodrow, *Analecta*, I, p. 166.
[17] James Balfour, *The Annales of Scotland*, III (London, 1825), p. 413.
[18] Of these three, only one can be said to have a specifically Scottish audience in mind: *The Last and Heavenly Speeches of Viscount Kenmuir* (1649) told the cautionary and edifying tale of Rutherford's noble patron, who had for a while deserted the radical Presbyterian cause only to be reconciled to it, and to God on his deathbed. Rutherford probably hoped that it would persuade recalcitrant nobles to give their full backing to the kirk party regime established in 1649.

stress on divine sovereignty a step too far.[19] Others believed that his attacks on Antinomianism in his English books introduced too strong an element of moralism into Reformed theology.[20]

However, Rutherford's ecclesiological treatises seemed to have aroused more controversy than his theology, particularly amongst the New England Puritans who had to defend their Congregationalism against the charge that it lay at the root of the sectarian anarchy of 1640s England. John Cotton, their foremost spokesman, took it upon himself to reply to Rutherford twice, in *The Way of the Congregational Churches Cleared* (1647), and *The Holinesse of Church Members* (1648). Thomas Hooker's Congregationalist classic, the *Survey of the Summe of Church Discipline* (1648), was also written in response to *The Due Right of Presbyteries*.[21] In England, too, Rutherford was famed as a champion of Scottish Presbyterianism and a scourge of the sects. His speeches in the Westminster Assembly, and the ecclesiological works he wrote whilst in London, provoked John Milton to name him among the 'New Forcers of Conscience under the Long Parliament'.[22]

However, Rutherford's polemical works attracted admirers as well as critics. As we shall see in Chapter 6, his anti-absolutist polemic, *Lex, Rex* (1644), was republished under different titles in 1648 and 1657, and may have influenced John Milton and John Lilburne. In addition, his ecclesiological works, his attacks on the sects, and his defences of orthodox Reformed theology were gratefully received by many conservative divines in Scotland, England and overseas.[23]

Besides being renowned for his polemics, Rutherford was also famed for his sermons. Robert Wodrow preserved the testimony of an English merchant who went to Scotland and was moved by the power of Rutherford's preaching, which 'shewed me the lovelyness of Christ'. 'The Englishman', Wodrow assured his Scottish readers, 'became an excellent

---

[19] See J. Owen, *A Dissertation on Divine Justice*, in *Works*, ed. W. H. Goold, X (London, 1967 edn), ch. 17; R. Baxter, *Catholick Theologie* (London, 1675), pp. 106–14. The works by Hagen and Strang, listed in the bibliography, also express similar concerns.

[20] See R. Towne, *A Reassertion of Grace . . . in a reply to Mr Rutherford's "Tryall and Triumph of Faith"* (1654).

[21] On the ecclesiology of the New England Puritans see P. Miller, *The New England Mind: From Colony to Province* (2nd edn: Cambridge, Mass., 1967). On the specific case of Rutherford's long-running debate with Thomas Hooker, see S. Bush, *The Writings of Thomas Hooker* (London, 1980), pp. 109ff.

[22] *John Milton*, ed. S. Orgel and J. Goldberg (Oxford, 1990), pp. 83–4.

[23] For example, the eighteenth-century New England revivalist and philosopher, Jonathan Edwards, recommended the *Survey of Spiritual Antichrist* in his classic work on *The Religious Affections*, ed. J. E. Smith (New Haven, 1959), pp. 72, 287. For further positive references to Rutherford's theological and ecclesiological treatises, see the *Calendar of the Correspondence of Richard Baxter*, ed. N. H. Keeble and G. Nuttall, 2 vols. (Oxford, 1991), I: 140; II: 17, 114.

Christian'.[24] Many thousands, mostly in Scotland, also heard Rutherford in person, and were similarly stirred by the passion of his preaching. Others encountered Rutherford the preacher through the printed page, particularly through two volumes of his sermons which were published in the 1640s.[25] These were not only read in Scotland; we know that both Isaac Newton and Richard Baxter owned one of these books, *The Tryal and Triumph of Faith* (1645),[26] and that Mary, Countess of Warwick, was an avid reader of Rutherford's devotional works.[27]

In contrast to his sermons, Rutherford's letters were not published in his lifetime. However, the contemporary historian John Row recorded that 'sundrie begouth to gather them together, and have whole books full of them',[28] and in 1652, Johnston of Wariston wrote in his diary: 'I found much lyfe and love in M. S[amuel] R[utherford's] lettres, written when he was banished to Aberdeen.'[29] Yet according to his earliest biographer, Robert McWard, Rutherford 'did not at all intend' the letters 'for publicke use', and 'did violence to the desires of many in refusing to publish them'.[30] Ironically, the letters were first published by McWard himself in 1664 and were to attract a far greater readership than did the rest of Rutherford's works put together.

Rutherford and the British Evangelical tradition

In the light of Rutherford's own reluctance to publish his letters, it is ironic that his posthumous reputation has rested upon them almost entirely, whilst the works he published in his lifetime have suffered almost complete neglect. Rutherford the controversialist was forgotten; Rutherford the Evangelical mystic remained. Since their original publication in 1664, the *Letters* have

---

[24] Wodrow, *Analecta*, III, p. 3.

[25] *The Tryal and Triumph of Faith* (1645) comprised sermons on the story of the Syro-Phoenician woman told in the Synoptic Gospels, and *Christ Dying and Drawing Sinners to Himself* (1647) was a book of 600 pages on John 12: 27–33.

[26] See J. Harrison, *The Library of Isaac Newton* (Cambridge, 1978), p. 230; G. Nuttall, 'A Transcript of Richard Baxter's Library Catalogue', *Journal of Ecclesiastical History*, 3 (1952), p. 80.

[27] See W. Lamont, 'The two "national churches" of 1691 and 1829', in A. Fletcher and P. Roberts, eds., *Religion, Culture and Society in Early Modern Britain: Essays in Honour of Patrick Collinson* (Cambridge, 1994), p. 342. The accounts of spiritual experiences recorded in her diary are almost identical to passages from Rutherford's letters: she wrote that a communion service 'set my heart a panting and breathing after Christ, longing to embrace him in the armes of my faith. I did there enjoy such sweet and ravishing communion with God.'

[28] J. Row, *The History of the Kirk of Scotland, From the Year 1558 to 1637* (Edinburgh, 1842), pp. 396–7. A book of seventeenth-century copies of Rutherford's *Letters* survives in St Andrew's University Library.

[29] Wariston, *Diary*, II, ed. D. H. Fleming (Edinburgh, 1919), p. 167.

[30] Robert McWard, preface to *Joshua Redivivus, or Mr Rutherfoords Letters* (1664).

been republished no fewer than eighty times in English in many editions, the fullest being that of Andrew Bonar which contains 365 letters and is still in print. They were also translated into Dutch in 1673, and there are at least fifteen editions in that language. In addition, they have appeared in German, French and Gaelic.[31]

For generations a copy of Rutherford's *Letters* was a cherished possession in the homes of Scottish peasants; the bibliographer Watt claimed that the *Letters* were particularly popular 'among the lower classes of Scotland'.[32] Images from them were woven into a hymn that has been sung by millions, 'The Sands of Time are Sinking'. They attained the status of a spiritual classic. Richard Baxter was said to have declared that he disagreed with Rutherford on several issues, 'But for that book of letters, hold off the Bible, such a book the world never saw the like!'[33] The great Victorian Baptist, C. H. Spurgeon, wrote: 'When we are dead and gone let the world know that Spurgeon held Rutherford's *Letters* to be the nearest thing to inspiration which can be found in all the writings of mere men'.[34] The Yorkshireman, Hudson Taylor, who founded the largest Protestant missionary society in China, often meditated on the *Letters*, and wrote a widely read devotional study of the Song of Songs with the very Rutherfordian title, *Union and Communion*.[35]

In sharp contrast to the *Letters* and sermons, however, Rutherford's controversial works lay buried in their seventeenth-century editions. None of the three Latin treatises on which his contemporary theological reputation rested have been republished or translated into English. Moreover, none of his polemical works in English have been republished, with the notable exception of *Lex, Rex*. Apart from *Lex, Rex*, the only works of Rutherford published in his own lifetime and later reprinted after his death are his sermons, the *Last and Heavenly Speeches*, *The Tryal and Triumph of Faith*, and *Christ Dying*, all of which can be read as inspirational rather than controversial works.

When we consider the writings of Rutherford that were first published after his death, our picture of his posthumous reputation becomes even clearer. An edition of 284 letters came first, published in Rotterdam in 1664 by Rutherford's secretary. Then in the early eighteenth century a number of

---

[31] A list of the many editions of the *Letters* is to be found in the bibliography.

[32] R. Watt, *Bibliotheca Brittanica, or a General Index to British and Foreign Literature*, II (Edinburgh, 1824), p. 823. See also G. Robertson, *Rural Recollections* (Irvine, 1829), p. 98.

[33] Wodrow, *Analecta*, III, p. 89. In his *Christian Directory* (London, 1673), p. 922, Baxter recommended that 'Mr Rutherfords letters' should be in 'the poorest or smallest library that is tolerable'.

[34] C. H. Spurgeon in *The Sword and the Trowel*, June 1891.

[35] H. Taylor and G. Taylor, *Hudson Taylor and the China Inland Mission: The Growth of a Work of God* (1918), p. 163.

his sermons were printed from the notes of hearers. These continued to be reprinted throughout the nineteenth century and were finally gathered together by Andrew Bonar in the *Communion Sermons* (1877) and *Quaint Sermons* (1885). Apart from the sermons and letters only three more Rutherford works were published posthumously; a catechism, *A Testimony to the Work of Reformation in Britaine and Ireland*, and *Examen Arminianismi*, a treatise drawn from his lectures to students at St Andrews.

The publishing history of Rutherford's writings and sermons reveals much about the history of British Protestantism. The ultimate failure of the Puritan revolution combined with the success of the Glorious Revolution to make Evangelical Protestantism more other-worldly and pietistic. The Evangelical revival of the eighteenth century under Wesley and Whitefield probably strengthened this tendency, and severely undermined cerebral Reformed scholasticism. The result was that Rutherford was appropriated by a quietist tradition that chose to ignore his polemical works but found his devotional writings of great value for the inner life of the soul. John Wesley himself included a selection of the letters in volume 28 of his *Christian Library* (1753). 'These letters', he commented, 'have been generally admired by all the children of God for the vein of piety, trust in God and holy zeal which runs through them'.[36] Arminian Evangelicals had no difficulty in extracting the gold of Rutherford's piety and leaving behind the dross of his scholastic predestinarianism.[37]

This neutering of Rutherford necessarily involved a certain amount of hagiographical romanticisation. This began soon after his death, probably even within his own lifetime. Wodrow tells the story of how as a boy of four Rutherford fell down a well 'several fathoms deep'. His sister ran to fetch her parents and when they returned they found young Samuel safe and well sitting on the grass, claiming that a 'bonny young man' had rescued him. According to Wodrow, Rutherford's parents 'concluded it was noe doubt ane angell'.[38] Later biographers were to retell the story of the well and make much of the romance of 'Fair Anwoth by the Solway'.[39] Rutherford became 'the small fair-haired letter-writer from Anwoth who showed . . . the loveliness of Christ'.[40] Anwoth became a place of pilgrimage for Scots and Ulster Protestants who came to see the place where the 'good pastor', the

---

[36] Quoted in F. Cook, *Samuel Rutherford and his Friends* (Edinburgh, 1992), p. 144.
[37] On Wesley's *Christian Library* and his selective use of the Puritans, see R. C. Monk, *John Wesley: His Puritan Heritage* (London, 1966).
[38] Wodrow, *Analecta*, I, p. 57. The story echoes those of two young boys in the Bible: Samuel and Jesus both showed themselves to be unusually sensitive to God when they were in the temple at an early age.
[39] Gilmour, *Samuel Rutherford*. The phrase is the title of ch. 4.
[40] Cook, *Samuel Rutherford and His Friends*, p. 147.

'Saint of the Covenant', had ministered. In the 1820s, the man who was to lead the Free Church Disruption, Thomas Chalmers, recorded that the masons who were told to demolish the manse in which Rutherford had once lived refused to do so because it would be 'an act of sacrilege'; Chalmers himself 'mourned over the rubbish of the foundation'.[41] A Roman Catholic historian noted ironically that 'men who would have shuddered at the idea of revering the relics of a catholic saint . . . have lain all night long on [Rutherford's] grave in the cold kirkyard of St Andrews, seeking inspiration from nearness to his sacred ashes'.[42] Although there may be a touch of hyperbole to this, we do know that when the Scottish theologian, Thomas Halyburton, lay on his deathbed at St Andrews in 1712, he had Rutherford's *Letters* read to him, spoke in phrases drawn directly from Rutherford, and rejoiced in the knowledge that he would be buried beside his great predecessor.[43]

A. T. Innes, in a short but perceptive essay, tried to understand why Rutherford was treated in this way by his later admirers. Innes believed that there were two men in Rutherford, the schoolman and the mystic, 'St. Thomas and St. Francis under one hood'. His logic was 'masculine and agressive rather than feminine and conservative', whilst his *Letters* revealed his 'somewhat feminine nature'. Innes recounted a story first recorded by Wodrow of how Rutherford, preaching on the dissensions of the time, was suddenly caught up with speaking about Christ alone. A bystander whispered, 'Ay, now you are right – hold you there!' 'And undoubtedly', Innes concludes, 'that has been the verdict of posterity'.[44] Eighteenth- and nineteenth-century Evangelicals, repelled by what they saw as the aridity of Rutherford's argumentation and disturbed by his uncharitable acrimony, often chose to pretend that they did not exist. The Rutherford *oeuvre* seemed to them 'a harsh and astringent cup, with a lump of sugar at the bottom'.[45] Believing in the religion of the heart they focused almost entirely on Rutherford the pastor, preacher and correspondent. Devout Protestants, seeing the home as a haven from the evils of the world, found in the private, homely, 'feminine' Rutherford, someone they understood.[46]

---

[41] *Memoirs of Thomas Chalmers*, ed. W. Hanna, III (Edinburgh, 1851), p. 130.
[42] M. G. J. Kinloch, *Studies in Scottish Ecclesiastical History* (London, 1898), p. 192.
[43] *Memoirs of the Life of the Reverend, Learned and Pious Mr Thomas Halyburton* (Edinburgh, 1733), pp. 170–228.
[44] A. T. Innes, 'Samuel Rutherford', *Studies in Scottish History, Chiefly Ecclesiastical* (London, 1892), p. 48.
[45] Innes, 'Samuel Rutherford', p. 50.
[46] S. Sizar, *Gospel Hymns and Social Religion* (Philadelphia, 1978), argues, from her analysis of Victorian Evangelical hymns, that the home, the woman's sphere, was portrayed as a haven from the stormy public world of the man.

Nearly all of Rutherford's biographers belong to this tradition. One of them, Alexander Whyte, the greatest preacher in late Victorian Scotland and an ardent admirer of Rutherford's piety, had no problems including this Reformed scholastic among the mystics, along with the Quaker, George Fox. He went so far as to make the *Theologica Germanica*, a book which Rutherford had castigated, the textbook for a course he gave on mysticism.[47] Robert Gilmour also declared that although Rutherford's scholastic works were 'a weariness to the flesh of even the most inveterate reader' and 'as good as dead' for modern people, his book of letters 'rank in the literature of the soul with the masterpieces of Augustine, Kempis, Taylor, Bunyan, Keble, and Martineau'.[48]

The Evangelicals who viewed Rutherford through pietistic spectacles also judged him from the standpoint of political liberalism. Nineteenth-century Evangelicalism was much more deeply imbued with liberal humanitarianism than was seventeenth-century Puritanism.[49] Consequently, Rutherford's Victorian biographers, whilst praising his piety and spirituality, felt an obligation to rebuke him for his intolerance. Grosart, an English Nonconformist, believed that the very title of Rutherford's *Free Disputation against Pretended Liberty of Conscience* was 'an offence and an opprobrium'. The real heroes of the seventeenth century were the 'elect few' who asserted the doctrine of freedom of conscience – Cromwell, Milton and the English Independents.[50]

For Scottish writers this was rather a bitter pill to swallow, for though as good Scots they wished to find a long liberal tradition in their country, as good Whigs they had to admit that there had been embarrassingly few Presbyterian advocates of toleration and freedom of conscience. Innes lamented the fact that because of Milton, 'Rutherford rhymes for ever to the

---

[47] G. F. Barbour, *The Life of Alexander Whyte* (London, 1923), pp. 648–9. Rutherford has found himself anthologised with equally bad company on many occasions. See M. W. Tileston, *Daily Strength for Daily Needs* (Boston, 1920), and P. Toon, *Spiritual Companions: An Introduction to the Christian Classics* (London, 1990), in both of which Rutherford shares a place of honour alongside Johannes Tauler and the author of *Theologica Germanica*, mystics whom he attacked in his *Survey of Spiritual Antichrist*.

[48] Gilmour, *Samuel Rutherford*, pp. 12, 15. The traditional pietist view of Rutherford is still found today; some of his letters have recently been put into verse by a minister's wife. See F. Cook, *Grace in Winter: Rutherford in Verse* (Edinburgh, 1989), and *Samuel Rutherford and his Friends*.

[49] Indeed, Joseph Altholz has argued that Evangelicalism fostered a humanitarianism which later undermined orthodox religion by raising questions concerning the morality of the traditional doctrines of hell and the atonement. See his 'The warfare of conscience with theology', in G. Parsons, ed., *Religion in Victorian Britain, IV: Interpretations* (Manchester, 1988), pp. 156–8.

[50] A. B. Grosart, *Representative Nonconformists* (London, 1874), p. 203.

civil sword'.[51] But he had to acknowledge that Milton was right, and that the Covenanters were mistaken in trying to persuade parliament to impose true religion on the whole of Britain. What could be said in their defence was that they were simply children of their times, and that we in our more enlightened age should remember this before criticising them too heavily.[52]

However, the Presbyterian Whigs of Scotland were not prepared to stop with a weak apology for their national religious heritage; instead they set out to offer a Whiggish interpretation of the Covenanting movement. In order to sustain this interpretation they stressed the post-Restoration period during which the Covenanters were persecuted, rather than the period of the 1640s when they wielded oppressive power. Covenanter opposition to royal absolutism and Erastianism was emphasised, and their desire for rigid theocracy conveniently overlooked. With the aid of such selective vision, it was possible to assert that the Scotsmen of the seventeenth century 'planted the roots of our liberties',[53] and maintain that Rutherford should be extolled as a hero in the Whig history of liberty. This was because he had written *Lex, Rex*, a book which Innes claimed had become 'the constitutional inheritance of all countries in modern times'.[54] Another biographer, Andrew Thomson, described the book as 'one of the most valuable contributions to political science, a help to human progress', and claimed that 'the bringing over of William of Orange was the living embodiment of the principle of *Lex, Rex*'.[55] Given that he had also been a staunch defender of the freedom of the church from state intervention, Rutherford could be portrayed as something of a liberal. Hence the inscription on the Anwoth monument lauding him for his 'distinguished public labours in the cause of civil and religious liberty'.

In the twentieth century, in an increasingly secular climate, Rutherford has lost his great nineteenth-century reputation. However, interest in him has not died. Nineteenth-century editions of his devotional works have recently been reprinted by small Reformed publishers for a popular

[51] Innes, 'Samuel Rutherford', p. 48. In his 'On the New Forcers of Conscience Under the Long Parliament', Milton had written:

> Dare ye for this abjure the civil sword
> To force our consciences that Christ set free
> And ride us with a classic hierarchy
> Taught ye by mere A. S. and Rutherford.

[52] A. Thomson, *The Life of Samuel Rutherford* (Edinburgh, 1884), p. 112.
[53] Innes, 'Samuel Rutherford', p. 53. G. D. Henderson claimed that the spirit of the Covenanters was 'the spirit of individualism and liberalism', a spirit which finally produced the Revolution settlement of 1688–9, *Religious Life in Seventeenth-Century Scotland* (Cambridge, 1937), p. 189.
[54] Innes, 'Samuel Rutherford', p. 5.
[55] Thomson, *Samuel Rutherford*, p. 119. See also Gilmour, *Samuel Rutherford*, p. 169.

readership,[56] and in 1983 a group of Evangelicals in the Church of Scotland founded Rutherford House, a research and publishing centre intended to foster the scholarly defence and promotion of orthodox Christianity. The House is both a residential library and a publisher of journals, theological monographs and the recent *Dictionary of Scottish Church History and Theology*. Rutherford appealed to its founders not as a devotional writer, but as a major Scottish defender of Reformed theology,[57] and this in itself reflects a growing dissatisfaction with pietism among conservative Evangelicals and a new desire to tap into the intellectual resources of the Reformed tradition.

Rutherford and the American Christian Right

Meanwhile, in the United States, there has been a revival of interest in Rutherford's political thought. It has coincided with the rise of the Christian Right, and the emergence of the fundamentalist movement from its subcultural ghetto into the mainstream of American politics. Feeling threatened by what they see as an increasingly corrupt world, fundamentalists have turned their backs on their traditional sectarian quietism, and have decided to raise their voices in the public arena, in the hope that they can get the world to leave them alone, or (better still) re-Christianise American society. Those who write about Rutherford in the USA exemplify both of these approaches; at one moment they see Rutherford as a liberal and call for the state to leave the church alone, while at another they claim him as a theocrat and dream of a godly nation. Their double-mindedness reflects a deep ambivalence among American fundamentalists, who feel attracted both to liberal values like voluntarism, individualism and the free market, and to the Puritan vision of a land ordered according to the laws of God.[58] Rutherford is a particularly appealing figure to these religious conservatives because he can be cited as an example of an orthodox, eminently pious Protestant who was also deeply political.

The man responsible for this Rutherford revival was Francis Schaeffer,

---

[56] *Letters of Samuel Rutherford* (Edinburgh: Banner of Truth Trust, 1984 [1891]); *The Tryal and Triumph of Faith* (Keyser, West Va.: Odom Publications, n.d. [1845]); *Communion Sermons* (Edinburgh: James A. Dickson, 1986 [1877]). In addition, a new edition of *The Power and Prevalency of Prayer* has been published as *The Power of Faith and Prayer* (Stornoway: Reformation Press, 1991).

[57] See the article on Rutherford House in the N. Cameron, ed., *Dictionary of Scottish Church History and Theology* (Edinburgh, 1993), pp. 734–5.

[58] See S. Bruce, *A House Divided : Protestantism, Schism and Secularisation* (London, 1990), ch. 8, and J. Garvey, 'Fundamentalism and American law', in M. Marty and R. S. Appleby, eds., *Fundamentalisms and the State: Remaking Polities, Economies, and Militance* (Chicago, 1993), ch. 3.

once described by *Newsweek* as 'the guru of fundamentalism'.[59] In *A Christian Manifesto* (1981), which he dedicated to Rutherford, Schaeffer claimed that 'Locke took Rutherford's *Lex, Rex* and secularised it', and that the ideas of *Lex, Rex* influenced the Founding Fathers through the Scottish minister John Witherspoon, who 'knew and stood consciously in the stream of Samuel Rutherford'.[60] Schaeffer had two purposes in resurrecting Rutherford. First, he wished to bolster the idea of a 'Christian America', showing that America had been built on a Christian base, which it was now in the process of betraying. Battling against 'secular humanists' and embarrassed by the obvious heterodoxy of the Founding Fathers, he was anxious to demonstrate the Christian roots of American liberties, and so justify his call for a return to them. However, Schaeffer's second purpose was to provide a justification for Christian civil disobedience. His book, *Whatever Happened to the Human Race* (1979), had converted large numbers of Evangelicals into fierce opponents of America's liberal abortion laws, but the pietistic conservatism of American fundamentalists led them to regard lawbreaking with the greatest horror. Schaeffer used Rutherford to argue that if a civil law conflicts with God's law, Christians have a right, indeed a duty, to disobey the government.

The impact of Schaeffer's arguments has been considerable. The 1843 edition of *Lex, Rex* was soon republished by a small Reformed press in Virginia, and Schaeffer's grand claims for Rutherford's historical importance were frequently recycled in the literature of the Christian Right, even after they had been thoroughly debunked by Evangelical academics.[61] Randall Terry – the founder of the anti-abortion protest movement, Operation Rescue – told the American political commentator, Garry Wills, 'You have to read Schaeffer's *Christian Manifesto* if you want to understand Operation Rescue', and he offered Wills a 'Rutherfordian' interpretation of America's past.[62] Terry has been described by Susan Faludi as 'the leading

---

[59] *Newsweek*, 1 November 1982, p. 88.

[60] F. Schaeffer, *A Christian Manifesto* (Westchester, IL, 1981), pp. 105–6. Numerous editions of this book have been published in America since 1981. Contrary to its assertions there is no evidence that either Locke or Witherspoon drew on Rutherford's ideas. As far as we know, neither writer owned a copy of *Lex, Rex* or quoted Rutherford even once. It would seem that Schaeffer was misled by the claims of J. Macleod, *Scottish Theology* (Edinburgh, 1943), pp. 71–3.

[61] See for instance, J. Eidsmore, *Christianity and the Constitution: The Faith of Our Fathers* (Grand Rapids, 1987), pp. 25–6, 90; and T. LaHaye, *A Nation Without a Conscience* (Colorado Springs, 1994), p. 62. The debunkers were M. Noll, N. O. Hatch and G. M. Marsden, *The Search for Christian America* (Westchester, Ill., 1983), p. 142; and R. V. Pierard, 'Schaeffer on History', in R. W. Ruegsegger, ed., *Reflections on Francis Schaeffer* (Grand Rapids, 1986), pp. 212–19.

[62] G. Wills, *Under God: Religion and American Politics* (New York, 1990), ch. 28; 'Evangels of Abortion', *New York Review of Books*, 15 June 1989, pp. 15–21.

figure' of the 1980s 'militant anti-abortion crusade'.[63] In the year 1988–9 alone, the action of Operation Rescue supporters who attempted to block the entrance to abortion clinics resulted in no less than 20,000 arrests.[64]

More extreme even than Terry were the Christian Reconstructionists. This group maintains that the Mosaic judicial law is still binding on Christians, and should be reimposed on modern America in the wake of a great revival of religion.[65] For them Schaeffer is 'half-hearted' in his reliance on Rutherford, appealing to 'a narrowly and even ultimately misleading selective segment of Rutherford's witness'. Rutherford, they claim, believed as they do in the continuing validity of Old Testament case laws. Schaeffer, seeing but not liking this, refrained from telling 'the full story regarding his proposed model theologian, Samuel Rutherford, who accepted the continuing validity of civil laws against homosexuals, witches and adulterers'.[66] Anxious to distance themselves from such theocratic harshness, the faculty of the Westminster Theological Seminary have published a book-length rebuttal of the theonomists' position, one chapter of which tries to demonstrate that Rutherford and his colleagues at the Westminster Assembly did not in fact believe that the Mosaic civil law should be re-instituted.[67]

Schaeffer admitted to being influenced by the Christian Reconstructionists, and one of his associates, John Whitehead, used their work to argue that America had departed from its Judaeo-Christian roots and been taken over by a secular-humanist elite.[68] However, Whitehead's work led him in a more 'liberal' direction. In 1982 he established the Rutherford Institute to defend religious liberties under threat from the secular state. The Institute takes its name from Rutherford because he 'resisted the European doctrine of divine right of kings . . . and argued that all men are subject to the law including the king. This same premise, that leaders are responsible to a law apart from and higher than themselves, was central to the formation of the US constitution.'[69] At its headquarters in Charlottesville, Virginia, the

---

[63] S. Faludi, *Backlash: The Undeclared War against Women* (London, 1992), p. 444.

[64] See F. Ginsburg, 'Saving America's souls: Operation Rescue's crusade against abortion', in Marty and Appleby, eds., *Fundamentalisms and the State*, ch. 23. Ronald Dworkin has argued that 'The war between anti-abortion groups and their opponents is America's new version of the terrible seventeenth-century European wars of religion', *Life's Dominion: an Argument about Abortion and Euthanasia* (London, 1993), p. 4. In the light of Rutherford's influence on Schaeffer and Terry, this seems strangely appropriate.

[65] For a fuller summary of their beliefs see M. Marty and R. S. Appleby, eds., *Fundamentalisms Observed* (Chicago, 1991), pp. 49–54.

[66] G. North, *Political Polytheism: the Myth of Pluralism* (Tyler, Texas, 1989), p. 197. For a theonomist reading of *Lex, Rex* see R. Flinn, 'Samuel Rutherford and Puritan political theory', *Journal of Christian Reconstruction*, 5 (1978–9), 49–74.

[67] S. Ferguson, 'An Assembly of theonomists?' in W. S. Barker and W. R. Godfrey, eds., *Theonomy: A Reformed Response* (Grand Rapids, Michigan, 1989), pp. 315–349.

[68] Especially in his *The Second American Revolution* (Eglin, IL, 1982).

[69] Rutherford Institute, publicity brochure.

Rutherford Institute employs around fifty full-time staff, and also draws on the volunteer services of approximately 500 lawyers in the United States. It airs a two-minute 'Freedom Under Fire' spot on 970 radio outlets across America each week, has offices in Bolivia, the United Kingdom and Hungary, and representatives in Romania, the Philippines and several Latin American countries.[70]

Typical cases taken up by Whitehead and other attorneys associated with the Institute are those of children prohibited from holding voluntary religious meetings in public schools, or of religious people penalised for expressing religious views in public forums. Whitehead is quite comfortable with the liberal language of 'rights' and 'autonomy', though in contrast to most liberals he applies it at least as much to families and religious groups as to individuals. He approves of J. S. Mill's conviction that 'the ideological control of public education' is dangerous,[71] and states that the aims of the Institute are to 'protect free speech in the public arena, protect the right of the religious organisation to operate freely without state intrusion, and defend parental rights and family autonomy'. Were the Institute's eponymous inspiration to see it at work, he would no doubt be bewildered to find that an organisation named after him has defended the religious liberties of the Krishna Consciousness Movement.[72]

The examples of Randall Terry, the Christian Reconstructionists and John Whitehead illustrate the many political 'lessons' that have been drawn from Rutherford's *Lex, Rex*, or at least from cursory readings of it. The book has been used to justify civil disobedience, a state run according to Mosaic law and the rights and liberties of religious people. Whilst partly reflecting the political confusion among conservative American Evangelicals, these views also point to ambiguities in Rutherford himself. Sometimes he appeared to be a constitutional liberal, at others a vengeful theocrat. Sometimes he rejoiced in the cross, at others he trusted in the sword. Those who claim to be inspired by him today reflect the same ambiguity.

Rutherford's interpreters, moreover, have also tended to focus on one aspect of his thought – be it his theology, piety, intolerance or constitutionalism – but they have failed to discuss them all. The self-confessed 'man of extremes' tends to provoke extreme reactions, and those who study him closely seem to find it impossible to look into both his eyes at once. To Buckle, the secular Enlightenment man, he was the archetype of the barbarous, superstitious and tyrannical Presbyterian cleric. To generations of Evangelicals he was the author of the 'seraphic' letters, 'the one supreme

[70] *Christianity Today*, 15 August 1994, p. 47.
[71] J.W. Whitehead, *The Rights of Religious Persons in Public Education* (Wheaton, Ill., 1991), p. 21.
[72] Information from Rutherford Institute publicity brochure and worldwide-web page.

Saint of Presbyterian Scotland',[73] the champion of British liberties. In short, no-one has yet provided a rounded, properly contextualised account of Rutherford's life and thought.

PREVIOUS RUTHERFORD SCHOLARSHIP

Rutherford has not been entirely ignored by modern scholarship, however. No less than nine academic dissertations have been written on Rutherford's life and thought. The most historically detailed is William Campbell's work on Rutherford's Presbyterianism, but it is seriously marred by a desire to enlist Rutherford as a good democrat.[74] The other dissertations vary in quality. Those by Webb, Strickland and Marshall are based on a careful reading of Rutherford, but perhaps because they emerge from divinity or politics departments they tend to be very weak on historical context. Strickland's thesis, however, contains an invaluable and almost comprehensive list of the seven hundred or more authors referred to in Rutherford's works.[75]

Fortunately, the published scholarly articles on Rutherford are rather better than these dissertations. Rutherford's political thought, in particular, has attracted a number of scholars. John Ford's '*Lex, rex iusto posita: Samuel Rutherford on the origins of government*' is by far the most thorough piece of scholarly work on Rutherford to date.[76] It has, however, a fairly specific focus, and the best article on Rutherford's political thought as a whole was written by J. F. Maclear some thirty years

---

[73] R. Gilmour, *Samuel Rutherford*, p. 3.

[74] W. Campbell, 'Samuel Rutherford: propagandist and exponent of Scottish Presbyterianism', unpublished Ph.D. thesis, Edinburgh University (1938). See also his '*Lex Rex* and its author', *Records Scottish Church History Society*, 7 (1939), 204–28.

[75] C. N. Button, 'Scottish mysticism in the seventeenth century, with special reference to Samuel Rutherford', unpublished Ph.D. dissertation, University of Edinburgh (1927); O. K. Webb, Jr, 'The political thought of Samuel Rutherford', unpublished Ph.D. dissertation, Duke University (1964); D. R. Strickland, 'Union with Christ in the theology of Samuel Rutherford', unpublished Ph.D. dissertation, University of Edinburgh (1972); T. D. Hall, 'Rutherford, Locke and the Declaration: the connection', unpublished M.Th. dissertation, Dallas Theological Seminary (1984); J. P. Burgess, 'The problem of Scripture and political affairs as reflected in the Puritan Revolution: Samuel Rutherford, Thomas Goodwin, John Goodwin and Gerrard Winstanley', unpublished Ph.D. dissertation, University of Chicago (1986); K. Rendall, 'Samuel Rutherford: the man and his ministry', unpublished M.A. dissertation, Durham University (1987); J. L. Marshall, 'Natural law and the covenant: the place of natural law in the covenantal framework of Samuel Rutherford's *Lex, Rex*', unpublished Ph.D. dissertation, Westminster Theological Seminary (1995).
In addition, there is one more thesis on Rutherford which I was unable to obtain when preparing this book: C. E. Rae, 'The political thought of Samuel Rutherford', unpublished M. A. dissertation, University of Guelph (1991).

[76] Published in R. Mason, ed., *Scots and Britons: Scottish Political Thought and the Union of 1603* (Cambridge, 1994), pp. 262–90.

ago.[77] Other writers tend to give us only a partial view of Rutherford's political ideas. Standard surveys of constitutionalist political theory – such as those by Allen, Zagorin and Tuck – describe Rutherford simply as a writer in the scholastic natural law tradition.[78] Works on the rise of toleration, on the other hand – like those by Jordan and Lecler – include Rutherford as a vociferous advocate of persecution.[79] This is also how Hugh Trevor-Roper views the man whom he calls 'the detestable Rutherford' (though since Trevor-Roper's pet hates include clerics, Scots and Calvinists, Rutherford was hardly likely to attract a balanced appraisal from that historian).[80] Finally, students of Scottish history like S. A. Burrell and Arthur Williamson follow yet another line of enquiry when they focus on Rutherford's apocalypticism, his belief in the imminent downfall of the popish Antichrist and Scotland's providential role.[81] Yet none of these scholars provide an in-depth account of Rutherford's political thought that explores the relationship between his natural-law constitutionalism, his belief in a godly, covenanted nation and his apocalypticism.

Even less has been written on other areas of Rutherford's thought. Charles Bell's *Calvin and Scottish Theology* (1985) contains a chapter on Rutherford's covenant theology, but it greatly exaggerates the gulf between Calvin and the Scottish divines. Two recent articles on Rutherford's *Letters* are more successful: a Dutch philologist, Hans Meier, has examined the 'extraordinary style' of Rutherford's prose with its images of 'love, law and lucre',[82] whilst

---

[77] J. F. Maclear, 'Samuel Rutherford: the law and the king', in G. Hunt and J. T. McNeill, eds., *Calvinism and Political Order* (Philadelphia, 1965), pp. 65–87.

[78] The following histories of early modern political thought all include a short discussion of *Lex, Rex*: G. P. Gooch, *English Democratic Ideas in the Seventeenth Century* (New York, 1959), pp. 98–9; J. W. Gough, *The Social Contract* (Oxford, 1936), pp. 93–4; J. W. Allen, *English Political Thought, 1603–44* (London, 1938), p. 285; P. Zagorin, *A History of Political Thought in the English Revolution* (London, 1954), pp. 5–6; R. Tuck, *Natural Rights Theories* (Cambridge, 1979), pp. 144–5; J. Sommerville, *Politics and Ideology in England* (Harlow, 1986); D. Wootton, ed., *Divine Right and Democracy* (Harmondsworth, 1986), p. 50; J. Sanderson, *But the People's Creatures: The Philosophical Basis of the English Civil War* (Manchester, 1989), ch. 1.

[79] W. K. Jordan, *The Development of Religious Toleration in England*, 4 vols. (London, 1932–40), III, pp. 292–7; J. Lecler, *Toleration and the Reformation*, II (London, 1960), pp. 451–3.

[80] H. Trevor-Roper, *Religion, the Reformation and Social Change* (London, 1967), pp. 216, 205–6.

[81] S. A. Burrell, 'The apocalyptic vision of the early Covenanters', *Scottish Historical Review*, 43 (1964), 1–24; A. H. Williamson, 'Latter day Judah, latter day Israel: the millennium, the Jews, and the British future', *Pietismus und Neuzeit*, 14 (1988), 159–60; 'The Jewish dimension of the Scottish apocalypse: climate, covenant and world renewal', in Y. Kaplan, H. Mechoulan and R. H. Popkin, eds., *Menassah Ben Israel and his World* (Leiden, 1989), pp. 24–30.

[82] H. Meier, 'Love, law and lucre: images in Rutherford's letters', in M. Arn and H. Wirtjes, eds., *Historical and Editorial Studies in Medieval and Early Modern English for Johan Gerritson* (Groningen, 1985), pp. 77–96.

Professor J. K. Cameron has suggested that the *Letters* force us to revise some traditional stereotypes of Scottish Presbyterian religiosity.[83]

Altogether, however, the small number of academic articles on Rutherford offers only patchy coverage of his ideas. Like seventeenth-century Scottish Presbyterians in general, Rutherford has not received sustained attention from professional historians.

THE HISTORIOGRAPHY OF PURITANISM AND SCOTTISH PRESBYTERIANISM

The meagreness of the academic literature on Scottish Presbyterianism is particularly obvious when one contrasts it with the enormous attention lavished on Puritanism in old and New England. The contrast is all the more striking, moreover, when one realises that devout Scottish Presbyterians were as 'Puritan' in their religious culture as the English and New English for whom the term is usually reserved. Historians nowadays tend to employ the term 'Puritan' to denote 'the hotter sort of Protestant',[84] the most zealous and strict of Protestants, those who called themselves 'the godly' and were called by others 'Puritans'.[85] Puritanism, it is now suggested, should be thought of as a distinctive religious culture characterised by 'a ceaseless round of . . . spiritual activities', including 'Bible-reading and Bible-study, sermon-attendance and sermon-gadding, fasting and whole-day sabbatarianism'.[86] Yet as we shall see in Chapter 4, this religious culture was as evident among Scotland's 'super-Protestants' as among their counterparts in England and New England.[87] Scots like Rutherford, therefore, should be considered part of the Puritan tendency within English-speaking Reformed Protestantism. To describe them simply as Presbyterians or Covenanters focuses attention on their particular ecclesiological or political positions, whilst obscuring the ethos and spiri-

---

[83] J. K. Cameron, 'The piety of Samuel Rutherford (c. 1601–61): a neglected feature of seventeenth-century Scottish Calvinism', *Nederlands Archief voor Kerkeschiedenis*, 65 (1985), 153–9.

[84] The phrase, taken from a sixteenth-century tract, was popularised by Patrick Collinson. See his *The Elizabethan Puritan Movement* (Oxford, 1967), p. 27.

[85] P. Lake, 'Puritan Identities', *Journal of Ecclesiastical History*, 35 (1984), 112–23, argues that Puritans were distinguished from other Protestants by their zeal rather than by their theology, ecclesiology, or social theory.

[86] C. Durston and J. Eales, eds., *The Culture of English Puritanism, 1560–1700* (London, 1996), p. 31.

[87] The phrase 'super-Protestants' comes from Patrick Collinson, 'Elizabethan and Jacobean Puritanism as forms of popular religious culture', in C. Durston and J. Eales, eds., *The Culture of English Puritanism* (London, 1996), p. 46. This article explicitly highlights the similarities between English Puritan and Scottish Presbyterian religious culture (pp. 53–5).

tuality that they shared with zealous Protestants beyond Scotland. To capture the latter we need to employ the term 'Puritan'.

In describing Scots like Rutherford as Puritan we are following the example of their contemporaries. When James VI revisited Scotland in 1617 he recalled that many English Puritans had yielded under royal pressure, and declared 'Let us take the same course with the Puritans here.'[88] Peter Heylyn too, did not hesitate to speak of 'the Presbyterian or Puritan Faction in Scotland'.[89] Rutherford himself noted that 'we be nicknamed Puritan' and complained that 'a strict and precise walking with God in everything' was scorned as 'Puritan'.[90] The nickname was given throughout the English-speaking world to people who were felt to be excessively zealous and strict in their religion, people whose intense desire to obey Scripture often brought them into conflict with royal ecclesiastical policy.

These godly people, moreover, were able to recognise their brethren in other countries. In the 1630s Rutherford closely followed the fortunes of the godly in England, and the emigration of some across the Atlantic. Another Scottish Presbyterian, John Livingstone, was a close friend of Rutherford who became a minister in Ulster, travelled to London in the mid-1630s to meet with other nonconforming Puritan clergy, attempted to sail to New England in 1636, and ended up being exiled in the Netherlands after the Restoration. His career amply illustrates the international connections between the hotter sort of Protestants.[91]

Despite all this, however, Scottish Presbyterianism has been largely ignored by historians of Puritanism. Those writing on Puritan theology, politics or spirituality frequently allude to Scots like Rutherford, thereby acknowledging that the Scots shared a great many of the characteristics of the English Puritans, but Scottish Puritanism as a movement has remained unexplored. Even a recent study of 'trans-Atlantic' Puritanism focuses exclusively on England and New England.[92] Because Scottish Puritanism is so widely disregarded, the myth has persisted that to study seventeenth-

---

[88] D. Calderwood, *The History of the Church of Scotland* (1678), p. 680.

[89] In his *History of the Presbyterians* (1670), quoted in I. Murray, *The Puritan Hope* (Edinburgh, 1971), p. xxv.

[90] *Letters*, p. 512; *Quaint Sermons*, p. 318. For other examples see *Communion Sermons*, p. 341; *Letters*, pp. 53, 134; and *The Last and Heavenly Speeches of John, Viscount Kenmuir*, p. 400.

[91] Livingstone's autobiography is to be found in W. K. Tweedie, ed., *Select Biographies*, I (Edinburgh, 1845).

[92] F. J. Bremer, ed., *Puritanism: Trans-atlantic Perspectives on a Seventeenth-century Anglo-American Faith* (Boston, 1993). This is in sharp contrast to another recent symposium on Evangelicalism, which compares examples of the phenomenon throughout the English-speaking world: M. Noll, D. Bebbington, and G. Rawlyk, eds., *Evangelicalism: Comparative Studies of Popular Protestantism in North America, the British Isles, and Beyond, 1700–1990* (Oxford, 1994).

century Scotland is to observe 'the dreary and irrational antics of backward and fanatical Scots obsessed by dark religion'.[93]

At one time, of course, such a myth would have applied equally well to the New England Puritans. Nathaniel Hawthorne's *The Scarlet Letter* (1850) illustrated the widespread belief that Puritans were narrow-minded, hypocritical, repressed and cruel, and H. L. Mencken famously described Puritanism as 'the haunting fear that someone, somewhere, may be happy'.[94] As one American historian put it recently, as far as the New England Puritans were concerned, 'Hawthorne built the coffin and Mencken nailed down the lid'.[95]

It is worth examining, therefore, why the historiographical fortunes of New England Puritanism rose so rapidly, whilst those of Scottish Presbyterianism continued to decline. The turning point for New England Puritan studies came in the 1930s with a series of books by American scholars which revised received opinion about the Puritans and rehabilitated their reputation. The historians who wrote these influential books believed – with Max Weber – that the Puritans were important because they were on the side of modernity. William Haller[96] and A. S. P. Woodhouse[97] associated Puritanism and liberty, arguing that the roots of modern liberal democracy could be found in the Puritan revolution. Perry Miller's *The New England Mind* (1939) argued that far from being irrational or Antinomian Calvinists, the Puritans injected large doses of rationalism and moralism into their religion which helped prepare the way for the Enlightenment.[98] Other historians and sociologists took a similarly Weberian line, arguing that Puritanism inadvertently contributed to the rise of modern individualism, modern science, the modern idea of progress, modern nationalism, the modern family and so on.[99]

[93] The quotation comes from D. Stevenson, *The Scottish Revolution, 1637–44: The Triumph of the Covenanters* (Newton Abbott, 1973), p. 14. Stevenson, of course, is concerned to undermine the myth.
[94] Quoted in W. Lamont, *Puritanism and Historical Controversy* (London, 1996), p. 3.
[95] D. Leverenz, *The Language of Puritan Feeling* (New Brunswick, NJ, 1980), p. 137.
[96] W. Haller, *The Rise of Puritanism* (New York, 1938).
[97] A. S. P. Woodhouse, *Puritanism and Liberty* (London, 1938).
[98] As he later recalled, Miller conceived the idea for his book whilst he was in the African jungle supervising 'the unloading of drums of case oil flowing out of the inexhaustible wilderness of America'. It was then that 'the mission of expounding what I took to be the innermost propulsion of the United States' was 'thrust upon me'. P. Miller, *Errand into the Wilderness* (Cambridge, Mass., 1956), p. viii. New England seemed to him 'the ideal laboratory for testing how, if not always why, the modern ethos emerged' out of Protestant scholasticism. Miller, *The New England Mind: The Seventeenth Century* (New York, 1939), p. xii.
[99] See, for example, the historian C. Hill, *The Century of Revolution* (London, 1961); and the sociologist R. Bellah, *Beyond Belief: Essays on Religion in a Post-traditional World* (New York, 1970), p. 38. For a survey and a trenchant critique see C. H. George, 'Puritanism as history and historiography', *Past and Present*, 41 (1968), 77–104.

The danger of imposing such a strong idea of modernisation on the seventeenth century, however, was that one could easily fall into teleological determinism and anachronism. The 'Puritan revolution' was too often seen as inevitable because modernity had to come and the revolution was the vehicle of modernisation. Puritanism itself was interpreted in largely secular terms, and studied more for its perceived world-historical role than for itself. Often this approach led to what we might call 'the booster-rocket theory of history', in which Puritanism was seen as fuelling the take-off towards modernity, only to fall away once its job was done.

In recent years, therefore, revisionist historians have reacted strongly against this kind of Whiggish history. Aspects of Puritanism that seem alien to modern eyes – such as its apocalypticism – have rightly been placed to the fore.[100] Rather than being viewed as the shock troops of a brave new world, the English Puritans are now portrayed as the conventional upholders of the established order.[101] The English revolution, once viewed as the first of the great modern revolutions, has been redescribed as 'the last of the Wars of Religion'.[102] The Civil Wars are said to have constituted a struggle over authority rather than a struggle against it. The Puritans sought a godly society rather than a liberal one, 'the freedom of God Almighty' rather than that of sinful human beings.[103] The connection Hill saw between Puritanism, capitalism and science, has been shown to be somewhat tenuous.[104]

Of course, some historians have always doubted the connection, and repudiated the Puritans' ferocious conviction politics in favour of what they see as the tolerant humanism of the Erasmian and Arminian tradition. Hugh Trevor-Roper's *Religion, the Reformation and Social Change* (1967) should be read as a sustained polemic against Weberian theories that link Calvinism and modernisation. Trevor-Roper agreed with Perry Miller that optimism about human nature and human reason is a key element of modernity, but he differed in seeing Puritanism as fiercely opposed to this optimism. The real progressives, he suggested, were those within the sceptical, Erasmian, Arminian tradition represented by men like Grotius and Selden. 'Calvinism', he wrote, 'was intolerant, fundamentalist, scholastic, determinist, while Erasmianism was tolerant, sceptical, mystical, liberal.' The religion of

---

[100] See especially W. Lamont, *Godly Rule: Politics and Religion, 1603–60* (London, 1969).

[101] P. Collinson, *The Religion of Protestants* (Oxford, 1982).

[102] J. Morrill, *The Nature of the English Revolution* (London, 1993), p. 68. Morrill says that his decision to describe the English Revolution in this way 'represented and represents what I still believe to be a salutary reaction against various forms of modernisation theory'.

[103] J. C. Davis, 'Religion and the struggle for freedom in the English Revolution', *Historical Journal*, 35 (1992), 507–30.

[104] See H. Kearney, 'Puritanism, capitalism and the scientific revolution', *Past and Present*, 28 (1964), 81–101; W. Lamont, 'The Puritan revolution: a historiographical essay', in J. G. A. Pocock, ed., *The Varieties of British Political Thought, 1500–1800* (Cambridge, 1993), pp. 127–38; Lamont, *Puritanism and Historical Controversy*, passim.

'intellectual reactionaries, scholastical bigots, blinkered Augustinians, Hebraic fundamentalists' had to be swept away before the Enlightenment could dawn.[105]

One powerful argument for this thesis, claimed Trevor-Roper, was the example of Scotland. Scotland after all was perhaps the most Calvinist country in Europe but it was also, he argued, hopelessly backward in its political, economic and intellectual life throughout the seventeenth century. Dominated by an intolerant, tyrannical and theocratic kirk, the only enlightenment that the Scots could hope to receive came from the English in the south, either during the conquest of the 1650s or after the Union of 1707. All this proved that rather than being an ideology especially conducive to the development of modernity, Calvinism – like Marxism – was suited to backwardness, and triumphed in underdeveloped countries.[106]

With this argument Trevor-Roper sought to slay two birds with one stone. As David Stevenson shows, he was aiming to discredit Scottish calls for devolution by demonstrating that historically the Scots had not been able to govern themselves.[107] But secondly, he was challenging all those who saw Calvinism as a particularly 'modern' ideology. The Enlightenment only came to Scotland after its kirk had been 'de-Calvinised', when the fanatical heirs of Rutherford had seceded and left the church to the Moderates. 'The detestable Rutherford', together with men like Perkins, Voetius, Jurieu and Turretini, formed 'a gallery of intolerant bigots, narrow-minded martinets, timid, conservative defenders of repellent dogmas, instant assailants of every new or liberal idea, inquisitors and witch-burners!'[108]

This vigorous diatribe clearly echoed the work of the nineteenth-century historian, Henry Buckle. Buckle's secularist tract, *On Scotland and the Scotch Intellect*, written (rather ironically) in a passionately biblical and prophetic style, deployed phrases from the writings of Scottish divines – particularly from Rutherford – to paint a picture of seventeenth-century Scotland as a superstitious and benighted land in a 'worse than Egyptian bondage'.[109] The clergy literally 'ruled the people' and the Scots 'had grown accustomed to look upon their minister as if he were a god, and to dwell

---

[105] H. Trevor-Roper, *Religion, the Reformation and Social Change* (London, 1967), pp. 221, 223.

[106] Trevor-Roper, 'Scotland and the Puritan Revolution' and 'The Union of Britain in the seventeenth century', in *Religion, the Reformation and Social Change*, chs. 8 and 9.

[107] D. Stevenson, 'Professor Trevor-Roper and the Scottish Revolution', *History Today*, 30 (1980), 34–40.

[108] Trevor-Roper, 'The religious origins of the Enlightenment', in *Religion, the Reformation and Social Change*, pp. 214, 216, 205–6.

[109] H. T. Buckle, *On Scotland and the Scotch Intellect*, edited by H. J. Hanham (Chicago, 1970), p. 194.

with rapture upon every word that dropt from his lips'.[110] 'The ablest Scotsmen wasted their energies on theological subjects',[111] and if they had never been born 'society would have lost nothing'.[112] Set alongside the genius of Milton or Selden in England, or that of Hume and Smith in eighteenth-century Scotland, 'the monkish rabble' of the Covenanting period could be made to seem a miserable bunch.[113]

Scottish historians have often concurred with this negative judgement on Scotland's pre-Enlightenment past. G. D. Henderson was apologetic about the fact that 'Scottish culture in the seventeenth century was not very impressive. Brilliant writers and thinkers were not plentiful . . . practically everyone was interested in theology'.[114] Similarly, David Reid writes that 'we need only compare it with what English writers of the time achieved or what Scottish writers would achieve in the next century to have the meagreness, the backwardness of the literary culture of the Scottish seventeenth century brought home to us'.[115]

A comparison with American historiography reveals how unnecessarily down-beat this attitude is. The fact that 'practically everyone' in seventeenth-century New England was interested in theology has not stopped American historians writing hundreds of articles and monographs about the Puritans. Nor has the absence of thinkers as original and influential as Grotius, Hobbes or Milton led them to apologise for the literary backwardness of their national past. The lack of historical studies of what I have called Scottish Puritanism is not necessarily a reflection on the dullness of the subject.

Fortunately, the last twenty years have seen a welcome revival in early modern Scottish historiography. The origins of the Scottish revolution have been analysed in detail by Maurice Lee,[116] Peter Donald[117] and Allan MacInnes,[118] and David Stevenson has provided us with a detailed political narrative covering the years 1637 to 1651.[119] Stevenson broke away from the stereotypes – perpetrated by Buckle and Trevor-Roper – of Scotland locked in the vice-like grip of clerical tyranny. He shifted attention from the clergy to the nobility, from the religious elements of Covenanter ideology to its secular-constitutional aspects, and successfully showed that the Scots

---

[110] Buckle, *On Scotland*, pp. 162, 172.   [111] Buckle, *On Scotland*, p. 384.
[112] Buckle, *On Scotland*, p. 155.   [113] Buckle, *On Scotland*, pp. 239, 385.
[114] G. D. Henderson, *Religious Life in Seventeenth-Century Scotland* (Cambridge, 1937), p. 117.
[115] D. Reid, *The Party Coloured Mind* (Edinburgh, 1982), p. 1.
[116] M. Lee, *The Road to Revolution: Scotland under Charles I* (Chicago, 1985).
[117] P. Donald, *An Uncounselled King: Charles I and the Scottish Troubles, 1637–41* (Cambridge, 1991).
[118] A. MacInnes, *Charles I and the Making of the Covenanting Movement* (Edinburgh, 1991).
[119] D. Stevenson, *The Scottish Revolution* (Newton Abbott, 1973) and *Revolution and Counter-Revolution in Scotland, 1644–51* (London, 1977).

influenced the English in far more positive ways than Trevor-Roper had allowed.[120]

Stevenson's stress on the *British* significance of the Covenanter revolution has been borne out by the trend among English historians towards writing the history of the three kingdoms, rather than that of England alone. John Pocock's seminal call for 'a new subject' has been heeded,[121] and Conrad Russell's work has demonstrated the critical role played by the Scots in the politics of Britain in the 1630s and 1640s. Russell argues forcefully that the Scottish troubles were 'the *primum mobile*' of the British crisis and 'that until well on the 1640s the major conflict in the British Isles was that between the king and the Scottish Covenanters'. Like Stevenson, he points out that the English parliament frequently followed the Scots example in the early years of the revolution.[122] John Morrill, while differing with Russell on some points, agrees that 'The stability of early Stuart England made civil war unlikely; it was the instability of early modern Britain that first made the war of 1642 possible.'[123]

In the light of the rise of a *British* history and also of the great emphasis among historians on the *religious* origins of the civil wars,[124] it is now time to reassess the Scottish clerics so vehemently denounced by Buckle and Trevor-Roper. There are encouraging signs that this is already being done. The work of Eric Schmidt and Marilyn Westerkamp has shown that the origins of the American revivalist tradition lie in Scotland among the radical Presbyterians in the 1620s and 1630s. Schmidt employs the tools of cultural anthropology to demonstrate that popular Presbyterian communions were characterised by the same vitality and colour as the eucharistic festivities of late medieval Catholicism.[125]

Other historians have begun to investigate early seventeenth-century Scottish religious thought. The books of G. D. Henderson still provide the most comprehensive introduction to religion in seventeenth-century

---

[120] See his 'Professor Trevor-Roper and the Scottish Revolution'.

[121] J. Pocock, 'British history: a plea for a new subject', *Journal of Modern History*, 47 (1975), 601–21; 'The limits and divisions of British history: in search of an unknown subject', *American Historical Review*, 87 (1982), 311–36.

[122] C. Russell, 'The British problem and the English civil war', *History*, 72 (1987), 415; *The Causes of the English Civil War* (Oxford, 1990), p. 29.

[123] Morrill, *The Nature of the English Revolution*, p. 5.

[124] See Lamont, *Godly Rule*; A. Fletcher, *The Outbreak of the English Civil War* (London, 1981), pp. 415–18; P. Collinson, *The Birthpangs of Protestant England* (London, 1988), ch. 5; Morrill, *The Nature of the English Revolution*, chs. 2 and 3; Russell, *Causes of the English Civil War*, chs. 2–5.

[125] L. E. Schmidt, *Holy Fairs: Scottish Communions and American Revivals in the Early Modern Period* (Princeton, 1989); M. Westerkamp, *The Triumph of the Laity: Scots-Irish Piety and the Great Awakening, 1625–1760* (Oxford, 1988).

Scotland,[126] but recently scholars have explored particular themes in
considerable depth. Arthur Williamson's work has investigated the impact
of apocalyptic ideas on Scottish national consciousness in the sixteenth and
seventeenth centuries,[127] whilst David Mullan has described the rather less
exciting but still significant literature of the Presbyterian/Episcopalian
debate up to 1638.[128] David Allan's recently published work on early
modern Scottish historiography highlights the continuing vitality of a
'Calvinist humanism' in the seventeenth century, and seeks to challenge the
deep-seated assumptions regarding the intellectual sterility and stagnation
of pre-Enlightenment Scotland.[129] This ambition is wholeheartedly shared
by Edward Cowan, who has gone so far as to maintain that those who led
the Covenanters included 'some of the brightest minds ever to grace a
Scottish leadership', men who have never received the credit they
deserve.[130] Gordon Marshall, an historically minded sociologist, has been
even more bold, and attempted what many have deemed impossible – a
defence of the Weber thesis with reference to Scotland. Marshall effectively
shows that Weber's claims are a great deal more subtle than his detractors
usually appreciate, but despite a final chapter entitled 'Weber vindicated', he
is unable to produce any hard evidence showing that anxiety over the
doctrine of election led to unusual entrepreneurial drive.[131] On a less
speculative level, the collection of essays edited by Roger Mason on
seventeenth-century Scottish political thought adds substantially to the
increasing discussion of Scottish intellectual history.[132]

However, much remains to be done. H. J. Hanham's verdict still applies:
'Scottish historians have in the past been prone to eschew ideas as
dangerous distractions from the main job of getting the facts right. Now
that Scottish history is in a relatively flourishing state there is perhaps room

[126] G. D. Henderson, *The Scottish Ruling Elder* (London, 1935); *The Religious Life of Seventeenth Century Scotland*; *The Claims of the Church of Scotland* (London, 1951); *Presbyterianism* (Aberdeen, 1954); *The Burning Bush* (Edinburgh, 1957).
[127] A. Williamson, *Scottish National Consciousness in the Age of James VI* (Edinburgh, 1979); 'Latter Day Judah, Latter Day Israel: The millennium, the Jews and the British Future', *Pietismus und Neuzeit*, 14 (1988), 149–65; 'The Jewish Dimension of the Scottish Apocalypse'.
[128] D. Mullan, *Episcopacy in Scotland: The History of an Idea, 1560–1638* (Edinburgh, 1986). Mullan is currently preparing a book on early seventeenth-century Scottish religion which should do much to improve our knowledge of the subject.
[129] D. Allan, *Virtue, Learning, and the Scottish Enlightenment: Ideas of Scholarship in Early Modern History* (Edinburgh, 1993).
[130] E. Cowan, 'The Making of the National Covenant', in Morrill, ed., *The Scottish National Covenant in its British Context* (Edinburgh, 1990), pp. 69, 75.
[131] G. Marshall, *Presbyteries and Profits: Calvinism and the Development of Capitalism in Scotland, 1560–1707* (Oxford, 1980).
[132] R. Mason, ed., *Scots and Britons: Scottish Political Thought and the Union of 1603* (Cambridge, 1994).

again for more of ideas.'[133] This Namierite aversion to studying ideas is even found among historians of religion. As Stevenson observes, for a country 'so obsessed with its religious history', there has been 'surprisingly little . . . published on the thought of Scottish theologians'. Historians have concentrated on the externals of church government, worship and routine whilst ignoring the faith and beliefs of the people they are studying.[134] As Nicholas Phillipson has pointed out, Scotland has never had its Perry Miller.[135]

One consequence of all this is that there is no modern intellectual biography of a Scot who lived between George Buchanan in the sixteenth century and Andrew Fletcher at the end of the seventeenth.[136] This book aims to rectify that deficiency. As the most prolific and wide-ranging of the Covenanter theorists, Samuel Rutherford is an ideal candidate for a study that seeks to discuss the period between these two great writers. This is especially so since Buckle repeatedly quoted Rutherford to demonstrate his thesis that seventeenth-century Scots were living in intellectual darkness. If this Enlightenment caricature of the Scots Calvinist as a dour, dull and dogmatic Presbyterian fanatic is to be replaced by a more vital and complex portrait, there is surely no better person to start with than Rutherford.

Given that Rutherford's writings amount to approximately 9,000 quarto pages, this book can hardly hope to provide an exhaustive treatment of his ideas. It does, however, present a thorough overview of his life and thought and will hopefully generate further interest in early modern Scottish history and in Rutherford himself. There is no good reason, after all, why Rutherford and other Scottish divines should not eventually attract the volume of high-quality scholarship which has hitherto been reserved for English and New English Puritans like Richard Baxter and John Cotton.

METHODOLOGY, SOURCES AND ARRANGEMENT

Methodologically, this study differs from most of the academic theses written on Rutherford in that it is thoroughly historical. I am indebted to the theoretical work of Quentin Skinner,[137] John Dunn[138] and John

---

[133] Hanham, introduction to Buckle, *On Scotland*, p. xxxv.

[134] D. Stevenson, 'Scottish church history 1600–60: a select critical bibliography', *Records of the Scottish Church History Society*, 21 (1982), pp. 213, 220.

[135] N. Phillipson, review of Sher and Smitten, eds., *Scotland and America in the Age of Enlightenment*, *Historical Journal*, 77 (1992), p. 433.

[136] I. D. McFarlane, *Buchanan* (London, 1981); P. Scott, *Andrew Fletcher and the Treaty of Union* (Edinburgh, 1992).

[137] See J. Tully, *Meaning and Context: Quentin Skinner and his Critics* (Cambridge, 1988).

[138] J. Dunn, 'The identity of the history of ideas', in P. Laslett, Q. Skinner, and W. G. Runciman, eds., *Philosophy, Politics and Society*, Fourth series (Oxford, 1982), pp. 158–73.

Pocock,[139] who argue that our understanding of the political ideas of past thinkers is greatly enhanced when we place them firmly in their historical context. These historians of ideas – sometimes known as 'the Cambridge School' – have criticised both the 'idealist' tendency to study the Great Books without reference to the circumstances in which they were written, and the 'realist' approach which sees ideas as the causally determined offspring of their social, economic or psychological context.[140] They argue for a method of reading historical texts which respects the intention of the author and is aware of the linguistic, political or ecclesiastical context in which he was working. The advantage of this approach is that it neither regards the author as a disembodied mind nor succumbs to various forms of reductionism. It neither puts the author into an artificial conversation with theorists writing in completely different historical situations, nor does it ignore what he himself claimed to be saying. It tries, so far as possible, to allow the natives to speak for themselves.

The basic raw materials for this book are of course the works of Rutherford himself. A substantial proportion of these – the *Letters* (1664), *Examen Arminianismi* (1668), *Testimony to the Work of Reformation* (1719), *Communion Sermons* (1802, 1876, 1877), *Quaint Sermons* (1885), and a catechism (1886) – were only published posthumously from seventeenth-century manuscripts. However, there seems to be no good reason to doubt the genuineness of these works. We know that manuscript copies of Rutherford's letters were circulating among the godly during his own lifetime, and these were gathered together and published in Rotterdam by his secretary, Robert McWard.[141] Subsequent editors added to the collection as further manuscript copies came to light; a number of such seventeenth-century copies exist in several libraries.[142] McWard was also responsible for editing *Examen Arminianismi* from Rutherford's lecture notes, and publishing it with the help of Dutch theologians.[143] Although no manuscript attestation survives for Rutherford's final *Testimony*, its substance was recorded by Wodrow, who had access to documents now lost,[144] and internal evidence (the opinions expressed and the people

---

[139] J. Pocock, 'The history of political thought: a methodological enquiry', in P. Laslett and W. G. Runciman, eds., *Philosophy, Politics and Society*, Second series (Oxford, 1962), pp. 183–202.

[140] See M. Goldie, 'Obligations, utopias and their historical context', *Historical Journal*, 26 (1983), 727–46.

[141] See McWard's preface to the first edition.

[142] National Library of Scotland, Mss. 15950 ff. 1–55; Wodrow papers Folio XXVII nos. 42 and 43, Folio LIV no. 9, Folio LIX no. 5, Quarto XXIV nos. 13, 21, 66, 88, Quarto XXXI no. 6; St Andrews University Library, Mss BX 8915; Bodleian Library, Oxford, Rawlinson Mss A.44.343.

[143] Cf. 'Epistola Dedicatoria' and MacWard's foreword to *Examen Arminianismi*.

[144] Wodrow, *Analecta*, I, pp. 225–36.

mentioned) firmly establishes its authenticity. All but two of the *Communion Sermons* and *Quaint Sermons* edited by Bonar can be found in manuscript,[145] and their style is thoroughly characteristic of Rutherford, often containing images that can also be found in other works.[146] The *Catechism* was transcribed in the nineteenth century from an original manuscript in Edinburgh University Library.[147] Among the works posthumously published in his name only *The Door of Salvation Opened* is wrongly attributed to him.[148]

Besides these printed works, I have also consulted a number of unpublished Rutherford manuscripts held in Scottish libraries. In Chapter 8, I refer to unpublished notes on thirty-four of his sermons; some of these are merely brief summaries, others almost verbatim reports.[149] I also discuss the fragment of a treatise Rutherford wrote on the relationship between church and state and on the nature of obedience to a usurper, which although only a few pages long contains Rutherford's providentialist justification for submission to Cromwellian rule.[150]

The principal aim of this work is to give a rounded and contextualised account of Rutherford's life and thought. Rather than portraying him as a precociously modern figure, it discusses in some detail his baroque spirituality, his apocalypticism and his attack on religious toleration. However, it also seeks to reawaken interest in Covenanter thought by depicting the range of Rutherford's concerns and the complexity of his mental furniture, and by setting his ideas in a broad intellectual context which reveals him to have been a cosmopolitan thinker rather than a backward and parochial bigot. Rutherford may have been deeply scholastic, but he was also imbued with humanist learning, and his well-stocked mind was thoroughly familiar with the work of classical poets and historians, early church Fathers, medieval Nominalists, Spanish Jesuits and contemporary Protestants. He was a complex man: a preacher, pastor, intellectual and ecclesiastical politician whose substantial body of writing covered theology, ecclesiology, political theory, spirituality and apocalypticism, and took the form not only of polemical treatises, but also of sermons, letters, a catechism and the testimony of a dying nobleman. His two most famous books, his *Letters*

---

[145] See MS 30386 in St Andrews University Library. Only Communion Sermons IX and XII are not to be found in this manuscript book.

[146] The images of bairns building sandcastles, the father wading across a river with his child, Christ as an apple and the world as a smoky inn can all be found in the *Letters* (pp. 203, 225, 79, 83) as well as in the *Communion Sermons* (pp. 234, 177, 286, 46–7).

[147] Dc. 8. 32.

[148] See the bibliography of Rutherford.

[149] National Library of Scotland, Acc 9270 no. 3; Edinburgh University Library, Dc. 5. 30–31; New College Library, Edinburgh, B. b. b. 12.

[150] 'Treatise on the nature of obedience to a usurped power and on the relation of the civil magistrate to religion', Edinburgh University Library, La. III. 69/5.

and *Lex, Rex*, could hardly be more different; here we have striking contrasts between nuptial mysticism and densely scholastic political theory, between apocalyptic and constitutionalist modes of political discourse.

This work surveys all these aspects of Rutherford's work. It begins in Chapter 2 with a narrative of his life, relating it to the political and ecclesiastical context of seventeenth-century Britain. Chapter 3 deals with Rutherford's scholarship, concentrating on his university education and the teachers who influenced him at an early stage, and discussing the authors whom he quoted and the traditions within which he stood. Chapter 4 attempts to understand Rutherford the Puritan pastor. It discusses his spirituality, his relationships with godly women and the literary style of his remarkable devotional prose. Chapter 5 turns to his public theological polemics, and explains his efforts to refute Arminianism and Antinomianism, and hold together divine sovereignty and human responsibility. Against those who see the Puritans and the Reformed orthodox as breaking with the theology of Calvin, I argue that there was substantial continuity. Chapter 6 then expounds Rutherford's most famous treatise, *Lex, Rex*. It uncovers a tension within the book between secular arguments drawn from natural reason, and religious arguments against popish idolatry inspired by the Old Testament. Chapter 7 discovers a similar tension in Rutherford's ecclesiology between his support for a comprehensive, national church, and his longing for a pure church. Finally, Chapter 8 looks in some detail at Rutherford the national prophet, calling the nation to maintain its covenant with the Lord and prepare for the apocalypse. These last two chapters are structured chronologically in order to emphasise the way in which the desire for purity came into conflict with the need for comprehension as the Covenanter revolution unravelled. Eventually, it is suggested, Rutherford's commitment to maintaining the integrity of the covenanted nation by purging 'malignants' from church and state undermined the idea of a comprehensive national church and subverted the logic of natural reason.

Besides providing a clearer understanding of Rutherford's own thought, these chapters also contain material of wider relevance. In many ways Rutherford was a microcosm of the learning and concerns of his age. As the foremost representative of Scotland's zealous Presbyterians, he obviously offers us an excellent summary of their approach to religion and politics.[151] But as I have argued above, he also has much to tell us about the Puritan ethos in general. Moreover, many of the themes dealt with in what follows – covenant theology, mystical spirituality, natural-law theory, the idea of the new Israel, apocalypticism – are of great interest to students of the

---

[151] Makey, *Church of the Covenant*, p. 59, rightly describes Rutherford as 'the theorist of the radical Presbyterians'.

Reformed tradition in Switzerland, France, the Netherlands, England and America. This book constantly interacts with studies of Calvinism and Puritanism in these nations, and uncovers many connections, while never losing sight of Rutherford's Scottish context. As I argue in the Conclusion, Rutherford's campaign for a godly Britain can be located within the much broader context of the pan-European shift from religiously unified to religiously pluralistic societies and from the Reformation to the Enlightenment. As one of the last full-blooded defenders of Reformed theocratic ambition, Rutherford died in the knowledge that most of what he had worked for was disintegrating. In the past his life story has often been retold as a romance; this book retells it as a tragedy.

$$2$$

Biography

Samuel Rutherford was born around the turn of the seventeenth century, at about the same time as both Charles I and Oliver Cromwell. Although the evidence for his early life is very fragmentary indeed, we know that he was born and grew up in the south-east of Scotland, almost certainly in the town of Nisbet in the parish of Crailing, not far from the English border. In his only personal reference to the first twenty years of his life – in a letter to the minister of Oxnam, the neighbouring parish to Crailing – Rutherford expressed his spiritual concern for the area, 'that place to which I owe my first breathing'.[2] Although it has one large hill, the parish is an area of rich and fertile arable land, and the lowest, warmest and most attractive part of the basin of the river Teviot, which wends its way eastwards between the small towns of Nisbet and Crailing.[3]

Rutherford's first biographer, Robert McWard, wrote that he was 'a gentleman by extraction',[4] and Robert Wodrow claimed that he was 'the son of an heretor [landowner]'.[5] Others have suggested that his father was a farmer or a miller, possibly Andrew or William Rutherford, both of whom were involved in a feud in the parish in 1596.[6] Although this cannot be

---

[1] Of all the biographical studies of Rutherford, only two have rested on substantial original research: those of Thomas Murray, *Life of Rutherford* (Edinburgh, 1828), and William Campbell, 'Samuel Rutherford, propagandist and exponent of Scottish Presbyterianism', unpublished Ph.D. dissertation, Edinburgh University (1937). This chapter draws on their biographies but also on further primary material not consulted by either writer.

[2] *Letters*, p. 680. Murray, *Life of Rutherford*, p. 2, recorded that in the early nineteenth century local people still pointed to the house in Nisbet where Rutherford was born.

[3] For a more detailed description of the parish see F. H. Groome, ed., *Ordnance Gazetteer of Scotland*, 6 vols. (London, 1894–5), II, p. 300; J. Sinclair, ed., *The Statistical Account of Scotland* (East Archley, 1979 edn), III, pp. 413–15.

[4] R. McWard, preface to *Joshua Redivivus, or Mr Rutherfoord's Letters* (1664).

[5] R. Wodrow, *Analecta, or Materials for a History of Remarkable Providences mostly relating to Scotch Ministers and Christians*, 4 vols. (Edinburgh, 1842–3), III, p. 88.

[6] K. Rutherford Davis, *The Rutherfords in Britain: A History and a Guide* (Gloucester, 1987), p. 86.

substantiated, it is clear that Rutherford's family was neither particularly poor nor especially distinguished. In this his social origins were typical of the Scottish ministry; in 1648 less than 5 per cent of the ministers were the sons of magnates, merchants, lawyers or doctors, whilst most were the sons of ministers or farmers. W. H. Makey exaggerates the humility of Rutherford's roots and his hostility to the nobility,[7] but the fact that he did not rise from even the lesser nobility does explain Rutherford's later egalitarianism and his willingness to attack the aristocracy.

Rutherford grew up with two younger brothers: George, who later joined him in Kirkcudbrightshire and became a schoolteacher, and James, who was to serve as a soldier in continental armies. It is likely that there were others of whom we do not know, who died without reaching adulthood. Almost certainly, they were educated at the grammar school in Jedburgh, just four or five miles south-west of Crailing, where they would eventually have progressed to learning Latin, in preparation for university.[8]

Yet more formative than his schooling was to be Rutherford's experience of growing up under the ministry of the man who was to become Scotland's most vociferous Presbyterian polemicist, David Calderwood. Calderwood was ordained as minister of Crailing in 1604, and remained there until he was deprived of his charge in 1617, the year in which Rutherford went to Edinburgh University. At a time when most Scots listened to preachers unwilling to attack the king's ecclesiastical policies, Rutherford had the rare experience of hearing a true exponent of the Melvillian theory of the two kingdoms asserting the independence of the church from the Crown and the need to eschew all popish ceremonies. The experience marked him for life, for he was to be a Melvillian in the mould of Calderwood.

Although his minister was godly and zealous, the same could not be said of the parish as a whole. Rutherford later complained that in his birthplace 'Christ was scarce named, as touching any reality or power of godliness'.[9] In Scotland, just as in England, and for the young Samuel Rutherford as much as for the young Richard Baxter, it felt hard to be in a godly minority. At parish level – as Rutherford was to discover in Edinburgh, Kirkcudbright and St Andrews too – there was always cultural conflict between the lax and ignorant majority and those whom they liked to call 'Puritans'.

As he grew up, Rutherford must have become more aware of another conflict, at a national level. For men like Calderwood, James VI was

---

[7] W. H. Makey, *The Church of the Covenant, 1637–51: Revolution and Social Change in Scotland* (Edinburgh, 1979), pp. 95–104.
[8] In 1669 the master of Jedburgh School was made rector of the High School of Edinburgh, so the town may have had a long tradition of academic excellence and links with Edinburgh. See Murray, *Life of Rutherford*, p. 5.
[9] *Letters*, p. 680.

destroying the fabric of the pure reformed church they believed had been set up after the Reformation. Since 1596 James had been asserting his control over the church and clamping down on the Melvillian faction. He had begun the restoration of episcopacy in 1600 by appointing three parliamentary bishops, and in 1606 he had had the Presbyterian leader Andrew Melville thrown into the Tower of London. The courts of High Commission were restored in 1609 and in 1610 three Scottish bishops were sent to London to be ordained, and diocesan episcopacy was returned to Scotland.[10] All this was anathema to Calderwood, and when in 1608 he refused to submit to the authority of the bishops, he was confined to his own parish and debarred from ecclesiastical assemblies.[11]

After this episode, life was relatively peaceful for Calderwood until 1617, when he went to Edinburgh to protest during a royal visit against the king's attempt to gain jurisdiction over the church. He told sympathetic ministers at this time, 'It is absurd, to see men sitting in silks and sattins, and to cry povertie in the kirk, when puritie is departing.' A Protestation was drawn up by these ministers, and handed in to the king, asking him to preserve the liberty and purity of the kirk. Calderwood, recognised as one of the leading dissidents, was summoned before the High Commission at St Andrews. On the 12 July he had an interview with James, reminiscent of Melville's famous exchange with him in 1596. The trial ended with the king crying 'in a great rage . . . "away with him, away with him" '.[12]

All this happened as Calderwood's young parishioner, Samuel Rutherford, prepared himself to begin his studies at Edinburgh University. The trauma of hearing that his minister had aroused the king's anger and been deprived of his parish was a forceful reminder that the vision of the church Rutherford had been brought up to hold was now unwelcome in Scotland. Yet Rutherford was to end up treading in his pastor's footsteps. Calderwood had been a student at Edinburgh in the early 1590s and seems to have spent the rest of the decade there, imbibing radical Presbyterian ideas before going to a parish in the south of Scotland.[13] Rutherford was to do almost exactly the same, and the likelihood has to be that this was exactly what Calderwood had planned for him.

---

[10] James's Scottish ecclesiastical policy is neatly summarised in G. Donaldson, *Scotland: James V–James VII* (Edinburgh, 1965), ch. 11.

[11] D. Calderwood, *The True History of the Church of Scotland: From the Beginning of the Reformation unto the Ende of the Reigne of James VI* (1678), pp. 573–4.

[12] Calderwood, *True History*, pp. 675–83. Calderwood's own description of the event invites comparison with the trial of Christ. An innocent man stands before the secular ruler and corrupt priests, refusing to bow to their demands. James's final cry is reminiscent of that of the Jewish crowd concerning Jesus.

[13] See A. MacDonald, 'David Calderwood: the not so hidden years, 1590–1604', *Scottish Historical Review*, 74 (1995), 69–74.

EDINBURGH UNIVERSITY (1617–1626)

In November 1617, Rutherford passed the strenuous Latin entrance exam for Edinburgh University. It involved translating texts from Scots to Latin in the morning and reading the translations out before the regents and the principals in the afternoon.[14] Proficiency in Latin was essential for students, because all lessons were conducted in it and, when together, whether in the college or outside, it was ruled that all students converse in Latin, and 'none be fund speiking scottes'.[15] In Chapter 3 I describe the curriculum and the way it shaped Rutherford's mind, but in this chapter I concentrate on his experiences in Edinburgh and the people who influenced him.

In the early seventeenth century, Edinburgh University was only a small college with two-thirds of the students living in the city, and a mere forty or fifty living in the college's twenty-three chambers, where they normally slept two to a bed. Bursars rang a bell to wake the students at 5 a.m. in summer and 6 a.m. in winter, summoning them to begin another long day of study. Every evening the principal would lead the college in daily worship, and on Wednesdays he would 'instruct theme in the knowledge of God and of thair deutyes', examining them on the previous week's lesson. On the Sabbath, the students were taken to church morning and afternoon and, back at college, were required 'to give accompt of the tuo sermones . . . and of the morning lessouns'. Academic, social and spiritual life was highly regimented and even monastic. But there were some moments of light relief from this regime; on 'play dayes' students were taken to the fields for two hours to practise wholesome sports like archery.[16]

When Rutherford entered the college in 1617 there were six academic staff – a principal who was also the professor of divinity, four rotating regents who each guided a class through its full four years of study, and a regent of humanity who prepared candidates for their Latin entrance exam.[17] Until 1620 the principal was Henry Charteris, an excessively modest man who did not take part in disputations. His influence on Rutherford was minimal, but Andrew Young, the regent who taught

---

[14] T. Crauford, *History of the University of Edinburgh from 1580 to 1646* (Edinburgh, 1808), p. 57. Crauford succeeded Rutherford as regent of humanity in 1626 and his contemporary account is our major source of information about the university in the early seventeenth century.

[15] *University of Edinburgh: Charters, Statutes, and Acts of the Town Council and the Senatus, 1583–1858*, ed. A. Morgan (Edinburgh, 1937), p. 124.

[16] For the original rules of discipline of the college see *University of Edinburgh*, ed. Morgan, pp. 117–25, 157–61. See also A. Grant, *The Story of the University of Edinburgh during its First Three Hundred Years* (London, 1884), pp. 136–43.

[17] *University of Edinburgh*, ed. Morgan, pp. 114–5.

Rutherford for four years, was probably responsible for instilling in the young student a profound respect for Aristotle and natural philosophy.

Besides Young, there were two more teachers at Edinburgh University who must have consolidated his Reformed orthodoxy. The professor of divinity in the college from 1620 was Andrew Ramsay, who had supported the Protestation against the state of the kirk in 1617 and was to play a prominent part in the Covenanting revolution in the late 1630s, providing a theological refutation of Arminianism at the 1638 Glasgow General Assembly.[18] The principal from 1623, John Adamson, was also to be a leading Covenanter. The militant Presbyterians who carefully stage-managed the 1638 Assembly placed Ramsay and Adamson on the committee to examine the High Commission, the Canons and the Service Book alongside their former student, Rutherford.[19] It seems possible that since the early 1620s these men had been part of a group of ministers who were dissatisfied with the direction in which the king and the bishops were taking their church.

However for all their commitment to Calvinist theology and unease with Episcopalian reform, Ramsay and Adamson were not in Rutherford's league when it came to zealotry. Ramsay quickly accepted innovations such as kneeling at communion, and was not averse to sitting on the Court of High Commission and seeking a bishopric. In the 1640s he opposed private meetings and supported the Engagement.[20] John Adamson was also a relatively moderate Covenanter. The changing fortunes of the Presbyterian cause would sort out the moderates from the militants. In 1635, when Charles I was pressing for innovations in worship, only Andrew Stevenson among the regents opposed royal policy; Ramsay and Adamson preferred to avoid open conflict. Edinburgh University was hardly a hot-bed of Presbyterian radicalism.[21]

---

[18] *Records of the Kirk of Scotland, containing the Acts and Proceedings of the General Assemblies, from the year 1638 downwards*, ed. A. Peterkin (Edinburgh, 1838), p. 159.

[19] R. Baillie, *Letters and Journals*, 3 vols., ed. D. Laing (Edinburgh, 1841–2), I, p. 148.

[20] See the article on Ramsay in N. Cameron, ed., *Dictionary of Scottish Church History and Theology* (Edinburgh, 1993), p. 691, and G. I. R. McMahon, 'The Scottish episcopate, 1600–38', unpublished Ph.D. dissertation, Birmingham University (1972), p. 42. Ramsay's support for the Engagement led to his ousting from the kirk in 1649. In the wake of this he wrote papers criticising alterations in the kirk's worship brought in by the Westminster Assembly, alterations which Rutherford and the radicals had promoted. He was restored to the ministry in 1655 by the Resolutioners. His position on private meetings was not entirely antagonistic, however. Baillie, *Letters and Journals*, I, p. 252, records that when Rutherford defended the legitimacy of private meetings among Christians at the 1640 Aberdeen Assembly, both Ramsay and Adamson 'greedilie handshit [snatched, caught up]' his argument, perhaps because Rutherford had stated his case in rather moderate terms.

[21] Glasgow produced more radical young ministers. See J. M. Barkley, 'Some Scottish bishops and ministers in the Irish Church, 1605–35', in D. Shaw, ed., *Reformation and Revolution: Essays Presented to Hugh Watt* (Edinburgh, 1967), p. 158.

Rutherford found the real radicals outside the University, in the private meetings or conventicles being organised in Edinburgh by a group of Presbyterian merchants led by John Mein and William Rigg. Many connections between these men and Rutherford in later years suggest that he had known them as a student. Rutherford wrote letters to both Mein and Rigg and also to Mein's wife, Barbara Hamilton, who was responsible for sparking off one of the 1637 Edinburgh Prayer Book riots, and to his son, John, who succeeded Rutherford as minister of Anwoth.[22] Barbara Hamilton's niece was to marry John Livingstone, and her sister married Robert Blair; both men were close friends of Rutherford and members of the 'radical party' in the kirk.[23] It is even possible that the Eupham Hamilton whom Rutherford married was related to Barbara Hamilton. Even if that was not so, this radical party was still a remarkably close and coherent group, motivated by a clear and fervent vision of ecclesiastical renewal.

It is highly probable that Calderwood was in contact with the Edinburgh radicals in 1617 and deliberately put them in touch with his promising young parishioner. In his *History of the Church of Scotland*, he describes in some detail the situation in Edinburgh when Rutherford was a student. He presents the ministers of Edinburgh as being at loggerheads with the magistrates, particularly the group of godly merchants led by Mein and Rigg. What drove them apart were the Five Articles passed by General Assembly at Perth in 1618, which ordered the observance of traditional holy days, confirmation of the laity by bishops, private baptism and communion for the infirm, and most controversially of all, kneeling at communion.[24] The radicals in Edinburgh regularly boycotted services held by their ministers on holy days or communions which required communicants to kneel in accordance with the Articles of Perth. They provocatively opened their shops at the time of the services, and tried to persuade others not to attend, arousing the fury of the ministers who attempted to have them banished. Censored books like Calderwood's attack on the Articles of Perth were circulating, and fierce arguments took place in town meetings between the ministers and the Presbyterians. Every communion was a dramatic event, as people watched to see who would kneel when the sacrament was given (according to Calderwood, there were few who did).[25] For a young student the Presbyterian subculture with its clandestine and

---

[22] There is one letter to Mein in the collection (no. 151), three to Rigg (nos. 114, 256, 273), two to Barbara Hamilton (nos. 311, 314), and two to John Mein jr. (nos. 81, 240).

[23] See D. Stevenson, 'Conventicles in the kirk, 1619–37: the emergence of a radical party', *Records of the Scottish Church History Society*, 18 (1973) 102–7.

[24] See I. B. Cowan, 'The Five Articles of Perth', in Shaw, *Reformation and Revolution*, pp. 160–77.

[25] For an often vivid description of events in Edinburgh from the beginning of the conflict in 1619 to the death of James VI in 1625 see Calderwood, *True History*, pp. 718–816.

subversive activities held a powerful attraction (though as an older man he would have trouble understanding the attractiveness of the separatist subculture to London Puritans). Having come from the countryside, Rutherford must have felt the exhilaration of being plunged into the middle of an ideological debate of national significance.

By 1620, however, it had become apparent that suffering as well as excitement was integral to the life of the godly. In April of that year, Mein, Rigg and several others were hauled before the High Commission to answer for their nonconformity, and charged to leave Edinburgh. Although eventually they were able to stay, the experience left its mark on Rutherford. When he himself was banished to Aberdeen in 1636, he wrote, 'That honour that I have prayed for these sixteen years . . . my kind Lord hath now bestowed on me, even to suffer for my royal and princely King Jesus, and for His kingly crown, and the freedom of His kingdom that His Father hath given Him.'[26] The example of Rigg and Mein had won a convert to the cause whose zeal would know no bounds. It was intensified when they were finally banished from Edinburgh by the Privy Council in 1624; in 1638, Rutherford wrote that his present spiritual ecstasies were something 'Christ hath been keeping these fourteen years for me'.[27] If Calderwood was the first crucial influence on Rutherford, Rigg and Mein were the second.[28]

His commitment was probably further strengthened by Robert Boyd, principal of the University for just one year, 1622. Boyd had been professor of theology at the Protestant seminary of Saumur in France for many years, and then was professor at Glasgow University 1615–22. He moved to Edinburgh in late 1622 and left early the next year, but it is probable that in this short time Rutherford joined 'the sundrie Noblemen, lawyers and countrey ministers' who 'resorted frequently to his [Boyd's] lessons in the schoole, and sermons in the kirk'.[29]

Boyd was a strict predestinarian, an opponent of ceremonies and the Articles of Perth, and a supporter of private conventicles. He was also the author of a huge commentary on Ephesians which quoted at length from the early church Fathers and from Bernard of Clairvaux and the Song of Songs.[30] Rutherford was to share many of these interests, and it is likely that he was inspired, at least in part, by hearing Boyd in 1622–3. Boyd's popularity in this period aroused the jealousy of less radical Edinburgh ministers like Andrew Ramsay,[31] and James VI came to distrust him too.

[26] *Letters*, p. 136.   [27] *Letters*, p. 556.
[28] I shall examine their ecclesiological position in chapter 7.
[29] Calderwood, *True History*, p. 801.
[30] See J. Walker, *The Theology and Theologians of Scotland, 1560–1750* (Edinburgh, 1982 edn), pp. 4–6.
[31] McMahon, 'Scottish episcopate', p. 42.

He demanded that Boyd be deprived of his position and expelled from the city of Edinburgh for refusing to conform to the Five Articles of Perth passed in 1618. Yet James had acted too late. Boyd had already made a significant impact on Rutherford and various other members of what was to become the 'radical party' in the kirk – David Dickson, John Livingstone and Robert Blair, who had been his students at Glasgow. Indeed the royal treatment of Boyd probably gave these men the extra inspiration they needed to carry on their underground crusade on behalf of high Calvinist theology and a pure Presbyterian Scotland.

In 1623 Rutherford was made regent of humanity at Edinburgh University, after a disputation with three other competitors. An older graduate, David Will, pleased the judges most because of his greater experience, but Rutherford was chosen for 'his eminent abilities of mind, and vertuous disposition'.[32] Before long, however, he became involved in two controversies. In 1625, another regent was appointed and 'there arose a contention between him and Mr Samuel Rutherford anent the precedency'.[33] It appears that Rutherford resented being made subordinate to a regent who had been appointed later than himself, but the case was decided against him. An ordinance that the regent of humanity was to be subordinate to the other regents was read out before the six academic staff and 'they promised to observe the same in all tyme coming'.[34]

One humiliation was swiftly followed by a far greater one. According to an entry in the burgh records of Edinburgh for 3 February 1626, it had been 'declaired be the principall of the colledge [John Adamson] that Mr Samuell Rutherfuird, regent of humanitie, hes fallin in furnicatioun with Euphame Hamiltoun, and hes committit ane grit scandle in the college'.[35] This passage has always caused great embarrassment to Rutherford's biographers, who have generally tried to demonstrate that Adamson's charge cannot have been true. Why else, they enquire, would Rutherford have been given an 'honest gratification' when he left his job, why else would it have been said that he 'has made demission' of his post rather than that he 'has been deprived' of it? If Rutherford really had 'fallin in furnicatioun' why did a staunch Presbyterian like Andrew Stevenson agree to be the godfather of an illegitimate child, why did Rutherford's critics never raise the issue at a later date to discredit him, why did the same burgh which registered the charge elect him as a minister in 1639 and a professor of divinity in 1649, and why did Viscount Kenmure appoint him to be minister of Anwoth just a year later in 1627? Rutherford's real

[32] Crauford, *History*, p. 97. [33] Crauford, *History*, p.103.
[34] A. Bower, *The History of the University of Edinburgh*, I (Edinburgh, 1917), pp. 167–8.
[35] *Extracts from the Records of the Burgh of Edinburgh, 1604 to 1626*, ed. M. Wood (Edinburgh, 1931), p. 296.

offence, his defenders suggest, was simply marrying 'without academic or episcopal authority', and the principal was looking out for an opportunity to dismiss him because of his conflict with the other regents or his uncompromising Presbyterianism. Rutherford resigned not because he was guilty, but simply for reasons of delicacy, to save the University further embarrassment over the affair.[36]

The strong point in favour of this view is that it is hard to understand how Rutherford could be a fornicator one year and a minister the next, especially when the exacting standards of the church of his day are taken into account. Yet such leniency was not unknown in the kirk – Baillie records an example of it in his journals.[37] Moreover, there do seem to be good grounds for considering Adamson correct in his charge. First, the committee appointed to investigate the scandal and appoint a successor if 'ane scandle sould happin to fall furth in his persone', did appoint a successor, suggesting that they did find a scandal. Secondly, it is hard to conceive how Rutherford could have sat on commissions with Adamson in the 1640s if the man had deliberately and falsely accused him of fornication. Thirdly, Rutherford's enemies did later mention the scandal in order to cast aspersions on his character; Sir James Balfour described the author of *Lex, Rex* as 'lousse in hes zouthe [youth]'.[38] Fourthly, a child was born to Hamilton and Rutherford in April 1626. If the couple really had married more than nine months previously, even without academic or episcopal approval, surely Adamson would not have made such a serious charge. Fifthly, Rutherford did speak in later life of his regret over the sins of his youth. This might have been typical Puritan self-deprecation, but more likely referred to the Edinburgh scandal. 'The old ashes of the sins of my youth are new fire of sorrow to me', he wrote to a young nobleman in 1637. 'The devil in his flowers (I mean the hot, fiery lusts and passions of youth) is much to be feared.'[39] Elsewhere he confessed that like a fool 'I suffered the sun to be high in the heaven, and near afternoon, before ever I took the gate by the end.' But the struggle with sexual temptation never really ceased. Late in his life, Rutherford wrote enigmatically to James Guthrie of 'my unseen and secret abominations; which would have been no small reproach to the holy name and precious truths of Christ'.[40]

[36] See, for example, Murray, *Life of Rutherford*, pp. 18–21.
[37] R. Baillie, *Letters and Journals*, II, 96.
[38] Sir James Balfour, *Historical Works*, 4 vols. (London, 1825), II, p. 413.
[39] *Letters*, p. 349. For other warnings about the lusts of youth see pp. 287, 311, 324, 364, 391, 398, 461, 477, 616.
[40] *Letters*, p. 701.

THE PARISH OF ANWOTH (1627–1636)

In April 1626, the month in which Rutherford's first child, Marie, was born, the Presbyterian John Livingstone was called to the parish of Anwoth in Galloway by the local nobleman, Sir John Gordon of Lochinvar. Livingstone eventually went elsewhere, but as he wrote in his diary, 'thereafter the Lord provided a great deal better for them, for they got that worthy servant of Christ, Mr Samuel Rutherfoord'.[41] Rutherford's first letter from Anwoth was dated June 1627, but since it suggests some familiarity with local people he may have arrived in the parish a month or so earlier.[42]

According to his earliest biographer, McWard, Rutherford entered his first charge 'without giving any engagement to the bishop'.[43] Although this was unusual in the late 1620s, a number of militant young ministers, including Rutherford's friends Blair and Livingstone, seem to have been presbyterially ordained, perhaps with the bishop taking his place among the other presbyters. In Rutherford's case this was made possible by his bishop, Lamb, who had himself been ordained in the Presbyterian manner and was a moderate Episcopalian, and by his patron, Gordon, who on his deathbed later exhorted the bishop 'most earnestly not to molest or remove the Lord's servants, and not to enforce or enthral their consciences to receive the Five Articles of Perth . . . but to behave himself meekly towards them as he would wish to have mercy from God'.[44]

Gordon's desire to find a zealous Presbyterian for his parish had its roots in the time he spent as a young man in France with John Welsh, who had been exiled along with Andrew Melville. Before his exile, Welsh had made a powerful impact on the area around Kirkcudbright and was famed for spending eight hours of every day in prayer. Along with Robert Bruce – whom Rutherford probably heard preach during the 1620s – Welsh was a pioneer of the intense style of extemporary conversionist preaching which was to be imitated by younger Presbyterians like Livingstone, Rutherford and Dickson. In the 1620s and 1630s, this new generation of ministers was to lead a series of revivals, the most famous of which occurred at Shotts in 1630, when around five hundred people were said to have been converted through a single sermon preached by Livingstone. These revivals greatly strengthened the cause of Presbyterianism, and they formed the backdrop to Rutherford's early ministry.[45]

---

[41] J. Livingstone, 'Life by himself', in *Select Biographies*, ed. W. K. Tweedie, I (Edinburgh, 1845), p. 135.
[42] *Letters*, p. 33.   [43] McWard, preface to *Joshua Redivivus*.
[44] *The Last and Heavenly Speeches of John, Viscount Kenmuir* (1649), p. 402.
[45] See L. E. Schmidt, *Holy Fairs: Scottish Communions and American Revivals in the Early*

The arrival of this young revivalist preacher in a country parish created some stir. Before he came, his parishioners wrote in 1639, 'our soules were under that miserable extreame femine of ye word, that we had onlie ye puir help of an sermone everie second Sabboth, by reasone of ane most inconvenient unione with uther twa kirkis'.[46] Rutherford changed the situation dramatically, for he was a whirlwind of enthusiasm.[47] As another minister explained to Wodrow, 'he seemed to be always praying, always preaching, always visiting families, always visiting the sick, always catechising, always teaching in the schools, always writing treatises, always reading and studying'.[48] 'He used ordinarly to rise be three a clock in the morning', wrote John Livingstone, and 'was the instrument of much good among a poor ignorant people, many of which he brought to the knowledge and practise of religion.'[49]

Yet Rutherford carried on his work at Anwoth amid personal tragedy, especially in the early years. In June 1630 his wife died after an illness of a year and one month. He had spoken of her 'exceeding great torment night and day'. 'God hath filled me with gall and wormwood', he wrote, 'but I believe.'[50] The children of their marriage all seem to have died before their mother. Rutherford himself had 'been diseased of a fever tertian for the space of thirteen weeks' while his wife was dying, and was unable to visit or examine his congregation.[51] He was to live as a widower for the rest of the 1630s, although his mother and brother moved to Anwoth to be with him.[52] Even in 1634 the 'wound' caused by his wife's death had 'not yet fully healed and cured'.[53] In his letters we can see the effect upon him of the experience of losing his children; he was highly conscious of affliction and the transience of life, and writing to numerous women who had lost children, husbands and friends he advocated a stoical, Job-like resignation to the inscrutable will of God, obviously born out of his own painful experience.

Traditionally, Rutherford's biographers have romanticised his ministry at

Modern Period (Princeton, 1989), pp. 21–32; M. Westerkamp, *The Triumph of the Laity: Scots-Irish Piety and the Great Awakening, 1625–1760* (Oxford, 1988), pp. 16–36.

[46] 'Petition of the parish of Anwoth', in Murray, *Life of Rutherford*, p. 355.
[47] He records in his *Letters*, p. 440, that his first sermon was on the text 'And Jesus said, For judgement I am come into the world, that they which see not might see; and that they which see might be made blind' (John 9.39).
[48] Wodrow, *Analecta*, III, p. 88.
[49] Livingstone, 'Memorable characteristics', in *Select Biographies*, ed. W. K. Tweedie, I, p. 320.
[50] *Letters*, p. 50.   [51] *Letters*, p. 51.
[52] *Letters*, p. 119. In this letter of early 1635, Rutherford writes that his mother is 'weak, and I think shall leave me alone'. His brother, George, was appointed schoolmaster of Kirkcudbright in 1630. See *Kirkcudbright Town Council Records, 1606–58*, ed. John, 4th Marquis of Bute and C. M. Armet (Edinburgh, 1958), pp. 405, 427.
[53] *Letters*, p. 100.

'leafy Anwoth' by the 'fair Solway', treating it as a model for the Evangelical pastor, and ignoring how intensely political Rutherford's work was.[54] In terms of population Anwoth was an obscure and minor parish, but as its parishioners were quick to point out, it had strategic importance. It was the parish of Rutherford's patron Viscount Kenmure, 'ye prym and most eminent man for power and commandement in these boundis', and it was 'cituat on ye hie way betwixt England and Ireland'.[55] Rutherford realised the strategic importance of his position and quickly began to establish connections with the various branches of the influential Gordon family and other local gentry. One of his closest friends was Jane Campbell, the wife of Viscount Kenmure and the sister of Lord Lorne, later the Earl of Argyll and the most powerful nobleman in Scotland. Rutherford was also in regular correspondence with Marion McNaught, a niece of Lord Lorne and the wife of the provost of Kirkcudbright.[56] His assiduous cultivation of noble connections was part of a farsighted campaign to promote the cause of Presbyterianism in the south-west. Its success is demonstrated by the fact that seventy-seven of Rutherford's correspondents signed the Kirkcudbright petition against the new Prayer Book in 1637.[57] But Rutherford was sowing on fertile ground. The 1625 Act of Revocation had alienated the nobility from the king by threatening to return the land they had gained at the Reformation to the church.[58] Moreover, the south-west of Scotland had traditionally been a radical stronghold, responsive to the message of the Lollards and the reformers.[59]

Building on this foundation, Rutherford turned his small parish into the local centre of opposition to episcopacy. He became engrossed in the Arminian controversy,[60] disseminated political information,[61] intervened in burgh elections,[62] wrote his own catechism,[63] organised seasons of fasting and humiliation over the corruption of the church,[64] prepared a Latin

---

[54] See, for instance, chapter 2 of A. Thomson's *The Life of Samuel Rutherford* (Glasgow, 1988 edn).
[55] 'Petition of the parish of Anwoth', Murray, *Life of Rutherford*, p. 356.
[56] Fifty-six of Rutherford's letters are written to Lady Kenmure, forty-four to Marion McNaught.
[57] J. D. Oglivie, 'The Kirkcudbright petition of 1637', *Transactions of the Edinburgh Bibliographical Society*, 14 (1926–30), 47–8.
[58] For the fullest and most recent account of the revocation scheme and its ramifications see A. MacInnes, *Charles I and the Making of the Covenanting Movement, 1625–41* (Edinburgh, 1991), chs. 3 and 4.
[59] On the radical tradition in the south-west of Scotland see G. Donaldson, 'Scotland's conservative north in the sixteenth and seventeenth centuries', in his *Scottish Church History* (Edinburgh, 1985), pp. 198–202.
[60] *Letters*, pp. 60, 64. [61] *Letters*, p. 92. [62] *Letters*, p. 99.
[63] 'Ane Catechisme conteining the Soume of Christian Religion', in A. F. Mitchell, ed., *Catechisms of the Second Reformation* (London, 1886).
[64] *Letters*, p. 92.

treatise against the theology of Arminius and the Jesuits,[65] and circulated manuscript treatises he had written to justify conventicles.[66] His letters and sermons in these years were jeremiads over the state of the kirk and the nation, stirring his hearers to pray for Scotland to be a worthy bride again.

By 1630 this message had brought Rutherford into conflict with his local presbytery. In June of that year he wrote that he had been summoned before the High Commission, after his nonconformist activities had been reported 'by a profligate person in the parish, convicted of incest'. However, nothing came of this – one of the local judges intervened on his behalf, and 'the sea and winds refused to give passage to the Bishop of St. Andrews', Spottiswoode, who was to try the case.[67] But in June 1631, Rutherford was still complaining about being 'most unkindly handled' by the presbytery.[68] In a letter probably written near the end of 1632, he claimed that while the faces of his fellow ministers smiled upon him, their tongues informed Spottiswoode about his activities.[69]

Charles I came to Scotland to be crowned in 1633. Rutherford's patron, Sir John Gordon, was created Viscount Kenmure and Lord Lochinvar on this occasion, and out of gratitude to the king and fear of coming into conflict with him, he withdrew from the parliament which was passing anti-Presbyterian legislation and returned to his own home, claiming to be ill. A year later in August 1634 he really did fall ill, and Rutherford was present at his bedside to chide him mercilessly over his betrayal of the Presbyterian cause and then help him to die in peace after he had repented. The encounter, an account of which was later published, illustrates how powerful a hold a minister could have over a religious nobleman.[70]

In the same year as Kenmure's death, Thomas Sydserff replaced Lamb as Bishop of Galloway. Sydserff had been in Edinburgh during the 1620s, and was probably well aware of Rutherford and his circle of friends. As one of the young Scottish Laudians or Canterburians, he was far more hardline than his predecessor, and determined to stamp out dissension in the church. His appointment was part of a renewed drive by Charles I for religious

---

[65] Though only published in Amsterdam in 1636, *Exercitationes Apologeticae pro Divina Gratia* is dedicated to Lord Kenmure, and appears to have been written before his death in 1634.

[66] Baillie, *Letters and Journals*, I, p. 8.   [67] *Letters*, p. 53.   [68] *Letters*, p. 61.

[69] *Letters*, p. 117. Bonar dates this letter December 1634, but since it refers to reports of the death of the Swedish king, Gustavus Adolphus, who was killed in 1632, it is more likely to have been written near the end of that year.

[70] See *The Last and Heavenly Speeches of John, Viscount Kenmuir*. The relationship between Lady Barrington and her family chaplain Roger Williams in late-1620s Essex provides another example of a Puritan minister berating a noble patron. See W. Hunt, *The Puritan Moment: The Coming of Revolution in an English County* (Cambridge, Mass., 1983), ch. 9, and L. Raymond Camp, *Roger Williams: God's Apostle of Advocacy* (Lewiston, 1989), pp. 83–99.

uniformity throughout the British Isles. In 1634 the Court of High Commission was reconstituted in Edinburgh, the Arminian William Forbes was made the capital's bishop, and the king issued new orders for the English liturgy to be observed in Scottish cathedrals and universities. Most ominously of all, the king had agreed on the need for a new Scottish prayer book and a book of canons to revise the liturgy and organisation of the kirk.[71]

Sydserff wasted no time in moving against nonconformists. He began by trying to imprison the elderly minister of Kirkcudbright, Robert Glenndinning, but Marion McNaught's husband and others came to his defence. Then Rutherford and another local minister, William Dalgleish, were threatened with summoning before the Court of High Commission. Dalgleish was deprived of his charge in 1635, and moves were being made against Rutherford too. In 1634 his treatise defending conventicles fell into the hands of the king himself.[72]

In mid-1636 Rutherford was summoned before the Court of High Commission in Edinburgh, deprived of his charge and sentenced to be confined in Aberdeen, where it was hoped he would come under the influence of the moderate Doctors of Divinity.[73] According to Baillie, 'the alleadged cause of their censure was onlie conformity'; Rutherford's preaching against the Articles of Perth and his advocacy of conventicles substantiated the charge. However, allied to his struggle against ceremonies were Rutherford's opposition to episcopacy and Arminian theology. He had refused 'to give the Chancellour or ony of the Bishops their styles' and his Latin treatise against the Arminians and Jesuits had attacked the theologian John Cameron and railed against Thomas Jackson, the dean of Peterborough.[74]

The case of Rutherford demonstrates the accuracy of Nicholas Tyacke's claim that the 1630s saw a three-pronged attack on the Calvinist *status quo*

---

[71] MacInnes, *Charles I and the . . . Covenanting Movement*, pp. 141–5. On the preparation of the Prayer Book see G. Donaldson, *The Making of the Scottish Prayer Book of 1637* (Edinburgh, 1954).

[72] *Letters*, p. 105. Baillie, *Letters and Journals*, I, p. 8. Hunt, *The Puritan Moment*, pp. 253–60, describes how the Laudians closed in on radical Puritan ministers in Essex from the late 1620s.

[73] *Letters*, p. 136. On the Court of High Commission and its moves against nonconformists in Scotland, see McMahon, 'Scottish episcopate', ch. 5.

[74] Baillie, *Letters and Journals*, I, p. 8. John Row, *History of the Kirk of Scotland, from the Year 1558 to 1637* (Edinburgh, 1842), pp. 396–7, also believed that the book against the Arminians was a key reason for Rutherford's deposition, since 'Sydserf now being turned an Arminian' was offended by it. Both John Livingstone and Rutherford himself agreed that the Latin treatise was a major reason for his trial and exile. See Livingstone, 'Memorable characteristics', p. 321; Rutherford, *Letters*, p. 135.

in Britain: on its liturgy, doctrine and polity.[75] Rutherford came into conflict with the Scottish bishops in each of these areas, and was eventually regarded as too dangerous to be allowed to remain at large, fomenting opposition to the policy of the king and the bishops. But by banishing him to Aberdeen, the bishops produced another martyr for the Presbyterian cause, and added to the smouldering resentment which had been aroused by the treatment of Lord Balmerino, who for the mere possession of a petition critical of the king's ecclesiastical policy had been sentenced to death for treason. Balmerino was eventually pardoned, but his case seemed to highlight the arbitrary style of government to which Scotland was being subjected, and the unwillingness of the new rulers to listen to any criticism.[76]

Yet in Scotland as in England, revolution seemed far from imminent in 1636. Rutherford was well aware that zealots of his stamp were the exception rather than the rule. Although there was substantial opposition to royal ecclesiastical reforms in Glasgow, Edinburgh and the south-west of Scotland, the north of the country was far more conservative and acquiescent. By and large, the reintroduction of episcopacy was quietly accepted, and because the Five Articles were never rigorously enforced, they failed to generate a broad-based opposition movement within the Church.[77] W. R. Foster's work on the church before the Covenants argues that 'the overwhelming impression is one of continuity and development', rather than of conflict and factionalism.[78] Future covenanting radicals like Johnston of Wariston took communion happily in the city under episcopacy right up until 1637, even enjoying the sermons of Thomas Sydserff.[79] So whilst with hindsight it may seem that Rutherford had placed himself on the side of the eventual winners, at the time the prospects for the Presbyterian cause looked much more bleak. As we shall see in Chapter 8, Rutherford foresaw disaster and suffering, not relief and the renewal of the nation's broken covenant with God. Christ was leaving Britain, and in late 1636 many of the godly felt like following him. Rutherford's friends, Blair and Livingstone, set sail for New England in September, but were forced to return because of a storm. Rutherford hoped that if they sailed again, he would be

---

[75] N. Tyacke, *Anti-Calvinists: The Rise of English Arminianism, c.1590–1640* (Oxford, 1987). For Tyacke's treatment of Rutherford and Scotland see pp. 230–5.

[76] On Balmerino's trial see M. Lee, *The Road to Revolution: Scotland under Charles I, 1625–37* (Chicago, 1985), pp. 157–62; MacInnes, *Charles I and the Making of the Covenanting Movement*, pp. 135–41.

[77] See H. Mackay, 'The reception given to the Five Articles of Perth', *Records of the Scottish Church History Society*, 19 (1977), 185–201.

[78] W. R. Foster, *The Church before the Covenants* (Edinburgh, 1975), p. 2.

[79] See G. Donaldson, 'Reformation to covenant', in D. Forrester and D. M. Murray, eds., *Studies in the History of Worship in Scotland* (Edinburgh, 1984), p. 48.

able to go with them. It seemed to be time for Christ and his people to go to a land where they would be more welcome.[80]

EXILE IN ABERDEEN (1636–1638)

However, in the meantime, Rutherford was exultant over the opportunity to carry his cross. 'Sweet, sweet is the Lord's cross', he wrote, 'I overcome my heaviness. My Bridegroom's love-blinks fatten my weary soul. I soon go to my King's palace at Aberdeen. Tongue, and pen, and wit, cannot express my joy.'[81] He arrived in Aberdeen in September 1636, just as proceedings were under way against his brother for his Presbyterian activities. In November, George Rutherford was forced to resign from his post as schoolmaster of Kirkcudbright and remove himself from the town.[82]

In the next year and a half, banned from preaching and pastoral work, Rutherford wrote scores of letters to friends who before long began to copy them, gather them together and circulate them among the godly. According to Row, these letters contained cases of conscience, commentary on 'the tymes and the Bishops' tyranny', and 'some prophecies'.[83] Two hundred and nineteen of these letters from Aberdeen have survived, almost two-thirds of the total collection of Rutherford's letters. They reveal a man alternating between spiritual ecstasy and deep frustration at the limits placed upon him. 'Under this black, rough tree of the cross of Christ', he writes, 'He hath ravished me with His love, and taken my heart to heaven with Him.'[84] But Rutherford was straining at the leash. 'My dumb Sabbaths stick in my throat', he wrote.[85]

It was from this pent-up frustration at his confinement that he released the torrent of letters to nobles, lairds, burgesses and ministers all over Scotland in the critical years of 1636 and 1637. In 1636 the Book of Canons was published in Aberdeen itself, and in July 1637 the new Prayer Book was read out in St Giles Cathedral, sparking off the famous riot which began the movement of resistance to the king's policy in Scotland. Rutherford lambasted the Arminian innovations in his letters. In a letter dated 13 July 1637 he urged his parishioners at Anwoth:

Hate, and keep yourselves from idols. Forbear in any case to hear the reading of the new fatherless Service Book, full of gross heresies, popish and superstitious errors, without any warrant of Christ, tending to the overthrow of preaching. You owe no obedience to the bastard canons; they are unlawful, blasphemous, and superstitious.

---

[80] *Letters*, pp. 298–301.   [81] *Letters*, p. 131.
[82] Row, *History of the Kirk*, pp. 406–7.   [83] Row, *History of the Kirk*, pp. 396–7.
[84] *Letters*, p. 269.   [85] *Letters*, p. 268; for the same phrase see also p. 502.

All the ceremonies that lie in Antichrist's foul womb, the wares of that great mother of fornications, the kirk of Rome, are to be refused.[86]

The list of the recipients of these letters reads like a *Who's Who* of mid-seventeenth-century Scottish life. As we shall see in Chapter 6, Rutherford followed Buchanan in seeing the nobility as the natural leaders of Scotland, and the defenders of the liberty and purity of its kirk. He wrote to eminent noblemen like Lord Balmerino,[87] Lord Loudon, who was to be head of the Covenanter's government in 1638,[88] and the Earl of Cassillis, who was also to become a leading supporter of the Covenanters.[89] He challenged them to consider the brevity and emptiness of this life, the duty and privilege of standing for Christ and his crown. He called on Cassillis 'to back Christ now, when so many think it wisdom to let Him fend for Himself'.[90] Writing to Loudon he said that the nobles of Scotland, 'stand looking on with their hands folded behind their back' while thieves run away with 'the spoil of Zion on their back'. 'Plead for your wronged Bridegroom and His oppressed spouse', Rutherford demanded.[91]

Besides writing to these national figures, Rutherford also agitated amongst the local nobility in the south-west. Thirty-four of his letters were written to various members of the Gordon family who exercised great local influence in the south-west of Scotland. Eight of these were to Alexander Gordon of Earlston who had, like Rutherford, been banished by Sydserff to the north of Scotland. Both men were to be rehabilitated by the Glasgow General Assembly on the same day.[92] When Rutherford's Galloway flock wanted to prevent his transportation to St Andrews, they testified that 'The principal means whereby the body of the gentry thair (at this time wanting a head) is stirred up, is some few ministers of whom he is the principal.'[93]

Rutherford also kept in contact with bailies, provosts and lairds,[94] and with other radical ministers like David Dickson, George Gillespie and Alexander Henderson, who were to be leaders of the Covenanting movement. His letters are fascinating political documents because they reveal the vigorous lobbying and politicking being carried out by these radical ministers in the years leading up to the revolution. Of course, for many of the nobles who supported their cause, religion was not as important a factor as their economic and political situation,[95] and in the long run it was to

---

[86] *Letters*, p. 440.   [87] *Letters*, no. 139.   [88] *Letters*, nos. 116, 258, 281.
[89] *Letters*, nos. 128, 268, 278.   [90] *Letters*, p. 252.   [91] *Letters*, p. 235.
[92] *Records of the Kirk*, ed. Peterkin, p. 150.
[93] 'Reasons why Mr Samuel Rutherford should not be transported from the place where he is', Murray, *Life of Rutherford*, pp. 353–7.
[94] Among his correspondents are five bailies, five provosts, and six lairds.
[95] K. Brown, 'Aristocratic finances and the origins of the Scottish Revolution', *English Historical Review*, 54 (1989), 46–87 explains the economic problems which made the Scottish nobility willing to support the covenant in 1638.

become obvious that they did not share their ministers' theocratic vision of society. But religious grievances were to be the spark that ignited the revolution in Scotland, and it was under a religious Covenant that resistance to royal policy was gathered. Rutherford's *Letters* reveal the religious indignation, spiritual ecstasy and national vision that lay behind the Scottish revolution.

Letter-writing was not to be Rutherford's only activity in Aberdeen. The town was a stronghold of episcopacy and moderate Calvinism, which to Rutherford was simply Arminianism. He was not impressed by the Aberdeen Doctors whose moderatism has been so attractive to ecumenical writers in the twentieth century.[96] Aberdeen was full of 'Papists and men of Gallio's naughty faith', Rutherford told a correspondent.[97] By February 1637 he was engaging in full-scale disputation with the Doctors, particularly Robert Baron.[98] 'Dr. Barron hath often disputed with me, especially about Arminian controversies, and for the ceremonies. Three yokings laid him by; and I have not been troubled with him since. Now he hath appointed a dispute before witnesses.'[99] Baron was not the only one to be subjected to Rutherford's attacks; Spalding recorded that hearing Dr Sibbald 'at that tyme preiche, [Rutherford] stude up and accusit him of Armenianisme [sic]'.[100]

It is hardly any wonder that in such a hostile environment Rutherford felt alienated. He was pointed out in the streets as 'the banished minister', and 'openly preached against in the pulpits' in his own hearing.[101] 'I find the town's men cold, general and dry in their kindness', he wrote, 'yet I find a lodging in the heart of many strangers.'[102] He began to have an influence on local people, so that the ministers in Aberdeen tried to exile him further north, to Orkney or Caithness.[103] Friends to the Presbyterian cause such as Lady Pitsligo, Lady Marischall and the fiery preacher Andrew Cant, came

---

[96] See for example D. MacMillan, *The Aberdeen Doctors* (London, 1909).

[97] *Letters*, p. 163. Gallio was the Roman official in the book of Acts who tolerated the Christians because of his own indifference to religion. He was to become a byword among the Covenanters; in Sir Walter Scott's *Old Mortality* the Covenanters insult their opponents by comparing them to Gallio.

[98] *Letters*, p. 189.

[99] *Letters*, p. 239. Baron was later to attack Rutherford's insistence on the limited nature of Christ's atonement in his 'Disputatio de universalitate mortis Christi, contra Rheterfortem'. See James Gordon, *History of Scots Affairs from 1637 to 1641* (Aberdeen, 1841), III, 238.

[100] J. Spalding, *Memorials of the Trubles in Scotland and in England, 1624–1645*, I, (Aberdeen, 1850), p. 312. McMahon, 'Scottish episcopate', ch. 9, suggests that probably neither Baron nor Sibbald were Arminians, and that the Scottish episcopalians were basically Calvinist in theology. However, Rutherford would have regarded the slightest deviation from Reformed orthodoxy as tantamount to Arminianism. Baron's willingness to defend the same thesis as John Cameron – that Christ had died for all men though his death was only effectual for the elect – was anathema to Rutherford.

[101] *Letters*, p. 189. [102] *Letters*, p. 145. [103] *Letters*, p. 301.

to visit him. But he still longed to return to Anwoth.[104] This must have seemed a forlorn hope in January 1637 when Baillie wrote, 'for our king's dominions, there is no appearance [Rutherford] will ever gett living into them'.[105]

However, events were moving fast. As news of the new Prayer Book spread, the Presbyterian radicals met secretly to plan protests against its introduction, and kept Rutherford informed of their strategy.[106] On 23 July 1637, their plots came to spectacular fruition, when the reading of the new Prayer Book was interrupted by a riot. The Covenanting Revolution had begun, and over the next few months, the disaffected were to organise themselves into a powerful opposition force. By the autumn, they had set up what amounted to an unofficial parliament, the Tables, and in February 1638 they signed the National Covenant, a document which bound its subscribers to maintain the kirk, laws and liberties of Scotland.[107]

THE COVENANTER REVOLUTION (1638–1643)

The National Covenant made possible Rutherford's return to Anwoth. He seems to have left for his parish very soon after its signing; his parishioners said that he had been confined in Aberdeen for 'six quarteris of ane yier', which suggests that he must have left the city in March 1638.[108] Wariston tells us that on 3 June Rutherford was preaching at the college kirk in Edinburgh, where he had often been as a student, on the book of Hosea, the prophet who condemned spiritual adultery.[109] Rutherford was among a group of preachers who at this time 'pressed for the extirpation of episcopacy', to the offence of Hamilton, the king's commissioner.[110] He and Cant were also appointed to preach in the High Kirk 'and receave the oaths of that people to the Covenant', oaths they made 'with many a sigh and teare'.[111] This must have been a triumphant return from exile for Rutherford. The prophecies of his letters were being fulfilled.

The triumph was perhaps heightened by the sweetness of revenge when the General Assembly met again in Glasgow in November 1638. This

---

[104] *Letters*, pp. 404–7, 508.   [105] Baillie, *Letters and Journals*, I, p. 9.

[106] See J. M. Henderson, 'An advertisement about the Service Book 1637', *Scottish Historical Review*, 23 (1925–6), 199–204.

[107] On these developments see MacInnes, *Charles I and the Making of the Covenanting Movement*, pp. 158–82; D. Stevenson, *The Scottish Revolution, 1637–44: The Triumph of the Covenanters* (Newton Abbott, 1973), ch. 2; Lee, *Road to Revolution*, chs. 6 and 7.

[108] 'Petition of the parish of Anwoth', in Murray, *Life of Rutherford*, p. 355. Bonar dates Rutherford's last letter from Aberdeen, 11 June 1638 (*Letters*, pp. 555ff.), but Rutherford was preaching in Edinburgh on 3 June. The last letter from Aberdeen appears to be dated 4 February 1638.

[109] Wariston, *Diary*, I: 1632–39, ed. G. M. Paul (Edinburgh, 1911), p. 349.

[110] Baillie, *Letters and Journals*, I, p. 86.   [111] Baillie, *Letters and Journals*, I, p. 89.

Assembly fulfilled Melvillian dreams, for it abolished episcopacy and restored the pure Presbyterianism that men like Rutherford had been fighting for.[112] Not only was Rutherford exonerated from all church censures, but he also acted as a witness against Thomas Sydserff, the bishop who had exiled him to Aberdeen, and against James Sibbald, whom he accused of Arminianism. Both were deposed; the tables had been turned.[113] Even the University of Aberdeen asked for him to be made professor of divinity there but Rutherford had no desire to be removed once more from Anwoth and his ministry of preaching to the cold northern city.[114]

Rutherford was now at the heart of the Church of Scotland. On 26 November, he met with Baillie, Dickson and Henderson in Loudon's chambers to persuade the principal of Glasgow University, John Strang, to withdraw his objections to lay elders being present at the Assembly.[115] On 29 November he was appointed to a committee to investigate the corruptions and errors of the books of Canons, Service and Ordination, and those of the High Commission. Sitting on the committee were his former professor of theology, Andrew Ramsay, and the principal who had accused him of fornication, John Adamson.[116]

Although he returned to Anwoth after the Assembly, many felt that Rutherford had now become a voice too important to be left in a rural parish. In 1639, the city of Edinburgh elected him as a minister in the city, and the University of St Andrews elected him as professor of divinity at the New College. The General Assembly of 1639 agreed that Rutherford should go to St Andrews, and they insisted on this despite petitions from Galloway and the parishioners of Anwoth and a plea from Rutherford himself. The struggle to get congregation and minister to agree to the parting demonstrates how close the relationship between them had become.

Rutherford arrived in St Andrews in October 1639. According to Robert McWard, who was Rutherford's student there, the University was at that time 'the seat of the Arch-Prelate . . . the very Nursery of all superstition in worship, and Error in Doctrine and the Sink of all Profanity in conversation amongst the students'. Under Rutherford's influence it was to become, in the eyes of McWard anyway, 'a Lebanon, out of which were taken Cedars for building the house of the Lord through the whole land'.[117] It is unlikely that Rutherford would have expressed it in quite such sanguine terms. His later years there were to be soured by bitter disputes with colleagues and

---

[112] On the Glasgow Assembly see Stevenson, *Scottish Revolution*, ch. 3.
[113] Gordon, *History of Scots Affairs*, III, pp. 28–9.
[114] *Records of the Kirk of Scotland*, ed. Peterkin, p. 189.
[115] Baillie, *Letters and Journals*, I, p. 134.   [116] Baillie, *Letters and Journals*, I, p. 148.
[117] McWard, preface to *Joshua Redivivus*.

lifelong friends like Robert Blair, and his early years were scarred by conflicts within the national church and with the St Andrews' presbytery.

Little can be ascertained about Rutherford's activities outside the General Assembly in these years. We know that he paid a brief visit to preach for Lord Brooke at Warwick at the end of December 1639 (the first record we have of him travelling outside Scotland),[118] and he may have travelled to England on other occasions before his departure for the Westminster Assembly at the end of 1643.[119] He certainly spent some time away from St Andrews in August 1640, in order to preach a series of crusading sermons to the Scottish army, which was preparing to invade England in the Second Bishops' War.[120] But when some of his colleagues travelled south to negotiate with the English in 1640–41, Rutherford stayed behind, and immersed himself in university teaching, domestic ecclesiastical politics and the writing of a defence of Presbyterianism. Perhaps he wished to spend time with his new wife, Jean McMath, whom he had married on 24 March 1640. Before they left for England they were to have three children: Catherine, born in February 1641, John, born in June 1642, and Robert, born in July 1643.[121]

It is disturbing to realise that while he was enjoying establishing a family again, Rutherford was probably also acting as an inquisitor in the trial of witches. The 1640s were one of the most intense periods of witch-hunting in post-Reformation Scotland. Acts condemning witchcraft were passed in 1640, 1643, 1644, 1645 and 1649, and the church petitioned parliament to make the Acts effective. Although we have no direct evidence of Rutherford's involvement, we know that many of his fellow clergy led the trials

---

[118] A. Hughes, 'Thomas Dugard and his circle in the 1630s: a parliamentary-Puritan connexion?', *Historical Journal*, 29 (1986), 788. Dugard recorded in his diary that he had heard 'Dr Rutterford, a Scot' preach. Hughes says 'There is no proof that the preacher was Samuel Rutherford but it is just possible, given what else is known of his schedule at this time.' This seems unnecessarily tentative; we do not know of anything else Rutherford was doing in December 1639 and I cannot think of another Scottish preacher with a name like 'Rutterford' who would be preaching for English Puritans. The chaplain of Warwick Castle, Simeon Ashe, was present on this occasion and as he and Rutherford became lifelong friends, it seems reasonable to suppose that they first met at Warwick, not at the Westminster Assembly. C. Russell, *The Fall of the British Monarchies, 1637–42* (Oxford, 1991), p. 62, writes that the probability that Rutterford was Rutherford is 'very great'.

[119] He seems to have visited England again in the first part of 1643. In March, the Marquis of Hamilton received a letter telling him that 'Mr Rutherford has arrived from Scotland', Historical Manuscripts Commission, *Supplementary Report on the Manuscripts of his Grace the Duke of Hamilton*, ed. J. H. McMaster and M. Wood (London, 1932), p. 69. Again we cannot be sure that this 'Rutherford' is our Rutherford, but it seems very likely. Given that both of Rutherford's early visits are only known from incidental references in other sources, it is quite possible that he visited England a number of times before late 1643.

[120] Several of these are published in *Quaint Sermons* (1885).

[121] Murray, *Life of Rutherford*, p. 374.

and attended the execution of witches. After Rutherford left for England, his St Andrews colleagues – Blair, Wood and Traill – were called upon to witness the execution of witches and to advise on similar cases.[122] In just a few months of 1643, around forty women were strangled at the stake and then burnt for witchcraft in St Andrews and other parts of Fife. Another wave of executions took place in 1649. In July of that year Sir James Balfour heard commissions being given in parliament for the trial and burning of twenty-seven women and three men and boys on charges of witchcraft. Given Rutherford's prominent position in the kirk, and his zeal to see Scotland purged of 'malignants', it would be very surprising if he was not active in these persecutions.[123]

Although the kirk was united in supporting these efforts to eradicate witchcraft, it was also – as we shall see in Chapter 7 – deeply divided. Militants like Rutherford were under attack for their liturgical innovations and their support for conventicling. In St Andrews, too, Rutherford and Blair faced opposition. In 1642 they protested against the presbytery's decision to appoint a new minister, Andrew Afflect; they felt that his doctrine was not 'so spirituall and powerfull as the case of St Andrews required'. Because of their protests 'almost the whole Toune did much storme, and refused to regard any of Mr. R[obert Blair] and Mr Sa[muel Rutherford's] desyres'. Both men were so unhappy with the situation that they applied for removal elsewhere. With Baillie's assistance Rutherford received an invitation to become the minister of the parish of West Calder in the presbytery of Linlithgow, but though he accepted it, the St Andrews' presbytery would not allow him to leave.[124]

On the political front, 1642 also saw the outbreak of civil war in England between the king and parliament. Desperate for assistance, the parliament drew up a Solemn League and Covenant with the Covenanters in August 1643 in which they promised to reform their religion 'according to the word of God and the example of the best reformed churches' in return for military support from the Scots. It was agreed that an Assembly of Divines should meet in London to decide on a form of church government, liturgy and

---

[122] 'Minutes of the presbytery of St Andrews, 1641–56', St Andrews University Library, MSS Deposit 23, f. 44. See also, *Catechisms of the Second Reformation*, ed. Mitchell, Appendix A, lxvii.

[123] For full details on this grisly theme see C. Larner, C. H. Lee, and H. V. McLachan, *A Source-Book of Scottish Witchcraft* (Glasgow, 1977); G. F. Black, *A Calendar of Cases of Witchcraft in Scotland, 1510–1727* (New York, 1971 edn), esp. pp. 51–9; and T. C. Smout, *A History of the Scottish People, 1560–1830* (London, 1969), pp. 184–92.

[124] R. Baillie, *Letters and Journals*, II, p. 49. See also Murray, *Life of Rutherford*, pp. 188–90. On 5 October 1642 the Synod of Fife agreed to send a letter to Rutherford 'earnestlie intreating him that he would not make use of his libertie of transportation till the nixt Generall Assemblie', *Ecclesiastical Records: Selections from the minutes of the Synod of Fife, 1611–1687*, ed. G. R. Kinloch (Edinburgh, 1837), p. 133.

catechism for England and Ireland. The Scots kirk was invited to send a number of commissioners to this Assembly at Westminster, and Rutherford was one of those chosen to go to London in this capacity. He was probably chosen because his *Peaceable Plea for Pauls Presbyterie*, published in 1642, had revealed him to be an authority on New England Congregationalism, which seemed like the most obvious alternative to the Scottish Presbyterian model available to the English. Also appointed were John Maitland, Earl of Lauderdale, the Earl of Cassillis, and Johnston of Wariston, all as ruling elders. The other ministers were Henderson, the leading figure in the Church of Scotland, Baillie, Robert Douglas, who never took up his seat, and the young George Gillespie, who had been the chaplain to Rutherford's patron, Viscount Kenmure.[125]

THE WESTMINSTER ASSEMBLY (1643–1647)

Baillie and Rutherford took up their seats in the Westminster Assembly on 20 November 1643, and were plunged straight into debate.[126] Throughout 1644 Rutherford and the other Scottish delegates vigorously defended the Presbyterian form of church government, exercising an influence out of all proportion to their numbers. At the same time he wrote his most famous treatise, *Lex, Rex*, a justification of Covenanter resistance to Charles I. By 19 August 1645 parliament had passed the first ordinance for Presbyterian church government, and the royalist army had suffered a heavy defeat at Naseby.

However, Rutherford was far from happy. The Scots army in England had enjoyed little success, Montrose was creating great problems for the Covenanters in Scotland, and the attacks on Scottish Presbyterianism in London were now loud and bitter. Rutherford had set out with great expectations of the Westminster Assembly but was now being rudely stripped of his illusions. In October 1643, he had rejoiced in 'the honour of being a mason to lay the foundation for many generations, and to build the waste places of Zion in another kingdom'.[127] By March 1644, however, he was writing home to complain about the multitude of sectarians, the clerical Independents, and the House of Lords. With the Scottish army in a strong

---

[125] Rutherford's stature in the Church of Scotland is confirmed by the fact that in 1644 Aberdeen University chose him before Robert Baillie and David Dickson as their professor of divinity. Rutherford, however, stayed at St Andrews. See *Extracts from the Council Register of the Burgh of Aberdeen, 1643–1747* (Edinburgh, 1872), p. 25.

[126] See John Lightfoot, *Journal of the Proceedings of the Assembly of Divines from January 1st 1643 to December 31st 1644*, in his *Complete Works*, XIII, ed. J. R. Pitman (London, 1824), p. 56.

[127] *Letters*, p. 615.

position at Newcastle, 'it may be thought the land is near a deliverance', he wrote, 'But I rather desire it than believe it'.[128]

The period spent in England was out of character with the rest of Rutherford's life, for whereas in Scotland he always seemed to be a radical, in England he appeared as the arch conservative, frightened of the fissiparous potential of Independency and Antinomian theology. Of course, there was no real contradiction, for Rutherford's radicalism was essentially authoritarian. Like the revolutionary mullahs of Iran in the late 1970s he was prepared to use the anarchic energies of private religious meetings to usher in the order and discipline of a Presbyterian theocracy.[129] In London he acted as the defender of a conservative Presbyterianism, taking on all its opponents. Within the Westminster Assembly he debated with Independents who placed ecclesiastical authority with the local congregation rather than with synods, and Erastians who gave it to the civil magistrate rather than the clergy. In *The Due Right of Presbyteries* (1644) and *The Divine Right of Church Government* (1646) – both over 750 quarto pages in length – he mounted an exhaustive critique of Independency and Erastianism respectively. But those who worried Rutherford most were the radical sectarians, particularly chaplains of the New Model Army like William Dell and John Saltmarsh. Their Antinomian and antiformalist theology was attacked in *The Tryal and Triumph of Faith* (1645), *Christ Dying* (1647), and *A Survey of Spiritual Antichrist* (1648). In his *Due Right* and *A Free Disputation against Pretended Liberty of Conscience* (1649), Rutherford did not hesitate to advocate their suppression by the magistrate.

Rutherford had brought his family with him to London, and in August 1645, his wife gave birth to a daughter, Jean.[130] But his joy was tempered by the wearisome nature of the ecclesiastical debate and by further bereavement. Two of his children had died before he left Scotland, and two more were to die in London.[131] He himself was in poor health. In July 1645 he went with Henderson to the Epsom Waters, and in the summer of 1646 he was in 'variable health'.[132] In August, Baillie wrote that he and Rutherford expected to return to Scotland in the near future.[133] But Rutherford was required to stay in England for two more years, despite petitioning his colleagues in Scotland for permission to return.[134]

Combined with public controversy and news of bitter warfare in

---

[128] *Letters*, pp. 618–9.

[129] See S. A. Arjomand, *The Turban for the Crown: The Islamic Revolution in Iran* (Oxford, 1988).

[130] Murray, *Life of Rutherford*, p. 374.

[131] *Letters*, p. 621. 'I was in your condition', he writes to a bereaved mother, 'I had but two children, and both are dead since I came hither.'

[132] Baillie, *Letters and Journals*, II, pp. 296, 392.

[133] Baillie, *Letters and Journals*, II, p. 311.   [134] Baillie, *Letters and Journals*, II, p. 406.

Scotland, these personal burdens contributed to Rutherford's apocalyptic morbidity. 'I conceive that Christ hath a great design of free grace in these lands', he wrote in April 1646, 'but His wheels must move over mountains and rocks. He never yet wooed a bride on earth, but in blood, in fire, and in the wilderness. A cross of our own choosing, honeyed and sugared with consolations, we cannot have.'[135]

In 1646, further ordinances for Presbyterian church government were passed, and in October episcopacy was finally abolished, having only been suspended previously. But the Independents were gaining in strength, and the months before Rutherford's departure saw them taking control of London government, and staging their own debates on the government of church and state. By the time he took his leave of the Westminster Assembly on 9 November 1647, all his work to establish Presbyterian government in England seemed in danger of collapse.

FINAL YEARS AT ST ANDREWS (1647–1661)

Rutherford reported back to the Commission of the General Assembly, of which he was a member, on 26 November 1647. Exactly a month later parliament signed the Engagement with the king, and set itself on a collision course with the kirk, which narrowly rejected it. The fact that the Engagement did receive substantial support from many ministers reveals how unrepresentative militants like Rutherford were of the church as a whole. However, they controlled the kirk through a Commission which had been set up in 1642, ironically employing the same means to control the church which they themselves had deplored in the 1630s. Although the Commission had a membership of around 190, on average only around 30 attended it regularly, the majority of them belonging to the radical party.[136]

Rutherford was one of the most regular attenders at the Commission, being present at nearly all its sessions after his return from England. For him the Commission was as critical for consolidating and furthering the Presbyterian revolution as was the conventicle. Throughout 1648 he actively lobbied and conferred with the Committee of Estates on behalf of the Commission. In March he presented a 'Declaration' against the Engagement to parliament, and then examined his old professor of theology, Andrew Ramsay, who had supported the Engagement. In April he presented a 'Protestation' from the Commission against a parliamentary declaration

---

[135] *Letters*, p. 641.
[136] See D. Stevenson, 'The General Assembly and the Commission of the Kirk, 1638–51', *Records of the Scottish Church History Society*, 19 (1975), 59–79.

calling for the return of the king, and in June the Commission issued a 'Vindication' of church authority.[137]

The radicals' moment finally arrived in August 1648, after Cromwell defeated the Engagers' army at Preston. In September a makeshift army from the south-west of Scotland, drawn from among the radical conventiclers whom Rutherford had stirred up when in Anwoth, marched on Edinburgh. The Whiggamore Raid, as it became known, placed power in the hands of a kirk party regime. The regime set about the process of purging the land of its wickedness. A campaign for the reformation of manners was instigated, and the persecution of witches intensified. On 23 January 1649, following the kirk's direction, parliament passed the Act of Classes, which excluded all those who had taken the Engagement from holding office in the government or the army.[138] The Melvillians were delighted; here was a system of government in which the church acted as the legislature and the state was merely the executive.

Rutherford was at the height of his influence in 1649. He had always defended the congregation's right to choose its own pastor, and on 9 March parliament passed an act for the abolition of patronage which he himself had drawn up. He was also elected to the professorship of divinity at his old university, and had been called to one at the new university of Harderwyck in Holland as well. He had thirteen treatises in print and was famed for his role in the Westminster Assembly. Most significantly, his dream of a godly, Presbyterian Scotland was never more fully realised than in 1649 and 1650.

However, the kirk party regime was far from secure. Besides having a very narrow support base in Scotland,[139] it forfeited English approval by proclaiming Charles I's son king of Great Britain and Ireland after his father was executed in January 1649. When Charles II eventually visited St Andrews in July 1650, he was subjected to a lengthy speech in Latin from Rutherford, 'running mutch upon what was the dewtie of kings', and

---

[137] See *The Records of the Commissions of the General Assemblies, 1648–9*, ed. A. F. Mitchell and J. Christie (Edinburgh, 1896). Baillie, *Letters and Journals*, III, pp. 33–5, records that in a public meeting during March an 'indiscreet challenge of Mr Rutherfoord' provoked the Engager, William Colville, to argue that the king should be unconditionally restored to full legal power.

[138] See D. Stevenson, *Revolution and Counter-Revolution in Scotland, 1644–51* (London, 1977), pp. 115–45.

[139] Sir Edward Walker, *Historical Discourses upon Several Occasions* (London, 1705), p. 194, claimed that the ruling party consisted of less than fifty persons. Among 'the Prime Rulers in the Assembly', he numbered Robert Blair, James Guthrie, Patrick Gillespie, Robert Douglas, Rutherford, David Dickson, Andrew Cant and James Durham. In 1651 this group was to split down the middle during the Protester/Resolutioner controversy. Guthrie, Gillespie, Rutherford and Cant were to lead the Protesters, Douglas and Dickson the Resolutioners. Blair and Durham worked for some kind of reconciliation.

reminding the king of his duty to keep the covenants.[140] Rutherford had good reason to doubt the king's sincerity on that score, but even more worrying was the apostasy of the Scottish aristocracy. The purge instigated by the Act of Classes had left only a handful of nobles in the Committee of Estates, and without the support of the most powerful men in Scotland the kirk party regime could hardly hope to last for long. With Colonel Pride's purge of the English parliament in December 1649, and the ascendancy of Cromwell and the Independents, the days of the radical Presbyterians in Scotland were numbered.

From August 1649 to May 1650 Cromwell was distracted by his crusade against the Irish, but once this was completed he turned his attention to Scotland.[141] Rutherford anticipated a holy war and the establishment of Christ's kingdom in Britain. The Scottish army could call Christ 'High Lord-General' he assured Colonel Gilbert Ker in August 1650. 'A throne shall be set up for Christ in this island of Britain . . . and there can be neither Papist, Prelate, Malignant, nor Sectary, who dare draw a sword against him that sitteth upon the throne.'[142]

The hopes Rutherford had of the imminent arrival of Christ's kingdom were shattered on 3 September 1650 when Cromwell inflicted a devastating defeat on the Covenanter army at Dunbar. Rutherford wrote immediately to assure Ker that God was not on Cromwell's side, despite all appearances. 'Cromwell and his army . . . fight in an unjust cause, against the Lord's secret ones.' The Scottish army had fallen simply because of its impurity.[143] Such was also the conclusion of the radical 'Gentlemen, Commanders and Ministers, attending the forces in the west' who signed the Western Remonstrance on 17 October. They condemned the treaty with the king, accused the Committee of Estates of covetousness and oppression, and opposed an invasion of England to force the king onto the English. Rutherford was not involved in drawing this up but he clearly shared many of its assumptions.

To more moderate ministers, however, it seemed that the army had been purged too thoroughly. Throughout November the Commission considered the Remonstrance, the sins of the land and malignancy. Eventually, the moderates were successful, and both state and church refused to endorse the Remonstrance. On 14 December the General Assembly ruled that purges of the army could be relaxed. Rutherford, Wariston, Patrick Gillespie, James Guthrie and Andrew Cant, together with other lesser known ministers,

[140] See John Lamont, *The Diary of Mr John Lamont of Newton, 1649–71*, ed. G.R. Kinloch (Edinburgh, 1830), p. 20; Walker, *Historical Discourses*, p. 160.
[141] See D. Stevenson, 'Cromwell, Scotland and Ireland', in J. Morrill, ed., *Oliver Cromwell and the English Revolution* (Harlow, 1990), ch. 6.
[142] *Letters*, p. 650.   [143] *Letters*, p. 651.

dissented from this decision. Arguing that what the country needed was another purge, not an amnesty, they became known as the Remonstrants, because of their support for the Remonstrance issued by the hardline Presbyterians in the west of Scotland. The division between Remonstrants and Resolutioners, which was to plague the Church of Scotland throughout the 1650s, had opened up.[144]

During the first half of 1651 the gulf between the two groups yawned wider. The Resolutioners crowned the young Charles king on 1 January. Rutherford could not agree that this was a wise move, given Charles's obvious lack of commitment to the covenants. A conference between the two sets of ministers in January brought no reconciliation. In April, Rutherford dissented from the Synod of Fife's approval of the Commission's decisions,[145] and he may have been present on the 23rd when Cromwell spent six hours debating with Remonstrant ministers in his lodgings, in the vain hope that he could come to an understanding with Scotland's godliest clergy.[146] By May Rutherford was organising a separate religious fast from that of his lifelong colleague and friend, Robert Blair, who had refused to take sides on the issue.[147] Given that he was 'heavilie seeke [sick]' around this time, life had rarely been more bitter.[148]

The decisive break with the rest of the church came at the St Andrews General Assembly of July 1651. On the 20 July Rutherford handed in a protestation against the lawfulness of the Assembly. When the Assembly reconvened on 22 July at Dundee, none of the Protestation's subscribers were present.[149] Rutherford was never again to attend a General Assembly of the Church of Scotland. To add to the bitterness of this alienation from the kirk, Cromwell's victory at Worcester on 3 September 1651 ensured that the very 'Sectaries' whom Rutherford had opposed so fiercely in the 1640s were now in control of Scotland itself.

The vision of a Britain united under Christ's rule now seemed to have only a distant fulfillment. Yet Rutherford clung on to this and fell back on the theology of suffering and submission to strange providence which he

[144] On the course of the controversy, see J. Ogilvie, 'A bibliography of the Resolutioner–Protester controversy, 1650–59', *Transactions of the Edinburgh Bibliographical Society*, 14 (1930), 57–86; G. Donaldson, 'The emergence of schism in seventeenth-century Scotland', in his *Scottish Church History*, ch. 16. We shall explore the ideological roots of the schism in chapters 7 and 8.

[145] *Ecclesiastical Records: Selections from the Minutes of the Synod of Fife*, p. 174.

[146] W. C. Abbott, *The Writings and Speeches of Oliver Cromwell*, 4 vols. (Oxford, 1937–47), II, p. 408, says that Rutherford was present, but the sources to which he refers do not mention Rutherford by name.

[147] Wariston, *Diary*, II: 1650–54, ed. D. Hay Fleming (Edinburgh, 1919), p. 57.

[148] *Ecclesiastical Records: Selections from the Minutes of the Presbyteries of St Andrews and Cupar, 1641–98*, ed. G. R. Kinloch (Edinburgh, 1837), p. 62.

[149] *Records of the Kirk*, ed. Peterkin, p. 628.

had developed in the hard days of his early ministry. As Makey puts it, once the institutions of the Covenanter revolution had collapsed, Rutherford luxuriated in the mysteries of the invisible church and the beauty of Christ.[150] 'The fairest things, and most eminent in Britain, are stained, and have lost their lustre; only Christ keepeth his greeness and beauty, and remaineth what he was.'[151] 'Christ must have a small remnant', he told Gilbert Ker, '(few nobles, if any; few ministers; few professors)', a remnant that bowed to the wise decree of Christ that 'Spoiling and desolation is best for Scotland.'[152]

Yet for all his jeremiads, Rutherford was not about to give up hope and simply wait for God's judgement. Twice in 1651 he was invited to become professor of divinity at the university of Utrecht[153] but he refused to abandon Scotland at a critical moment. 'I would rather be in Scotland beside angry Jesus Christ', he declared, 'knowing that He mindeth no evil to us, than in Eden or any garden in the earth.'[154]

Rutherford had good reason to remain in Scotland. Some of the Protesters in Aberdeen were moving towards Independency, whilst others were showing considerable sympathy towards Cromwell. Cromwell had tried to persuade some that God was on his side; to Ker he 'had spoken baisly of the ministry of Scotland, and particularly of Mr S. Rutherfoord as a lyer, and that readily som judicial stroak would light upon them'.[155] But Cromwell also fostered the Protesters' cause and succeeded in attracting some of them into his government. Patrick Gillespie, the brother of George, became principal of Glasgow University and a close friend of Cromwell. Alexander Jaffray became one of his Scottish advisors.[156] Rutherford had no sympathy for Cromwell, and did his best to stop the Protesters compromising with the English, knowing that this would only strengthen the Resolutioners' accusation that their rivals were really Independents in disguise. In January 1652, a number of Protester leaders issued a 'Letter to Cromwell' in which they protested against the toleration the English had introduced and what they saw as the subordination of the church to the state.[157] In March 1653 a 'Declaration as to English Actings' was so strong in its condemnation of Cromwell's policies that Gillespie refused to sign it.[158]

---

[150] W. H. Makey, *The Church of the Covenant, 1637–51: Revolution and Social Change in Scotland* (Edinburgh, 1979), p. 165.

[151] *Letters*, p. 664.   [152] *Letters*, pp. 660–1.

[153] See Nethenus's preface to Rutherford, *Examen Arminianismi* (Utrecht, 1668). Also, Murray, *Life of Rutherford*, pp. 258–61.

[154] *Letters*, p. 662.   [155] Wariston, *Diary*, II, p. 39.

[156] H. Trevor-Roper, 'Scotland and the Puritan Revolution', in his *Religion, the Reformation and Social Change* (London, 1967), pp. 412–44.

[157] Printed in *Register of the Consultations of the Ministers of Edinburgh*, I: 1652–7, ed. W. Stephen (Edinburgh, 1921), pp. 1–12.

[158] *Consultations*, ed. Stephen, pp. 13–36.

The most bitter controversy of the 1650s was not, however, with Cromwell or the separatists, but with the Resolutioners. Various attempts were made to reunite the church, most notably a twenty-day conference in Edinburgh in November 1655, but to no avail.[159] Rutherford himself stoked the embers of the controversy on two occasions. In 1656 he wrote to the London Presbyterian minister, Simeon Ashe, whom he had known at the Westminster Assembly, claiming that the Resolutioners 'do persecute the godly, and in pulpits and presbyteries declaim against us as implacable and separatists'.[160] The Resolutioner ministers quickly sent their own account of the division to the London ministers, expressing their sorrow that Rutherford had used his reputation to 'render them odious abroad'.[161] In January 1657, Ashe responded to Rutherford by telling him that 'your tartnesse in language did not a little trouble mee', and advising him to be more conciliatory.[162]

Rutherford did not follow Ashe's advice. Early in 1658 his *Survey of Hooker* came off the presses with a preface which repeated the charges made against the Resolutioners in his letter to Ashe. The Resolutioners were understandably furious; Rutherford had probably a greater reputation abroad than any other man in the Scottish church at the time, and he had now slandered them before an international audience.[163] Robert Blair is said to have avowed 'that before he had written any such things, he could have rather choiced to have had his right-hand stricken off at the Crosse of Edinburgh by the axe of the hangman'.[164] Resolutioner ministers were urged to 'provide them selves coppies of the said book' that they might know how to counter its propaganda.[165]

At a local level in St Andrews, Rutherford's passion for the 'Godlie party' was also causing strife. All his colleagues were Resolutioners and even in the Synod of Fife only six members supported him, but as Baillie put it 'Mr Rutherfoord to the uttermost of his power, advances the other partie.'[166] In September 1656 Baillie reported that James Wood was seeking removal from his position in New College because 'Mr Rutherfoord's daily contentions

---

[159] The papers from this conference are printed in *Consultations*, ed. Stephen, pp. 90–201.

[160] *Letters*, p. 681.

[161] *Consultations*, ed. Stephen, pp. 213, 232–3, 276–80, prints four letters from the Resolutioners to Ashe, Calamy and Manton.

[162] *Consultations*, ed. Stephen, pp. 288–9.

[163] Ashe had written to him, 'many more eyes are upon you than any other man in Scotland', Stephen, ed., *Consultations*, p. 289.

[164] R. Baillie, *Letters and Journals*, III, p. 375. Baillie wrote a long letter to Douglas criticising Rutherford's preface, pp. 375–81.

[165] *Consultations of the Ministers of Edinburgh*, II: 1657–1660, ed. W. Stephen (Edinburgh, 1930), p. 140.

[166] Baillie, *Letters and Journals*, III, p. 248.

with him made him wearie of his place exceedingly.'[167] Wood moved to St Salvators in 1657 leaving a vacancy which involved Rutherford in more acrimonious debate. The second master, Alexander Colville, wanted to appoint James Sharp, who had been a student at Aberdeen during Rutherford's exile there, and a regent at St Andrews in the early 1640s. Rutherford had no intention of appointing Sharp and lobbied strenuously for William Raitt.[168] Colville won out in the end and Sharp was inducted in February 1661, a month before Rutherford's death.

In the midst of all this controversy Rutherford's life had some brighter moments. He preached at communion festivals for the godly at Scone, sometimes before large crowds,[169] and friends from Galloway seem to have attended his meetings in St Andrews.[170] In March 1654 Wariston reported him preaching to 'such a throng in the Grayfreers in the forenoon and in the Tron kirk in the afternoon' as had not been seen since 1638.[171] Three more children were born to him and Jean MacMath after his return from England but Agnes, born in 1649, was the only child to be alive at his death, the five-year-old Margaret having died some weeks before.[172] Jean MacMath was to live until 1675, but in 1656 Rutherford had written to Wariston 'about his wyfes feared death'.[173] Affliction had plagued him throughout his life.

On 14 May 1660, Charles II was proclaimed king in Edinburgh. In September the Committee of Estates issued a declaration against *Lex, Rex*, 'a book inveighing against monarchie, and laying ground for rebellion'; every person with a copy who did not return it to his Majesty's solicitor by 16 October was to be regarded as an enemy of the king. The seditious book was burnt at the Cross in Edinburgh in the following month, and then under the windows of New College in St Andrews. Rutherford was deprived of his position in the University, his charge in the church, and his stipend, and confined to his own house. He was cited to appear before parliament on a charge of treason,[174] and his friends feared that he might be executed, just as Wariston, James Guthrie and the Earl of Argyll, Archibald Campbell,

---

[167] Baillie, *Letters and Journals*, III, p. 316.
[168] *Ecclesiastical Records: Selections from the Minutes of the Presbyteries of St Andrews and Cupar*, pp. 74–6.
[169] Lamont, *Diary*, pp. 15, 31–2, 58, 66.   [170] Wodrow, *Analecta*, II, p. 147.
[171] Wariston to Guthrie, in Historical Manuscripts Commission, *Report on the Laing Manuscripts*, (London, 1914), p. 293.
[172] Murray, *Life of Rutherford*, p. 374; Lamont, *Diary*, p. 133. Out of at least eight children from two marriages, all but one died before Rutherford.
[173] Wariston, *Diary*, III, p. 27.
[174] Baillie, *Letters and Journals*, III, p. 447. Baillie also recorded that Andrew Cant was accused before the magistrates of treason for daring to preach against 'Mr Rutherfoord's hard usage'.

were to be.[175] In December, Baillie wrote to Sharp asking him to make sure that the authorities went no further with his old friend.[176]

As it turned out, he need not have bothered. Rutherford fell seriously ill early in 1661 and was unable to appear before parliament to face the charges. On 8 March he issued a last will and testimony. When asked about *Lex, Rex* he is reported to have said that 'he would willingly dye on the scaffold for that book with a good conscience'.[177] He died near the end of March 1661, speaking rapturously of Christ's glory: 'I shall live and adore Him. Glory, glory to my Creator and to my Redeemer for ever. Glory shines in Emmanuel's land.'[178]

---

[175] Baillie, *Letters and Journals*, III, p. 467, wrote after Guthrie's execution that 'Mr Rutherfoord, had not death prevented, was in the same hazard'.

[176] Baillie, *Letters and Journals*, III, p. 418. [177] Wodrow, *Analecta*, I, pp. 165–6.

[178] *A Testimony to the Work of Reformation in Britaine and Ireland* (Lanark, 1739), p. 15. Rutherford was to live on in the minds of his admirers. Later in 1661, when Wariston was flitting around the continent trying to avoid being sent back to Scotland for trial and as delirious as any character from Dostoyevsky, he dreamt of being condemned by the 'king's absolut decree' as the greatest traitor of all, and saw himself falling beside the king's bedside swearing to his innocence. It was then that Rutherford 'spake som seasonable instructing word at my one eare and then a comforting word at the uther . . . which refreshed me, and I thought the king was calmer'. Wariston, *Diary*, III, p. 185.

3

The scholar

This chapter will explore the furniture of Rutherford's mind, and (to mix metaphors) the mental tools with which he hammered out his ideas. In particular, it will draw attention to the catholicity of his intellectual taste in the hope that this will do something to dispel the stereotype of the bigoted, narrow-minded Presbyterian cleric drawn by Buckle and Trevor-Roper. Rutherford was certainly an intolerant advocate of religious persecution and divine-right Presbyterianism, but he was also a writer with a genuine appreciation for the learning and eloquence of Spanish Jesuits, Roman orators and medieval scholastics. He may have been a passionate revivalist preacher, but we ought not to forget that for over twenty years he was a university professor. This chapter aims to evoke something of the richness, complexity and sophistication of his mental world. We shall begin by examining the formative role played by his education, and then go on to examine the intellectual sources mined by his books.

UNIVERSITY EDUCATION

Something has been said in the previous chapter of the personal influences on Rutherford as a young man. Those of David Calderwood and the Edinburgh privy kirk were the most formative. But Rutherford was also a conscientious and clever student, and the Melvillians had never been averse to learning; indeed Melville himself was an educational pioneer who promoted humanism and Ramism in Scottish universities. So it is necessary to consider the course of study pursued by Rutherford at university, and the way in which it shaped his mind.

Rutherford's personal library has not survived intact and seems to have been dispersed after his death, but we do know the books possessed by Edinburgh University Library. The core of the library was the collection of Clement Little which had been donated to the town college in the 1580s. Rutherford would probably have used this library in the five or six years between his graduation and his appointment at Anwoth in 1627. According to James Kirk the library shows 'a catholicity of taste in theological treatises'. There was an ample collection of patristic, medieval, humanist, Lutheran, anti-Protestant and Calvinist texts.[1] As we shall see, Rutherford himself was to demonstrate a similar range in his reading.

The curriculum of Edinburgh college began in the first year (called the 'bajan' year) with the students translating Cicero from the Latin; proficiency in Latin was essential since the entire MA course was taught in what was still the *lingua franca* of all European intellectuals. Then the students' attention was turned towards Greek. They learnt grammar by reading examples of it from the New Testament and Isocrates, and then studied the poetry and prose of various authors, including Homer. The final four or five months of the year were spent poring over the *Dialectic* of Petrus Ramus (1517–72). The second year 'Semi-Bajan' class started by translating Greek to Latin and then turned to the study of rhetoric using the textbooks of Talaeus (Ramus's colleague and collaborator), Cassander, and Aphthonius of Antioch (AD 234–305). Both dialectic and rhetoric were practised using concrete examples from Cicero and Demosthenes. At this point in their course, after a year of Greek, the students first encountered Aristotle. They were to work through five of his logical treatises: the *Organum*, *De Interpretatione* (and the commentary upon it by the neo-Platonist Porphyry), *Priora Analytica*, the *Topicks* and *De Sophisticis Elenchis*. The year was rounded off with the study of arithmetic. In the third year the 'Bachelor' class learnt Hebrew grammar, and then proceeded to read Aristotle's *Posteriora Analytica* and then his *Ethica*. The year ended with anatomy classes using the textbook of Servelius. The fourth year 'Magistrand' class read more Aristotle (*De Caelo, De Ortu, Metrologica, De Anima*), Hunter's *Cosmographia* and Joan de Sacrobosco's *Sphere*.[2]

Perhaps the first point to make about this course is that it was strikingly 'secular', a fact worth bearing in mind considering that it was designed mainly for future ministers of the church; this does something to undermine the old belief in the tyranny of a superstitious kirk over the Scottish mind of the seventeenth century. As Walter Ong remarked, the only scholastics we tend to read or remember today are theologians, and we forget that 'arts scholasticism' was actually more important in the university curriculum than was scholastic theology. Universities were not absorbed by theological

---

[1] J. Kirk, 'Clement Little's library', in J. R. Guild and A. Law, eds., *Edinburgh University Library 1580–1980* (Edinburgh, 1982), pp. 1–42.

[2] *University of Edinburgh: Charters, Statutes and Acts of the Town Council and the Senatus 1583–1858*, ed. A. Morgan (Edinburgh, 1937), pp. 110–15. T. Crauford, *History of the University of Edinburgh from 1580 to 1646* (Edinburgh, 1808), pp. 57–62. See also A. Grant, *The Story of the University of Edinburgh During its First Three Hundred Years* (London, 1884), pp. 148–50; A. Bower, *The History of the University of Edinburgh*, I (Edinburgh, 1917), pp. 82–92.

questions but had a strong orientation towards the material world.[3] Of course Latin, Greek and Hebrew were very useful languages for a would-be theologian, but the MA course at university was to influence the methodology rather than the content of Rutherford's later theological writings. The imprint of three distinct intellectual traditions can be found on this curriculum: scholasticism, humanism and Ramism, and I shall assess the relative importance of each in turn.

As Alasdair MacIntyre and James McConica have recently pointed out, the revival of Aristotelian scholasticism in the sixteenth and seventeenth centuries, particularly in the Protestant world, is one which has not yet been properly studied.[4] Yet its impact on Edinburgh University was significant. According to Alexander Bower, the theses of the regents which survive for the years between 1610 and 1624 were all thoroughly Aristotelian, showing a complete commitment to the idea that logic should be centred on syllogism and deduction.[5] Early seventeenth-century student notebooks were also essentially commentaries on Aristotle, and were subdivided according to the traditional scholastic categories of questions and answers, objections and replies.[6] The methods of learning were also thoroughly medieval, revolving around lectures (probably often dictation) on set texts, and disputations in which the student was given a thesis and then asked to defend it, probably with reference to Aristotle. Even anatomy was taught using textbooks, not through observation of dissections. Edinburgh also retained a regenting scheme of teaching, and did not adopt the professorial one advocated by Melville. The result was that it was not a university with various faculties and specialist teaching, but merely a college of arts and philosophy, with rather amateurish regents teaching all the subjects.[7]

By far the most prominent author studied was Aristotle. Ten of the set texts, comprising almost half of the total, were by the philosopher. Aristotle dominated this curriculum almost as much as he had done those of the medieval period. The minds of Rutherford's teachers at Edinburgh were immersed in his writings. In 1617 James VI had listened to one of the regents, Andrew Young, 'pressing many things by clear testimonies from Aristotle's text'. He was duly impressed, declaring 'Mr Young is very old in Aristotle.' He is also said to have told some English doctors sitting by

[3] W. Ong, *Ramus: Method and the Decay of Dialogue: From the Art of Discourse to the Art of Reason* (Cambridge, Mass., 1958), pp. 132–5.

[4] A. MacIntyre, *Whose Justice, Which Rationality?* (London, 1988), p. 209; J. McConica, 'Humanism and Aristotle in Tudor Oxford', *English Historical Review*, 94 (1979), 291.

[5] Bower, *History*, pp. 129–31.

[6] C. Shepherd, 'University life in the seventeenth century', in G. Donaldson, ed., *Four Centuries: Edinburgh University Life 1583–1983* (Edinburgh, 1983), p. 11.

[7] On the regenting scheme of teaching see D. Stevenson, *Kings College, Aberdeen 1560–1641: From Protestant Reformation to Covenanting Revolution* (Aberdeen, 1990), p. 51.

him, 'These men know Aristotle's mind as well as he himself did while he lived.'[8]

Alexander Bower concluded from all this that the education offered at Edinburgh 'was very superficial; consisting of a short introduction to geography, a comparatively long time spent on the abstractions of Aristotle, and some attention paid to scholastic divinity'. Bower charged that the system taught at the university did injury to the progress of science since it failed to see that general principles are not the foundation but the point at which we arrive at the end of an empirical investigation.[9] Similarly, G. D. Henderson claimed that the method of university study in seventeenth-century Scotland was 'pure scholasticism'.[10]

It is no doubt true that this was no *curriculum à la Descartes*, but concentration on Aristotle led Bower and Henderson to ignore vital differences from the medieval university curriculum.[11] There was, for instance, no teaching of metaphysics. This was quite natural in a Protestant university deeply suspicious of the traditional textbooks that had been so tainted by their use of fine metaphysical distinctions to defend Catholic doctrines such as transubstantiation. Although Suarez and other Catholic neo-scholastics had written metaphysics textbooks shorn of such controversial theological issues and designed to have a more universal appeal, these had not found their way into the curriculum at Edinburgh. For good Protestant and humanist reasons metaphysics was still suspect, and this indicates that the university did not have a full-blown scholastic curriculum.

Bower also missed the important humanist elements in the Edinburgh University curriculum. In this he shares the same blind spots as historians of the English universities such as Costello, Curtis, Kearney and Hill.[12] James McConica has argued that they have exaggerated the conservatism and sterility of the official teaching, and ignored the influence of humanism. The curriculum may have been largely Aristotelian but a cosmopolitan Protestant and humanist culture was arranged around it. Aristotle was not an ossified legacy but a convenient vehicle through which to mobilise vast amounts of new intellectual material in the sixteenth century.[13] Margo Todd makes a similar point in her *Christian Humanism and the Puritan*

---

[8] Crauford, *History*, pp. 83–5.   [9] Bower, *History*, I, pp. 92, 129–30.

[10] G. D. Henderson, *Religious Life in Seventeenth-Century Scotland* (Cambridge, 1937), p. 122.

[11] A more balanced assessment of the Edinburgh curriculum is given by Alexander Grant, *Story of the University of Edinburgh*, p. 150.

[12] W. T. Costello, *The Scholastic Curriculum at Early Seventeenth Century Cambridge* (Cambridge, Mass., 1958); M. Curtis, *Oxford and Cambridge in Transition 1558–1642: An Essay on Changing Relations between the English Universities and English Society* (Oxford, 1959); H. Kearney, *Scholars and Gentlemen: Universities and Society in Pre-industrial Britain, 1500–1700* (London, 1970); C. Hill, *The Intellectual Origins of the English Revolution* (Oxford, 1965), appendix.

[13] McConica, 'Humanism and Aristotle in Tudor Oxford', pp. 291–317.

Social Order. She takes issue with the claim of Costello, Kearney and Hill that neo-scholasticism overtook the humanist element in the curriculum of early seventeenth-century Oxford and Cambridge.[14] Many of her arguments apply equally well to the arts course at Edinburgh University, and they draw our attention to its important humanist features. Todd points out that the dominance of Aristotle in the university syllabus was not an indication of the weakness of humanism or Ramism. Erasmus had approved of Aristotle's logic, and even Ramus quoted the philosopher when he was in agreement with him. Protestants and humanists were not opposed to Aristotle as such, but only to his pagan metaphysics and to what they saw as the corruption of the philosopher by the scholastic tradition. They intended to strip away the layers of interpretation and commentary that had obscured Aristotle, and read him again in the original Greek, without the distraction of scholastic commentaries.[15]

This concern to read Aristotle and the Bible in the original Greek and Hebrew reflects the influence of the humanist slogan *ad fontes* (back to the sources). It was in sharp contrast to Catholic universities, where notebooks still contained basically Thomistic commentaries on the Latin text of Aristotle and comments by Schoolmen.[16] In keeping with humanism, great attention was paid to purity of Greek and Latin style, rather than to the acquisition of standard medieval Latin, and the inclusion of Homer, Isocrates, Demosthenes and Cicero in the course reflected the impact of humanist assumptions on the framers of the Edinburgh curriculum.

Rutherford was particularly well acquainted with humanist thought because from 1623 to 1626 he was employed as regent of humanity in the university. In this position he had to ensure that those who were applying to begin the MA course in the following year had a good grounding in Latin and some elementary knowledge of Greek grammar. He was required to teach Latin poets and orators like Horace, Juvenal, Plautus and Cicero, and on Saturday afternoons he taught his class some part of the *Psalms* in the edition of the great Scottish humanist, George Buchanan.[17]

The faculty of the university seems to have preserved the humanist interest in Latin verse so elegantly mastered by Buchanan. The principal, John Adamson, edited a volume of verse entitled *The Muses Welcome to King James VI* which included a long poem by the most eminent Scottish poet of the time, Drummond of Hawthornden. Drummond was a graduate of the University and donated 550 books to the college in 1626–7.[18] It is

---

[14] M. Todd, *Christian Humanism and the Puritan Social Order* (Cambridge, 1987), ch. 3.
[15] Todd, *Christian Humanism*, pp. 63–8.   [16] Todd, *Christian Humanism*, pp. 79–80.
[17] See Morgan, ed., *University of Edinburgh*, pp. 114–15.
[18] See C. Finlayson and S. Simpson, 'The history of the library, 1580–1710', in Guild and Law, eds., *Edinburgh University Library*, p. 46.

important to remember that although he was certainly the most accomplished of the humanist poets in Scotland at the time, he was not the only one. Adamson and the professor of theology, Andrew Ramsay, were among the minor poets who provided the context in which Drummond produced his work. Unfortunately, as John MacQueen has observed, this is often ignored, and the cultural history of Renaissance Scotland is written as if the great intellectuals lived in a vacuum.[19]

The third aspect of the course we must consider is its Ramism. Students spent several months of their first year studying Ramus's *Dialectic* and in their second year the *Rhetoric* of Ramus's colleague Talaeus was used as a guide. The creator of this new system of logic and rhetoric had first attained notoriety when, as a student in Paris, he defended the iconoclastic thesis that everything Aristotle said was wrong. He later developed his *Dialectic* as an alternative to the Aristotelian logic being taught in universities, and it became enormously popular and controversial – particularly in Protestant countries – even leading to outbreaks of rioting in some universities.[20]

The first university in Britain to be influenced by Ramism was St Andrews, where Andrew Melville promoted Ramist reforms in the face of Aristotelian opposition in the 1570s and 1580s. Robert Rollock, the founder of Edinburgh College, had known Melville well, and it was through him that Ramus and Talaeus were incorporated into the Edinburgh syllabus.[21] Crauford tells us that Rollock was 'of eminent knowledge in the dogmatick philosophies of Aristotle', and that 'He esteemed also much of Ramus his Dialectick, and hardly any man made better use thereof', a reminder that Aristotelianism was as compatible with Ramism as it evidently was with humanism.[22] Besides having the textbooks of Ramus and Talaeus on the curriculum, Rollock also followed the Ramist advice to use concrete examples from writers like Cicero and Demosthenes when studying both dialectic and rhetoric. Moreover, he included Talaeus on the course taught by the regent of humanity, who from 1623 to 1626 was Rutherford himself.[23]

Perhaps the major reason for Ramus's appeal was his radical simplification of logic, something for which the teachers of the adolescent boys who studied at universities must have been deeply grateful. He has been hyperbolically described as 'the greatest master of the short-cut the world

---

[19] J. MacQueen, 'Conclusion' to his *Humanism in Renaissance Scotland* (Edinburgh, 1990), p. 178.

[20] For a description of the uproar caused at Cambridge when the Puritan, William Gouge, defended Ramus in public debate see Curtis, *Oxford and Cambridge in Transition*, pp. 118–19.

[21] On Melville and Ramism at St Andrews see H. Kearney, *Scholars and Gentlemen*, pp. 53–9.

[22] Crauford, *History*, p. 44.   [23] See Morgan, *University of Edinburgh*, pp. 112, 115.

has ever known'.[24] Ramus did away with the abstruse predicables of Aristotle, and proceeded to lay out the various aspects of logic in a neat table with dichotomous organisation. He began by breaking logic down into the two categories of invention and judgement, then divided invention into artificial and inartificial and proceeded until he had arrived at what he saw as the irreducible building-blocks of logic. For Ramus, dialectic was not the art of syllogism but the art of classification by dichotomy.

Quite what the significance of this was and why it provoked such enthusiasm has puzzled many scholars. Perry Miller believed that it provided the New England Puritans with a kind of common-sense realism freeing them from nominalist doubts,[25] but Walter Ong suggested that Ramist logic was typical of the modern trend from an oral to a visual culture, where thinking was conceived of in spatial terms.[26] Christopher Hill saw Ramism as a precursor of the modern scientific attitude,[27] and Hugh Kearney has argued that it appealed particularly to the Puritan merchants in the towns, whilst humanism appealed to the Puritan gentry in the country.[28]

The claim that Ramism was a big step towards the modern scientific method is problematic since it did not stress experiment or observation as most of the really seminal thinkers of the seventeenth century were to do. Similarly, there does not appear to be much evidence for Kearney's claim that intellectual traditions corresponded neatly to conventional social divisions. The most plausible interpretation is probably still that of Perry Miller, one of the first modern historians to draw attention to Ramus's importance. Miller argued that the key innovation of Ramus was to see logic as a matter of properly classifying axioms, rather than as a difficult process of syllogistic deduction. This appealed greatly to the Puritans, for instead of having to provide painstaking proof for their beliefs they could simply state the teaching of Scripture as axiomatic and then proceed to break it down into logical order. 'It was a logic for dogmatists', said Miller; 'it assumed that decency and order prevailed both in the mind and among things.' Ramists were realists who believed that concepts were real things, and not just mental constructs. Each word in the Ramist system stood for something objective, and the distance between the idea and the thing-in-itself was annihilated.[29]

[24] Hardin Craig, quoted in Curtis, *Oxford and Cambridge in Transition*, p. 254.
[25] P. Miller, *The New England Mind*, I: *The Seventeenth Century* (New York, 1939), chs. 5 and 6.
[26] Ong, *Ramus, Method and the Decay of Dialogue*. In making this judgement, Ong was influenced by the ideas of Marshall McLuhan.
[27] Hill, *Intellectual Origins of the English Revolution*.
[28] Kearney, *Scholars and Gentlemen*, pp. 46–70.
[29] Miller, *The New England Mind*, ch. 5.

Although one might think that this realism would be attractive to Rutherford, it is hard to find much trace of Ramist logic in his work. He certainly did not assemble the sort of dichotomous tables that made Perkins's *Golden Chain* so famous. He also seems to have become somewhat notorious for his syllogisms and the scholastic arrangement of his works, suggesting that he was influenced by the Protestant neo-scholastic revival in the early seventeenth century. One of his critics, James Gordon, found his style unbearably scholastic: 'Mr Samuel Reterfortis soars with sublime distinctions, *et caput intra nubila condit*; most pairt of which are not to be understood by ordinar capacityes; for many of which he is beholding to Gregory de Valentia, a Jesuit; which is but to robbe the Egyptian for a better ende.'[30] Gordon was not the only one to be exasperated by Rutherford's form of argument. Baillie records that during the controversial debate on conventicles at the 1640 Aberdeen Assembly, 'in the midst of the jangleing' Rutherford 'cast in a syllogisme'. However, his painstaking contribution was abruptly dismissed: 'my Lord Seafort would not have Mr Samuell to trouble us with his logick syllogismes'.[31] Perhaps, as David Stevenson has suggested, Scottish universities continued to pay 'lip-service to Ramism' whilst largely accepting the renewal of neo-scholasticism.[32] If this is the case, it reminds us that whilst avoiding the mistake of neglecting the humanist and Ramist elements on the curriculum, we should not go to the other extreme and emphasise them to the point of excluding scholasticism.

Rutherford's love of syllogism, his constant use of Aristotelian distinctions between ends and means, essence and form, and his scholastic obsession with amassing authorities to support his case, were natural to a mind educated through this curriculum, but so were the classical quotations and philological skills also evident in his works. As Margo Todd has urged, it is time that we took seriously the eclecticism of seventeenth-century thinkers; it was quite possible to be an Aristotelian and a humanist at the same time.[33] False dichotomies between scholasticism and humanism, scholasticism and Ramism fail to do justice to the complexity of early modern intellectual method.[34] The sort of neat chronological scheme presented by Hugh Kearney (scholasticism in the first generation of the sixteenth century, humanism in the second, Ramism in the third, and neo-

[30] J. Gordon, *History of Scots Affairs from 1637 to 1641* (Aberdeen, 1841), p. 170. 'Reterfortis' was the Latinised version of Rutherford; Gordon no doubt used it to reinforce the impression that Rutherford was a pretentious scholastic.
[31] R. Baillie, *Letters and Journals*, 3 vols., ed. D. Laing (Edinburgh, 1841–2), I, p. 252.
[32] Stevenson, *Kings College, Aberdeen*, p. 52.   [33] Todd, *Christian Humanism*, p. 70.
[34] A point made very forcefully by R. Muller, 'Calvin and the "Calvinists": assessing continuities and discontinuities between the Reformation and orthodoxy', *Calvin Theological Journal*, 30 (1995), 360–72.

scholasticism from the 1590s) is not convincing.[35] Far from being incompatible, these were intertwined in the curriculum of Scottish universities, which helps to explain the methodological pluralism and heterogeneous sources of Rutherford's own writings.

ERUDITION

Throughout his life Rutherford was concerned to reconcile word and spirit, form and substance, mind and heart. He vigorously opposed those who purveyed anti-intellectual and antiformalist piety. His own works displayed formidable erudition. Like Boyd and Calderwood, the two men who probably influenced the course of his life most directly, he showed extraordinary familiarity with a very wide range of authors and ideas.[36] In the course of his works he referred to over seven hundred different authors: Spanish Jesuits, rabbinical commentators, Greek and Latin Fathers, classical philosophers, contemporary Protestants, medieval scholastic theologians, and of course, the sixteenth-century Reformers.[37] The writers he quoted can be roughly divided into five broad categories: classical, patristic, medieval, post-Reformation Catholics, and Protestants. I shall examine each of these categories in turn and then conclude by discussing Rutherford's use of the most significant source-book of all, the Bible.

Classical references in Rutherford's works were few in number compared to those in the other categories, no doubt because the pre-Christian writers were difficult to introduce into any study of Christian theology and practice. In *Pro Divina Gratia* for example, there were only around twenty references to classical authors or characters, seven of which were to Aristotle. *Lex, Rex* clearly allowed more scope for quotation from pagan authors since its subject was political, and there were forty-five classical references here. Again Aristotle was the most quoted author; he was referred to nineteen times altogether and Rutherford declared him to be 'the flower of nature's wit'.[38]

The preponderance of references to Aristotle reveals the scholasticism and conservatism of Rutherford's outlook. Cicero, the favourite classical writer of the early Renaissance, was only mentioned twice in *Lex, Rex*, and although Tacitus was cited six times, it is clear that Rutherford was mining him for examples of the terrors of tyranny and not for the cynical attitude

---

[35] Kearney, *Scholars and Gentlemen*, p. 77.   [36] Henderson, *Religious Life*, pp. 127–8.

[37] For an almost complete list of authors quoted by Rutherford see the appendix to David Strickland, 'Union with Christ in the theology of Samuel Rutherford', unpublished Ph.D. dissertation, Edinburgh University (1972), pp. 210–55.

[38] *Lex, Rex*, p. 79 [45].

that made him a favourite with Renaissance sceptics such as Lipsius and Montaigne.[39]

Rutherford's preference for Aristotle was common among second- and third-generation Protestants, but it would have been out of place in Luther and Calvin. Luther once declared 'no man can become a theologian unless he becomes one without Aristotle', and 'the whole of Aristotle is to theology as darkness is to light'.[40] Rutherford, therefore, shared the renewed enthusiasm for scholastic method that Brian Armstrong has detected among second- and third-generation Protestants.[41]

However, it is important not to set this scholasticism against humanism, as Armstrong seems to do. Rutherford's use of classical quotations reveals a moralistic and didactic purpose characteristic of Christian humanism. He saw in the ancient Greek and Latin authors a mine of examples that illustrated the evils and tragic end of tyrants. It was for this purpose that he referred to the writings of historians such as Plutarch, Xenophon, Sallust and Herodotus, and chose a dialogue between Nero and Seneca as the frontispiece of *Lex, Rex*. In *The Covenant of Life Opened* he also gave examples from classical history to convince his readers (and no doubt himself) of the necessity of mortification to 'book-vanity'. He wrote that Ptolemaeus Philadelphius, king of Egypt, had gathered 40,000 books into his great library in Alexandria only for them all to be destroyed by fire, and that Serenus Sanmionicus had a personal library of 2,060 books, but had to leave them behind at death.[42] Rutherford's familiarity with such stories shows that he was very much a part of the Calvinist humanism described by Margo Todd and David Allan.[43]

As Allan points out, Rutherford was also well aware of the great Scottish historical tradition, and in the forty-third chapter of *Lex, Rex* he appealed for support to Boethius, Fordun, Major and Buchanan. *Lex, Rex* also referred several times to the historical works of Josephus (the *Antiquities* and *The Jewish War*), in order to draw moral examples from them. Although he never wrote an historical work, Rutherford showed a typical humanist concern for historical argument.[44] *A Survey of Spiritual Antichrist* was equally historical in approach because it presented its case against the

[39] On the popularity of Tacitus among early-modern sceptics, see R. Tuck, *Philosophy and Government, 1572–1651* (Cambridge, 1993).

[40] J. P. Donnelly, *Calvinism and Scholasticism in Vermigli's Doctrine of Man and Grace* (Leiden, 1976), p. 7.

[41] B. Armstrong, *Calvinism and the Amyraut Heresy* (Madison, Wis., 1969), pp. 15–41. See also A. Clifford, *Atonement and Justification: English Evangelical Theology 1640–1740: An Evaluation* (Oxford, 1990), pp. 95–105.

[42] *Covenant of Life*, p. 269.

[43] Todd, *Christian Humanism*; D. Allan, *Virtue, Learning, and the Scottish Enlightenment: Ideas of Scholarship in Early Modern History* (Edinburgh, 1993), part I.

[44] See Allan, *Virtue, Learning and the Scottish Enlightenment*, pp. 34–5.

Antinomians not just through straightforward theological refutation but also by tracing the lineage of the heresy back to the sixteenth-century Anabaptists and beyond. It complemented the more abstract and ahistorical heresiography of Thomas Edwards's *Gangraena*, and has been seen as a precursor of the classic attacks on religious enthusiasm by Henry More and Meric Casaubon.[45]

Another indication of Rutherford's humanism was his correspondence. The letter was an important Renaissance literary form, particularly popular with the Reformers; 12,000 of Bullinger's letters have survived, 7,000 of Melancthon's, and 4,000 each of Luther and Calvin's.[46] By comparison only 365 of Rutherford's letters are extant but they show him to have been a tireless correspondent. The style of these epistles, however, clearly owed more to the language of the Hebrew prophets than it did to the exacting standards of Renaissance prose.

Nevertheless, the *Letters* point us towards another classical and humanist trait of Rutherford, and that is his Stoicism. Many of his letters were written to the bereaved and his advice to those in grief was always to avoid strong attachment to this world and earthly relationships. He thought 'that there went letters between Paul and Seneca, who was a very learned man, and that they conversed with another',[47] and clearly believed that the philosopher had much to teach Christians. His debt to the Stoics was explicitly brought out in a fascinating passage on mortification in *The Covenant of Life Opened*. He pointed to various types of mortification, including the 'philosophick' which he illustrated by reference to Archimedes 'and other great spirits' who desired knowledge so much that they despised 'honour, gain, pleasure, the three idols of ambitious, of covetous and voluptuous men'. Seneca, Diogenes and Cato were offered as examples of civil or moral mortification. Although none of these were 'crucified with Christ' and experienced Christian mortification, Rutherford still held them up as examples to shame Christians. When arguing that Christians should be dead to injuries he pointed to the example of Socrates whose response after being kicked by a young man was simply 'If an Asse lift his heels against me, shall I lift my heels against an Asse?'[48]

As Margo Todd demonstrates, this admiration for the Stoics was common among Puritans and indicative of their Christian humanism.[49] However, Rutherford's neo-Platonist streak is far more surprising. The best

[45] See E. Walker, *William Dell* (Cambridge, 1970), p. 92.
[46] See E. Cameron, 'The late Renaissance and the unfolding Reformation in Europe', in J. Kirk, ed., *Humanism and Reform: The Church of Scotland in Europe, England and Scotland, 1447–1643* (Oxford, 1991), pp. 28–9.
[47] *Quaint Sermons*, p. 365.   [48] *Covenant of Life*, pp. 263–81.
[49] Todd, *Christian Humanism*, pp. 153–4.

example of it is found in the preface to *Christ Dying*, where he described the whole of creation – 'dainty flowres of being, Heavens, Sunne, Moone, Starres, Seas, Birds, Fishes, Trees, Flowres, Herbes' – as 'created emanations and twigs that sprang out of Christ . . . chips, created leavings, small blossomes, daughters, and births of goodnesse and grace' which have 'streamed out of him'.[50] Rutherford rarely quoted neo-Platonist thinkers like Porphyry directly, but as this extract illustrates he showed a remarkable willingness to use their theological language. Yet despite this willingness to learn from classical pagan sources, Rutherford did not hold out much hope for the salvation of these writers. He rebuked Prynne for arguing that men might be saved without hearing the Word, because 'this may make us fancie somewhat of the salvation of Aristotle, Seneca, Cicero, Aristides, Scipio, Regulus, without the Law or the Gospel'. Rutherford was sure that the sacrament did not say, 'Christ died for thee, O Seneca'![51]

The second major group Rutherford quoted were the early church Fathers. There were generally more references to patristic than to classical sources in Rutherford's works. In *Lex, Rex*, for example, there were approximately sixty references to the Fathers compared with only forty-five to the classics.[52] As Aristotle was always the most frequently quoted of the classical writers, so Augustine dominated Rutherford's citation from the Fathers. In *Lex, Rex* he was cited on ten occasions, followed by Jerome (six) and Ambrose (five). However, in a theological treatise like *Pro Divina Gratia*, Augustine's prominence was understandably greater. He was referred to twenty-two times, with Jerome, the next most frequently quoted Father, only being cited in three places. Moreover, the treatise finished with a string of quotations from Augustine, and Rutherford made it clear that he saw himself as defending an Augustinian theology.

However, recognition of Augustine's significance should not be allowed to obscure the wide range of patristic sources with which Rutherford was familiar. In *Lex, Rex* he referred to twenty patristic writers besides Augus-

---

[50] *Christ Dying*, sig. A4.   [51] *Divine Right*, pp. 522, 526.

[52] Something should be said about these tallies. In the first place it must be realised that absolute statistical accuracy is unattainable because: (1) quotations from and allusions to an author may be made without the reference being given; (2) several quotations from a single author may be made in one passage, though I have usually chosen to count these as one; (3) some of the authors Rutherford quoted are so obscure that their identity cannot be easily established; (4) often quotations are indirect, so that texts are quoted through a third source without there necessarily being any familiarity with the original. Secondly, not too much reliance should be placed on such statistical counts because a large number of quotations from a particular author does not necessarily imply agreement with him. For instance, Rutherford's quotations from Suarez were numerous, but most of the time he was pointing out why Suarez was wrong. However, the large number of references to Suarez suggests that Rutherford was framing his own ideas in conscious opposition to the thought of the Spanish Jesuit, and reveals the importance of his influence, albeit a mostly negative one.

tine, some famous (Chrysostom, Cyprian) and others not (Optatus Mile-
vitanus), some Latin (Ambrose) and others Greek (Irenaeus), some staunch
defenders of Catholic orthodoxy (Athanasius) and others suspiciously
heterodox (Origen). Thus Rutherford's eclectic and catholic intellectual
tastes are apparent even when focusing on one particular group of sources.

His citations of medieval sources were roughly equal in number to those
of the Fathers. *Pro Divina Gratia* contained thirty-nine medieval references
and forty-three patristic references, and in *Lex, Rex* there were sixty in each
category. Naturally Thomas Aquinas featured prominently (twelve and five
references respectively) but he did not dominate in the way that Aristotle
and Augustine did among the classics and patristics. Lyranus, Durandus
and Hugo Cardinalis were often quoted for their biblical exegesis, and
Gerson, Almain, Ockham and the Scot, John Mair, for their conciliar view
of the church and populist account of the origins of government.[53]

Rutherford, like the early Reformers, was well aware of the Augustinian
tradition in medieval thought and borrowed from it freely. In his Latin
theological treatises he constantly referred to scholastics like Ockham,
Scotus and Thomas Bradwardine, the fourteenth-century Archbishop of
Canterbury. However, Rutherford combined a Scotist vision of God with a
Thomist stress on natural law and natural reason; God himself may have
been unknowable and unpredictable, but he had created a law-bound world
intelligible to the reason of man. The tension here was derived from
Rutherford's complex borrowing from medieval theologians.

His spirituality – as we shall see in the next chapter – was also influenced
by medieval writers, particularly Bernard of Clairvaux's sermons on the
Song of Songs. Rutherford's *Letters* represent an almost mystical spirituality
more common in medieval Christianity than in the Reformed tradition. It is
another indication of the 'catholic' outlook of a Protestant who believed in
the validity of Roman Catholic baptism and ordination and relied heavily
on various aspects of medieval thought. His 'medievalism' may be taken as
further evidence of his narrow scholasticism or as striking proof of the
breadth of his sympathies.

However, by far the majority of Rutherford's references were not to
classical, patristic or medieval writers, but to both Catholics and Protestants
after the Reformation. In *Pro Divina Gratia*, for example, there were 180
citations of Catholic writers after 1500, and 244 references to Protestants.
Similarly, in *Lex, Rex* there were 157 references to post-Reformation
Catholics, 245 to Protestants.

Perhaps the most conspicuous group among the post-Reformation Catholics were the Spanish. That Spanish Catholics were quoted far more than

---

[53] See, for example, his appeal to them in *Peaceable Plea*, p. 3.

any others is another indication of the extent to which Rutherford had been influenced by the scholastic revival that had originated in the Spanish universities.[54] In his Latin works he devoted considerable attention to attacking the theology of Jesuits like Fonseca, Suarez (1548–1617) and Molina (1535–1600), particularly their notion of *scientia media*, and he drew on the work of Dominicans like Báñez to do so. In *Lex, Rex* he was concerned to refute Catholic theorists like Bellarmine (1542–1611), but also to draw on the support of Covarrubias (1512–77), Mendoza, Fernando Vásquez (1506–56), and Cornelius à Lapide.[55]

However, as one would expect, the most significant grouping of writers Rutherford quoted were his fellow Protestants. Yet, contrary to the common assumption, Calvin did not tower above all other Reformed theologians in importance.[56] In *Pro Divina Gratia* Rutherford referred to Calvin only four times; William Twisse, later to be prolocutor of the Westminster Assembly, was referred to twelve times. It is true that in *Lex, Rex* Rutherford appealed to Calvin on fourteen occasions, but most of these were over exegetical controversies, rather than over doctrine. He clearly had great respect for the French Reformer, calling him 'a man endued with the Spirit of God above any Papist'.[57] However, Rutherford never called himself a 'Calvinist', and the tendency of historians to prefer the term 'Calvinist' to the more accurate 'Reformed', suggests a movement dominated by a single man, rather than one shaped by a group of like-minded theologians as was in fact the case. Much of the debate over Calvin and the theology of the 'Calvinists' would be avoided were we to realise that seventeenth-century Protestants aimed to be faithful not to Calvin but to Scripture as interpreted by the Reformed tradition in general.[58]

Nearly all of Rutherford's polemical works were directed against Protestant thinkers. Even when in his Latin works he attacked the 'pelagian' theology of the Spanish Jesuits, his real targets were the Dutch Remons-

[54] See Q. Skinner, *The Foundations of Modern Political Thought*, II (Cambridge, 1978), pp. 135–73.
[55] It is no doubt significant that Rutherford was considerably more hopeful about the salvation of Catholics than about the salvation of pagans. Yet his one statement on the issue suggests that polemicists for the Catholic Church were not among the elect: 'We are sure God hath thousands in the bosome of that Church [the 'Romish Church'], who believe in Christ, and do not defend Popery with obstinacie', *Due Right*, p. 417.
[56] See Donnelly,*Calvinism and Scholasticism*, p. 1.   [57] *Divine Right*, p. 62.
[58] Indeed, Rutherford never treated Calvin in the same depth as he dealt with Luther. The reason for this was that Rutherford felt he needed to demonstrate that the Antinomians' reading of the Reformer was false. He devoted one hundred pages of his *Survey of Spiritual Antichrist* (pp. 68–163) to this task and revealed his close knowledge of Luther's writings and respect for his theology. However, Luther was not quoted as often as Calvin in the rest of Rutherford's books, partly because the latter was more theologically acceptable, but, more significantly, because he was a great biblical commentator. Rutherford tended to quote like-minded Protestants for their exegesis rather than for their own theology.

trants, and British theologians like Thomas Jackson and John Cameron, whom he hoped to discredit by identifying their theology with that of the Jesuits.[59] In his campaign against the Five Articles of Perth, he took on the ceremonialists in Scotland (such as Thomas Sydserff and the Aberdeen Doctors) and in England (Richard Hooker). In the 1640s, his theological and ecclesiological works were also focused on debates among English-speaking Protestant theologians. At great length he refuted the Antinomian errors of English preachers like John Saltmarsh, William Dell and Tobias Crisp, the Congregational ecclesiology of the New England Puritans and the English Independents, and the ceremonialism of British Episcopalians. Even in *Lex, Rex*, Rutherford's fire was mainly directed against Protestants: Henry Ferne, Symmons, Grotius and, most of all, the 'Popish Prelate' John Maxwell, former Bishop of Ross. Yet although the debates in which Rutherford participated were generally restricted to the English-speaking world, he always drew on a wide range of authors from other nations and eras to support his case. Behind the immediate parochial debate lay comprehensive learning.

However, there is a group of seventeenth-century writers who are noticeable by their absence from Rutherford's works. This is the group associated with Descartes who are now credited with paving the way for the Enlightenment. Descartes and Gassendi were never mentioned in all Rutherford's works, nor were English thinkers like Francis Bacon and Thomas Hobbes. In ignoring them Rutherford was not unusual among Scottish writers.[60] Not until the 1660s did Edinburgh University begin to show receptivity to Cartesian ideas, and overturn the Aristotelian consensus.[61] However, lest this be taken as another sign of Scottish backwardness it should perhaps be noted that in the 1640s references to any of these now-revered thinkers were rare in England too. Only with hindsight can it be said that Rutherford was largely blind to the most important intellectual movement of his day.

Two other striking omissions were Shakespeare and Milton. Again, the neglect of Shakespeare was common among Scottish writers; even Drummond the poet had only two plays by the English dramatist among over six hundred books which he donated to the library of Edinburgh University.[62] The omission of Milton is more surprising since Rutherford would surely have known about him during his time at the Westminster Assembly. However, the Scot clearly felt he had more immediately important targets to

---

[59] The Remonstrants cropped up throughout Rutherford's writings and he obviously regarded them as one of the main threats to Reformed orthodoxy. Not only did they challenge strict Calvinism, they also advocated the kind of 'licentious toleration' that Rutherford deplored.

[60] Henderson, *Religious Life*, pp. 132–3.

[61] C. Shepard, 'The inter-relationship between the library and teaching in the seventeenth and eighteenth centuries', in Guild and Law, eds., *Edinburgh University Library*, pp. 68–76.

[62] Finlayson and Simpson, 'History of the library', p. 46.

hit. The neglect of contemporary drama and poetry in Rutherford's writings does remind us that, as Henderson has put it, 'the mental background of the century was theological to an extent utterly unknown to us'.[63]

The barrage of quotations with which Rutherford assaulted his readers demonstrated his scholastic compulsion to pile up authorities.[64] When challenging Robert Parker's Independency he was undeterred by the fact that Parker could quote Fathers in his support: 'we may oppose Fathers to Fathers', he happily retorted.[65] Yet there was also a catholic concern to establish his agreement and continuity with the whole church through the ages. 'Fathers, Doctors, Councels, our Divines Protestants and Lutherans, popish writers, Schoolemen, canonists, casuists' were all called in to prove his point about the keys of the kingdom being given to the apostles and not to the church of believers.[66] 'Ignatius very ancient', Rutherford claimed, 'describeth our very Scottish presbyterie'.[67] And in every age of the church, no matter how dark, there had been 'Orthodox Doctors' who had stood against corruption.[68]

Even more important than the testimony of the church was the testimony of Scripture. The authority of Scripture was not to be compromised by adding the authority of tradition, for 'traditions beside the Scripture, are also traditions against the Scripture'.[69] Rutherford adhered to a very strict view of biblical inspiration. In the *Divine Right* he seems to have offered something very close to a dictation theory: 'In writing every jot, tittle, or word of Scripture, [the authors] were immediately inspired, as touching the matter, words, phrases, expression, order, method, majesty, stile and all. So I think they were but organs, the mouth, pen and Amanuenses . . . God borrowed the mouth of the prophet.' This belief led to the position that it was necessary to accept the statement that 'Paul left his cloak at Troas' as of no less authority than the statement that 'Christ came into the world to save sinners', 'in regard of Canonical authority stamped upon both'.[70]

Despite such unequivocal statements, two American scholars, Jack Rogers and Donald McKim, have claimed that Rutherford substantiates their argument that the Puritans did not subscribe to a strict theory of biblical infallibility. They acknowledge that Rutherford was, 'on occasion, driven to a theory of dictation', but maintain that he did not regard Scripture as the rule in arts and sciences (such as Latin and astronomy), but only in the fundamentals of salvation. In contrast to the Aristotelian-

---

[63] Henderson, *Religious Life*, p. 139.   [64] See Henderson, *Religious Life*, p. 138.
[65] *Peaceable Plea*, p. 22.   [66] *Peaceable Plea*, p. 37.   [67] *Peaceable Plea*, p. 18.
[68] *Due Right*, pp. 230–1.   [69] *Due Right*, p. 57.   [70] *Divine Right*, pp. 64–6.

Thomistic scholasticism of High Church divines, claim Rogers and McKim, Rutherford and the Puritans generally espoused an anti-Aristotelian Augustinianism, eschewing natural theology and relying on Scriptural revelation alone for knowledge of God. They refused to treat Scripture as an inerrant encyclopedia for every sort of question, and did not bother to defend the traditional authorship of biblical books, stressing that the persuasion that the Bible was authoritative came from the internal witness of the Spirit rather than from external evidences. Rutherford, in short, turns out to be something of a Barthian *avant la lettre*.[71]

This, however, is hardly credible. Rogers and McKim are quite right to argue that Rutherford and other Puritans do not take the trouble to articulate a formal theory of biblical inspiration, but the reason for this is simply that they felt no need to do so, as biblical authority in the strictest sense was rarely challenged. Early-modern theologians went to great lengths to reconcile Scripture and scientific discoveries and to harmonise apparent discrepancies in the biblical text. The option of treating Scripture as fallible in matters of history and science was simply not open, at least not until sceptical writers like Spinoza, Simon and La Peyrère began to attack strict notions of infallibility.[72] Rutherford did indeed declare that 'Scripture giveth not to us, precepts of Grammar, of War, of Trades, and Arts, teaching us to speak right Latine'.[73] But he was not asserting that the Bible was unreliable in matters of history or science, only that it did not provide an exhaustive guide to them. Actions which were merely natural (like growing), animal (like sleeping), or artificial (like learning Latin), might not have been prescribed by Scripture, but all morality in these actions was regulated by Scripture – one must not lie in Latin, or ride ten miles with a friend if this would waste time.[74]

Rutherford never suggested, as Rogers and McKim think he did, that Scripture was intended only to bring people into a relationship with God, and not to communicate interesting information in all branches of learning. As far as he was concerned, this was a false dichotomy. The preaching of the Word did indeed produce conversions, but the historical books of the Old Testament also provided man with the ultimate political textbook, showing how natural-law principles were applied in practice. Our study of *Lex, Rex* will demonstrate that, contrary to what Rogers and McKim claim,

---

[71] J. B. Rogers and D. K. McKim, *The Authority and Interpretation of the Bible: An Historical Approach* (New York, 1979), pp. 272–15, 250 n. 23.

[72] See J. Woodbridge, *Biblical Authority: A Critique of the Rogers/McKim Proposal* (Grand Rapids, Mich., 1982). For a comprehensive study of the doctrine of Scripture in scholastic Protestantism see R. Muller, *Post-Reformation Reformed Dogmatics, II : Holy Scripture: The Cognitive Foundation of Theology* (Grand Rapids, Mich., 1993).

[73] *Divine Right*, p. 108.   [74] *Divine Right*, pp. 104–7.

Rutherford was both an exponent of Aristotelian-Thomist scholasticism, and a believer in the absolute accuracy of biblical history.[75]

This is not to deny that Rutherford acknowledged other sources of authority besides Scripture – his ready acceptance of Aristotelian natural-law theory shows that he saw the Protestant slogan *sola scriptura* as quite compatible with a belief in the powers of natural reason, though he regarded reason as damaged by the Fall, and in need of constant regulation by Scripture. As will become very clear when we study *Lex, Rex*, Rutherford believed that grace complemented nature, it did not destroy or replace it. Aristotle and Reformed theology could (and did) sit happily side by side on the university curriculum.

This conviction that reason and revelation complemented each other became most evident in Rutherford's attacks on the spiritualism and anti-intellectualism of Antinomians such as William Dell. Although he declared that 'we hate with our soules that Christians should adore and fall downe before an inke-Divinity and meere paper-godlinesse', Rutherford was sure that the Holy Spirit was against 'wilde logicke' and that Scripture was 'a book of discoursive refined reason'.[76] Christ knew Hebrew and used logical consequences, Paul quoted the heathen poets, 'in the books of Moses, are secrets of Physick', Samuel and Kings introduced man to 'sacred politicks', and Job taught him astronomy. 'The naturall sinlesse knowledge of sciences, arts, tongues' was, therefore, the candlelight by which Christians studied the Bible.[77] The tools of textual and philological humanist scholarship had to be applied to Scripture if it was to be properly understood. As we shall see in Chapter 7, Rutherford was deeply committed to the humanist historical-grammatical hermeneutic championed by the Reformers.[78]

Whenever the native sense of a biblical text was unclear, Rutherford referred to the biblical commentaries of Protestants like Calvin and Piscator, Catholics like Cornelius à Lapide, and Jewish scholars like Rabbi Solomon and Rabbi Levi ben Gersom. Although he could not quite match Baillie, who was said to be able to read thirteen languages, his learning was still impressive. For example, in order to demonstrate the error of the Socinian claim that when Scripture said, 'Christ died for us' it meant that he died 'for our good' rather than 'instead of us', Rutherford assembled three pages of textual evidence, showing that this was not the clear meaning in other texts

[75] It follows that it is a mistake to see the fundamentalist doctrine of Scriptural inerrancy as an innovation either of scholastic Protestants in the mid-seventeenth century (as Rogers and McKim do) or of American Calvinist theologians in the late nineteenth century (as George Marsden claims). See G. Marsden, *Fundamentalism and American Culture: The Shaping of Twentieth Century Evangelicalism, 1870–1925* (Oxford, 1980).

[76] *Survey of Antichrist*, pp. 314–15.   [77] *Survey of Antichrist*, pp. 50–2.

[78] On the Reformers' doctrine of Scripture and its interpretation, see A. McGrath, *Reformation Thought: An Introduction* (Oxford, 1993 edn), ch. 7.

where the phrase was used. He referred to Demosthenes, Isocrates, Homer's *Iliad*, Stephanus's *Thesaurus*, the Septuagint, the Syriac version, the Chaldean paraphrase, the Hebrew, Tremellius, and Trostius, and rounded off with a triumphant clincher from the Old Testament: Hoshea slew the king and then reigned 'for him'. Clearly the phrase had to mean 'instead of', not just 'on behalf of'.[79] Such an example could be multiplied many times over, but even on its own it gives a fair idea of Rutherford's application of the critical tools of humanist scholarship, and his deep commitment to its historical-critical method of exegesis.

Although Rutherford's writings were saturated with quotations from every part of Scripture, it is clear that he was particularly fond of the Psalms, and the other poetic and prophetic books of the Old Testament. In *Pro Divina Gratia* he quoted the Wisdom literature (Job, Psalms, Proverbs, Ecclesiastes, Song of Songs) forty-eight times, and referred on sixty-seven occasions to the writings of the major prophets (Isaiah, Jeremiah, Ezekiel, Daniel). He meditated often on the book of Job, and it gave him an overpowering sense of divine sovereignty and of the duty of the believer to accept suffering without complaint against the Almighty. Moreover his spirituality was profoundly shaped by a traditional Christian spiritualisation of the Song of Songs, and his apocalyptic writings were written in the language of the Old Testament prophets and the psalmist. From the sermons of Rutherford that have survived we can see that he liked to preach on these parts of the Bible. Five of his thirty-four published sermons were on the Song of Songs, and eight on the prophetic books, including one on Hosea which provided a picture of the adulterous spouse to contrast with the image of the faithful one given in the Song. Rutherford's forty unpublished sermons confirm his liking for the most vividly poetic parts of Scripture: ten were on the Psalms, four on Isaiah and two on the Song of Songs.

However, in *Lex, Rex* it was the historical books of the Old Testament that were most commonly referred to. This was, of course, because these books were crammed with historical references to kings and covenants, and provided a mine of political quotations for Rutherford. *Lex, Rex* stood in sharp contrast to its obvious Scottish predecessor, *De Jure Regni*, in that it constantly appealed to biblical example whereas Buchanan had used the tools of humanist exegesis to relativise the biblical stories, confining them to their distant historical context and taking away their power to provide precedents. Mining Scripture for political examples was also a humanist trait, however, for it involved a didactic reading of the Bible as a source-book of moral examples. References to the New Testament in Rutherford's

---

[79] *Covenant of Life*, pp. 247–55.

political theory were overwhelmingly outnumbered by those to the Old Testament. As we shall see, he believed that Israel was still to be a model for contemporary Christian nations.

In his theological writings Rutherford, as one would expect, continually cited the Epistles. However, his sermons seem to have been based rather on the Gospels or the Book of Revelation, suggesting that he felt either narratives or poetic passages to be most appropriate and accessible to an ordinary audience. Eleven of his thirty-four published sermons were based on Gospel narratives, another three were on Revelation, and only three were from the Epistles. Similarly, out of sixteen unpublished sermons on the New Testament, seven were on the Gospels, four on Revelation and although seven treated texts from the epistles, six of these were on the most metaphorical of all New Testament books, Hebrews. As we would expect from the author of the effusive letters, Rutherford seems to have been deeply attracted to the poetic parts of the Bible.

This should serve as a reminder of the folly of trying to understand the ideas of Puritan writers without reference to their principal intellectual source, the Bible itself.[80] In later chapters, we shall focus on the deep tension in Rutherford's political thought between 'secular' discourses that can ultimately be traced back to classical sources (natural-law contractualism and ancient constitutionalism) and religious discourses derived from the Old Testament (religious covenantalism and apocalypticism). Often this tension is hard to detect, because in early modern Europe – and in Rutherford's own education – the Greek and Roman classical heritage was thoroughly interwoven with the Hebrew biblical heritage. In the end, however, this particular tapestry was to unravel, and when it did, it was not the classical sources but the Old Testament that guided Rutherford's political thinking.

---

[80] This is probably the greatest weakness of Perry Miller's classic study of the 'New England Mind'. Miller pays full attention to the scholastic, humanist and Ramist influences on Puritan thinking, but conspicuously fails to assess the importance of biblical language and categories to their thought. See G. Marsden, 'Perry Miller's rehabilitation of the Puritans: a critique', *Church History*, 39 (1970), 93.

4

The Puritan pastor

Rutherford's admirers have focused so intently on the pious pastor of Anwoth that they have forgotten his scholarly output. Yet a modern historian who concentrated on Rutherford's controversial writings at the expense of his devotional letters and sermons would be making an equally great mistake. For Rutherford the Puritan pastor is a fascinating figure, a man with an intense spirituality, close friendships with godly women, and an extraordinary way with language. By examining these features of his life and work we can shed new light on the role of women within the Puritan movement, the style of Puritan preaching and the relationship between Puritanism and popular culture. I will begin with an exposition of Rutherford's own spirituality.

A SPIRITUALITY OF PRESENCE AND ABSENCE

To some readers the exotic (and erotic) imagery of Rutherford's *Letters* has marked him out as a rare example of that paradoxical phenomenon, the Presbyterian mystic. As we shall see, mysticism is perhaps not the best term to apply to Rutherford, and he would no doubt be horrified to find himself anthologised with Jacob Boehme, George Fox, Goethe and Virginia Woolf.[1] Nevertheless, it is striking to find in an intolerant seventeenth-century Scottish Presbyterian, passages that would seem more at home in the works of St Bernard or St Teresa.[2]

Despite its obvious interest, Rutherford's spirituality has been a neglected

[1] As he is in A. Freemantle, ed., *The Protestant Mystics* (London, 1964).
[2] A point made by J. M. Ross, 'Post-Reformation spirituality 3: Samuel Rutherford', *The Month* (July 1975), p. 207. One scholar has written that encountering Rutherford's *Letters* 'recalled one's first contact with women: they were softer, warmer, heavier, and sweeter than one had expected'! H. H. Meier, 'Love, law and lucre: images in Rutherford's letters', in M.-J. Arn and H. Wirtjes, eds., *Historical and Editorial Essays in Medieval and Early Modern English for Johan Gerritsen* (Groningen, 1985), p. 77.

feature of seventeenth-century Scottish Calvinism.[3] Perhaps this is not altogether surprising when we consider the historiographical context. Twentieth-century historians have tended to ignore Puritan spirituality, and concentrate instead on Puritanism as an intellectual or social movement. Perry Miller's famous work on the New England Puritans began with a description of their Augustinian piety, but mostly he was concerned to emphasise the 'Mind' of the Puritans, and tended to focus on intellect rather than emotion. The works of Christopher Hill, on the other hand, have attempted to reveal the social and political implications of Puritanism. The problem with the work of Hill and other Marxist and Weberian historians has been pithily summed up by Colin Davis, who suggests that looking for the non-theological reasons for being a Puritan is like looking for the non-socio-political reasons for being a Marxist.[4]

Recently, historians have begun to put spirituality back at the centre of the Puritan movement.[5] Trying to define and distinguish Puritans according to their ecclesiological, theological or political opinions has proved very difficult. What really made them stand out was their zeal and fervour; they were 'the hotter sort of Protestants'. 'At its heart', writes Charles Hambrick-Stowe, 'Puritanism was a devotional movement, rooted in religious experience.'[6] The Puritan theologians became known as the 'affectionate practical' school, because of their great stress on spiritual experience. They were the leaders of 'a movement of revival',[7] a movement not only found within the Church of England, but in Scotland too.

The spirituality of this revival movement was rooted in a powerful emphasis on the need for conversion. Rutherford was convinced that although the unconverted man might 'have a good smell outwardly' and might be honest and civil, he was really 'only a man buried in a grave' with

---

[3] See J. K. Cameron, 'The piety of Samuel Rutherford (c. 1600–61): a neglected feature of seventeenth-century Scottish Calvinism', *Nederlands Archief voor Kerkgeschiedenis*, 65 (1985), 153–9.

[4] J. C. Davis, 'Puritanism and revolution: themes, categories, methods and conclusions', *Historical Journal*, 33 (1990), 704.

[5] C. E. Hambrick-Stowe, *The Practice of Piety: Puritan Devotional Disciplines in Seventeenth-Century New England* (Chapel Hill, 1982); C. L. Cohen, *God's Caress: The Psychology of Puritan Religious Experience* (Oxford, 1986). Two excellent older studies of Puritan spirituality are G. Nuttall, *The Holy Spirit in Puritan Faith and Experience* (Oxford, 1946), and G. Wakefield, *Puritan Devotion: Its Place in the Development of Christian Piety* (London, 1957). Louise Yeoman's dissertation has done a valuable job in filling the lacuna that existed with regard to specifically Scottish spirituality. It does however, tend to exaggerate the subjective nature of Presbyterianism. At times her Presbyterians sound just like Quakers! Yeoman, 'Heart-work: emotion, empowerment and authority in covenanting times', unpublished Ph.D. dissertation, St Andrews University (1991).

[6] Hambrick-Stowe, *Practice of Piety*, p. vii.

[7] J. I. Packer, *Among God's Giants: The Puritan Vision of the Christian Life* (Eastbourne, 1991), pp. 40–63.

a few flowers growing on top. He lacked life itself, being spiritually dead; he lacked reason, for everything he did was guided by worldly calculation; and he lacked sense of life, for he did not feel wounded when he sinned.[8] 'As beautiful as he looks without, yet within he is nothing else but the work-house of the devil.'[9]

It followed from this uncompromising statement of the Calvinist (and Augustinian) doctrine of human depravity that 'All the natural and civil honesty in the world will not do the turn to bring us to heaven, till we once see that by nature we are in a damnable case.'[10] People could only see their 'damnable case' when God intervened directly in their lives. Repentance 'is a thing altogether supernatural and not proceeding at all from nature', Rutherford preached.[11] Although certain preparations were to be made before God came to lodge in a person, 'the king himself sends [these]'. 'Our love to Christ is nothing else but an effect of His love to us . . . So may we ever learn to sing a song of free grace shown in our conversion.'[12] Rutherford's theology remained loyal to the Reformation insistence on *sola gratia*, and did not – as some have argued – attempt to rehabilitate natural man or shift towards salvation by works.[13]

More than that, his high Calvinist theology seems to have been shaped by his own conversion experience. He declared that 'few whoever kent [knew; experienced] what the power of the grace of God meant – durst take upon themselves to be an Arminian'. Rutherford had experienced the power, and he suspected that Arminians were not really converted: 'It has been very well observed by learned men, that there were never any who opposed themselves unto it [the idea of irresistible grace], but those who kent nothing of the grace of God themselves.'[14]

For Rutherford, an experience of the grace of God left a deep mark on a person's psyche. He admitted that the children of God might not always be able 'to tell the very first mathematical point of the time of their conversion . . . But for the most part I say this is His dealing, that when sinners have been going on into a course of rebellion, running away from Him, after their humiliation ordinarily He fills them with a feast of the sense of His love, that all their days they cannot forget it.'[15] If we place Rutherford's conversion in 1626, after the Eupham Hamilton scandal and his public

---

[8] *Quaint Sermons*, pp. 291–5.   [9] *Quaint Sermons*, p. 333.
[10] *Quaint Sermons*, p. 338.   [11] *Quaint Sermons*, p. 307.
[12] *Quaint Sermons*, p. 251.
[13] As Hambrick-Stowe says, 'It must be emphasized that in the eyes of all Puritans, despite charges during the Antinomian controversy that the orthodoxy had lapsed into Arminianism, the entire journey to heaven was the result of God's work in the soul . . . They understood preparation for conversion to be of a sinner by Christ', *Practice of Piety*, pp. 79–80.
[14] *Quaint Sermons*, p. 332.   [15] *Quaint Sermons*, p. 353.

humiliation, this description seems to reflect clearly that unforgettable personal experience. It marked him for life, and shaped his spirituality.

Conversion, for Rutherford, was trauma followed by ecstasy. It began with 'a humiliation and downcasting' when 'God begins to batter at the hearts' of his elect. The experience of grace was a painful one, for grace began by lopping off branches so that sinners could be grafted into the stock, and by casting down the walls and 'towers of pride, of worldly-mindedness, of filthiness'. After being shaken by the discovery of their own depravity, sinners began 'to make syllogisms of their own': I am in trouble, I cannot save myself, therefore I need Christ. This was followed by an earnest desire for Christ, by looking to God's promises to sinners, and finally by the experience of loving communion with Him.[16] 'At the Lord's first meeting with a sinner, the Lord opens his heart by grace to let Him in, and there they sup together. There is a feast of love between them.'[17]

Rutherford's conversion, therefore, made his spirituality intensely experiential. True religion was not ultimately a matter of form (though as a Presbyterian Rutherford was certainly not an antiformalist in the way Cromwell was) it was a matter of the heart. 'Woe's them that know no more of religion but only the name of it!' he declared. Signing the National Covenant was not enough; one had also to be 'a heart-covenanter'.[18] As Hambrick-Stowe argues, this fundamental distinction between experiential heart religion and formal ritualistic religion was crucial to the Puritans, setting them against the ungodly and the 'mere professors'.[19]

It was also this concern for spiritual experience which led Rutherford to that Old Testament love poem, the Song of Songs. He read the book as a description of the relationship between Christ (the bridegroom) and the soul (the bride). In this he followed a long hermeneutical tradition stretching back to Origen in the fourth century, but one that until the twelfth century had taken second place to the allegorical interpretation (also found in Origen) which treated the Song as a picture of Christ and the church. It was Bernard of Clairvaux's eighty-six sermons on the Song that firmly established the tropological or moral mode of exegesis. Bernard and numerous medieval commentators and mystics read the poem 'as a dynamic guide to the quest of each human being for union with God'.[20] The Puritans with their deep concern for heart religion followed them, though Rutherford continued to apply the Song to the church as well.

One consequence of this use of the Song of Songs was that spiritual experience was described in frankly sensual terms.

---

[16] *Quaint Sermons*, pp. 339–46.   [17] *Quaint Sermons*, p. 252.
[18] *Quaint Sermons*, p. 61.   [19] Hambrick-Stowe, *Practice of Piety*, p. 43.
[20] E. A. Matter, *The Voice of My Beloved: The Song of Songs in Western Medieval Christianity* (Philadelphia, 1990), p. 123.

Oh, what a sight to be up in heaven in that fair orchard of the new paradise; and to see, and smell, and touch, and kiss that fair field-flower, that evergreen Tree of life! . . . Christ, Christ, nothing but Christ can cool our love's burning languor. O thirsty love! wilt thou set Christ, the well of life, to thy head, and drink thy fill? Drink, and spare not; drink love, and be drunken with Christ! Nay, alas! the distance betwixt us and Christ is a death. Oh, if we were clasped in other's arms. We should never twin again, except heaven twinned and sundered us; and that cannot be. [21]

Rutherford wanted his readers to discover that Christ delighted 'all the spiritual senses', just as the bridegroom in the Song of Songs was beautiful to smell, see, hear, taste and touch.[22] He exhorted Lady Kenmure to 'put up your own sinful hand to the tree of life and take down and eat the sweetest apple in all God's heavenly paradise, Jesus Christ, your life and your Lord'.[23] He wrote of 'Christ's God-like and soul-ravishing countenance',[24] of 'Christ's soft and sweet kisses to me',[25] and testified that 'the King's spikenard casteth a fragrant smell'.[26] He described being 'feasted with love banquets with my royal, high, high, and princely King Jesus . . . now he hath taken the mask off his face, and saith, "Kiss thy fill"; and what can I have more when I get great heaven in my little arms?'[27]

Language, however, even biblical language, could not adequately describe the beauty of Christ. Anyone who writes of Christ, said Rutherford, 'his heart may censure his pen'. For 'in regard of any comprehensive knowledge we but speak and write our guessings, our far-off and twylight apprehensions of him'. Christians simply played 'as children doe with the golden covering and silken ribbens of an Arabicke Bible that they cannot read, about the borders and margent of the knowledge of Christ'.[28] Not only was language incapable of capturing the glory of Christ, but the human body would be unable to survive a full revelation of his glory: 'Would Christ in his fulness of the irradiations of his glory breake in upon us, he should breake the bodily organs, and over-master the soules faculties, that all the banks of the soule should be like broken walls, hedges or day channels.'[29]

That Rutherford could write this is an indication of the sheer emotional power of his spiritual experiences. Evangelical Presbyterianism was highly 'affectionate', and its worship could be physically expressive too. The Lord was thought to welcome crying, breathing, lifting up the eyes, moaning, sighing, sobbing and stretching out the hands as acceptable forms of prayer.[30] Gilbert Burnet wrote that the Presbyterian preachers, including Rutherford, 'affected great sublimities in devotion: they poured themselves out in their prayers with a loud voice and often with many tears'.[31] If this

---

[21] *Letters*, p. 173.   [22] *Christ Dying*, p. 294.   [23] *Letters*, p. 79.
[24] *Letters*, p. 165.   [25] *Letters*, p. 158.   [26] *Letters*, p. 150.
[27] *Letters*, p. 148.   [28] *Christ Dying*, sig. A2v.   [29] *Christ Dying*, p. 45.
[30] *Quaint Sermons*, pp. 257–9.
[31] G. Burnet, *The History of My Own Time*, I, ed. O. Airy (Oxford, 1897), p. 56.

makes Rutherford sound like a revivalistic preacher, that is because he was. As Westerkamp and Schmidt have recently demonstrated, the Great Awakening was not so much an American innovation, as a Scottish import.[32]

The 'love feasts' of which Rutherford wrote from exile in Aberdeen, were private affairs: 'I eat my feasts my lone.'[33] However, Rutherford was not a solitary mystic; he longed to see his 'flock' again; 'O that my Lord would bring me among them, that I might tell unco [uncommon] and great tales of Christ to them.'[34] Not only did Rutherford want to preach to his flock, he also desired to share communion with them, for it was through the Word and the sacraments that God revealed himself and visited his people. Communion seasons were the time 'wherein our Well-beloved Jesus rejoiceth and is merry with His friends'.[35] As the day of a communion service approached, Rutherford could write that 'Jesus Christ will be welcome, when he comes'.[36]

Bouyer has observed that the Scots believed – in a manner strikingly close to the counter-Reformation – that if communion was taken in faith it brought substantial union with Christ.[37] Rutherford's was a deeply sacramentalist piety, far removed from the Zwinglian memorialism of later Evangelicalism. In his *Due Right of Presbyteries*, he complained that the New England Puritans denied 'all reall exhibition of grace in the sacraments', thus making them 'but a naked sign'. The truth, however, was that by using the sacrament in faith the believer received an increase in 'sacrament grace'.[38]

Such a theology of the sacrament clearly shaped the practice of men like Rutherford. As Leigh Eric Schmidt has vividly demonstrated, it was the radical Presbyterians, the most Puritan group in Scotland, who recovered much of the eucharistic festivity of late medieval Catholicism. They espoused an 'evangelical ritualism' that combined sacred and secular; at their outdoor communion festivals people ate, drank, conversed and courted, prayed, meditated and covenanted.[39]

The fellowship of the godly was also sustained by close spiritual relation-

---

[32] M. Westerkamp, *Triumph of the Laity: Scots–Irish Piety and the Great Awakening, 1625–1760* (Oxford, 1988); L. E. Schmidt, *Holy Fairs: Scottish Communions and American Revivals in the Early Modern Period* (Princeton, 1989).
[33] *Letters*, p. 150.   [34] *Letters*, pp. 173–4.   [35] *Letters*, p. 58.
[36] *Letters*, p. 95.
[37] L. Bouyer, *Orthodox Spirituality and Protestant and Anglican Spirituality* (London, 1969), p. 136.
[38] *Due Right*, pp. 212–17. Ironically, those who drew up the 'popish' Scottish Prayer Book of 1637 had tried to guard against what James Wedderburn, the Bishop of Dunblane, described as 'the Zwinglian tenet that the sacrament is a bare sign taken in remembrance of Christ's passion'. See N. Tyacke, 'Archbishop Laud', in K. Fincham, ed., *The Early Stuart Church* (London, 1993), p. 70. Their sensitivity on this point was not understood or appreciated by men like Rutherford.
[39] Schmidt, *Holy Fairs*, pp. 18–37, 214–8.

ships between individuals, by family devotions, and by private meetings. It was his separation from the company of the godly that made Rutherford's exile in Aberdeen so painful. Letter-writing was the only means of maintaining fellowship with them, and so he was hurt when he received few letters: 'I complain that Galloway is not kind to me in paper. I have received no letters these sixteen weeks but two.'[40] He himself wrote voluminously, testifying to the love feasts he had with Christ.

Letter-writing was one of the spiritual disciplines and devotional exercises that nourished Rutherford's piety. By writing, he was giving an exact account of 'the comings and goings of Christ'. His letters were a sort of spiritual journal. He later wrote that 'To be able to write a spiritual Chronicle and History of all Christ's stirrings towards your soul, saith ye have letters daily, and good intelligence of the affairs of the Spirit, and of the kings court, and that he writes to you.'[41]

Disciplines like this were essential to spirituality because life was far from being one long love feast. Indeed love feasts were often followed by periods of Christ's absence: 'Often the time of some extreme desertion and soule-trouble is, when Christ hath been in the soule with a full, high spring-tyde of divine manifestations of himself.'[42] This was an experience of great pain; the believer at such times was, like Christ on the Cross, cut off from the 'out-breathings' of eternal love by a great cloud.[43] Christ at such times was a *Deus absconditus*, an absent God, one who hid his face behind a mask.

Rutherford referred many times in his letters to the spiritual depression brought on by God's withdrawing. To Lady Kenmure he wrote 'Madam, I am in exceeding great heaviness',[44] and in a 1634 letter he told Marion McNaught, 'I left you in as great heaviness as I was in since I came to this country.'[45] A man capable of rapturous exultation, he was also vulnerable to deep depression and morbidity. Although due in part to his personal psychology, his beliefs and commitments clearly intensified his gloom. In conscious imitation of the Hebrew prophets, Rutherford wrote from Aberdeen to warn of Scotland's impending doom. 'I see the Lord's vineyard laid waste, and the heathen entered into the sanctuary: and my belly is pained, and my soul in heaviness, because the Lord's people are gone into captivity, and because of the fury of the Lord, and that wind (but neither to fan nor to purge) which is coming upon apostate Scotland.'[46]

Rutherford's spirituality was thus intimately connected with his apocalypticism, and the welfare of his soul with the welfare of the nation. The Song of Songs was about Christ and the soul, but also about Christ and the church, and the ecclesiological reading of the Song was linked – as it had

---

[40] *Letters*, p. 168.   [41] *Covenant of Life*, p. 142.   [42] *Christ Dying*, p. 44.
[43] *Christ Dying*, pp. 19–20.   [44] *Letters*, p. 79.   [45] *Letters*, p. 114.
[46] *Letters*, p. 156.

been in the medieval period – to a fascination with the prophecies of the Book of Revelation.[47] Because of this Rutherford tended to see the soul as almost a microcosm of the kirk and the nation. Christ's withdrawal from the kirk cast him into profound melancholy, but Christ's visitations to his soul made him long for the day when the whole of Scotland would experience the same revelation: 'O that this nation knew what is betwixt Him and me; none would scar [take fright] at the Cross of Christ.'[48]

True spirituality was, therefore, far from being a personal or private matter. It was public and political, a fact usually missed by those who read Rutherford from an Evangelical pietist perspective. When urging the House of Commons to support Christ's cause, Rutherford declared that 'Grace's end is the most publick end of the world, even God's glory . . . The more gratious men bee, the more publick they are'. Linking this explicitly with the Song of Songs he said 'hee who is for the Bridegroome, cannot bee against the Bride [the kirk].'[49]

The fate of the bride (the soul and the kirk) ultimately lay, of course, in the hands of God not of men. The 'desertions' and 'withdrawals' of Christ were 'a worke of omnipotent dominion'. An 'absolute freedom of an independent dominion acteth in the Lord's covering of himselfe with a cloud, and putteth an iron-crosse-barre on the doore of his pavilion; and can you stirre omnipotency, and remove it?'[50] Because he was utterly sovereign, God was free to act towards different people in completely different ways. Rutherford's high Calvinist stress on divine sovereignty pervaded his spirituality as much as his theology:

Christ walks in a path of unsearchable liberty, that some are in the suburbs of heaven, and feele the dainties of the Kings higher house, ere they be in heaven; and others, children of the same Father, passengers on the same journey, wade through hell, darkness of fears, thornes of doubtings, and have few love-tokens till the marriage day.[51]

Still, the mysteries of God's providence could seem baffling and cruel. Rutherford was aware that believers often felt they had a case against God, and he himself was not beyond quarrelling with the divine will. Shortly after his move to Aberdeen he wrote 'I took up an action against Christ, and brought a plea against His love, and libelled unkindness against Christ my Lord, and I said, "This is my death; He hath forgotten me."'[52] Christ was in covenant with his elect, but seemed to have broken his part of the bargain.

---

[47] See Matter, *Voice of my Beloved*, ch. 4. I shall explore this further in Chapter 8.
[48] *Letters*, p. 150.   [49] *Sermon to Commons*, pp. 5–6.
[50] *Christ Dying*, pp. 87–8.   [51] *Christ Dying*, pp. 49–50.
[52] *Letters*, p. 156. Cf. p. 151: 'At my first coming hither, I took the dorts [the sulks, offence] at Christ, and took up a stomach against Him; I said, He had cast me over the dike of the vineyard, like a dry tree.'

Yet it was wrong to 'upbraid grace' or murmur against God, thought
Rutherford (though he was in the good company of the psalmist in doing
so). If God 'restraines the clouds and bindeth up the wombe of heaven in
extreme drought' that was his prerogative. Moreover, the silence of God did
not mean that he had changed. 'Is the God of Nature changed, because its
not ever summer and daylight?' One had to live not according to feeling,
but by faith. To 'calculate Christs love by our own elevation, not by his'
was a great mistake.[53] To live on divine love was 'a life liable to many
clouds . . . when Christs love-letter from heaven miscarries and is inter-
cepted the soul swoons: its surer to live by faith'.[54] Put more pithily: 'Faith
saith, sense is a liar.'[55]

Moreover, it was manifestly wrong for the Christian to expect better
treatment on earth than Christ himself received.

We would have a silken, a soft, a perfumed crosse, sugered and honeyed with the
consolations of Christ, or wee faint . . . But Christs crosse did not smile on him, his
crosse was a crosse, and his ship sailed in bloud, and his blessed soule was sea-sicke,
and heavie even to death . . . The crosse to all the saints must have a bloody bit, and
lyons teeth, it was like it selfe to Christ, gallie and soure, so it must be to us. Wee
cannot have a Paper-crosse.[56]

One of the reasons Rutherford reacted so fiercely against the Antinomians
was that they seemed to be denying the continuing reality of struggle and
pain in the lives of Christians. Yet effort was essential: 'Take pains, above
all things, for salvation; for without running, fighting, sweating, wrestling,
heaven is not taken.'[57]

The right attitude of the believer under desertion was one of humility and
submission. 'Faith thinketh no evil of Christ; blame thyselfe and thy
unbeleefe if Christ hide his face.'[58] 'Patient submission to God under
desertion is sweet.' Aware of the 'Infinite sovereignty' of God, one could
only say 'It is an act of Heaven; I bear it with silence.'[59] This was more than
mere pious rhetoric; amid the crushing sorrows of life it had to become a
practical reality. Bereavement loomed large in the lives of seventeenth-
century people. Famines, plagues and epidemics were common, and there
was a strong sense of the precariousness of human existence. Rutherford
himself saw his wife die in agony in 1630 and his letters contain vivid
descriptions of her suffering:

my wife's disease increaseth daily, to her great torment and pain night and day. She
has not been in God's house since our communion, neither out of her bed. I have
hired a man to Edinburgh to Doctor Jeally and to John Hamilton. I can hardly

---

[53] *Christ Dying*, pp. 52–5.   [54] *Christ Dying*, p. 51.   [55] *Tryal of Faith*, p. 157.
[56] *Christ Dying*, pp. 15–6.   [57] *Letters*, p. 399.   [58] *Sermon to Lords*, p. 55.
[59] *Tryal*, p. 156.

believe her disease is ordinary, for her life is bitter to her; she sleeps none, but cries as a woman travailling in birth.[60]

When Eupham died, 'after long disease and torment, for the space of a year and a month', Rutherford's response was that of Job: 'The Lord hath done it; blessed be His name.'[61]

His reaction to his loss was almost identical to that of the New England poet Anne Bradstreet as she saw her house (with all her manuscripts) burnt to the ground in 1666. She wrote:

> And, when I could no longer look
> I blest his Name that gave and took
> that layd my goods now in the dust
> Yea so it was, and so twas just.

Coming to terms with such loss was a central feature of Puritan spirituality. Following Calvin, the Puritans undermined the *contemptus mundi* tradition with their emphasis on the earthly calling of the believer. The saint was not called out of the world but was required to live a holy life in it. Puritanism was a spirituality of householders, for even the clergy were family men. Yet this position led to a crisis, for the world was transitory and love for the creatures inevitably led to grief, for they too would pass away.

The Puritan response to loss and bereavement was to turn to prayer and devotional exercises. The New England pastor, Cotton Mather, went through the same experience as Rutherford when his own 'lovely Consort' was close to death. He was in deep distress, emotionally and spiritually, but he too turned to prayer, and these 'prayers, rooted in grief over the loss of a finite creature, lifted him into "intimate Communion with Heaven"'. Loss, therefore, became the occasion for spiritual growth. Puritans did not abandon the world, but they were careful to live as pilgrims and strangers in it, and not to rely too heavily on any created thing. Theirs was a spirituality of 'weaned affections, rooted always in this world but reaching toward the other world'.[62]

This is particularly evident in the seventeen letters Rutherford wrote to those who had been bereaved. Lady Kenmure, to whom he wrote three times on the death of her children, was told that 'faith will teach you to kiss a striking Lord; and so acknowledge the sovereignty of God (in the death of a child) to be above the power of us mortal men . . . If our dear Lord pluck up one of His roses, and pull down sour and green fruit before harvest, who can challenge Him?' Yet the workings of providence were not entirely inscrutable, for the experience of loss made sanctification easier: 'All these

---

[60] *Letters*, p. 49.   [61] *Letters*, p. 53.

[62] See Hambrick-Stowe, 'Loss and hope in Reformed spirituality: the example of Anne Bradstreet', in B. C. Hanson, ed., *Modern Christian Spirituality* (Atlanta, 1990), pp. 85–112.

crosses (and indeed, when I remember them, they are heavy and many – peace, peace be the end of them!) are to make you white and ripe for the Lord's harvest-hook. I have seen the Lord weaning you from the breasts of this world.'[63] To another bereaved gentlewoman he wrote, 'You must learn to make your evils your great good; and to spin comforts, peace, joy, communion with Christ, out of your troubles, which are Christ's wooers, sent to speak for you from Himself.'[64]

Even in times of trouble and desertion, then, there was the possibility of joy and Christ's presence. Faith had eyes to see Christ 'in the night as in the daylight', and faith's eyes could 'pierce through Christs maske, and the vaile or cloud that covers his face'.[65] In the midst of suffering faith could believe that God had a purpose for it, that something good could come out of it, just as redemption emerged from Christ's death on the Cross. Believers should 'count it exceeding joy when we fall into divers temptations', for Christ had 'fastened heaven to the far-end of the cross'.[66] Just as Christ's Cross had been the means of believers' salvation, so the crosses of believers were the means of their sanctification.

It was for this reason that Rutherford repeatedly spoke of 'the white side of Christ's cross'[67] and could say ' "Welcome, welcome, sweet, sweet cross of Christ". I verily think the chains of my Lord Jesus are all overlaid with pure gold, and that His cross is perfumed, and that it smelleth of Christ.'[68] The cross of Golgotha may have been terrible, but the Lord of glory hung there, and 'O! it was made a fair tree when such an Apple grew on it!'[69] In the same way, 'those who can take that crabbed tree handsomely upon their back, and fasten it on cannily, shall find it such a burden as wings unto a bird, or sails to a ship'.[70] In embracing pain one could rise above it.

The agony and the ecstasy lay side by side in Rutherford's spirituality. The dialectic of Christ's absence and presence was expressed by a host of dichotomies which engaged all the senses. 'Both sweet and sour feed my soul', he wrote from Aberdeen; although he was delighted by Christ's presence, the remembrance of his 'dear flock' was 'vinegar to my sugared wine'.[71] The reek of this world's smoky house, the inn in which the elect stayed as they passed through this life,[72] was nothing in comparison to the perfumed beauty of Christ, 'the sweetest rose that God ever planted'.[73] It was in times of pain and anguish that Christ came with 'his soft and sweet kisses to me in the furnace'.[74] Christ was the one who 'mixeth our cup', said Rutherford, and this should give us confidence:

---

[63] *Letters*, p. 98.   [64] *Letters*, p. 246.   [65] *Sermon to Lords*, p. 55.
[66] *Letters*, p. 247.   [67] *Letters*, pp. 150, 152.   [68] *Letters*, p. 141.
[69] *Communion Sermons*, p. 286.   [70] *Letters*, p. 148.   [71] *Letters*, p. 143.
[72] *Communion Sermons*, pp. 46–7.   [73] *Letters*, p. 187. See also pp. 80, 89.
[74] *Letters*, p. 158.

he can sugar the salt and bitter wine with mercy. There is no desertion of the saints that we read of, but there is as much of Christ in it, as giveth it some taste and smell of heaven. Heaven is stamped upon the hell of the saints, life is written on their death: their grave and dead corpse are hot, and do breathe out life and glory; their ashes and dust smell of immortality and resurrection to life. Even when Christ is gone from the church, he leaveth a pawn or a pledge behind him, as love-sickness for the want of him (Canticles 3. 5.).[75]

After his absences, moreover, Christ was sure to return, and his presence would be better than before. During his desertion, the saints had learnt to desire him more, trust in him more fully, and rely on faith not on sense.[76] When his presence was felt again, 'The first warm smile of a new return, is sufficient to recompense all sorrow in his absence, to say nothing of everlasting huggings, and embracings.'[77]

This dialectic of Christ's absence and presence was well illustrated by the Song of Songs, in which the bride experiences times of blissful union with her bridegroom, but then finds that he has deserted her, leaving her longing for his return. St Bernard had used the Song to illuminate the alternation and fluctuation which characterise spiritual experience.[78] He believed that 'the Word of God, who is himself God and the bridegroom of the soul, comes to the soul and leaves it, just as he wishes'. The reason for this withdrawal was 'that he may be sought with greater eagerness and held with even greater strength'.[79] Christ's absences, then, were the occasion for spiritual growth. However, the immediate effect of Christ's withdrawal was that the soul fell into sin: 'When God seems to withdraw from someone, it is inevitable that sin will result, *necesse est*. The removal of the divine support confronts the human being with his overwhelming frailty, and this happens repeatedly.'[80] These words could easily have been written by Rutherford, and they remind us of the revival of medieval currents of inward religion within Protestantism, something which, as Gordon Rupp points out, has received less attention than the parallel revival of scholasticism among Reformed theologians.[81] Rutherford's devotional writings belong to a predominantly Catholic tradition of affective spirituality stemming from Bernard and drawing on the Song of Songs.[82]

---

[75] *Tryal*, p. 179.   [76] *Christ Dying*, p. 59.   [77] *Christ Dying*, p. 83.
[78] This is explored in detail by M. Casey, *Athirst for God: Spiritual Desire in Bernard of Clairvaux's Sermons on the Song of Songs* (Kalamazoo, Mich., 1988), ch. 6: 'Desire as dialectic'.
[79] *Sermons on the Song of Songs*, no. 74. Quoted in Casey, *Athirst for God*, p. 271.
[80] Quoted in Casey, *Athirst for God*, p. 260.
[81] G. Rupp, 'A devotion of rapture in English Puritanism', in R. B. Knox, ed., *Reformation, Conformity and Dissent: essays in Honour of Geoffrey Nuttall* (London, 1977), p. 126.
[82] Matter, *Voice of My Beloved*, p. 8, argues that commentaries on the Song constitute in themselves a separate sub-genre of medieval literature. Rutherford referred to Bernard's sermons on the Song of Songs on several occasions. See, for example, *Communion Sermons*, p. 251; *Covenant of Life*, p. 307.

Rutherford was not alone among the Reformed in sharing this affinity with Catholic spirituality. John Calvin was strongly influenced by Bernard's teaching on union with Christ,[83] and as Louis Bouyer has pointed out, 'the hot-house mysticism that seems to many people a characteristic essential and proper to post-Tridentine Catholicism . . . was nevertheless widely shared in the spiritual world of the Puritans'.[84] One of the writers who ensured that this was so was the Cambridge Puritan, Richard Sibbes. Sibbes's sermons drew heavily on the Song of Songs, but he tended to favour the ecclesiological interpretation of the Song, and he made it clear that Christ came to the soul 'in His appointed ways and not, as a rule, through special and private raptures'.[85] Rutherford also emphasised the way in which Christ visited believers through means (especially communion) but his letters testified to his many 'special and private raptures'. He was thus closer to Francis Rous (1579–1669) whose commentary on the Song treated the bride as the soul and saw the beloved's desertions as purifying dark nights of the soul, in a way strikingly similar to St John of the Cross.[86] Further similarities between Catholic and Puritan spirituality can be found in the Westminster divine Thomas Goodwin's *The Heart of Christ in Heaven towards Sinners on Earth* (1635), which has been described as the earliest example of what has often been regarded as a quintessentially Catholic devotion to the Sacred Heart.[87] Rutherford himself was anxious to tell his listeners that Christ had as much love for his kirk in heaven as he had for it when he was on earth; 'all Christs affections be in heaven with him' like 'a rose planted in better soyle, keepeth the same smell'.[88] His *Christ Dying* (1647) also closely resembles Catholic devotion to the Passion of Christ,[89] and his devotional writings have been compared to the nuptial mysticism of some Catholic hymnology.[90]

All this reminds us that Puritanism can be seen as part of a devotional revival which swept both Catholic and Protestant Europe in the late sixteenth and seventeenth centuries.[91] In the Netherlands the beginnings of

---

[83] D. E. Tamburello, *Union with Christ: John Calvin and the Mysticism of St Bernard* (Louisville, Ky, 1994).

[84] Bouyer, *Orthodox Spirituality* pp. 134–5.

[85] Quoted in Wakefield, *Puritan Devotion*, p. 103. See also M. E. Dever, 'Richard Sibbes and the "Truly Evangelical Church of England"', unpublished Ph.D. dissertation, University of Cambridge (1991), ch. 6.

[86] Bouyer, *Orthodox Spirituality*, pp. 136–8; Wakefield, *Puritan Devotion*, pp. 103–6.

[87] Bouyer, *Orthodox Spirituality*, pp. 140–2; E. I. Watkin, *Poets and Mystics* (London, 1953), ch. 4.

[88] Sermon on Hebrews 4.15 in Edinburgh University Library, Dc. 5. 30.

[89] Wakefield, *Puritan Devotion*, p. 98.

[90] R. Stuart Louden, 'Samuel Rutherford', in G. Wakefield, ed., *The Westminster Dictionary of Christian Spirituality* (Philadelphia, 1983), p. 345.

[91] Hambrick-Stowe, *Practice of Piety*, p. 23.

pietism could be observed in two Reformed scholastics very similar to Rutherford, Gisbert Voetius (1589–1676) and William Ames (1576–1633), although neither wrote in his effusive style. The devotional writer and hymnist Jodocus van Lodensteyn (1620–77) was perhaps closer to Rutherford in this respect, but he avoided the scholastic theology that delighted the Scotsman.[92] Among the French and Swiss Calvinists there was apparently less emphasis 'upon piety, upon inward religion', than there was among the Puritans, who tended on the whole to leave the scholastic theology to the continentals and concentrate on affectionate and practical writings.[93] Rutherford, therefore, may have been somewhat unusual among Protestants in mixing scholasticism and mysticism in an almost medieval cocktail.

However, the term 'mysticism' needs to be used with care. If by 'mystic' we mean someone with 'an intense desire for immediacy of communion with God', then Rutherford certainly was one. But if we are thinking of an individual who seeks the absorption of their human personality into the divine, or direct access to personal revelation which bypasses Scripture, then he most definitely was not. He believed that perfect communion with Christ would only be enjoyed at the marriage supper of the Lamb, which was to be at the end of all things and a corporate rather than a personal experience. In the meantime, effort, struggle and spiritual exercises were to occupy every Christian. It is because of these beliefs that Rutherford can be described by Wakefield as an 'anti-mystic'. Indeed, in his *Survey of Spiritual Antichrist* he attacked Familists and *Theologica Germanica* because they failed to understand these tough spiritual realities.[94] Perhaps we would be wise to follow Mark Dever's suggestion that instead of describing Puritans as 'mystics' (which implies a rather vague and undogmatic spirituality), we would do better to follow their own terms and call them 'affectionate theologians' (thereby highlighting their belief that doctrine must be internally appropriated and felt).[95] Yet having said this, it should be added that there were times when Rutherford did use the language of mystical absorption. 'O sweet communion', he wrote to Lady Kenmure, 'when Christ and we are through-other, and are no longer two!'[96] For all his theological reservations, he was perhaps temperamentally closer to being a mystic than most other Puritans.

If Puritan spirituality is not to be confused with mysticism, neither is it to be identified wholly with Catholic spirituality. Watkin has claimed that

---

[92] M. H. Prozesky, 'The emergence of Dutch pietism', *Journal of Ecclesiastical History*, 28 (1977), 29–37.
[93] B. Armstrong, 'Puritan spirituality: the tension of Bible and experience', in E. R. Elder, ed., *The Roots of the Modern Christian Tradition* (Kalamazoo, Mich., 1984), p. 229.
[94] Wakefield, *Puritan Devotion*, pp. 102, 107–8.
[95] See Dever, 'Richard Sibbes', pp. 119–20. [96] *Letters*, p. 47.

there was 'a tendency among the Protestants to return to the Catholic type of spirituality rejected by the Reformers'. He argues that although 'the Puritans may spill ink and energy in abuse of the "Roman Antichrist", smash stained-glass windows, and fast on Christmas Day – their devotional leaders are all the while preaching a spirituality substantially Catholic and, to a considerable extent, consciously drawn from Catholic sources'. As we have seen, this is largely true of Rutherford; he did share what Watkin calls 'a tender, a deeply Catholic, devotion to Jesus'.[97] But it would be a mistake to ignore his differences with Catholic piety. He did not believe in an 'inner light' or 'divine spark' within every human being which could naturally lead them to God. Rather, he stressed the deadness of natural man, and the need for God's supernatural intervention in conversion. Whilst this Augustinian piety did not separate him from all Catholics – as we have seen, Bernard was thoroughly Augustinian in his emphasis on the bridegroom's sovereignty – it did distinguish him from many of the mystics who appear to have been almost Pelagian in their stress on the human ability to rise towards God.[98]

Moreover, because his deep spirituality was grounded on his belief in God's justification open to all the elect, Rutherford did not make the Catholic distinction between *ascetic* experience available to all Christians and *mystical* experience reserved for a saintly elite. He believed that the 'love feasts' he experienced were available to all justified believers. It was for this reason that Puritanism fostered a lay spirituality which flourished among those engaged in secular pursuits, rather than a monastic spirituality for those in holy orders. As Hambrick-Stowe puts it, 'While the Catholic saint was an extraordinarily gifted mystic separated from the world by the cloister, the Puritan saint was an ordinary believer sanctified by God living and praying in the world.'[99]

The influence of Rutherford on Scottish Presbyterian piety has been very great. As Stuart Louden has written, 'In Scottish homes for some two centuries the most widely read devotional classic, apart from the Bible, was Rutherford's *Letters*.' The *Letters* 'infused a gentle and tenderhearted quality into evangelical faith which so easily became rigid and legalistic . . .

---

[97] Watkin, *Poets and Mystics*, pp. 56–8.

[98] Hambrick-Stowe, *Practice of Piety*, pp. 44–5, argues that whilst the Puritan asked 'Am I one of the elect?', the Catholic's goal was to elect God. Rutherford's strong Augustinianism still separated him from much of contemporary Catholicism. Bouyer is mistaken when he follows Perry Miller in thinking that Ramism and covenant theology had thoroughly rehabilitated human reason and nature among the Puritans after their Calvinian Fall, and had thus made Protestant theology far closer to that of the Catholic church (Bouyer, *Orthodox Spirituality*, pp. 143–5).

[99] Hambrick-Stowe, 'Loss and hope in Reformed spirituality', p. 97. Of course, Rutherford was a minister and no 'ordinary believer', and arguably he came to be seen as 'an extraordinarily gifted mystic', locked away in his cloister in Aberdeen.

Rutherford's wide influence engendered a spirituality of ardent and almost passionate love, with a Jesus-centred yearning for heaven'.[100]

Some have found it remarkable that this type of spirituality should be found in Scottish Calvinism, especially in one of the most rigid of supralapsarian Calvinists. Yet as Louise Yeoman has recently shown, those who see the Presbyterians as obsessed by external form rather than by inner spirituality are wide of the mark. Outer actions were emphasised 'in the name of maximising spiritual experience and inner contact'. Rutherford's *Letters*, she suggests, reveal that

the seeming outer emphasis in Presbyterianism came, in the most part, from a desire to protect the inner world from being smoored [smothered] by exposure to a lifeless time-serving episcopal ministry, and ceremonies which were perceived to be either useless in stirring up inner experience or threatening to the headship of Christ and thus likely to lead to him withdrawing his inner spiritual presence in disgust.[101]

Theology, ecclesiology and apocalypticism were therefore intimately connected with Rutherford's spirituality. The claim that Rutherford was simply practising revived Catholic piety is, therefore, as misleading as the claim that Scottish Presbyterianism was intellectually arid and emotionally frigid.

GODLY WOMEN

If Rutherford's piety is not what one expects from a Scottish Presbyterian, his close relationships with godly women are no less surprising. One hundred and seventy-one of Rutherford's surviving letters were addressed to women. This in itself is a striking fact, for although countless other religious leaders had maintained regular correspondence with women, it was usually slight compared with the overall bulk of their letter-writing. For instance, only sixty of Calvin's four thousand extant letters are addressed to female correspondents, and with Ignatius Loyola the figure is ninety out of seven thousand.[102] It would be hard to find another religious leader whose surviving correspondence is almost half addressed to women.

Like Calvin and Loyola, Rutherford wrote to women with some political influence. Fifty-six of his letters were addressed to Jane Campbell (Lady Kenmure), the wife of his patron, Viscount Kenmure, and the sister of one of the most powerful nobles in Scotland, Archibald Campbell (Lord Lorne, later marquis of Argyle). Rutherford pressed Jane Campbell to influence her husband and uncle. Because of this personal contact, Lorne tried unsuccessfully to defend Rutherford against the Court of High Commission in

---

[100] Louden, 'Samuel Rutherford', p. 345.   [101] Yeoman, 'Heart-work', pp. viii–ix.
[102] C. Blaisdell, 'Calvin and Loyola's letters to women: politics and spiritual counsel in the sixteenth century', in R. V. Schnucker, ed., *Calviniana: Ideas and Influence of Jean Calvin* (Kirksville, Missouri, 1988), pp. 235–6.

1636.[103] Many of the women to whom Rutherford wrote enjoyed similar influence.

This being so, was it the case that Rutherford simply wrote to these women for political purposes? Were his letters, like Calvin's, 'devoid of spiritual support and pastoral care'? The answer must be negative. These letters do not show the kind of evenhanded businesslike approach that Blaisdell has observed in Calvin's letters.[104] They are instead deeply personal, full of pastoral advice to women suffering from depression, bereavement and lack of spiritual assurance. When Jane Campbell lost a daughter, Rutherford comforted her with the thought that 'She is not sent away, but only sent before, like unto a star, which going out of our sight doth not die and evanish, but shineth in another hemisphere.'[105] When Marion McNaught fell into great 'heaviness' due to 'the temptations that press you sore', he assured her that she was undergoing the same trials and assaults as her Lord had endured.[106]

However, these were not merely one-way relationships in which the pastor was the dispenser and the woman the recipient of advice. Rutherford depended on these women as much as they depended on him. The number of letters he wrote to each perhaps indicates this: fifty-six to Jane Campbell and forty-four to Marion McNaught. Campbell was the younger of the two women, and almost the same age as Rutherford. When she left Galloway to move to England in 1629 Rutherford had already established a close friendship with her. 'I have received many and divers dashes and heavy strokes since the Lord called me to the ministry', he lamented, 'but indeed I esteem your departure from us amongst the weightiest. But I perceive God will have us to be deprived of whatsoever we idolise, that He may have His own room.'[107]

Marion McNaught was around fifteen years older than Rutherford and appears to have been his mentor and fellow-conspirator for the Presbyterian cause. In 1632 he wrote to John Kennedy, and sang McNaught's praises: 'Blessed be the Lord! that in God's mercy I found in this country such a woman, to whom Jesus is dearer than her own heart.'[108] In August 1633 he

---

103 *Letters*, p. 138.
104 C. J. Blaisdell, 'Calvin's letters to women: the courting of ladies in high places', *Sixteenth Century Journal*, 13 (1982), 67–84.
105 *Letters*, p. 41.   106 *Letters*, p. 106.   107 *Letters*, p. 43.
108 *Letters*, p. 77. McNaught's piety was such that she seems to have fasted to the detriment of her health. In 1632 Rutherford wrote to warn her of the sin of 'fasting against your weak body'. Her body was 'the dwelling-house of the Spirit' and hence 'you may not, without offending the Lord, suffer the old walls of that house to fall down through want of necessary food' (*Letters*, p. 85). This is a fascinating reference, for not only does it show us Rutherford's Reformed refusal to regard the human body as something corrupt or evil, it also confirms Caroline Walker Bynum's point that fasting has traditionally held more symbolic force for women than it has for men. McNaught's 'anorexia' seems very similar to

tells McNaught herself that he 'longed much to have conferred with you at this time'.[109] McNaught lived in Kirkcudbright, a few miles from Anwoth, and Rutherford appears to have visited her frequently.

This dependency of Presbyterian pastors like Rutherford on godly women aroused the contempt of more self-reliant Episcopalians. 'Many of [the Presbyterian ministers] were fawning and servile', wrote Gilbert Burnet, 'especially to the ladies that were much esteemed for piety.'[110] The Irish bishop, Henrie Leslie, felt that such attitudes subverted social order and hierarchy. 'The special meanes whereby [the Presbyterians] have advanced their faction', he claimed, 'is by insinuating into the weaker sexe in whom there is least ability of Judgement.' He alleged that the Presbyterian pastors enabled women 'to prattle of matters of divinity', and that wherever they had prevailed 'husbands have learned to obey their wives'.[111]

The level of intimacy that could develop between the godly woman and her pastor is only fully revealed in a manuscript copy of Rutherford's letters kept in St Andrews University Library. The fourth letter in the notebook is addressed to Margaret Grahame, and although printed in the first edition of the *Letters* it was significantly altered. In the manuscript copy, Rutherford wrote to the woman, 'I think you dearest to me then ever ye was for howbeit since my covenant with you in the garden of the man of God I have named you to my Lord and your case.'[112] The printed edition omitted this sentence altogether, probably because it was thought too intimate. We know nothing else about Margaret Grahame, but if we read it literally the statement means that she had made a personal covenant with Rutherford, probably at the home of another minister or prominent Puritan layman. Covenanting was not just for groups and nations, but also took place among godly individuals. That it took place between a minister and a woman is an indication of just how remarkably close such friendships could be. It confirms Diane Willen's argument that if women became dependent on their pastors the reverse was also the case; these relationships were fully reciprocal.[113]

Whether Rutherford's relationships with godly women ever became decidedly ungodly is a question to which it is difficult to give a definitive

that of the pious medieval women studied by Bynum in her *Holy Feast and Holy Fast: The Religious Significance of Food to Medieval Women* (London, 1987). Nor was hers a unique experience in seventeenth-century Scotland; as Yeoman, 'Heart-work', p. 268, shows, other godly women also practised such extreme fasting. Here we see another intriguing link with medieval spirituality.

[109] *Letters*, p. 89.   [110] Burnet, *History of my own Time*, I, p. 273.

[111] H. Leslie, *A Treatise of the Authoritie of the Church* (Dublin, 1637), Epistle Dedicatory.

[112] MS BX 8915 R8L4C37, n. p., St Andrews University Library.

[113] D. Willen, 'Godly women in early modern England: Puritanism and gender', *Journal of Ecclesiastical History*, 43 (1992), 561–80. As Willen observes, women 'were much more likely than men to develop strong, perhaps intense, and long-lasting relationships with their clergy', *Ibid*. p. 570.

answer, though it has to be said that there is no evidence that they did. The sexual scandal of his early years, and the many warnings he gave against youthful lusts certainly suggest that Rutherford struggled with his sexual passion, but so far as we know he never repeated the sin of his youth.

It is not clear how much Rutherford discussed fine theological points with his female correspondents. Perhaps, like Loyola and Calvin, he did not do so. However, he certainly discussed the state of the church, and passed on news of the latest ecclesiastical developments. In January 1634 he wrote to tell Campbell that the 'best affected of the ministry' had decided to hold a week of prayer and fasting for the state of the church. He knew that she was among those who 'love the beauty of Zion, and are afflicted to see the Lord's vineyard trodden under foot by the wild boars out of the wood', and he urged her to pass the information on to her husband.[114] Marion McNaught was given 'secret' news, which Rutherford dared not reveal 'to any but to yourself, whom I know'.[115] Clearly these women were fully informed about kirk politics and deeply implicated in Presbyterian plots to bring about radical change. They were trusted with important political information and were key members of a network of the godly in south-west Scotland.

As the wife of William Fullerton, provost of Kirkcudbright, Marion McNaught seems to have become embroiled in a battle for control of the town, the details of which are not clear. What does seem obvious is that in the early 1630s the Puritan party was struggling against a moderate group whom Rutherford refers to as 'the devil's instruments'.[116] McNaught was involved behind the scenes in trying to get a godly minister appointed[117] and in attempts to ensure the election of a godly commissioner to the Scottish parliament.[118] In July 1635 Rutherford advised her to write to lawyers in Edinburgh to see what her husband could do 'in opposing any intruded minister', and how far he could disobey the bishop without breaking the law.[119] McNaught was clearly an extremely active and competent woman, whose godliness (combined with the position of her husband) gave her a great deal of social influence.

The cases of Rutherford's female correspondents are obviously relevant to the long-standing debate over Puritanism and the position of women. The argument that Puritanism promoted the 'companionate marriage' and gave women more personal autonomy and social space has been challenged by those who argue that Puritan attitudes were both intellectually derivative and heavily patriarchal.[120] However, as Peter Lake has suggested, we can

---

[114] *Letters*, p. 92.   [115] *Letters*, p. 114.   [116] *Letters*, p. 113.
[117] *Letters*, p. 85.   [118] *Letters*, p. 99.   [119] *Letters*, p. 125.
[120] K. M. Davies, 'The sacred condition of equality: how unique were Puritan doctrines of marriage?', *Social History*, 5 (1977), 563–78; M. Todd, *Christian Humanism and the Puritan Social Order* (Cambridge, 1987), ch. 4.

accept this but continue to argue that Puritan zeal and piety may well have led to either a certain easing of patriarchal pressure or an increased number of opportunities 'for piecemeal acts of resistance and assertion against the overbearing presence of male authority'. Godliness was a source of 'personal potency and charisma' for women, and enabled them to circumvent the usual constraints of female existence.[121] Amanda Porterfield,[122] Diane Willen and Debra Parrish take up essentially the same position as Lake. Willen claims that 'godliness tempered patriarchy' and that 'Puritanism offered women enhanced status and reciprocity without demanding a cloistered life, martyrdom or mysticism'.[123] Parrish argues that women's religious influence was not confined to the household sphere, and that rather than being 'silent and struggling background figures' they were 'active participants' in the Puritan movement.[124]

The cases of Marion McNaught and Jane Campbell reinforce this line of argument. Both women were highly respected among the godly, and their political influence seems to have been quite substantial. On occasions they could resist the authority of their husbands on religious grounds. Rutherford clearly urges Campbell to take a stand against her lukewarm husband. It was her duty 'to drop words in the ears of your noble husband continually of eternity, judgement, death, hell, heaven, the honourable profession, the sins of his father's house'.[125] The principle underlying Rutherford's advice was the same as that underlying his political thought: when the will of God and the will of man conflicted, God must be followed and man disobeyed. Puritanism could undermine patriarchalism in sexual relations just as much as it did in political thought. However, as was the case in the political realm, by undermining the authority of one patriarch – be it the king or the husband – the Presbyterian clergy inevitably exalted their own authority, for they were the experts who could most clearly discern God's will.[126]

The influence of women like McNaught and Campbell within the Puritan movement helps to explain its attraction for women. As Blaisdell has observed, dynamic new movements in the early modern period – such as the Society of Jesus and Calvinism – seem to have had an 'enormous appeal' for women. They offered 'a means for expressing the ambitions of some powerful and enterprising women'. Although the social ethics of these movements were still firmly patriarchal, they valued the support of the

---

121 P. Lake, 'Feminine piety and personal potency: the "emancipation" of Mrs Jane Ratcliffe', *The Seventeenth Century*, 2 (1987), 143–65.
122 A. Porterfield, *Female Piety in Puritan New England: The Emergence of Religious Humanism* (Oxford, 1992).
123 Willen, 'Godly women', pp. 577–80.
124 D. Parrish, 'The power of female pietism: women as spiritual authorities and religious role models in seventeenth-century England', *Journal of Religious History*, 17 (1992), 33–45.
125 *Letters*, p. 91.   126 On this point, see Chapter 6.

godly regardless of gender.[127] Hambrick-Stowe has even gone so far as to call Puritanism 'a women's movement', since it 'tended to elevate the status of women', albeit within an 'obviously patriarchal' context.[128]

It seems clear, therefore, that Covenanter women were able to exercise a great deal of charismatic influence over the godly. Evangelical Presbyterianism, with its stress on the gulf between formal religion and heart-religion, created substantially more social space for the godly woman than did the much more formal structure of an Episcopalian kirk. However, in the years when the Covenanters were in power, governing through office rather than acting as charismatic agitators, women had less scope and influence than in the period before 1638 and after 1651. The records of the General Assembly for this period contain almost no references to women.[129] It was the conventicle rather than the committee that empowered the female sex. In the Quaker movement of the 1650s, where the stress on charisma as opposed to office was more complete, sexual egalitarianism was the inevitable result.[130] 'Heart religion' could be a great leveller.[131]

RUTHERFORD'S LANGUAGE

If Rutherford's close relationships with godly women do not fit our stereotype of the austere Presbyterian cleric, neither does the luxuriant and earthy prose of his letters, sermons and devotional works. His vocabulary is so distinctively Scottish that the Oxford English Dictionary quotes from the *Letters* and the *Tryal and Triumph of Faith* around seven hundred times to illustrate the use of obscure, colloquial or obsolete words.[132] Here we come across many words and phrases that are quintessential Rutherford. He speaks of having 'a wombful of love' for Christ, of being 'handfasted [betrothed] to Christ', of falling 'aswoon'. He talks of 'jouking' [darting], of

---

[127] Blaisdell, 'Calvin and Loyola's letters to women', p. 248.

[128] Hambrick-Stowe, *Practice of Piety*, pp. 47–8. Yeoman, 'Heart-work', pp. 253–60, after considering some of the Scottish evidence concludes that 'the role of presbyterian women does seem to show a brand of female activism and assertion which is rarely seen in other seventeenth-century contexts'.

[129] *Records of the Kirk of Scotland, 1638–51*, ed. A. Peterkin (Edinburgh, 1838).

[130] K. Thomas, 'Women and the Civil War sects', *Past and Present*, 13 (1958), 42–62; P. Mack, 'Women as prophets during the English Civil War', *Feminist Studies*, 8 (1982).

[131] See D. Hempton and M. Hill, eds., *Evangelical Protestantism in Ulster Society, 1740–1890* (London, 1992), ch. 7; J. Rendall, *The Origins of Modern Feminism: Women in Britain, France and the United States, 1780–1860* (London, 1985), ch. 3.

[132] By comparison there are only 252 references to Gillespie, and 63 to Baillie. Only the most famous of seventeenth-century English writers are referred to more often: Baxter (1,526), Locke (1,529), Hobbes (2,283), and Milton (12,845). Numbers are taken from the second edition on CD-Rom; included among them may be a few quotations taken from other authors with the same name.

'loons' [rogues], of 'unheartsome' [disheartening] events, and of the need to 'lippen' [trust] in Christ.

Yet Rutherford's prose was characterised as much by vivid images as by quaint vocabulary. The best study of the imagery in Rutherford's writing is that of the German philologist Hans Meier. His approximate count of images in Rutherford's *Catechism* showed that, of a total of 100, around 20 concerned rural domestic life, 15 were drawn from aristocratic life (including courtly, military and sports), but more than half were erotic, legal or commercial. Meier argues that 'love, law and lucre' were the three major metaphor clusters in Rutherford's writings, from his time in Anwoth through to his final days in St Andrews. Yet although 'Rutherford may be said to have always written the same letter', Meier is impressed by 'the absence of actual verbal repetition and the variation in phrase and appeal'.[133]

The power of Rutherford's writing is best seen in those passages in which he couched abstract theological concepts in daring, colourful and homely images which were not to be found in the Bible. A number of his most striking images centred on children. The Jews refused the rich banquet God offered them, Rutherford declared, and 'like daft bairns [children], ran to the play, and had more mind of their play than of their meat'.[134] Similarly, unbelievers were 'like bairns holding the water at a river side with their hands. They think (daft things) they hold the water, while in the meantime it runs through their fingers'. When they chased after earthly riches they were just like children building 'sandy burrocks' [sandcastles], whose play is disturbed by a shower or a speat of water.[135]

Images involving children and books are particularly noticeable in Rutherford's letters and sermons. We have already noted his description of Christians playing around the margins of Christ, as children play with the ribbons and gilt covering of an Arabic Bible. Elsewhere he complained that people 'seek truth as a wanton child doth his book, wishing he may not find it, and fearing the finding of his book cost him the loss of his pastime'.[136] Relying on feelings distracted sinners from the truth, just as 'while the bairn eateth an apple the book is laid by'.[137] Moreover, just as a child's first book had 'fair and large letters', so a believer's first experience of Christ in conversion was large and powerful so that he would not forget it.[138] If, when he began to pray, his first prayers seemed weak and foolish, he should not worry; 'young children rive [tear up] two or three books ere they learn one'.[139] This combination of children and books in Rutherford's imagery

---

[133] Meier, 'Love, law and lucre', pp. 77–96.   [134] *Communion Sermons*, pp. 133–4.
[135] *Communion Sermons*, p. 234.   [136] *Quaint Sermons*, p. 120.
[137] *Quaint Sermons*, p. 98.   [138] *Communion Sermons*, p. 213.
[139] *Quaint Sermons*, p. 134.

suggests the peculiarly Protestant phenomenon of the stern, academic pastor trying to cope with his rumbustious children.

Yet Rutherford was obviously convinced that domestic imagery was not enough. His readers and hearers also needed to be shaken up by more startling and aggressive pictures. He wrote, for instance, of foolish men 'tigging [toying, playing 'tig']' with a wrathful Christ,[140] like children 'thrusting up a stick in the nose of a sleeping lion'.[141] He pictured 'the great Shepherd' unable to walk because he had been bitten on the heel by 'that great hell's hound, the devil'.[142] When preaching before a communion, he compared Christ's body to a meat dinner: Christ had been boiled in his own blood in Gethsemane, roasted on the cross, carved by nails and spears and covered in the sour sauce of his Father's rejection. Christians were to 'eat heartily' of this body, and to reject all those who brought to the table 'Mary's milk' or 'Martyr's blood' as a dessert.[143] On another occasion he preached that sin lurked around a man like a ghost, blew in his face like wind, wrapped itself round his legs like weedbind, bit his heel like a serpent, and promised much but delivered nothing just like a joker.[144] Satan was like a warship 'with twenty pieces of ordnance, shooting at all who are sailing to Canaan', but 'Christ will mend the gap that Satan's bullet has made'.[145]

Above all, Rutherford employed feminine imagery.[146] He positively revelled in the nuptial metaphors provided by the Song of Songs, so much so, according to one eighteenth-century source, that lecherous drunkards were wont to use the *Letters* as pornographic reading material.[147] Rutherford clearly believed that the only language capable of expressing longing for Christ and the bliss of union with him was the language of sexual desire and sexual union:

What heaven can there be liker to hell than to lust, and green [long for], and dwine [pine after], and fall a swoon for Christ's love and to want it? . . . I would that Christ would let us meet and join together, the soul and Christ in each other's arms. Oh what a meeting is like this, to see blackness soul and Christ, kiss each other! Nay, but when all is done, I may be wearied in speaking and writing; but, oh, how far am I from the right expression of Christ or of His love? I can neither speak, nor write feeling, nor tasting, nor smelling: come feel, and smell, and taste Christ and his love, and ye shall call it more than can be spoken. To write how sweet the honeycomb is, is not so lovely as to eat and suck the honeycomb. One night's rest in a bed of love with Christ will say more than heart can think, or tongue can utter.[148]

---

[140] *Letters*, p. 119.   [141] *Communion Sermons*, p. 15.
[142] *Communion Sermons*, pp. 46–7.   [143] *Communion Sermons*, p. 68.
[144] *Communion Sermons*, p. 96.   [145] *Communion Sermons*, p. 101.
[146] Diane Willen is preparing a study of religious self-imagery, particularly imagery of the self as a bride, and intends to take Rutherford as 'a striking example'. See Willen, 'Godly women', p. 568n.
[147] P. Walker, *Six Saints of the Covenant* (London, 1901), p. 358.   [148] *Letters*, p. 448.

Such erotic language could not only convey the ecstasy of religious experience, it could also remind Rutherford's readers of their moral obligations. Here the sensual met the ethical. Just as the marriage bed ought only to be shared with the covenanted bridegroom, so the believer (or Scotland) ought to devote herself to Christ alone. When the world or the devil tried to seduce the soul she could say 'You are too long a-coming; I have many a year since promised my soul to another, even to my dearest Lord Jesus, to whom I must be true.'[149] If the Song of Songs told of the union of Christ and the soul, the prophet Hosea warned of the danger of spiritual adultery. If Rutherford used seductive images to describe Christ, he also reminded his readers of the seductive attractiveness of the world with its 'childish toys and earthly delights'.[150] Christ was a jealous husband who demanded absolute faithfulness and did not want to share his wife with any other rival. In a remarkable passage, Rutherford assured Lady Kenmure that the death of her husband would allow her to devote herself wholly to Christ and his cause: 'since you lie alone in your bed, let Christ be as a bundle of myrrh, to sleep and lie all the night betwixt your breasts (Cant. i. 13), and then your bed is better filled than before'.[151]

Occasionally Rutherford used mothering metaphors. In one of his sermons he compared Christ to 'a mother that has a bairn with a broken face, all bloody and bleared with tears, and it comes to her (and woe's her heart to see him so), and she sits down and wipes the tears from his eyes and lays her hand softly on the wound, and his head in her breast, and dights [wipes] away the blood, and lays her two arms about him, and there is no end of fair words.'[152] Here God is feminine and her child is masculine. Such metaphors are rare, however, compared to nuptial images.

A number of scholars have seen in feminine imagery like this the key to various aspects of social reality or attitudes to gender. While there is little doubt that in the hands of a sensitive practitioner like Caroline Walker Bynum[153] this approach can be illuminating, the whole area is an intellectual minefield, and not everyone who enters it avoids being blown skywards. Several attempts to examine Puritan sexual imagery, for example, seem less than successful.

A neo-Freudian interpretation of this language has been advanced by David Leverenz, who argues that the mothering imagery used by the Puritans reflects their experience of being parented by weak, anxious fathers

---

[149] *Letters*, p. 83.   [150] *Letters*, p. 70.

[151] *Letters*, p. 100. Unsurprisingly, this is one of those passages in Rutherford's *Letters* that critics have found both insensitive and indecent.

[152] *Communion Sermons*, p. 224.

[153] See C. W. Bynum, *Jesus as Mother: Studies in the Spirituality of the High Middle Ages* (London, 1982).

and strong, confident mothers, an experience that led them to imagine ideal parental types of commanding fathers and nurturing mothers in their sermons. These types produced two contradictory traits: an anal-obsessive character expressed in Puritan intolerance of ambiguity, dirt and sin, and their meticulous dogmatic precision; and an oral family romance fantasy expressed in a desire for nurture and fluidity and articulated in the frequent images of feeding on the breasts of Christ and his ministers.[154] This is certainly ingenious, but it fails to convince. Psychoanalysis of living individuals is difficult and controversial in itself; psychoanalysis of the dead is even more so, and psychoanalysis of dead *movements* is simply beyond the pale.

An alternative reading of the gender imagery of the New England Puritans is offered by Margaret Masson. She suggests that because they saw the female as a model for the regenerate person, and believed themselves capable of assuming a 'feminine' attitude towards God, they did not see gender differences as innate, but rather as a product of nurture. For this reason, she claims, Puritanism should be credited with 'a limited kind of egalitarianism'.[155] Yet this argument seems to carry the unlikely implication that every Christian writer who saw himself as a bride of Christ was a proto-feminist.

Recognising this problem, Amanda Porterfield has argued that the Puritans were unique because they used feminine self-imagery in the context of domestic life. By making wifely devotion a model for all Christians at the same time as putting great stress on the home as the locus of moral authority and ritual activity, they enhanced women's status. Good wives gained influence because they were admired as exemplary Christians, male aggression and ambition were restrained, and a new cultural significance was imparted to the social settings in which women worked.[156] Yet even here, as Porterfield realises, there are complications, because by identifying submissiveness as the definitive 'feminine' posture, Puritan language could be said to underwrite patriarchal attitudes.[157]

Another problem with all of the above theories is that they work on the assumption that attitudes towards gender roles are somehow encoded in

---

[154] D. Leverenz, *The Language of Puritan Feeling: An Exploration in Literature, Psychology and Social History* (New Brunswick, 1980).

[155] M. Masson, 'The typology of the female as a model of the regenerate: Puritan preaching, 1690–1730', *Signs*, 2 (1976), 304–15.

[156] Porterfield, *Female Piety*, pp. 3–10.

[157] Alison Weber has argued that although St Teresa employed a rhetoric of femininity in a way that served her own need of self-assertion (through it she reassured men and so avoided being silenced), her use of such rhetoric reinforced the ideology of women's intellectual and social subordination, making it more difficult for other women. See A. Weber, *Teresa of Avila and the Rhetoric of Femininity* (Princeton, 1990), p. 165.

language. It is quite possible that this was not the case, and that we are in danger of reading far too much into the feminine language of Christian spirituality. In the first place, feminine imagery was taken almost wholesale from the Song of Songs and formed an entirely conventional part of the language of spiritual expression for over a millennium. It is difficult to know if it can tell us much about the attitudes towards gender of a particular group at a particular time. Secondly, because an 'egalitarian' language of spiritual expression could co-exist with highly patriarchal social structures, it would seem that its significance was compartmentalised. Before God, men and women were equal and had to adopt a posture of submissiveness and receptivity, but this had no implications beyond the devotional sphere. For all his willingness to regard himself as a bride of Christ, Rutherford was still heavily patriarchal. When he wished to discredit the Independent idea that ultimate authority in a church lay with the members of the congregation, he simply said this would make women rulers, something he clearly saw as self-evidently ridiculous.[158] Any argument which claims that Rutherford could temper this with a degree of sexual egalitarianism must rest on his concrete practice rather than on the flimsy and highly contentious basis of the supposed significance of his feminine imagery. And as we have seen, a study of Rutherford's *Letters* does indeed suggest that godly women enjoyed respect, authority and even emulation among Puritans and their ministers.[159]

If the attempt to use feminine imagery as a key to social attitudes is contentious, judgements regarding the literary merit of Rutherford's prose seem almost equally tricky. As J. H. Millar observed, it is difficult to read Rutherford's *Letters* with indifference: 'They inspire either enthusiastic admiration or an antipathy amounting almost to disgust.'[160] To Rutherford's enthusiastic admirers, the *Letters* were 'the most seraphic book in our literature', 'the Golden Book of Love', and simply 'angelic'.[161] Those who thought little of them were said to be guilty of gross impiety. 'The haughty

---

[158] *Peaceable Plea*, p. 247.

[159] The volume of Rutherford's correspondence with women, and his positive attitudes towards his female correspondents, perhaps helps to explain why women have been prominent as editors and versifiers of his *Letters*. Editions of the letters compiled by women include Eva S. Sandeman, ed., *Daily Thoughts for a Year from the Letters of Samuel Rutherford* (Edinburgh, 1897); Eleanor C. Gregory, ed., *The Upward Way* (London, 1903); and Ellen C. Lister, ed., *The Loveliness of Christ* (London, 1893). Rutherford's words have also been put into verse by two women. Mrs Cousin wrote a well-known hymn, 'The Sands of Time are Sinking' based on Rutherford's *Letters*, and Faith Cook has recently written a book of verse based on them, *Grace in Winter: Rutherford in Verse* (Edinburgh, 1989).

[160] J. H. Millar, *A Literary History of Scotland* (London, 1903), p. 262.

[161] A. T. Innes, *Studies in Scottish History, Chiefly Ecclesiastical* (London, 1892), p. 5; A. Philip, *The Devotional Literature of Scotland* (London, 1920), p. 116; F. E. Gaebelin, *The Letters of Samuel Rutherford* (Chicago, 1951), p. 16.

contempt of that book which is in the heart of many', warned one fan, 'will be ground of condemnation when the Lord cometh to make inquisition after such things.'[162]

Unperturbed by threats of judgement, a number of critics have expressed outrage or hilarity at Rutherford's prose style. *The Scotch Presbyterian Eloquence*, published by Episcopalians in 1692, reproduced fifty-nine quotations from Rutherford's *Letters*, believing that in themselves they would demonstrate the absurdities of the Presbyterians. The author wrote that when the Presbyterians 'speak of Christ, they represent him as a Gallant, courting and kissing, by their fulsome, amorous Discourses on the mysterious Parables of the Canticles'.[163]

Modern authors have often concurred. Louis Bouyer complained that Rutherford was proof positive that Protestants were just as capable as Catholic mystics of 'sinking into bad taste and turbid emotionalism'. In Rutherford 'we find as much slumbering in the arms of Christ as we could wish, and swooning on his breast, and the exchange of languorous and sophisticated kisses. All that is lacking is a touch of real poetry.'[164] In a similar vein, J. H. Millar regarded Rutherford as 'a particularly gross offender against decency and good taste'. He compiled a little anthology of his 'erotic sallies', but declared that 'on going over my notebook, I frankly confess that I am unable to face up to regaling you with this heavenly Christian's odious ecstacies'.[165] Rutherford had no sense of proportion or of what was fitting, and his lack of tact and discretion with the Song of Songs led him to ride every metaphor to death. His language was 'ludicrous', 'vulgar', and made worse by virtue of being mixed up with excessive forensic terminology.[166]

---

[162] Dr Love, quoted in Millar, *Literary History*, pp. 262–3.

[163] Jacob Curate, *The Scotch Presbyterian Eloquence Display'd, or the Teaching of their Folly discover'd from their Books, Sermons and Prayers* (Rotterdam, 1738 edn), pp. 23, 98–108. See T. Maxwell, 'The Scotch Presbyterian Eloquence: a post-Revolution pamphlet', *Records of the Scottish Church History Society*, 8 (1944), 225–53. The pamphlet provoked outraged – and equally scurrilous – Presbyterian replies. Rutherford's defenders pointed to his undoubted piety, the fact that the letters were not written for publication, and their great popularity in Holland. They also expressed disgust that the Episcopalian author could ridicule Scots dialect. See [George Ridpath], *An Answer to the Scotch Presbyterian Eloquence* (London, 1693), and [Gilbert Rule], *A Just and Modest Reproof of a Pamphlet called the Scotch Presbyterian Eloquence* (Edinburgh, 1693).

[164] Bouyer, *Orthodox Spirituality*, p. 139. Wakefield, *Puritan Devotion*, pp. 107–8, agrees with Bouyer. He states that Rutherford's unrestrained erotic images are to be deprecated. His language does not have 'the numinous quality which saves the more realistic Puritan descriptions of Christ's sufferings from unhealthy sentimentalism'.

[165] J. H. Millar, *Scottish Prose of the Seventeenth and Eighteenth Centuries* (Glasgow, 1912), pp. 51–2.

[166] Millar, *Literary History*, pp. 264–5.

The poet Maurice Lindsay follows Millar in dismissing Rutherford as a serious literary talent. Rutherford, he says,

passed his time writing unctuously and at great length to a troubled soul with an insatiable appetite for rhetoric, one Marion McNaught . . . Unfortunately, Rutherford had become an early addict to the sexual imagery and seductive word-music of the Song of Solomon. These inspired him to devise word-play, which, to a modern reader, seems as absurdly comical as it would no doubt be deeply revealing to a psychologist.[167]

The 'effusions' of Rutherford, argues Lindsay, were largely responsible for the 'muddled imagery and inflated rhetoric' of much Scottish preaching from the seventeenth century onwards.[168]

One can sympathise with such negative reactions to Rutherford's prose. To a literary critic who values restraint and discipline, Rutherford's prose will appear marred by apocalyptic bombast and overblown emotionalism.[169] However, when we remember that his use of erotic and legal imagery stands in a broad biblical and Catholic tradition, it appears to be neither 'absurdly comical' nor 'deeply revealing'. Such imagery hardly requires a profound psychoanalytic explanation, since its use had been utterly conventional for centuries. Rutherford may have been less restrained in his erotic imagery than were most other writers, but he rarely went beyond the formulations of the biblical books on which he drew, and when he did he hedged his metaphors with phrases such as 'if we may say so'.[170]

Critics who focus on Rutherford's florid nuptial imagery, moreover, invariably ignore his tougher metaphors, and his hard-headed reflections on affliction. Gordon Rupp is quite right to argue that Bouyer's dismissal of Rutherford as 'a trivial sentimentalist' is unfair: 'What he says about devotion to Christ is set against a background of persecution and physical suffering.'[171] David Reid makes a similar point when he quotes a passage of 'fitful imaginative brilliance' from *Christ Dying*. Here Rutherford speaks of a sinner haunted by the fear of hell; even when he goes to church 'there is a dog as great as a mountain before his eye'. Reid remarks that Rutherford forms 'images crowded thick with visionary grotesqueness'; 'someone who can write like that about wretchedness is an extraordinary force at least'.[172]

Reid has also argued that Rutherford should be recognised as one of only three writers in pre-Restoration Scotland who 'developed elaborately mannered prose'. The others were the poet Drummond of Hawthornden, and

---

[167] M. Lindsay, *History of Scottish Literature* (London, 1977), pp. 154–5.
[168] M. Lindsay, *Scotland: An Anthology* (London, 1974), p. 340.
[169] The fervent pomposity into which Covenanter preachers could lapse is brilliantly caricatured by Sir Walter Scott in *Old Mortality*.
[170] *Communion Sermons*, p. 46.   [171] Rupp, 'A devotion of rapture', pp. 125–6.
[172] D. Reid, 'Prose after Knox', in R. D. S. Jack, ed., *The History of Scottish Literature*, I: *Origins to 1660* (Aberdeen, 1988), p. 194.

the eccentric prose stylist Thomas Urquhart. In contrast to both, Rutherford's extravagances were unconscious. 'His is an enthusiastic prose, language bent to convey religious excitement.'[173] As Agnes Machar indicated a century ago, his *Letters* are full of unconscious poetry: 'the "little birds of Anwoth", the mayflower, the fallow field, the moonlight and dews, the rising storm, the summer shower, the river, "flowing over bank and brae"'.[174] The plethora of images in Rutherford's sermons and letters are a welcome break from the otherwise unrelieved plainness of Scots ecclesiastical prose, and we may well be inclined to agree with one literary critic who suggests that 'our current neglect of Rutherford seems to me a much more puzzling phenomenon than his earlier fame'.[175]

Ultimately, however, judgements about the literary quality or gender implications of Rutherford's prose tend to miss the more obvious historical point – that Rutherford was not aiming for literary grace, but for the maximum rhetorical effect on his audience. His language possessed a raw, colloquial energy precisely because it was intended to grab the attention of a congregation.[176] The earthiness of his imagery supports Frank Gatter's thesis that we find in the radical Presbyterian writings of the seventeenth century 'a theology of the people', expressed in the diction of the simple folk and illustrated by metaphors of pantries, ploughs and children's games. Biblical language is often used to great effect, argues Gatter, and Presbyterian writings amaze 'by the simpleness and transparency of their idiom as well as by the air of human dignity that distinguishes them'.[177]

Gatter's analysis reminds us that Presbyterian preachers like Rutherford were deeply committed to communicating evangelical Protestantism to a popular audience. For all his Calvinist stress on the printed word, Rutherford was determined to present doctrine in a highly visual and pictorial way, even if the images he employed were verbally constructed. In letters and sermons of great imagination, he fused the apocalyptic and the nuptial, the sublime and the homely, constantly surprising and assaulting the senses. His prose stands as a powerful testimony to the populist impulses of the Puritan preachers.

---

[173] Reid, 'Prose after Knox', p. 186.
[174] A. M. Machar, 'A Scottish Mystic', *The Andover Review*, 6 (1986) p. 388.
[175] R. D. S. Jack, ed., *Scottish Prose 1550–1700* (London, 1971), p. 41.
[176] As Owen Watkins has said, when the Puritans produced literature 'they did so in the same way as the British were said to have acquired the Empire – in a fit of absentmindedness'. Quoted in Leverenz, *Language of Puritan Feeling*, p. 163.
[177] F. Gatter, 'On the literary value of some Scottish Presbyterian writings in the context of the Scottish Enlightenment', in D. Strauss and H. W. Drescher, eds., *Scottish Language and Literature, Medieval and Renaissance* (Frankfurt, 1986), pp. 175–92.

PURITANISM AND POPULAR CULTURE

Puritan populism, however, would sound like a contradiction in terms to many historians, who are struck by the mutual hostility that developed between the godly and the population they were trying to evangelise. The intensity of the Puritan drive for collective godliness, these scholars argue, provoked widespread resentment and resistance at a local level, whilst the appealing visual spectacle of the mass was replaced with sermons too intellectually demanding for a popular audience. Like the Pharisees, the Puritans laid heavy and grievous burdens on men's shoulders and did not lift a finger to help their victims.[178]

The standard social history of early modern Scotland draws a somewhat contrasting picture. Although it emphasises the disciplinary control imposed by the kirk, it also claims that by 1630 the church had 'won deep respect and exercised a powerful influence' among all classes except the nobility and vagrants.[179] Rutherford's letters and sermons, however, suggest that the godly in Scotland may have aroused the same kind of opposition as their counterparts in England. On several occasions he urged his correspondents not to be intimidated by those who nicknamed them 'Puritans'. 'Be not cast down', he wrote to Alexander Gordon of Earlston, 'for what the servants of Antichrist cast in your teeth, that ye are a head to and favourer of the Puritans, and leader to that sect.'[180] Of course, the Scottish Puritan 'sect' was a good deal more rigorous than its equivalent in England, for it espoused full-blown Presbyterianism and was utterly opposed to any compromise with episcopacy. Nevertheless, what seems to have set Puritans at odds with many of their contemporaries was not so much their ecclesiology, as their passionate concern for moral reformation, reformation resisted and resented by a substantial section of the population. In his sermons, Rutherford complained of those who 'dow [can] not bide heat and forwardness in religion', who 'love still a moderation in God's matters'. The 'middoway man' said

I love Christ . . . but I would not make a blowing horn of my religion. They shall never know upon what side I am . . . ill may I thrive if I endure too great preciseness, and that men should start at a strae [straw] and carry so kittle [squeamish] stomachs, and they will not do as neighbours do, having forgotten what common people say, 'Too holy was hanged'.[181]

---

[178] See, in particular, K. Wrightson and D. Levine, *Poverty and Piety in an English Village: Terling, 1525–1700* (London, 1979); W. Hunt, *The Puritan Moment: The Coming of Revolution in an English County* (Cambridge, Mass., 1983), ch. 6; D. Underdown, *Revel, Riot and Rebellion: Popular Politics and Culture in England, 1603–60* (Oxford, 1985); and R. Hutton, *The Rise and Fall of Merry England: The Ritual Year 1400–1700* (Oxford, 1994).

[179] T. C. Smout, *A History of the Scottish People, 1560–1830* (London, 1969), pp. 67–93; quotation from p. 74.

[180] *Letters*, p. 134.   [181] *Quaint Sermons*, pp. 136–7.

Clearly such attitudes were widespread among the common people, as well as among the complacent nobility forever chasing baronies, whom Rutherford continually assaulted in his sermons. 'I have exceeding small fruit of my ministry, and would be glad to know of one soul to be my crown and rejoicing in the day of Christ', he told Lady Kenmure in 1629.[182] A year later, in 1630, he wrote, 'For myself, I have daily griefs, through the disobedience unto, and contempt of, the word of God.'[183] In a communion sermon preached at Anwoth in 1634 he complained of 'our people', who say 'If this religion were away we will get the good, old merry, sonsy [plump, thriving] world again, wherein there was much luck and grace.' Only 'barking prophets' like Rutherford, who cried 'The burden of the Lord, the burden of the Lord', stood in the way of this.[184]

All this suggests that cultural conflict between the godly and those who defended traditional popular culture was to be found in Scotland, as in England. It is well illustrated by a story told of Rutherford, one that may be apocryphal, but which perhaps preserves an incident transmitted over the generations by oral tradition. The story goes that one Sabbath in Anwoth, Rutherford found some of his parishioners playing football. He exploded with rage and called on a group of stones nearby as witnesses against them.[185] The zealous Puritan minister, the 'barking prophet', was taking the offensive against his lukewarm and worldly parishioners.

However, it would be a mistake to see Puritanism as resolutely opposed to popular culture. Various aspects of enthusiastic Protestantism – psalm-singing, the sociability of the godly, even moral reformation itself – had considerable popular appeal.[186] The tendency of Puritans to see everything in terms of manichaean dichotomies – Christ versus Antichrist, tyranny versus liberty, idolatry versus true religion – meshed easily with a popular culture that also arranged the world into binary oppositions.[187] Moreover, the much-maligned Puritan sermon was far from being a dull affair; two modern historians have even described it as 'performance art'. Puritan preachers like John Rogers and Stephen Marshall in Essex were often highly theatrical and dramatic in their presentation; Rogers once took hold of the pulpit canopy and began 'roaring hideously, to represent the torments of the damned', whilst Marshall preached with such fervour that his sister was on hand to give him a towel and a clean shirt after his strenuous pulpit exertions.[188]

---

[182] *Letters*, p. 43.   [183] *Letters*, p. 52.   [184] *Communion Sermons*, p. 148.
[185] A. Thomson, *The Life of Samuel Rutherford* (Edinburgh, 1884 edn), p. 30.
[186] This is emphasised by P. Collinson, 'Puritanism as popular religious culture', in C. Durston and J. Eales, eds., *The Culture of English Puritanism, 1560–1700* (London, 1996), pp. 32–57.
[187] A point made by P. Lake, 'Anti-popery: the structure of a prejudice', in R. Cust and A. Hughes, eds., *Conflict in Early Modern England* (London, 1989), pp. 72–106.
[188] See F. Bremer and E. Rydell, 'Performance art? Puritans in the pulpit', *History Today*, 45 (September 1995), pp. 50–4.

Rutherford's own preaching style seems to have been equally enthusiastic. One of his students told Wodrow that his teacher 'had a strange utterance when preaching, a kind of screigh which he never heard the like'. Another claimed that 'many times he thought Mr Rutherford would have flown out of the pulpit when he came to speak of Christ, the Rose of Sharon'.[189] He was, declares Wodrow, 'one of the most moving and affectionate preachers in his time, or perhaps in any age of the church'.[190]

Such 'moving and affectionate' preaching came into its own at the time of the great Scottish communion festivals, whose intensely communal nature and sacramental piety are spoken of with such warmth in Rutherford's letters and sermons. According to Gilbert Burnet, the Protester communions of the 1650s drew people from a forty or fifty mile radius, leading to crowds so large that several sermons would be preached simultaneously to different sections of the gathering. On the Wednesday before the communion, a fast day was held with prayers and sermons continuing for eight or ten hours. Saturday was preparation day, and communion itself was administered on Sunday, with the rituals lasting for up to twelve hours. All this, says Burnet, 'was performed with great shews of zeal', and concluded with a day of thanksgiving on Monday. Those who attended told stories of 'many signal conversions that were wrought upon these occasions', though Burnet himself was more inclined to believe stories of 'much lewdness' resulting from the gathering of such multitudes.[191]

As Collinson points out, these Scottish communions demonstrate that early modern evangelical Protestantism had plenty of populist potential. Indeed, they seem to have combined the characteristic features of two Christian traditions famed for their popularity: the eucharistic festivity of medieval Catholicism and the enthusiastic preaching of American revivalism. These communions remind us that Puritanism, like later Evangelicalism, had a soft as well as a hard side. As well as being deeply concerned with moral discipline and godly reformation, it fostered popular enthusiasm.[192] Our assessment of the movement must remember both.[193]

[189] R. Wodrow, *Analecta or Materials for a History of Remarkable Providences Mostly Relating to Scotch Ministers and Christians* (Edinburgh, 1842–3), III, pp. 88–9.
[190] R. Wodrow, *The History of the Sufferings of the Church of Scotland from the Restoration to the Revolution*, I (Glasgow, 1828), p. 205.
[191] Burnet, *History of My Own Time*, I, p. 113.
[192] These two facets of American Evangelicalism are noted by D. W. Howe, 'Religion and politics in the antebellum North', in M. Noll, ed., *Religion and American Politics: From the Colonial Period to the 1980s* (Oxford, 1990), pp. 123–4.
[193] For Scotland, therefore, Smout's emphasis on the disciplinary side of the kirk must be balanced by Yeoman's stress on Presbyterian enthusiasm.

5

The Reformed theologian

For over twenty years of his life, Samuel Rutherford was a professor of divinity. Altogether he published eight theological works – three of them in Latin – amounting to almost 4,000 printed pages.[1] He was the most distinguished theologian among the Scottish Covenanters,[2] with an international reputation as a champion of Reformed orthodoxy.[3] Throughout his life he saw that orthodoxy threatened by two equal and opposite errors – Arminianism and Antinomianism – and he produced extensive polemical refutations of both positions. Given the range and depth of his output, it is inevitable that this chapter will leave much untouched. The detailed arguments of Rutherford's Latin works against Arminianism, in particular, require a more extended treatment. However, what we can provide here is a general overview of Rutherford's theology. We shall begin with a brief look at the historiography.

---

[1] In chronological order these works are: *Exercitationes Apologeticae pro Divina Gratia* (Amsterdam, 1636), *The Tryal and Triumph of Faith* (London, 1645; republished Edinburgh, 1845), *Christ Dying* (London, 1647), *A Survey of Spiritual Antichrist* (London, 1648), *Disputatio Scholastica* (Edinburgh, 1649), *The Covenant of Life Opened* (Edinburgh, 1655), *Influences of the Life of Grace* (London, 1659), and *Examen Arminianismi* (Utrecht, 1668).

[2] Of the other Covenanter ministers, Alexander Henderson and Robert Douglas were more statesmen than theologians, David Calderwood and George Gillespie dealt more with ecclesiological issues than with theology, and David Dickson, James Durham and George Hutcheson specialised as biblical commentators. Rutherford, Dickson, Durham, William Guthrie and Patrick Gillespie all wrote works of covenant theology, but only Robert Baillie approaches the range of Rutherford's theological writings. The best introductory works on Scottish theology are J. Walker, *The Theology and Theologians of Scotland, 1560–1750* (Edinburgh, 1982 edn); J. Macleod, *Scottish Theology* (Edinburgh, 1974 edn). But see now the articles by Donald Macleod and others in N. Cameron, ed., *Dictionary of Scottish Church History and Theology* (Edinburgh, 1993) on assurance, atonement, covenant theology, justification, and systematic theology.

[3] Rutherford's Latin works against Arminianism brought him to the attention of Dutch theologians, and prompted the universities of Harderwyck and Utrecht to offer him professorships of divinity. See R. Baillie, *Letters and Journals*, 3 vols., ed. D. Laing (Edinburgh, 1841–2), III, p. 82.

THE HISTORIOGRAPHICAL DEBATE OVER
REFORMED THEOLOGY

Surprising as it may seem to the outside observer, the subject of early modern Reformed theology has generated intense debate among historians and theologians in recent years. The literature on the topic is now very extensive indeed, and can be thoroughly bewildering. However, we can begin to make sense of it when we understand the reasons why three distinct groups of scholars have thought this subject worthy of their attention.

In the first place, a number of secular historians and sociologists have studied Calvinist theology because they have suspected that it was connected in some way or other with the process of modernisation.[4] Max Weber's *The Protestant Ethic and the Spirit of Capitalism* (1904) suggested that the unintentional psychological consequence of the Calvinist doctrine of predestination was to produce believers who were intensely anxious about their salvation and threw themselves into ascetic economic activity in a subconscious effort to gain through their productive lives the assurance that they were members of the elect.[5] Michael Walzer and Kevin Sharpe, in contrast, see the 'Puritan' doctrine of election as important because it undermined the holistic Elizabethan world picture.[6] Christopher Hill is most interested in the 'covenant' motif in Reformed theology. He has argued that its emergence in the late sixteenth and early seventeenth centuries reflected the growing significance of the contracts and debtor-creditor relationships associated with capitalist development.[7] The most distinguished historian of American Puritan thought, Perry Miller, believed that the covenant idea had softened the theology of Calvin by binding his tyrannical God and by giving an active role to human effort. Miller was convinced that the covenant theology of the Puritans 'carried us . . . to the very threshold of the Age of Reason'.[8] Like the rest of this group, he

---

[4] By 'Calvinist' theology they mean the sort of predestinarian theology for which Calvin himself is famed. Calvin's theology, of course, involved much more than a doctrine of predestination, and later theologians preferred to call themselves 'Reformed' rather than 'Calvinist', since Calvin was only one of the sixteenth-century theologians whom they admired. However, the term 'Calvinist' is so widely used and understood, that I shall follow convention throughout this chapter, using it interchangeably with 'Reformed orthodox'.

[5] For a sophisticated assessment of Weber's thesis and an attempt to apply it to Scottish Calvinism, see G. Marshall, *Presbyteries and Profits: Calvinism and the Development of Capitalism in Scotland, 1560–1707* (Oxford, 1980).

[6] M. Walzer, *The Revolution of the Saints* (Cambridge, Mass., 1965), ch. 5; K. Sharpe, *Politics and Ideas in Early Stuart England: Essays and Studies* (London, 1987), pp. 28–31.

[7] C. Hill, 'Covenant theology and the concept of "A public person"', in *The Collected Essays of Christopher Hill*, III (Brighton, 1986), pp. 301–3.

[8] P. Miller, *The New England Mind from Colony to Province* (Cambridge, Mass., 1953), p. 67. Miller's thesis was first advanced in 'The marrow of Puritan divinity', republished in

thought he saw Calvinist theology as reflecting and facilitating modernisation.

A second group of historians has been generally sceptical about such grand theories, but it has been interested in developments within Reformed theology as a possible factor in the origins of the English Civil War. Nicholas Tyacke was the first historian to suggest that the rise of Arminian theology in the Jacobean Church of England fractured a Calvinist consensus and led to a bitter ecclesiastical conflict which eventually erupted in the Civil War of 1642.[9] His thesis – which sees Arminianism rather than Puritanism as the innovatory and destabilising force in English affairs – has attracted much support, notably from Conrad Russell.[10] It has also come under fierce attack from Peter White and Kevin Sharpe, who question the existence of a Calvinist consensus in the sixteenth century and even of widespread Arminianism in the early seventeenth.[11] The debate is one to which we shall return at the end of this chapter.

In the meantime, however, we will concentrate on a third debate, which is largely – though not exclusively – a family quarrel among theologians in the Reformed tradition. What interests these scholars is the relationship between the theology of John Calvin and the Reformed orthodoxy of the late sixteenth and seventeenth centuries. Whilst one group insists that the 'orthodox' were essentially faithful to Calvin's legacy, the other maintains that they corrupted the Reformer's pure theological milk. These discontinuity or betrayal theorists commonly level two major charges against the Reformed orthodox. They suggest, first, that the later Calvinists moved away from Calvin's biblical and Christocentric theology and acquired a speculative and scholastic obsession with theories of predestination. Secondly, they claim the covenant theology of the orthodox reintroduced a legalistic strain into the Reformed tradition, drawing attention away from salvation by grace alone.

Although endorsed by many scholars, these claims have met with growing criticism, and my own view is that they are considerably exaggerated. I will attempt to show that this is so with reference to Rutherford who, as a Reformed scholastic and a Puritan covenant theologian, offers a prime example of the theological orientation that is widely seen as diverging

his *Errand into the Wilderness* (Cambridge, Mass., 1956), pp. 48–98. See also his *The New England Mind: The Seventeenth Century* (New York, 1939), pp. 365–97.
[9] N. Tyacke, 'Puritanism, Arminianism and counter-revolution', in C. Russell, ed., *The Origins of the English Civil War* (London, 1973), pp. 119–43; *Anti-Calvinists: The Rise of English Arminianism, c. 1590–1640* (Oxford, 1987).
[10] C. Russell, *The Causes of the English Civil War* (Oxford, 1990), ch. 4.
[11] P. White, 'The rise of Arminianism reconsidered', *Past and Present*, 101 (1983), 34–54; *Predestination, Policy and Polemic* (Cambridge, 1992); K. Sharpe, *The Personal Rule of Charles I* (New Haven, 1992), pp. 292–301.

sharply from Calvin. I shall look first at what Rutherford has to say about predestination and divine sovereignty, and then discuss his covenant theology and stress on human agency. Towards the end of the chapter I shall move beyond the narrow confines of the historical theology debate and investigate the political implications of Rutherford's theology.

PREDESTINATION AND DIVINE SOVEREIGNTY

To read Rutherford's scholastic theology is to enter the world evoked so vividly in Umberto Eco's novel, *The Name of the Rose*. As one nineteenth-century scholar put it, '[Rutherford] was born too late to take part in the controversy which divided the schoolmen, as to whether an angel could pass from star to star without traversing the intermediate space, but he delights in raising and discussing questions no less abstruse.'[12] Rutherford, indeed, showed considerable respect for the medieval scholastic theologians. He particularly admired one of the Nominalist schools, the *schola Augustiniana moderna*, which included Thomas Bradwardine (c.1290–1349) and Gregory of Rimini, and drew on the ideas of both Thomas Aquinas and Duns Scotus. In common with other Reformed theologians in the first half of the seventeenth century, he was swept along by a powerful revival of scholasticism, and published vast, philosophically sophisticated treatises in defence of Calvinist orthodoxy.

Ironically, many scholars have seen this scholastic Reformed orthodoxy as undermining Calvin's legacy rather than defending it.[13] The orthodoxy of the later Calvinists, they suggest, had more to do with Aristotelian metaphysics than with the biblical exegesis of which Calvin was a master. The Calvinist scholastics placed far more trust in reason and logic than did Calvin. They made predestination an organising principle, and then by means of the Aristotelian syllogism they deduced a logically watertight system from it. Whereas Calvin warned against speculation into the hidden will of God, the Calvinists were quite prepared to pontificate about the

---

[12] A. Milroy, 'The doctrine of the Church of Scotland', in R. H. Story, ed., *The Church of Scotland Past and Present*, IV (London, 1891), p. 230. The notorious angel debates, however, are far better known to the detractors of scholasticism than they were to the Schoolmen themselves.

[13] See, for example, B. Hall, 'Calvin and the Calvinists,' in G. E. Duffield, ed., *John Calvin* (Abingdon, 1966); B. Armstrong, *Calvinism and the Amyraut Heresy: Protestant Scholasticism and Humanism in Seventeenth Century France* (London, 1969); S. Strehle, *Calvinism, Federalism, and Scholasticism: A Study in the Reformed Doctrine of the Covenant* (Bern, 1988); A. E. McGrath, *Reformation Thought: An Introduction* (Oxford, 1993 edn), pp. 123–31; A. C. Clifford, *Atonement and Justification: English Evangelical Theology 1640–1790: An Evaluation* (Oxford, 1990), pp. 95–105. All these books lay heavy emphasis on the scholastic methodology of the high orthodox and contrast it with the humanist method of Calvin and his supposedly faithful followers like Amyraut.

precise order of God's eternal decrees. Moreover, their approach to
Scripture was unhistorical since they read it through their own metaphysical
theology.

Richard Muller, however, has presented a devastating critique of this
account of theological development within the Reformed tradition, arguing
that it greatly exaggerates the differences between Calvin and the
orthodox.[14] He points to scholarship that emphasises how much the
Reformers themselves owed to medieval Augustinianism,[15] and suggests
that neither Calvin nor his followers can be understood apart from their
scholastic background. Scholasticism was a rigorous methodology that did
not yield any particular set of doctrines, and it was employed by Calvin and
Arminius as well as by the Reformed orthodox.[16] By and large the orthodox
used scholastic argument to defend Calvin's doctrine of absolute double
predestination. Faced with a new wave of sophisticated attacks that Calvin
himself did not have to deal with, they probably had little choice but to use
the new tools of scholastic logic. They never made the eternal decree the
heart and soul of their theology, or allowed it to displace Calvin's biblical
and Christological orientation. Those who assert otherwise invariably soft-
pedal Calvin's predestinarianism while exaggerating that of his followers.[17]
Later Reformed theology, asserts Muller, did not distort the heritage of the
Reformation.

The case of Rutherford tends to confirm Muller's argument. If Rutherford's major Latin treatises focused more obsessively on the issue of
predestination than did the works of Calvin, this was simply because
Rutherford was aware of the pressing need to counteract a rising tide of
anti-Augustinianism across Europe. Within Catholicism, Jesuit theologians
had advanced novel variations or even alternatives to traditional Augustin-

---

[14] Muller's voluminous writings include *Christ and the Decree: Christology and Predestination
in Reformed Theology from Calvin to Perkins* (Durham, NC, 1986); *Post-Reformation
Reformed Dogmatics, Volume I: Prolegomena to Theology* (Grand Rapids, Mich., 1987);
'Arminius and the scholastic tradition', *Calvin Theological Journal*, 24 (1989), 263–77;
God, Creation and Providence in the Thought of Jacob Arminius (Grand Rapids, 1991);
'The myth of decretal theology', *Calvin Theological Journal*, 30 (1995), 159–67; and
'Calvin and the "Calvinists": assessing continuities and discontinuities between the Refor-
mation and orthodoxy', *Calvin Theological Journal*, 30 (1995), 345–75.

[15] For a discussion of how medieval Augustinianism influenced the Reformers see A. McGrath,
Intellectual Origins of the European Reformation (Oxford, 1987), pp. 86–93, and his
Reformation Thought, ch. 4.

[16] On Calvin see, for example, his *Institutes of the Christian Religion*, trans. H. Beveridge
(Grand Rapids, Mich., 1989 edn), III. 14. 17, where he employs Aristotle's fourfold division
of causality: efficient, material, instrumental and final. On Arminius, see Muller, 'Arminius
and the scholastic tradition', 263–77.

[17] See for example, McGrath, *Reformation Thought*, pp. 123–31. K. Barth, *Church Dogmatics* (Edinburgh, 1936–81), II/2, p. 86, is more balanced when he suggests that predestination was neither central nor peripheral in Calvin's system. Muller, *Christ and the Decree*,
argues something similar for the Reformed scholastics.

ianism, and anti-Calvinist ideas had begun to emerge in England during the 1590s. In the Netherlands, the resistance to Calvin's predestinarianism had been led by Jacob Arminius (1560–1609), and by the 1640s Arminianism had even begun to take hold among 'the Godly party' in England, championed by men like the Independent divine, John Goodwin.[18]

Arminians disagreed sharply with Calvin's claim that God had sovereignly decreed the election to salvation of certain individuals without any consideration of their future choices, while also decreeing that the rest of mankind would be damned.[19] In their influential Remonstrance (1610), the Dutch Arminians argued that election was based on foreknowledge; God had predestined to glory all those whom he foresaw would freely cooperate with his prevenient (but resistible) grace by believing in Christ and persevering in the faith to the end.[20] The contrast with the Genevan reformer was stark. For Calvin, God's decree was *absolute* and irresistible; for Arminius it was *conditional* on human decision. In Calvin's scheme, God was radically free and humans only enjoyed a *compatibilist* freedom to follow their own predetermined desires; in Arminius's theology God was bound by his own loving character to make salvation available to all, and it was the human individual who enjoyed *libertarian*, non-determinist freedom. Whereas Calvin taught that God's decree involved the specific selection of particular individuals, Arminius viewed the eternal decree as a general determination to save that corporate body of people who responded to the Gospel in faith. For Calvin, whether one was saved or damned ultimately depended on God's mysterious decision in eternity; for Arminius, by contrast, it depended on the human individual's free decision in time.

Rutherford had many objections to Arminianism, but foremost among them was his complaint that it detracted from the glory of God and boosted the pride of man. 'A God electing on faith forseen', argued Rutherford, 'maketh God go out of himself, looking to this or that in the creature, upon which his will may be determined to elect. Now this is against the alsufficiencie of God.'[21] By denying that grace determined the decisions of free agency, and by claiming that both acted together as 'two joynt causes, the one not depending on the other', Arminians effectively admitted that

---

[18] *Christ Dying*, p. 400. Rutherford's first book, *Exercitationes Apologeticae pro Divina Gratia* (1636), criticised not only the Dutch Arminians, but also the Jesuits and English anti-Calvinists like Thomas Jackson.

[19] See Calvin, *Institutes*, III. pp. 21–4. The idea of double predestination was introduced by the monk, Godescalc of Orbais (c. 805–c. 868), whose extreme Augustinianism generated intense debate in the ninth century.

[20] See H. Bettenson, ed., *Documents of the Christian Church* (Oxford, 1943), pp. 374–6.

[21] Unpublished manuscript, 'Fragments of a discourse on Ephesians 1.4', in Edinburgh University Library, Laing II: 394, n. p.

'free-will divideth the spoyl with Christ'.[22] The great Reformation doctrine of *sola gratia* was destroyed – salvation was no longer by grace alone, but by the works of free will too. Men were made the 'Artists, causes and masters of the decrees of Election, or Reprobation'; ultimately, it was not divine free will but human free will that had 'the free and absolute casting of the balance' as to whether the individual would be saved or not.[23] The God of the Arminians had to confess, 'I can but dance as free-will pipeth'.[24] Because God's determination of second causes was denied, he was no longer 'Master of events, nor hath he a dominion of providence in all things that fall out, good and evill.'[25]

Arminianism was also objectionable because it made salvation uncertain. Christ may have died for everyone, and God may have given his grace to everyone, but that atonement and that grace were useless unless the individual chose to avail himself of them. The Arminian assurance that God loved all and willed to save all turned out to be 'cold comfort'.[26] The God of the Arminians was a mere well-wisher, and his love turned out to be mere 'lip-love, not reall', since it was not efficacious or irresistible. Christ's death had merely secured 'a possible salvation'. Arminianism, concluded Rutherford, was a 'most abominable and comfortlesse doctrine'.[27]

Moreover, argued Rutherford, Arminianism did not really avoid the problems of theodicy encountered by Calvinists. Calvinists might find it difficult to explain why God had predestined some to salvation and passed over others, but Arminians faced an equally perplexing problem: why had God created people who he knew would not respond freely to him but would instead have to be 'cast in a river of fire, to be burnt quick, where they shall be tormented ten thousand yeares, ever dying, and not able to find death, to end their miseries'.[28] Arminians made God guilty of 'double dealing', for they pictured a Deity who willed that all be saved, and yet failed to provide them with the effectual means necessary for salvation.[29]

Finally, Rutherford feared that the Arminian assertion of free will was somehow linked to scepticism, doubt and uncertainty. Arminians taught that the eternal will of God was 'loose, lubrick, potential, disjunctive', 'tottering' and unfixed, and that 'all the contingent acts of men' were cast upon 'loose uncertainties'.[30] But they seemed to be implying something similar about reason. Free will and free thought seemed to go together, or so Rutherford claimed in his *Free Disputation Against Pretended Liberty of Conscience* (1649). The Dutch Arminians and the radical Independent, John Goodwin, had advocated religious toleration on the grounds that uncer-

---

[22] *Christ Dying*, pp. 469–70.   [23] *Christ Dying*, p. 410.   [24] *Christ Dying*, p. 430.
[25] *Christ Dying*, p. 469.   [26] *Christ Dying*, p. 427.
[27] *Christ Dying*, pp. 440, 393–5.   [28] *Christ Dying*, p. 416.
[29] *Christ Dying*, p. 417.   [30] *Influences*, sigs. a3–a3v.

tainty and disagreement over 'non-fundamentals' was inevitable, and their relativistic indifferentism was to be seen in their theology too – even the decree of God was 'dubious and indifferent toward things and persons'. In an Arminian world, chance reigned supreme; events were unhinged from the strong post of God's providence, guided only by 'the sway of Nature, and blind Fortune'. The world would be like chariot wheels running down a huge mountain for hundreds of years 'after the man who set them first a work, were [sic] dead'.[31] Arminianism led naturally to the mechanistic universe of the Deist, a universe which, for all its apparent stability, was actually ruled by contingencies and chance.[32]

In contrast to Arminianism, the doctrine of absolute predestination evoked awe and gratitude to God. 'No doctrine so endeareth Christ to a soule, as this of particular redemption and free grace separating one from another', wrote Rutherford. When the elect sinner contemplated that 'the Lord passed by so many thousands and millions, and the lot of free grace fell upon me precisely by name, and upon us, and not upon thousands, besides no less eligible than I was', he would be sure to cry out 'behold what love!'[33]

Rutherford's belief in the awe-inspiring particularity of God's love was the source of his opposition to the ideas of the French Calvinist, Moises Amyraut (1596–1664). Heavily influenced by the Scotsman, John Cameron, Amyraut had argued that God desired the salvation of all men, and that Christ died to atone for the sins of the whole world, not for those of the elect alone. However, he did not abandon the idea of absolute predestination. The universality of Christ's atonement was purely hypothetical, he explained; Christ's sacrifice only became effectual for the elect, in whom God would irresistibly produce saving faith.[34]

Amyraut's ideas divided the French Reformed Church for several decades and aroused controversy across Reformed Europe. In England, for example, his position was supported by moderate Calvinists like James Ussher, Richard Baxter and Edmund Calamy, but it was opposed by John Owen, who regarded it as a half-way house to Arminianism.[35] Rutherford was firmly among the critics, and he wrote at considerable length against

---

[31] *Influences*, p. 8.
[32] The link between Arminianism and Pyrrhonianism is made by N. Tyacke, 'Arminianism and English culture', in A. C. Duke and C. A. Tamse, eds., *Britain and the Netherlands, Volume VII: Church and State Since the Reformation* (The Hague, 1981).
[33] *Christ Dying*, pp. 437–9.   [34] See Armstrong, *Calvinism and the Amyraut Heresy*.
[35] D. Wallace, *Puritans and Predestination: Grace in English Protestant Theology, 1525–1695* (Chapel Hill, NC, 1982), contains a useful analysis of moderate Calvinism. For debates between Rutherford and the Amyraldians at the Westminster Assembly see the *Minutes of the Westminster Assembly of Divines*, ed. A. F. Mitchell and J. Struthers (London, 1874), pp. 152–60. Owen's *The Death of Death in the Death of Christ* was entirely devoted to defending the idea of a definite or limited atonement.

Amyraut and in defence of limited or definite atonement.[36] He insisted that the universalist texts of the Bible were not to be interpreted literally; 'all' was regularly used as a synecdoche meaning 'many', so that Scriptural verses declaring that God loved all the world could reasonably be read to mean that God loved the elect.[37] As far as Rutherford was concerned, Amyraut's support for universal atonement demonstrated that he was nothing but an Arminian.[38] The claim that God willed the salvation of all and made provision for it in the atonement was the first step on a slippery slope. Once one accepted that it was God's will to save all, it would not be long before one adopted Arminianism or even outright universalism.[39]

Moreover, Amyraut's position as it stood seemed to make God's will and Christ's atonement ineffectual; God willed the salvation of all, but not all were saved, and Christ died as a ransom for all, but not all the ransomed benefited. To cope with this problem Amyraut had had to posit two wills in God; a conditional will that ineffectually desired the salvation of all, and an absolute will that effectually desired the salvation of the elect only.[40] But the scholastic distinction seemed to make things little better. What, Rutherford asked, was the comfort in knowing that God willed one's salvation or had provided an atonement for it when that will and atonement could be wholly ineffectual? 'A salvation purchased by Christ without an efficacious intention in God to apply it to all' was nothing but 'a shadow and a mere nothing'.[41] And where did the Bible teach that the ransomed of the Lord could be thrown into hell?[42] The doctrine of definite atonement, by contrast, assured people that Christ's death made salvation not just possible but certain.

Whether Calvin would have sided with Amyraut or Rutherford is difficult to determine. Amyraut claimed that he was only repeating Calvin's position, and it is certainly the case that some passages from the Reformer seem to stress the universality of Christ's atonement.[43] However, Calvin never explicitly engaged with the debate about the extent of the atonement, or formulated a precise position on it as Amyraut did, and a number of scholars suggest that what he does say on the matter is consistent with the Reformed orthodox doctrine of a definite atonement.[44] Given the ambiguity

---

[36] See especially, *Christ Dying*, pp. 364–438.   [37] *Christ Dying*, pp. 402–9, 421–42.

[38] *Christ Dying*, p. 367, 425. Article two of the Arminians' Remonstrance had taught universal atonement (Bettenson, *Documents*, p. 374).

[39] *Christ Dying*, p. 440.   [40] Armstrong, *Calvinism and the Amyraut Heresy*, pp. 185ff.

[41] *Christ Dying*, p. 378.   [42] *Christ Dying*, p. 429.

[43] See R. T. Kendall, *Calvin and English Calvinism to 1649* (Oxford, 1979), pp. 13–18.

[44] See W. R. Godfrey, 'Reformed thought on the extent of the atonement', *Westminster Theological Journal*, 37 (1975), 133–71; R. Nicole, 'John Calvin's view of the extent of the atonement', *Westminster Theological Journal*, 47 (1985), 197–225; Muller, *Christ and the Decree*, pp. 33–4; and especially J. Rainbow, *The Will of God and the Cross: An Historical and Theological Study of John Calvin's Doctrine of Limited Redemption* (Allison Park, PN, 1990).

of Calvin's formulations, it can hardly be said that Rutherford was making a sharp break with the Reformer in matters of substance, though his willingness to brand Amyraut an Arminian highlights the tendency of the scholastic Calvinists to define Reformed orthodoxy with a greater strictness than was the case in the early Reformation.

As well as countering heresies within the Reformed tradition, Rutherford was also aware of the development by Jesuit theologians of a startlingly original theory of predestination. The new kid on the theological block was the theory of middle knowledge (*scientia media*). First formulated by Pietro de Fonseca, the doctrine received its classic statement in the Jesuit theologian Luis de Molina's *Concordia liberi arbitrii cum gratiae donis, divina praescientia, providentia, praedestinatione et reprobatione* (1588). Molina pointed out that theologians had traditionally ascribed two sorts of knowledge to God. First, God possessed *natural knowledge*; by knowing his own omnipotent nature, he knew every possible state of affairs that he could create. Secondly, God possessed *free knowledge*; by knowing his own free decision to instantiate a particular state of affairs, God knew the actual world that would obtain. But Molina suggested that God also had a third type of knowledge, *middle knowledge*; God knew the contingent future choices that would be made by free creatures in every specific set of circumstances. He knew, for example – as Jesus had done – that if Tyre and Sidon had seen the miracles performed in Corazin and Bethsaida they would have repented long ago in sackcloth and ashes (Matthew 11).[45]

The genius of Molina's position was that it allowed him to chart a course between absolute and conditional predestinarianism, apparently securing both divine predetermination and libertarian free will. Like Arminians, Molina insisted that all people were given sufficient grace to be saved and enjoyed the freedom to choose contrary options. Like Calvinists, however, he maintained that whether one was saved or damned depended on God's decision in eternity; by deciding to actualise a particular possible world, God effectively determined the fate of individuals. The actual world that God chose to create, for example, could be one in which William would freely choose to use God's sufficient grace because he was surrounded by other devout people, and James would freely choose to reject this grace because he was surrounded by bad company. Molina's position, however, was basically anti-Augustinian.

---

[45] In recent years there has been a revival of interest in Molinism and *scientia media* among philosophers of religion, prompted by the unwitting re-invention of the concept by the philosopher Alvin Plantinga in his *The Nature of Necessity* (Oxford, 1974), pp. 174–80. Part IV of Molina's *Concordia* has recently been translated and published with a full introduction to the contemporary debate by A. J. Freddoso, ed., *Luis de Molina's 'On Divine Foreknowledge'* (Ithaca, NY, 1988).

By contrast, his fellow Jesuit, Suarez, defended the doctrine of absolute predestination and simply used middle knowledge to explain how God's predestination worked. According to his doctrine of Congruism, God first selected William for salvation and then used his middle knowledge to choose the grace that he knew William needed if he was to respond positively to God. Whereas Molina seemed to imply that God inadvertently predestined individuals while going about creating a particular world, Suarez defended the Augustinian claim that God deliberately and freely chose certain individuals for salvation while passing over others.[46]

However, although Molina may have moved closer to absolute predestinarianism than Arminius, and Suarez closer still, traditional Augustinians were equally hostile to both the Jesuit positions. The Dominicans, led by Domingo Báñez, were the first to criticise middle knowledge, committed as they were to the theology of the most famous theologian of their order, Thomas Aquinas. They were soon joined by orthodox Calvinists, who noticed the attraction of Jesuit ideas to the Arminians,[47] and by the French Jansenists.[48] Dominicans, Calvinists and Jansenists rejected the very concept of middle knowledge, because according to their theologies, God's foreknowledge was based entirely on his knowledge of his own decrees of foreordination.[49] But their fundamental objection to Molinism and Congruism was that both led to a synergistic understanding of redemption; salvation was no longer the work of grace alone, but of grace working alongside human effort. Orthodox Augustinians could not abide this cooperationalist model of divine concurrence, according to which God conserved the independent activity of secondary causes and worked with them to produce their effects. They saw the Jesuits' defence of a libertarian concept of free will as undermining divine sovereignty and exalting human effort. As Rutherford expressed it, Jesuit Congruism was 'the Pelagian way, sacrilegiously robbing the grace of God'. The Arminians and Jesuits saw free will as 'essentially a power absolutely loosed from predeterminating Providence'. Human free will was turned into something sovereign and

---

[46] For a lucid exposition of the ideas of Molina and Suarez see W. L. Craig, *The Problem of Divine Foreknowledge and Future Contingents from Aristotle to Suarez* (Leiden, 1988), chs. 7 and 8.

[47] Rutherford wrote of Jesuit ideas that they were 'once maintained by Arminius and his disciples at the conference at Hage; but now, for shame, forsaken by Arminians', *Christ Dying*, p. 311. Arminius's use of the Jesuit theologians is demonstrated in Muller, 'Arminius and the scholastic tradition', and *God, Creation and Providence*.

[48] See L. Kolakowski, *God Owes Us Nothing: A Brief Remark on Pascal's Religion and on the Spirit of Jansenism* (Chicago, 1995).

[49] They also suggested that undetermined free choices logically cannot be foreknown, an argument that is also advanced by modern critics of middle knowledge. See, for example, R. M. Adams, 'Middle knowledge and the problem of evil', in R. M. Adams and M. M. Adams, eds., *The Problem of Evil* (Oxford, 1990), pp. 110–25.

independent, so that God, 'that moulded and created the horologe, and all the pins, pieces and parts, hath not power to turn the wheel as he pleaseth'. Molina and Suarez seemed to teach that for God's grace to work it had to be given to people in favourable states of affairs; as Rutherford noted sarcastically, 'Jesuits dream that Christ cannot conquer the will to a free consent, except he lie in wait to catch the man when he hath been at a banquet, hath slept well, is merry, and when he sees the man is in a good blood, then he draws and invites and so catches the man.' But this, Rutherford argued, was to attribute far too much to man's weak will, and far too little to God's omnipotent grace. 'Heaven and hell, salvation and damnation' were made to turn upon 'such good or ill humours . . . as a banquet, no banquet, a crabbed disposition, or a merrie'.[50]

In contrast to the Jesuits, Rutherford and other orthodox Calvinists followed Aquinas and the Dominicans in defending the 'premotionist' theory of concurrence, which insisted that God acted *upon* secondary causes to produce their actual operations. In the case of a medicine, for instance, the premotionist saw God as activating the natural powers of the medicine every time it was applied in order that it produced the desired effect, whilst a co-operationalist argued that God merely allowed the coming into being of the effect, which was a natural product of the medicine. For the former, God was intimately involved in every event that occurs in the physical universe, whereas for the latter, God had a much more *laissez-faire* role. The great Dutch Calvinist, Gisbertus Voetius – who was an admirer of Rutherford – believed that co-operationalism opened the way to Descartes' mechanical philosophy, in which the natural world moves automatically by itself, without divine *concursus*.[51]

Rutherford was in full agreement with Voetius on this subject, though he never confronted the new philosophy as directly as Voetius did at Utrecht. He held to 'the Lord's invincible predetermination of second causes'.[52] At times he expressed almost mystical rapture over the thought of such exhaustive sovereignty. The God who was quite distinct from his creation and transcendent above it was also the source of it all, and the one who pervaded the whole. Sun, moon, stars, seas, birds, fishes, herbs and 'dainty flowres' were all 'created expressions', 'twigs', 'chips', and 'small blossomes' emanating and streaming forth from Christ.[53] The believer was filled with 'precious thoughts' when he considered the 'millions and numberless numbers of influences' which lay behind the rain, the hail and the dew.[54]

---

[50] *Christ Dying*, pp. 308–13.
[51] J. A. van Ruler, 'New philosophy and old standards: Voetius's vindication of divine concurrence and secondary causality', *Nederlands Archief voor Kerkgeschiedenis*, 71 (1991), 61–6.
[52] *Influences*, p. 6.   [53] *Christ Dying*, sig. A4.   [54] *Influences*, p. 7.

Scholarly meditation on the eternal decrees of an absolute God could inspire intensely emotional piety. Scholastic predestinarianism was not as emotionally arid as it has often been assumed to be; the Dominican, Domingo Báñez – whose defence of Augustinianism Rutherford admired – was after all the spiritual director of St Teresa of Avila.

However, although a high doctrine of divine *concursus* might inspire something akin to nature mysticism, it also raised thorny theological problems. It was one thing to say that 'God shot the Arrow' that killed evil king Ahab,[55] but it was quite another to claim that God caused the Fall of Adam by withdrawing his *concursus*. Doing so seemed to turn God into a cosmic puppetmaster. Recognising the problem, Rutherford tried to extricate himself by means of one of his beloved scholastic distinctions. He acknowledged that the 'real' or 'physical' cause of Adam's sin was 'the Lord's withdrawing of his concurring influence', but claimed that the 'moral' cause of Adam's Fall lay in his refusal of that influence at the same moment in time as it was withdrawn.[56] Thus Rutherford felt able to say that God's decree did make things necessary without destroying free will.

Rutherford's Scottish critic, John Strang, found this reasoning 'dark and not intelligible'.[57] Other critics of premotionism had the same problems. Cardinal Bellarmine, who was appointed by the Pope to investigate the Jesuit–Dominican dispute, could not see how the Dominican position allowed free will to emerge unscathed and how it avoided making God the author of sin.[58] Richard Baxter, like John Strang, believed that Rutherford had taken his stress on God's influences too far. He pointed to the resemblances between Rutherford's necessitarianism and that of Thomas Hobbes,[59] just as later writers have noted its affinities to the heterodox, materialist determinism of Scottish Enlightenment thinkers like Lord Kames.[60] To Baxter, such necessitarianism, though born out of piety, was

---

[55] *Sermon to Commons*, p. 62.
[56] 'God out of holy sovereignty withdraws in the same moment his influence, in which Adam sinfully rejects the same influence', *Influences*, sig. A4.
[57] Quoted in *Influences*, sig. a2. Rutherford wrote that Strang's own position 'destroys all eternal decrees of God, under pretence of eschewing a necessity' (sig. a3).
[58] A helpful summary of the debate is to be found in J. Brodrick, *Robert Bellarmine: Saint and Scholar* (London, 1961). See also C. Brown, *Christianity and Western Thought*, I (Leicester, 1990), pp. 161–4.
[59] R. Baxter, *Catholick Theologie: Plain, Pure, Peaceable, for Pacification of the Dogmaticall Word-warriors* (London, 1675), p. 113. For more on Hobbes and Calvinism see N. Malcolm, 'Thomas Hobbes and voluntarist theology', Ph.D. dissertation, Cambridge University (1983), especially part 3.
[60] See Walker, *The Theology and Theologians of Scotland*, pp. 61–6, and R. B. Sher, *Church and University in the Scottish Enlightenment: The Moderate Literati of Edinburgh* (Princeton, NJ, 1985), p. 73, who reveals that Scottish Enlightenment philosophers sometimes even quoted Rutherford to show that their views were not heterodox. William Cunningham, the Free Church professor of theology from 1847–61, highlighted the discontinuities

deeply impious. He was vexed to 'read a good man Voluminously proving God to be a willer of sins existence, and a prime-predetermining Cause of all prohibited Volitions and acts'. Baxter argued that God only willed the *effect* of sin, not its *existence*. By attacking Jesuits, Arminians and Socinians for not endorsing this opinion, Rutherford 'would tempt the world to think that Socinians were in the right, and that Jesuits, Lutherans and Arminians were the only defenders of the Holiness of God, whilst Calvinists made Him the Lover of all the sin in the World, as the most appetible conducible Medium to his Glory'.[61] In reality, according to Baxter, the Reformed Confessions did not endorse the extreme positions of Rutherford, Beza and Twisse, and moderate Calvinists like Davenant, Ussher, Strang, Cameron and Amyraut were strongly opposed to necessitarianism.

Baxter may well have been right about the widespread rejection of necessitarian ideas among Reformed theologians, and there can be little doubt that high Calvinists like Rutherford had defended precise scholastic concepts of divine premotion not present in Calvin. Nevertheless, it is not clear that Rutherford and Twisse were the real aberrants from the mainstream Reformed tradition. Baxter himself had moved in a decidedly Arminian direction in the 1640s, and arguably it is he and other moderates who had broken with the doctrine of exhaustive divine sovereignty laid out in Calvin's *Institutes*. Calvin, after all, had stated emphatically that 'men do nothing save at the secret instigation of God, and do not discuss and deliberate on anything but what he has previously decreed with himself, and brings to pass by his secret direction'. Evil deeds were not merely permitted by God, but decreed, willed and impelled by him, and evil actors were 'merely the instruments' in his hands.[62] Other Reformed theologians, recognising the problems raised by this teaching, attempted to state the doctrine of divine sovereignty so as to avoid the implication that God was the author of sin. They reinstated, for example, the distinction between permission and volition that Calvin had boldly rejected, and argued that whilst God was responsible for the physical 'matter' of a sinful act, man was responsible for its sinful 'form'.[63] Rutherford, however, rejected such distinctions, and it was perhaps his willingness to press Calvin's necessitarianism to its logical conclusion that made his work embarrassing to men like Baxter.

Rutherford's determination to defend the highest possible doctrine of divine sovereignty can also be seen in his supralapsarianism.[64] According to

between Calvinism and later determinisms in 'Calvinism and the doctrine of philosophical necessity', in his *The Reformers and the Theology of the Reformation* ([1862]; Edinburgh, 1989), pp. 471–524.
[61] Baxter, *Catholick Theologie*, p. 112.   [62] Calvin, *Institutes* I. 18. 1.
[63] See Muller, *Christ and the Decree*.
[64] For useful introductions to the supralapsarian/infralapsarian debates see Cunningham, *Reformers*, pp. 358–71; Barth, *Church Dogmatics* II/2: *The Doctrine of God*, Part 2, trans.

this doctrine, the object of God's predestination in eternity was not the human race as created and fallen (as infralapsarians believed), but the human race as not yet created and not yet fallen (hence the term supralapsarian, meaning above or before the Fall). The logic behind this seemingly abstruse theory was actually quite simple. 'God's electing of us cannot be after the consideration of our creation and fall', explained Rutherford, because this would suggest that God was reacting to contingencies beyond his control by electing people to salvation as a kind of Plan B emergency measure. 'To make God choose after the Fall, maketh him to have willed ineffectualie some other end', Rutherford wrote. It made God 'look out of himself for determining his will', and made him 'like man, to do as he may, when he is hindred from that [which] he would'. Supralapsarianism, on the other hand, saw God's glory as being his end; he chose the salvation of men as the means to that glory, and the Fall as the means to make their salvation necessary. God had therefore decreed everything from eternity, not as a response to what he foresaw, but simply in the course of the pursuit of his own glory.[65]

Although it was always a minority opinion among the Reformed, and although it was never enshrined in any of the confessions of the Reformed churches such as Dort and Westminster, supralapsarianism nevertheless attracted some of the greatest theologians in the Reformed tradition, including Theodore Beza, William Perkins, Franciscus Gomarus, Gisbertus Voetius and the Scotsman, Robert Boyd. There were, however, serious objections to the position. It could, for instance, be seen as a speculative doctrine, one that ignored Calvin's warnings against prying into the secret will of God.[66] Yet Calvin's own doctrine of double predestination can itself be seen as speculative,[67] and it is not at all clear that he would have rejected the Bezan position.[68] Moreover, supralapsarians believed that far from dispelling mystery their position intensified one's awe of the divine will. Rutherford himself was clear that 'That which doth take away the unsearchable mysterie of election, and reprobation, is not to be admitted.'[69]

G. W. Bromiley et al. (Edinburgh, 1957), pp. 127–45; L. C. Boughton, 'Supralapsarianism and the role of metaphysics in sixteenth-century Reformed theology', *Westminster Theological Journal*, 48 (1986), 63–96; White, *Predestination, Policy and Polemic*, ch. 2.

[65] Unpublished manuscript, 'Fragments of a discourse on Ephesians 1.4', n. p.

[66] See Calvin, *Institutes*, III. 21.1.

[67] Barth, *Church Dogmatics*, II/2, pp. 17–18, wished that Calvin's doctrine of predestination had been 'less speculative and more in accordance with the biblical testimony', and recognised that the later dogmaticians were writing 'in the spirit of Calvin'.

[68] Boughton, 'Supralapsarianism and the role of metaphysics', p. 80, points out that Calvin knew about Beza's supralapsarianism and never openly criticised it. Moreover, as Barth noted in *Church Dogmatics* II/2, p. 127, some of Calvin's statements do seem to lean towards supralapsarianism. He refers to the *Institutes*, III. 21. 5 and 23. 7.

[69] 'Fragments of a discourse on Ephesians 1.4'.

A second objection to supralapsarianism was that it turned God into the author of sin. As Rutherford himself put it, 'God is the chief insuperable cause of all the sin of Devils and men for which he damneth them, and that both as to the matter and the form.' To those who complained that this made God responsible for human sin, Rutherford had a simple reply: 'thus to do is no sin in God himself, because he is under no Law'.[70] Law was simply a creation of the divine will, and whatever God willed was by definition just. 'His will is before His justice, by order of nature', declared Rutherford, 'and what is His will is His justice.'[71] No other theodicy was needed; God was under no law and it was blasphemous to question his actions.

Rutherford's intense voluntarism led to another startling conclusion. He argued that although God was under a necessity of nature to love himself, he was under no such necessity to promote his own glory or to punish human sin. The claim that he was under such a necessity 'utterly destroys the libertie and freedom of God in all his works of Providence and Creation, and so God shall be a natural agent in all his works without himself, not a free agent in creating and Redeeming'.[72] Moreover, if it was true that God must by the necessity of his own justice punish sin, it followed that he would also be under a necessity to punish men for their *own* sin, and could not justly lay it on Christ. 'Punitory justice exists not in God by necessity of nature, but freely', Rutherford declared. The reason why Christ's atonement was just was that God's free choice of punishment and remedy determined what was just and right. When God told Adam and Eve that if they ate the fruit of the Tree of Knowledge they would die, it was not because there was any necessary connection between eating and death but because God freely and arbitrarily decided what was sin and how it should be punished.[73] Christ was sent to bear the sins of the elect not because that was the only way out but simply because that was the way God chose to redeem us. The English Independent, John Owen, feared that by using this argument Rutherford was providing ammunition for the Socinians who, in their desire to refute the doctrine that Christ had died to satisfy God's justice, argued that justice was merely a free act of the divine will and hence that a propitiatory atonement was not necessary.[74]

It has been said that Rutherford's doctrine of divine justice is almost the only instance in which 'he deviates from the path of strict orthodoxy'.[75] However, his extreme voluntarism had strong precedents among the Schoolmen, and in Calvin. Duns Scotus (1265–1308) had argued that

[70] Quoted from Baxter, *Catholick Theologie*, p. 113.   [71] *Letters*, p. 468.
[72] *Covenant of Life*, p. 31.   [73] *Covenant of Life*, p. 32.
[74] J. Owen, *A Dissertation On Divine Justice* (1653), in W. H. Goold, ed., *The Works of John Owen*, X (London, 1967), pp. 607–18.
[75] Milroy, 'Doctrine of the Church of Scotland', pp. 230–2.

although God had chosen to redeem men through the Cross, he had been free to redeem them in any way he chose, and both Calvin and Peter Vermigli insisted that Christ's substitutionary atonement was not 'absolutely necessary'.[76] This, however, created a problem. If God was not bound by necessity, then his will and his actions did not necessarily reveal his nature. God's decree to punish sin and his decision to send Christ as an atoning sacrifice revealed only his will, not his being. Even if Rutherford thought of God's being as essentially just, his definition of justice – that which God willed – seemed to vacate the concept of any clear content. Will took precedence over being, and God's nature remained quite inscrutable.

Perry Miller once wrote that Calvin had 'required men to stare fixedly and without relief into the very center of the blazing sun of glory. God is not to be understood but to be adored.'[77] Rutherford required no less. The contemplation of God's absolute sovereignty, he believed, would drive men to deep humility and self-abasement; God owed them nothing, they owed him everything. The notion that 'we are profitable to God' was a false one. God did not need us and he was certainly under no obligation to create us. 'God shall make morter of thee, O Fool! who makes a god of borrowed I, great I and poor Nothing-self', Rutherford thundered.[78] His God was as awesome in his sovereignty as the God of Calvin, and human beings were just as humbly and utterly dependent on God's grace as they were in the theology of the Genevan Reformer.

COVENANT THEOLOGY AND HUMAN AGENCY

If the God of Rutherford and other Puritans was as awesome in his unconditioned sovereignty as the God of Calvin, why did Perry Miller think otherwise? The answer lies in Puritan 'use of the covenant concept as an architectonic principle for the systematising of Christian truth'.[79] Covenant theologians argued that the salvation history recorded in the Old and New Testaments could be explained by reference to two covenants. The covenant of works was the covenant made between God and mankind through Adam, mankind's federal head. In this covenant, God promised to grant eternal life to those who perfectly fulfilled the demands of the natural law written on the conscience of every individual. However, 'Man by his fall having made himself incapable of life by that covenant, the Lord was

---

[76] See *Institutes*, vol. II. 17. 1; Muller, *Christ and the Decree*, pp. 28, 61; and on the similarities between Duns Scotus and Calvin see F. Wendel, *Calvin: The Origins and Development of his Religious Thought*, trans. P. Mairet (London, 1963), pp. 127–9.

[77] Miller, 'Marrow of Puritan divinity', p. 51.   [78] *Covenant of Life*, pp. 37, 39.

[79] D. Macleod, 'Covenant theology', in N. Cameron, ed., *Dictionary of Scottish Church History and Theology*, p. 214.

pleased to make a second, commonly called the Covenant of Grace; whereby he freely offereth unto sinners life and salvation by Jesus Christ, requiring of them faith in him, that they may be saved.'[80]

For Perry Miller the significance of covenant theology lay in the fact that it made the transcendent, arbitrary God of Calvin 'less inscrutable, less mysterious, less unpredictable'. The Lord had bound himself to act in a regular and reasonable manner. Moreover, by stressing the conditions that human beings had to fulfil, covenant theology rehabilitated natural man and his capacities. Like Descartes, Bacon and Hobbes, the Puritans were taking the first steps towards the Age of Reason.[81]

Other scholars have also detected in covenant theology a shift away from Calvin, but they interpret it in a less positive light. Covenant theology for them marks a departure from the Reformation doctrine of *sola gratia*. The covenant by its very nature was bilateral and implied a synergistic under-standing of salvation – man could and must co-operate as a fellow-worker with God in order to be saved. R. T. Kendall, who popularised this reappraisal, has gone so far as to argue that the 'Calvinists' at the Westminster Assembly were 'crypto Arminian'. In their desire to refute Antinomianism, Kendall claimed, they fell over backwards into legalism and lost Calvin's emphasis on salvation by grace.[82]

Among the many who have argued for the discontinuity between Calvin and the 'Calvinists', two have focused particularly on Scotland. In a series of articles, James Torrance has vigorously maintained that the federalist orthodoxy of seventeenth-century Scotland reversed Calvin's insistence that grace comes before law in God's relation to mankind.[83] Covenant theology

---

[80] *Westminster Confession of Faith*, VII. 2,3. Rutherford expounds the two covenants in various works, but see especially 'Ane Catechisme conteining the soume of Christian Religion', pp. 175–8; and *The Covenant of Life Opened, passim*.

[81] Miller, 'Marrow of Puritan divinity', pp. 48–98; *The New England Mind: The Seventeenth Century*, ch. 13.

[82] Kendall, *Calvin and English Calvinism*, pp. 208–9. See also Barth, *Church Dogmatics*, IV/1: *The Doctrine of Reconciliation*, Part 1, trans. G. W. Bromiley (Edinburgh, 1956), pp. 54–66; N. Pettit, *The Heart Prepared: Grace and Conversion in Puritan Spiritual Life* (New Haven, 1966); Armstrong, *Calvinism and the Amyraut Heresy*; Holmes Rolston III, *John Calvin versus the Westminster Confession* (Richmond, 1972); A. P. Sell, *The Great Debate: Calvinism, Arminianism and Salvation* (Worthing, 1982); D. Zaret, *The Heavenly Contract: Ideology and Organisation in Pre-Revolutionary Puritanism* (London, 1985); Strehle, *Calvinism, Federalism and Scholasticism*; Clifford, *Atonement and Justification*; D. A. Weir, *The Origins of Federal Theology in Sixteenth-Century Reformation Thought* (Oxford, 1990).

[83] J. B. Torrance, 'Covenant or contract? A study of the theological background of worship in seventeenth-century Scotland', *Scottish Journal of Theology*, 23, (1970), 51–76; 'The covenant concept in Scottish theology and politics and its legacy', *Scottish Journal of Theology*, 34, (1981), 225–43; 'Strengths and weaknesses of Westminster theology', in A. Heron, ed., *The Westminster Confession in the Church Today* (Edinburgh, 1982); 'The incarnation and "limited atonement"', *Evangelical Quarterly*, 55 (1983), 83–94; 'Inter-

replaced the absolute promise ('Christ has done this for you, therefore repent') with the conditional message ('If you repent you will be forgiven'). In short 'a subtle kind of legalism began to creep in' during the seventeenth century in Scotland, a legalism and rationalism that was ironically to open the way for Moderatism in the church.[84]

Charles Bell largely concurs with the criticisms of Kendall and Torrance, and applies them in some detail to Rutherford, 'the prince of the federal theologians'.[85] He argues that the concept of a covenant of works and a covenant of grace reinforced the belief that only the elect were related to Christ in love and that the rest of mankind only knew a God of justice. Moreover, the covenant concept – couched in mercantile metaphor – strengthened the idea that salvation is conditional on man's works and led to an emphasis on 'preparations' for salvation. All this undermined assurance of salvation, for it no longer seemed to rest on Christ's work and his free grace. Rather, it seemed to depend on human works – assurance was found by looking within at one's own deeds, it was not of the essence of faith.

In contrast to these discontinuity theorists, however, a growing number of scholars now argue that the covenant theologians did not depart from Calvin in any substantial way.[86] Calvin's own teaching contained the germ-seed of covenant theology (see, for example, *Institutes* II. 9–11), and Puritan federalism maintained a balance between divine initiative and human response that was wholly consonant with the French Reformer. The idea that there was a gulf between Calvin and the Calvinists can only be sustained by persistently misrepresenting both.

That such misrepresentation takes place can hardly be doubted. Writers like Torrance, for example, often succumb to 'the temptation to press Calvin into their ranks and to make him Karl Barth's first and greatest disciple'.[87] Although their critique of covenant theology is framed around

---

preting the Word by the light of Christ or the light of nature? Calvin, Calvinism and Barth', in R. V. Schnucker, ed., *Calviniana: Ideas and Influence of Jean Calvin* (Kirksville, Missouri, 1988), 256–67.

[84] Torrance, 'Covenant or contract?', pp. 52–60.

[85] M. C. Bell, *Calvin and Scottish Theology: The Doctrine of Assurance* (Edinburgh, 1985), ch. 3.

[86] See especially E. Kevan, *The Grace of Law: A Study in Puritan Theology* (London, 1964); A. Hoekema, 'The covenant of grace in Calvin's teaching', *Calvin Theological Journal*, 2 (1967), 133–61; G. Marsden, 'Perry Miller's rehabilitation of the Puritans: a critique', *Church History*, 39 (1970), 91–105; W. K. B. Stoever, '*A Faire and Easie Way to Heaven': Covenant Theology and Antinomianism in Early Massachusetts* (Middletown, Conn., 1978); P. Helm, *Calvin and the Calvinists* (Edinburgh, 1982); Wallace, *Puritans and Predestination*; J. von Rohr, *The Covenant of Grace in Puritan Thought* (Atlanta, Ga, 1986); D. McWilliams, 'The covenant theology of the Westminster Confession of Faith and recent criticism', *Westminster Theological Journal*, 53 (1991), 109–24; R. C. Gleason, *John Calvin and John Owen on Mortification: A Comparative Study in Reformed Spirituality* (New York, 1995).

[87] The phrase is taken from A. Lane, 'The quest for the historical Calvin', *Evangelical Quarterly*, 55 (1983), 107.

its alleged departure from Calvin they credit the reformer with some remarkably Barthian beliefs, such as the rejection of natural law in favour of a Christocentric holism, and the conviction that God relates to all mankind as a God of love.[88] Yet Calvin did not reject the idea of natural law as Barth did,[89] and as a believer in double predestination he had no time for the universalist idea that God was equally loving towards all mankind.

Furthermore, the claim that Rutherford and other covenant theologians were guilty of a semi-Pelagian synergism is very difficult to sustain. It is certainly true that Rutherford stressed the conditionality of the covenant of grace and the role of 'preparations' for justification, but he also insisted that the conditions and the preparations were themselves supplied by divine grace. 'Never Protestant divine taught that without the actuall influence of omnipotent Grace, can faith or spirituall sense that we are justified, be produced by the Word, work, or created light alone.'[90] Instead, the orthodox Reformed position emphasised both divine predetermination and human agency:

Grace and free will doth work so as Grace is the principall, first inspiring and fountaine cause . . . And also actually it determineth, sweetly enclineth and stirreth the will to these acts; yet so as free-will moveth actively, freely, and conferreth radicall, vitall, & subordinate influence & is not a meer patient in all these.[91]

Moreover, Rutherford was careful to say that although preparations of faith and repentance might be conditions of justification, they were not the cause, ground, or meritorious qualification for it.[92] No Protestant divine, he asserted, ever taught that 'Faith, new Obedience, Repentance, are grounds upon which God justifieth a sinner'.[93] 'Conditions' were neither acts of free will as Arminians conceived them to be, nor, as papists taught, were they meritorious acts which God rewarded.[94] Well aware of the accusation that he and other orthodox divines were 'Legalists, Antifidians, Pharisees',[95] Rutherford responded: 'we conceive the bottome of no mans faith is within himselfe, but the common ground and Royall charter, warranting all to beleeve is the free and money lesse offer of a precious Saviour'.[96]

The response of Torrance or Bell to this is that the Calvinist emphasis on *sola gratia* was still maintained in theory whilst at the level of practical

---

[88] See, for example, Torrance, 'Interpreting the Word', an article which notes Barth's criticism of Calvin's natural-law assumptions but then goes on to set up a false dichotomy between a Christocentric Calvin and naturalistic Calvinists.

[89] See P. Helm, 'Calvin and natural law', *Scottish Bulletin of Evangelical Theology*, 2 (1984), 5–22; and the discussion of Rutherford's natural-law theory in the next chapter.

[90] *Christ Dying*, p. 116.   [91] *Christ Dying*, p. 470.

[92] *Survey of Antichrist*, II, p. 116   [93] *Christ Dying*, p. 77.   [94] *Tryal*, p. 93.

[95] *Survey of Antichrist*, II, p. 1.   [96] *Survey of Antichrist*, II, p. 3.

preaching it was drowned out by the stress on the conditionality of the covenant and the importance of 'preparations'. However, Rutherford was careful to advocate a balance in preaching; preachers should preach duties 'running in a Gospel-channel of Free Grace'. 'Litterall, and moral preaching of dead and letter-works, too Seneca-like, is farre from the Gospel-free-Spirit', he warned. But the preacher must also:

Beware of licence to the flesh, under the coat of liberty of the Spirit; and let none thinke that law-curses, looseth us from all law-obedience; or that Christ hath cryed downe the tenne commandments; and that Gospel-liberty is a dispensation for law-loosenesse; or that free grace is a lawlesse Pope.[97]

This did not so much strike a balance between law and grace, as maintain that the dichotomy between them was false. If the Spirit was at work by grace, this would be evident in repentance, faith and obedience to the law.

It was this conviction that led Rutherford to oppose the Antinomian doctrine of justification propagated by popular preachers and pamphleteers like John Saltmarsh,[98] John Eaton and Tobias Crisp.[99] Justification did not occur in eternity, as they had taught. This would have implied that the elect were sinless in God's eyes even before their conversion. Rather, God had decreed in eternity that justification would occur in time when the elect responded to the evangel in repentance and faith.[100] The saints, therefore, were not uninvolved in their justification, but 'the acts of the begger doe in no wayes impeach the freedome of the grace of the giver',[101] particularly given that the beggar's acts were themselves caused by God.

Secondly, justification was not to be seen as 'an abolition of sin in its real *essence* and physical indwelling'.[102] Justification did not make the believer sinless or perfect; the event of God's declaring one justified before him did not remove the need for the process of sanctification. Indeed, sorrow for sin was a part of all true believers' lives.[103] But as Rutherford wrote to a correspondent, 'Sanctification and mortification of our lusts are the hardest part of Christianity.' Many were happy to take Jesus as Saviour but they did not want him as Lord; they eschewed the cumber-some task of obeying and working out their own salvation.[104] Antino-mianism told Christians that they did not need to worry about this at all, and it had to be countered with a correct view of justification. Justification was a legal action; it removed the accidental penalty and *condemnation* of sin. The Christian was no longer under the tyranny of sin, but he was still

---

[97] *Survey of Antichrist*, II, p. 29.
[98] On Saltmarsh see A. L. Morton, *The World of the Ranters* (London, 1970), pp. 44–69.
[99] On Crisp see C. Hill, 'Tobias Crisp', in *The Collected Essays of Christopher Hill*, III (Brighton, 1986).
[100] *Survey of Antichrist*, II, pp. 129–30.   [101] *Survey of Antichrist*, II, p. 114.
[102] *Tryal*, p. 195.   [103] *Tryal*, pp. 188–94.   [104] *Letters*, p. 467.

under its righteous *commands*.[105] Or, to put it another way, justification gave the saint the positive freedom to live under 'the law of God, honeyed with the love of Christ'.[106] Antinomians were utterly mistaken when they taught that justification gave the believer a negative freedom from the commanding power of the law.[107]

In his *Survey of Spiritual Antichrist* (1648), Rutherford traced Antinomian doctrines back to the German Anabaptists, the Family of Love and the New England followers of Anne Hutchinson. Like these groups, the English Antinomians were deluded enthusiasts, following their own spirit or inner light instead of the objective, external standards of God's law. It was a theme that he developed at length in *A Free Disputation* (1649). Though claiming to be avoiding legalism, these seventeenth-century New Agers were actually committing idolatry, setting themselves up as gods by speaking of themselves as having been 'Godded' and 'Christed'.[108] Deifying their own inclinations and feelings, they refused to be subject to 'sense, nature and reason',[109] to the Word or to external ordinances. The result was that they were abandoning the discipline of established religion for their own subjective experiences.

Rutherford, of course, was far from being an opponent of subjective experience, of affectionate religion or of the doctrine of grace. Indeed, he was himself accused of Antinomianism and enthusiasm.[110] However, he refused to create a dichotomy between the external and the internal, the spirit and the law. Grace would always produce works, and the Spirit would help the Christian to live by the law. Internal, subjective life had to be regulated by external, objective standards.

In this Rutherford was once again walking in the path of Calvin. Calvin's had been a theology of grace, but it was also a religion of discipline, one which took God's commands and the human duty to obey them with great seriousness. As David Little has pointed out, Calvin was unique among the major Reformers in his stress on the third use of the law and on the reformation of society in conformity with the law of God.[111] His *sola gratia* theology, like that of Rutherford, did not rule out strenuous moralism.[112] Christians, wrote Calvin, should 'prepare for a hard, laborious, troubled

[105] *Survey of Antichrist*, II, p. 5.   [106] *Tryal*, p. 164.
[107] *Survey of Antichrist*, II, pp. 94–9.   [108] *Survey of Antichrist*, I, p. 3.
[109] *Survey of Antichrist*, II, p. 10.
[110] Most famously in J. Curate, *The Scotch Presbyterian Eloquence Display'd, or the Teaching of their Folly Discover'd from their Books, Sermons and Prayers* (1692).
[111] D. Little, 'Reformed faith and religious liberty', in D. K. McKim, ed., *Major Themes in the Reformed Tradition* (Grand Rapids, Mich., 1992), pp. 197–9.
[112] On Calvin's moralism see H. Hopfl, *The Christian Polity of John Calvin* (Cambridge, 1982), pp. 175–8; and W. Bouswma, *John Calvin: A Sixteenth-Century Portrait* (Oxford, 1988), esp. pp. 85, 97.

life', one characterised by 'constant endeavour to become better'.[113] As
Rutherford was keen to point out, Calvin had been intensely hostile to
Antinomians, and had insisted that Christians were 'not freed from the law'
but had an obligation to mortify their lusts.[114] Indeed, Calvin's *Contre la
Secte Phantastique et Furieuse des Libertins, que se nomment Spirituelz*
(1545) is uncannily similar to Rutherford's *Survey of Spiritual Antichrist*,
for both works condemn the moral and hermeneutical laxity of sectarian
Protestants. The Calvinist project of building disciplined, godly societies
regulated by righteous rules depended on profound respect for the external:
the written Word, the moral law, the proper ecclesiastical forms. Antinomianism, with its emphasis on the Spirit within, represented a threat that
could not be ignored.

But did the Puritan emphasis on law undermine Calvin's doctrine that
assurance of salvation was of the essence of faith? Kendall and Bell argue
that it did. By stressing the conditionality of the covenant and by claiming
that Christ had only died for the elect, covenant theology shifted the focus
from God's objective work in Christ to the subjective state of the sinner, and
in doing so made assurance very difficult to acquire.

This picture, however, oversimplifies.[115] As Joel Beeke has demonstrated,
all Calvinists believed that the surest ground of assurance lay in the promises
of Christ to redeem. Rutherford, for example, wrote that 'faith grippeth the
promises and maketh us to goe out of ourselves to Christ as being homelie
with Christ',[116] and declared 'it is adultery to seek a sign, because we
cannot rest on our husband's word'. Christ's promises, and the concluded
atonement, were far surer than human sense and feelings.[117] The 'first
assurance of justification' came from faith.[118]

However, as a pastor, Rutherford was painfully aware that many people
who had faith did not have assurance of salvation. It would not do, he
suggested, to keep repeating that assurance was of the essence of faith, when
quite clearly it was not. To do so was cruel to weak believers, for it
reinforced their doubts.[119] It also reflected a seriously distorted view of the
Christian life, one which saw it all through rose-tinted spectacles. Antinomians, significantly, interpreted Romans 7 – in which Paul describes an
internal battle between the flesh and the Spirit – as a description of the

---

[113] Calvin, *Institutes* III.8.1; III.6.5.
[114] *Christ Dying*, pp. 500, 505. The basic agreement between Calvin and the Puritans on the
   need for believers to participate actively in the struggle against the flesh is demonstrated in
   Gleason, *John Calvin and John Owen on Mortification*.
[115] J. R. Beeke, *Assurance of Faith: Calvin, English Puritanism and the Dutch Second
   Reformation* (New York, 1991); 'Personal assurance of faith: the Puritans and chapter 18.2
   of the Westminster Confession', *Westminster Theological Journal*, 55 (1993), 1–30.
[116] *Ane Catechisme*, p. 176.   [117] *Tryal*, pp. 131–3.   [118] *Christ Dying*, p. 110.
[119] *Christ Dying*, p. 104.

spiritual struggle of a 'half renewed man'.[120] They failed to see that the Christian life was characterised by struggle, doubting and the 'sad absences' and 'desertions' of Christ.[121] Some believers might live on 'the suburbs of heaven' but others were destined to 'wade through hell'.[122] Antinomian theology was inadequate because it failed to take account of the reality of the suffering of the elect, presuming that Christ would provide 'a broad, a faire and easie way to heaven'.[123]

The orthodox pastor, aware of the reality of desertions and doubt, was therefore quite justified in pointing the 'afflicted soul' towards other grounds of assurance. In the first place, he could advise the doubting Christian to look for 'some inherent qualification' as evidence that Christ was in him (a method sometimes known as the practical syllogism).[124] To look to the good works produced by the Spirit in the believer in order to gain assurance was quite legitimate, advocated as it was by the apostle John in his epistles.[125] Secondly, one might also appeal to another subjective ground of assurance mentioned in the Johannine letters, the witness of the Spirit within the believer. All three grounds – the promises of God to save those who believed, the evidence of the Spirit's work in the believer's life, and the internal witness of the Spirit – could contribute to the achievement of a full and firm assurance of salvation. If this view went beyond Calvin in looking within for grounds of assurance, it was always accompanied by a thoroughly Calvinian determination to credit everything to the work of the Spirit.[126]

The claim of Kendall and Bell that assurance was undermined by the doctrine of limited atonement is also highly questionable. Indeed, the whole point about limited or definite atonement was that it reinforced assurance. The Cross did not just make salvation possible or hypothetical, it made it certain; if Christ had died for a person, that person's salvation was guaranteed. The doctrine of universal atonement, on the other hand, granted no such assurance. It was cold comfort to be told that Christ had died for you, when you did not know whether Christ's atonement for you was effectual or merely hypothetical. Ultimately, the problem of assurance arose for Calvinists because of their doctrine of absolute predestination, not because of a doctrine of limited atonement.

Finally, in discussing Rutherford's treatment of assurance we must not forget the significance he attached to the covenant of redemption. Rutherford was probably following his friend and colleague David Dickson in adding this covenant to the covenant of works and the covenant of grace. It was not present in his *Catechisme*, but did appear in later works after

---

[120] *Christ Dying*, p. 24. [121] *Christ Dying*, pp. 24–51. [122] *Christ Dying*, p. 50.
[123] *Christ Dying*, p. 79. [124] *Christ Dying*, p. 82. [125] *Christ Dying*, p. 105.
[126] See Beeke, 'Personal assurance of faith', pp. 28–30.

Dickson had introduced it in *Therapeutica Sacra* (1656). The covenant of redemption (or suretyship) was a covenant made between the Father and the Son in eternity, in which the Father agreed to give the elect to the Son on condition that he died to redeem them. It was thus a covenant in which man played no part and one which preserved the federal theology from the idea that salvation is dependent on man. The covenant of redemption was a ground for assurance according to Rutherford, for it told the elect that their salvation was wrapped up in a deal struck between the Father and the Son in eternity, and was not ultimately dependent on human works.[127] Thus, the threefold covenant scheme contained the necessary safeguard against Arminianism. When David Dickson delivered a speech refuting Arminian errors at the 1638 Glasgow Assembly, it was to the covenant of redemption that he appealed so as to demonstrate that salvation was by God's grace alone.[128]

CALVIN AND THE CALVINISTS

The case of Rutherford, therefore, amply demonstrates the difficulties with the claim that the later Calvinists betrayed Calvin. Like the Reformer, Rutherford was concerned to do justice to both God's grace and God's law, to divine sovereignty and human responsibility.[129] The creative tension between these poles was a central feature of Reformed orthodoxy. Rutherford devoted his life's work to combatting the twin threats of Arminianism and Antinomianism, both of which seemed to wish to eliminate the tension by emphasising only one side of it:

the Papist and the Arminian on the one extremity, enthroneth Nature, and extolleth proud merit, and abaseth Christ and free grace. The Familist, libertine, and Antinomian, on a contrary extremity and opposition, turn man into a block, and make him a mere patient in the way to heaven.[130]

The preservation of a fine balance between nature and grace, divine sovereignty and human responsibility, man as both patient and agent, lay at the heart of Calvinist religion. However, the twin foci of Rutherford's theology have meant that he has been read in quite contrasting ways by succeeding generations. Cotton Mather numbered him among the 'champions of grace',[131] whilst Baxter praised the *Survey of Spiritual Antichrist* as

---

[127] *Covenant of Life*, pp. 283–301.
[128] See *Records of the Kirk of Scotland*, ed. A. Peterkin (Edinburgh, 1838), pp. 156–9.
[129] I am here following the interpretation of Puritan theology advanced in Stoever, 'A Faire and Easie Way', and von Rohr, *Covenant of Grace*.
[130] *Tryal*, pp. 294–5.
[131] C. Mather, *Student and Preacher: Or Directions for a Candidate of the Ministry* (London, 1789), p. 190. The English Puritan, Robert Greville (Lord Brooke) also praised the 'mighty

'one of the fullest' works written against the Antinomians.[132] When the so-called Marrow Controversy raged between 'Antinomian' Marrowmen and their more legalistic opponents in the early eighteenth century, both sides appealed to Rutherford to support their case. David Lachman, the author of the definitive study of the case, suggests that the Marrowmen were probably correct in claiming Rutherford for their side. For all his polemic against Antinomianism he always guarded against the kind of legalism into which the church fell in the later seventeenth century.[133] More recently, scholars have had a hard time deciding whether Rutherford was a hyper-Calvinist or a proto-Arminian.[134]

The confusion surrounding Rutherford's theology is replicated in the treatment of Reformed orthodoxy in general. On the one hand the orthodox are accused of believing in a God who predetermined everything from eternity by his absolute decrees, and on the other they are accused of teaching that people were saved because of their own repentance and faith. Hence, Baker criticises Perkins for advancing a testamental understanding of God's relationship to man derived from Calvin,[135] whereas Kendall attacks him for precisely the opposite reason, that he bases the relationship on a contract instead of on free grace as Calvin did.[136]

The problem here is that historians fail to acknowledge that the orthodox believed in both divine predetermination and human agency. As well as repudiating Arminianism they wished to counteract the Antinomian claim that the elect person simply had to 'let go and let God'. Too many scholars have concentrated on one of these at the expense of the other, so producing seriously distorted accounts of theologians like Rutherford. To comprehend the orthodox Calvinists we must remember that they were 'combining furious opposites by keeping them both, and keeping them furious', to borrow a phrase from G. K. Chesterton.[137] By reminding individuals of their responsibility to repent, believe and obey, they never intended to undermine dependence on divine grace. Human agency, for preachers like Rutherford, was always a result of divine predetermination. *Sola fide* was underpinned

---

Rutherfort' for his critique of Arminianism. See Robert Greville, *The Nature of Truth* (London, 1640), p. 52.

[132] In the postscript to his *Apology* (cited in Kevan, *Grace of Law*, p. 29).

[133] D. Lachman, *The Marrow Controversy, 1718–23* (Edinburgh, 1988), p. 14.

[134] P. Toon, *The Emergence of Hyper-Calvinism in English Nonconformity* (London, 1967), pp. 100, 138, identifies Rutherford as one of the sources of hyper-Calvinism, whereas R. Greaves, 'John Bunyan and covenant theology in the seventeenth century', *Church History*, 36 (1967), 152, classifies Rutherford with Baxter as a 'moderate Calvinist' because of his use of covenant theology.

[135] W. Baker, *Heinrich Bullinger and the Covenant* (Athens, Ohio, 1980), p. 166.

[136] Kendall, *Calvin and English Calvinism*, p. 75.

[137] Quoted from M. E. Dever, 'Richard Sibbes and the "truly evangelicall Church of England"', unpublished Ph.D. dissertation, University of Cambridge (1991), p. 107.

by *sola gratia*. 'All we doe', wrote Rutherford, 'the least good thought, or gracious motion in the soule, is a flower, and a rose of Christ's planting.'[138]

In failing to listen to such insistent declarations, discontinuity theorists have seriously misrepresented many early modern Reformed theologians. They have also distracted us from the real theological innovator in the Reformed tradition, Jacobus Arminius. Arminius broke decisively with Calvin's understanding of predestination as an unconditioned eternal decree. The orthodox, by contrast, continued to adhere to Calvin's fundamental stress on God's absolute sovereignty over history, deviating from him in only minor respects. They were, for example, more willing than Calvin to engage in speculation and philosophical theorising about divine sovereignty. Rutherford, for one, followed the idea of absolute predestination through to what he saw as its logical entailments: necessitarianism, definite atonement, extreme voluntarism and supralapsarianism. Yet such scholastic speculations hardly constituted a basic betrayal of Calvin, who can be read either way on all of these issues. The history of Reformed dogmatics from Calvin to scholastic orthodoxy is notable more for its continuity than for its change.

ARMINIANISM AND THE ROAD TO CIVIL WAR

Having concentrated on the developments within Reformed theology after Calvin, it is now time to focus on the debate that rages over the rise of Arminianism and the origins of the British troubles. It is true that the scholars involved in this controversy have been overwhelmingly concerned with England, but Nicholas Tyacke has appealed to Scottish evidence, including the case of Rutherford, something entirely appropriate given the recent rediscovery of the British dimension of the mid-century crisis. So how does an analysis of Rutherford relate to the debate over the origins of the British troubles?

At one level our treatment of Rutherford's theology may be said to reinforce Peter White's points about the complexity of the issues involved. White argues that we should stop thinking in terms of a straightforward conflict between a monolithic Calvinism and a monolithic Arminianism. As we have seen, there was in fact a bewildering multitude of theological positions, including supralapsarianism, infralapsarianism, Amyraldianism, Antinomianism, Molinism, Congruism and Arminianism proper. It was often difficult to summarise an individual theologian's position under a single category; Rutherford both held a very high doctrine of divine sovereignty and insisted on the reality of human agency, and one can easily

---

[138] *Christ Dying*, p. 79.

distort his position by ignoring one or the other. Moreover, theologians were often labelled Arminian by their polemical opponents simply because they did not toe the high Calvinist line on the extent of Christ's atonement. Rutherford regarded Cameron and Amyraut as Arminian, for example, even though they accepted Calvin's doctrine of absolute predestination and claimed to be following his teaching on the universal scope of the atonement.

However, although White rightly draws attention to the complexity of the theological issues, his work can still be viewed as an elaborate attempt at obfuscation. When everything has been said about the variety of possible positions theologians adopted, the fact remains that there was a stark contrast between Calvinists who claimed that what determined whether one was saved or damned was God's election in eternity, and Arminians who claimed that it was one's own free decision in time. The Jesuits may have tried to synthesise both claims, but few Protestants followed them. White's work draws attention away from the fact that Arminianism represented a full-frontal assault on traditional Calvinism.[139]

It is of course possible that some of those accused of anti-Calvinism were actually innocent, but Arminian and other anti-Calvinist theologies did exist and many Calvinists believed that they were growing apace. White's failure to come to terms with the *perceptions* of a rising Arminianism is almost as misleading as his determination to confuse us about the positions involved. As we know from the study of anti-popery in seventeenth-century England, the belief in a popish plot could powerfully shape political action whether or not such a plot actually existed.[140] Laud may or may not have been an Arminian, but there can be no doubt that many Puritans were convinced that he was.[141] In his final chapter, White does concentrate on perceptions of the Laudians' theology rather than on the theology itself, but his conclusion that Arminianism was not prominent among the charges brought up against them is not supported by the Scottish evidence, which he completely ignores.[142] Rutherford had no doubt that Arminianism was a

---

[139] It is, however, possible that some anti-Calvinists did not repudiate the traditional Calvinist doctrines of unconditional election and irresistible grace. Instead, they may have broken with the Calvinist claim that all those who experienced justification would persevere to the end and be saved. By breaking the traditional link between justification and election they robbed Calvinists of assurance of salvation and seemed to be heading back towards Catholic doctrine. I owe this point to Sean Hughes, whose forthcoming work on theologies of predestination in England promises to provide us with a much more sophisticated understanding of anti-Calvinism.

[140] See C. Hibbard, *Charles I and the Popish Plot* (Chapel Hill, NC, 1983); and J. Miller, *Popery and Politics in England, 1660–88* (Cambridge, 1973).

[141] N. Tyacke, *Anti-Calvinists: The Rise of English Arminianism, c. 1590–1640* (Oxford, 1987), pp. x–xi and Appendix II argues that Laud was an Arminian, whilst White, *Predestination, Policy and Polemic*, p. xiii, claims that he was not.

[142] White, *Predestination, Policy and Polemic*, pp. 307–11.

rising threat to pure Reformed theology,[143] and in 1637 he was planning to publish a second treatise against Arminianism.[144] As Tyacke rightly points out, he had been exiled to Aberdeen in 1636 partly because he had dared to publish a Latin treatise attacking Arminians like Thomas Jackson.[145] Moreover, the records of the 1638 Glasgow General Assembly show that Arminianism was one of the major charges brought against the bishops and some of the clergy. Robert Baillie, David Dickson and Rutherford's former teacher, Andrew Ramsay, all made speeches before the Assembly explaining the differences between Arminian doctrine and their own.[146] Rutherford was called as a witness against James Sibbald,[147] who had already had the misfortune of being heckled by Rutherford when preaching in Aberdeen. A number of bishops and clergy were deposed for their supposedly Arminian doctrine.[148] Fear of Arminianism, whether real or imagined, was certainly one of the factors contributing to anti-government agitation in Scotland in 1637–8, and as such it must count as one of the causes of the British troubles, even if not the most important.

THE DISRUPTIVE POTENTIAL OF CALVINIST THEOLOGY

The role played by Arminianism in the British crisis has led some historians to portray its advocates as the true revolutionaries, the Calvinists as the conservative establishment.[149] But the awe-inspiring Calvinist vision of a predestinating, covenanting God always possessed disruptive potential of its own, particularly in the hands of Puritans.[150] Rutherford's sermons to the English parliament in January 1644 and June 1645 are particularly powerful examples of the way in which Calvinist doctrine could be used to shape political attitudes. As such they provide us with a valuable bridge from Rutherford's theology to his political theory, which we will consider in the next chapter.

---

[143] See his *Letters*, pp. 56, 64, 135–6, 141, 181, 275, 370. Writing in the early 1640s, Rutherford still counted the promotion of Arminianism among Charles I's gravest sins in the previous decade. See *Lex, Rex*, pp. 223 [122], 225 [123], 267–8 [145].

[144] *Letters*, p. 404.   [145] Tyacke, *Anti-Calvinists*, p. 33.

[146] *Records of the Kirk of Scotland*, ed. Peterkin, pp. 156–9.

[147] J. Gordon, *History of Scots Affairs from 1637 to 1641* (Aberdeen, 1841), pp. 54–8, 228–9.

[148] *Records of the Kirk*, ed. Peterkin, pp. 165–6, 170–4. See also M. C. Kitshoff, 'Aspects of Arminianism in Scotland', unpublished M.Th. dissertation, University of St Andrews (1967), pp. 54–142.

[149] See, for example, P. Collinson, *The Religion of Protestants: The Church in English Society, 1559–1625* (Oxford, 1982), ch. 4.

[150] A point stressed by Walzer, *Revolution of the Saints*; Sharpe, *Politics and Ideas*, pp. 28–31; and P. Lake, '"A charitable Christian hatred": the godly and their enemies in the 1630s', in C. Durston and J. Eales, eds., *The Culture of English Puritanism, 1560–1700* (London, 1996), ch. 5.

Both of these sermons to parliament were saturated with a Calvinist insistence on the exhaustive sovereignty of God and the awesome responsibility of man. The texts chosen on both occasions spoke of God's control over history and nature. Before the House of Commons, Rutherford preached on Daniel 6, where Darius the Mede acknowledges the dominion of the God of Israel, and before the House of Lords, he expounded the story of Christ's stilling of the storm.

The theological doctrines preached so passionately by Rutherford in these sermons served important political purposes. The doctrines of the hiddenness and sovereignty of God reassured anxious and bewildered opponents of the king that the war was in God's hands, that victory was sure. 'God seemeth to sleepe, as if God were dead', Rutherford admitted, just as Christ had slept in the disciples' boat during the height of a storm.[151] Yet it was wise to remember that providence was 'a great mystery'; 'Our senses cannot reach the reason of his counsell.'[152] It was common for Christ to 'hide his face', but faith thought no evil of Christ and 'faiths eye' could 'pierce through Christs maske and the vaile or cloud that covers his face'.[153] Instead of looking at 'the darke side of God's providence', the saints should look to its 'faire and smiling side', believing that 'God is now drawing an excellent portrait of a refined Church, but with the Inke of the innocent blood of his people'.[154]

Such faith in the ultimate triumph of providence was not fanciful to those convinced of God's exhaustive sovereignty over human affairs. 'God shot the Arrow' that killed King Ahab, Rutherford assured his hearers, determining that it struck him precisely 'betweene the joints of his harnesse'. With the Lord there was 'no contingency, no such thing as maybee, and may not bee'.[155] The 'Bullets, Arrows and Fire-works' that flew in civil war battles were 'his souldiers flying in the Aire'.[156] He had sent 'Stormy Winds to destroy Armado's'. He could 'take up the whole Ile of Brittaine in his hand, and . . . hang the weight of the massie body of Heaven and Earth on the top of his finger'.[157] Such a sovereign God would not fail to bring victory to his people: 'Christ hath endured more than the wrath of the King of Britaine, and beleeve it, he shall be victorious and shall prevaile.'[158] Those who had deserted parliament for Oxford were fools to place their hope 'in a king that shall die', rather than in a God who endured for ever.[159]

Calvinism also steeled Covenanters and parliamentarians for the cruelties of war. This was no time for sensitivity and the Calvinist God was himself

---

[151] *Sermon to Lords*, p. 46. [152] *Sermon to Lords*, p. 11.
[153] *Sermon to Lords*, p. 55. [154] *Sermon to Commons*, pp. 9–10.
[155] *Sermon to Lords*, pp. 60–1. [156] *Sermon to Commons*, p. 62.
[157] *Sermon to Commons*, pp. 40–2. [158] *Sermon to Lords*, p. 20.
[159] *Sermon to Commons*, p. 53.

no bleeding-heart liberal. He had, after all, predestined millions of people to damnation before they had even been born simply for the sake of his glory. And he had every right to do so, for in comparison to the Lord, what was man 'but a weeping, groaning, dying, nothing?' For reprobates to complain that God had not given them the grace necessary for salvation was blasphemous; 'the clay should not dispute with the potter'. 'Millions and hosts of men are Millions and Hosts of vanities', preached Rutherford, 'God is all and an infinite all.'[160] Such an attitude had the potential to dehumanise the opposition and desensitise the godly. If God was all and men were mere vanities, then a holy war that extinguished many lives did not have to lie heavy on the conscience, particularly when one's enemies were 'malignants, bloody Irish, rotten hearted men . . . backsliders and perjured Apostates'. Rutherford did not deny, of course, that even 'God's enemies' were made in the image of God, but in the heat of righteous indignation this seemed less important than the fact that they were malignants. Because the royalist malignants were idolaters and enemies of God, Rutherford suggested, war against them was more justified than if they had been merely enemies of parliament.[161]

By stressing the utter transcendence of God over puny mankind the Calvinist preacher was also able to overcome qualms about opposing earthly kings. He reminded his hearers that they belonged to God and not to the king. The mistake of cavaliers, courtiers and prelates was to make the king the absolute Lord of their religion, when their souls should be subject to God alone.[162] 'Make not clay and the creature . . . pure meere nothing, your last end', Rutherford urged. 'Let God, only God, be your last end.' 'Court, court is made of glasse, and can glitter and be broken in one houre.' God, however, was infinite, 'an instant standing always still'. The leaders of the nation ought to 'stoope, stoope before this monarch, cast down your Crownes and Scepters at the feet of the King of Kings'.[163]

Rutherford's stress on divine sovereignty, therefore, was accompanied by a call to human action. As in his theological treatises, he castigated Antinomians for denying the importance of good works and waiting passively for the Spirit to stir them. 'God blesseth right precisenesse and strictnesse in his way', he declared.[164] The Lord might have predetermined all things, but he still made great demands upon his creatures. Just as his covenant with the elect was conditional and called for their response, so his covenant with Britain demanded action. Rutherford condemned the English parliamentarians for their passivity during the previous decades when the

[160] *Sermon to Commons*, pp. 14, 42.
[161] *Sermon to Commons*, p. 23; *Sermon to Lords*, p. 40.
[162] *Sermon to Commons*, p. 61.   [163] *Sermon to Commons*, pp. 45–8.
[164] *Sermon to Commons*, p. 37.

servants of God had been persecuted and corruptions had been brought into the church.[165] Now was the time for them to throw themselves behind the Reformation, to pray for the success of the Gospel, to build God's temple, and 'to send the Glory of Christ over Sea, to all Europe'.[166] For Rutherford, divine sovereignty and human agency were not merely abstract theological doctrines, they were practical political truths.

[165] *Sermon to Commons*, p. 59.
[166] *Sermon to Commons*, pp. 5–7, 64; *Sermon to Lords*, p. 6.

The political theorist

THE LITERARY AND POLITICAL CONTEXT OF *LEX, REX*

If Rutherford's posthumous popularity was secured by his *Letters*, it is his political treatise, *Lex, Rex*, which is best known to historians.[1] Published in London in 1644, it presented a thorough defence of the Covenanters' armed resistance to Charles I. Although for this reason it was very much a product of the post-1638 period, it is possible that Rutherford had held some of its

[1] The following histories of early modern political thought include a short discussion of *Lex, Rex*, usually in the context of English ideas: G. P. Gooch, *English Democratic Ideas in the Seventeenth Century* (New York, 1959 edn.), pp. 98–9; J. W. Gough, *The Social Contract: A Critical Study of its Development* (Oxford, 1936), pp. 93–4; J. W. Allen, *English Political Thought, 1603–44* (London, 1938), p. 285; P. Zagorin, *A History of Political Thought in the English Revolution* (London, 1954), pp. 5–6; J. Salmon, *The French Religious Wars in English Political Thought* (Oxford, 1959), pp. 87–8; R. Tuck, *Natural Rights Theories: Their Origin and Development* (Cambridge, 1979), pp. 144–5; J. Sommerville, *Politics and Ideology in England, 1603–40* (Harlow, 1986); D. Wootton, ed., *Divine Right and Democracy: An Anthology of Political Writing in Stuart England* (London, 1986), p. 50; J. Sanderson, *'But the People's Creatures': The Philosophical Basis of the English Civil War* (Manchester, 1989), ch. 1.
  Four American theses that deal with Rutherford's political thought are all weak on the historical context: O. Webb, 'The political thought of Samuel Rutherford', unpublished Ph.D. dissertation, Duke University (1964); T. Hall, 'Rutherford, Locke and the Declaration', unpublished M.Th. dissertation, Dallas Theological Seminary (1984); J. P. Burgess, 'The problem of Scripture and political affairs as reflected in the Puritan Revolution', unpublished Ph.D. dissertation, University of Chicago (1986); J. L. Marshall, 'Natural law and the covenant: the place of natural law in the covenantal framework of Samuel Rutherford's *Lex, Rex*', unpublished Ph.D. dissertation, Westminster Theological Seminary (1995).
  However, the most detailed published studies of *Lex, Rex* are all written from a Scottish perspective: W. Campbell, '*Lex, Rex* and its author', *RSCHS*, 7 (1941), 204–28; J. F. Maclear, 'Samuel Rutherford: the law and the king', in G. L. Hunt and J. T. McNeill, eds., *Calvinism and the Political Order* (Philadelphia, 1965), pp. 65–87; I. M. Smart, 'The political ideas of the Scottish Covenanters, 1638–88', *History of Political Thought*, 1 (1980), pp. 175–80; J. Ford, '*Lex, rex iusto posita*: Samuel Rutherford on the origins of government', in R. Mason, ed., *Scots and Britons: Scottish Political Thought and the Union of 1603* (Cambridge, 1994), pp. 262–90.
  A recent thesis on Rutherford's political thought which I was not able to read for this book is: C. Rae, 'The political thought of Samuel Rutherford', unpublished MA dissertation, University of Guelph (1991).

radical tenets since his student days in the 1620s. There is no direct evidence for this, but an incident in the life of his radical Presbyterian colleague, Robert Blair, is revealing. Blair lost his position as a regent at Glasgow University in 1623 because his lectures on Aristotle's *Politics* and *Ethics* were regarded as subversive. He was accused of teaching that the people did well in rescuing Jonathan out of the hands of Saul, and that election to the throne was better than succession.[2] Both of these points are to be found in *Lex, Rex*,[3] and it is significant that when Rutherford drafted a political treatise in manuscript form before leaving Scotland, he asked Blair to read it. It seems possible that these men did not just develop a radical political theory after 1638, but had remained substantially loyal to the tradition of natural-law contractualism stemming from Buchanan.

What is certain is that the success of the Covenanter revolution led Rutherford to write about political theory. According to the biographer of Robert Blair, Rutherford wrote 'a great part' of *Lex, Rex* before he went to London at the end of 1643, and submitted it to Blair, who advised him to set the project to one side, since it was better tackled by experts such as lawyers and politicians. Only when he was at Westminster Assembly, and at Wariston's prompting, did Rutherford complete the work.[4] *Lex, Rex*, it

---

[2] See D. Calderwood, *The True History of the Church of Scotland* (1678), pp. 799–800. See also [Walter Balcanquhall], A *Large Declaration concerning the Late Tumults in Scotland* (1639), p. 324. Blair himself claimed that the controversy actually arose because 'I taxed that Arminian poynt [election based on 'foirsein faith'] in my notes upon Aristotles Ethicks and Politicks.' See *Records of the Kirk of Scotland*, ed. A. Peterkin (Edinburgh, 1838), pp. 148–9.

[3] Rutherford's scepticism about hereditary monarchy is seen in *Lex, Rex*, Questions X and XI, and the example of the rescue of Jonathan is used on pp. 348–9 [171]. Figures in square brackets refer to the 1843 edition, reprinted in 1846 and 1982.

[4] *The Life of Robert Blair*, ed. T. McCrie (Edinburgh, 1848), pp. 365–6. William Campbell, '*Lex, Rex* and its author', pp. 204–6, argued that the section of *Lex, Rex* devoted to justifying defensive wars (Questions XXVIII–XXXVII) had been written in the summer of 1643, before Rutherford went to London. In support of this claim he pointed to two pieces of internal evidence: first, the 'popish prelate', Maxwell, was attacked only twice in these chapters (in what Campbell took to be insertions) whilst he was the main opponent elsewhere; secondly, the frequent references to the 'bloody Irish' suggest that Rutherford wrote it after Argyll's exposé of the king's dealings with the Irish rebels in late May 1643. The purpose of this pamphlet on 'Defensive Wars', Campbell concluded, was to support Argyll's hawkish policy and strengthen the hand of those negotiating the Solemn League and Covenant with the English parliament.
However, there are major difficulties with this interesting proposal: Row wrote that Rutherford submitted to Blair 'a great part' of *Lex, Rex*, not just one section of it; Maxwell was mentioned in these chapters more than Campbell claimed; Rutherford quoted the third part of Prynne's *Soveraigne Power of Parliaments* (p. 371 [183]) published only in late June 1643; Question XXXVII on the legitimacy of the Scots assisting their English fellow Protestants, declared that the two nations have 'now, by the mercy of god, sworn one covenant' (p. 382 [189]), a clear reference to the Solemn League and Covenant of September 1643; the statement, 'The king hath now made a cessation with the bloody Irish' (p. 337 [165]) surely refers to the formal cessation made in September 1643 rather than to earlier

would seem, was based on the earlier manuscript treatise, but was thoroughly rewritten in 1644 for the new political context.

The immediate reason for the rewriting of the earlier manuscript was the publication, in January 1644, of a royalist treatise, *Sacro-Sancta Regum Majestas; or The Sacred and Royal Prerogative of Christian Kings*. Its author was John Maxwell, the deposed 'Canterburian' Bishop of Ross and one of the major architects of the notorious Scottish Prayer Book. Rutherford found this treatise by an old enemy deeply provocative,[5] and over the winter, spring and summer of 1644, he spent much of his free-time away from the Westminster Assembly writing a detailed refutation. *Lex, Rex, or the Law and the Prince*, was published 'by authority' in October. It ran to some 450 quarto pages, and was packed with vituperative attacks on the 'Popish Prelate'.[6]

Lex, Rex has usually been lumped together with the English parliamentarian justifications of resistance produced by 'the men of 1642'. John Sanderson, for instance, calls it 'the most comprehensive justification of resistance (which summed up two years of resistance theorizing)'.[7] Yet although it is true that *Lex, Rex* repeated the familiar arguments of English writers like Parker, Goodwin, Prynne and Hunton, it was also the distinctive contribution of a Scottish divine, peppered with references to Scottish resistance, and marked by explicitly theological arguments.[8] Even Prynne, who dealt with biblical and natural-law arguments in some detail,[9] had focused primarily on legal and historical precedents, and Rutherford probably felt that the theological case needed a fuller treatment. Maxwell had written his book because he felt that it was appropriate for a divine to put the case for absolutism, since it had already been convincingly argued by eminent lawyers like Bodin and Barclay, and since it was so strongly

---

negotiations; and the mention of the battle of Marston Moor (p. 360 [177]), fought in July 1644, seals the case.

[5] He had probably picked out Maxwell as a dangerous heretic back in the early 1620s when the latter was a minister at Edinburgh. See *Lex, Rex* (p. 271 [147]). George Mackenzie, Lord Advocate of Scotland during the Restoration, later claimed that the author of *Lex, Rex* was known to have written 'those libels from pigue [*sic*] against the Government, because [he] had justly suffered under it'. G. Mackenzie, *Jus Regium, or the Just and Solid Foundations of Monarchy* (London, 1684), p. 6.

[6] Maxwell was called a drunkard, a heretic and a plagiarist, who was only worth answering because more learned authors could be refuted in the process. See, for example, *Lex, Rex* (p. 270 [146], pp. 366–7 [181]).

[7] J. Sanderson, 'Conrad Russell's ideas', *History of Political Thought*, 14 (1993), 94.

[8] *Lex, Rex* was far more scholastic in style than the brief, straightforward and orderly pamphlets of Parker, Hunton and Goodwin; only Prynne's sprawling four-part *Soveraigne Power of Parliaments* (1643) compared with Rutherford in style. So far as content was concerned, Parker and Hunton offered largely secular, constitutionalist arguments, whilst Goodwin summarised the religious argument for resistance.

[9] See part III of the *Soveraigne Power of Parliaments*. Pages 1–60 discussed natural-law principles, and pages 61–150 the biblical data, especially Romans 13.

supported by Scripture and Christian tradition.[10] Rutherford clearly could not let this go unchallenged. The natural-law contractualism of the Scottish–parliamentarian alliance needed to be defended by a theologian.

Yet why publish such a comprehensive defence in late 1644? Who remained to be convinced by that late stage in the war? Who was Rutherford writing for?

The clue to his intent may lie in the fact that he published his treatise whilst negotiations were taking place between the king, the English parliament and the Scots. Arguably, he wanted to make clear to the royalists, and to Charles himself, just how angry the Scots were at what they saw as his betrayal of the Reformed religion. He also wished to highlight the drastic limitations that the Presbyterians wanted to impose on royal authority. His ultimate aim was to push a very hard line in the negotiations, perhaps because he suspected Loudon and Lauderdale of compromising too much.[11]

In this respect, Wariston's role in the publication of *Lex, Rex* is significant. According to Row, Wariston 'did not only assist to, but did also wholly complete and finish that work'. Although the work was published anonymously, there is no other evidence to suggest that Wariston wrote any of it, and contemporaries always took it to be Rutherford's work.[12] Wariston probably only helped Rutherford with the legal and historical details of question XLIII (on the Scottish constitution). But his enthusiasm for the work was no doubt inspired by his desire (and perhaps that of Argyll) to ensure that the achievements of the Covenanting revolution were not forfeited by moderates who were prepared to pay a high price for peace. *Lex, Rex* was intended to close the possibility of compromise. It demonstrated to royalists and to moderates on the Covenanter and parliamentarian side just how much the godly felt alienated from the king, and how much they wanted his powers restricted. The fact that *Lex, Rex* was published 'by authority' in London suggests that the militant Scots had

---

[10] Maxwell, *Sacro-sancta*, epistle dedicatory.

[11] This line of argument was originally suggested by Campbell, '*Lex, Rex* and its author', pp. 211–13.

[12] See Henry Guthry, *Memoirs of Henry Guthrie, late Bishop of Dunkel in Scotland* (London, 1702), p. 139; John Livingstone, 'Memorable characteristics', in W. K. Tweedie, ed., *Select Biographies*, I (Edinburgh, 1845), p. 321; James Gordon, *History of Scots Affairs from 1637 to 1641* (Aberdeen, 1841), pp. 169–70; James Balfour, *The Annales of Scotland*, 3 vols. (London, 1825), III, p. 410; Robert Baillie, *Letters and Journals*, III (Edinburgh, 1842), p. 447; *Life of Blair*, p. 365; John Lamont, *The Diary of Mr John Lamont of Newton 1649–71*, ed. G. R. Kinloch (Edinburgh, 1830), p. 126. Most convincingly of all, Wariston calls it 'Mr Rutherfurds Lex, Rex', *Diary*, III, ed. J. D. Ogilvie (Edinburgh, 1940), p. 64, and Rutherford himself was said to have declared on his deathbed that 'he would willingly die on the scaffold for that book with a good conscience', Robert Wodrow, *Analecta*, I (Edinburgh, 1842), pp. 165–6.

allied themselves with those Presbyterians in the English parliament who were equally concerned to drive a hard bargain.

The ferocity and bitterness of *Lex, Rex* fits very well with this conception of its purpose. Rutherford's work was more passionate in tone than that of the earlier parliamentarian theorists. Parker and Hunton wrote in a relatively calm style, and Prynne's zeal was a little crushed under the weight of legal and historical data. But Rutherford fulminated against the 'bloody' and 'cut-throat' Irish,[13] and against a king who was 'drinking the blood of innocents, and wasting the church of God'.[14] The king had invited 'a bloody conqueror [the confederate Irish] to come in with an army of men to destroy his people, [and] impose upon their conscience an idolatrous religion'.[15] Moreover, he had not done this in a fit of madness, but after he had 'slept upon this prelatical resolution many months'.[16] That this was a settled disposition in the king was confirmed by the popish religious policies of the 1630s,[17] and the terrible failure to assist the Protestants at La Rochelle and the Palatinate in the 1620s.[18] Charles had not only failed to break 'the images and idols of his queen, and of papists about him'[19] but he had also commanded good Protestants to commit worse than Babylonian idolatry.[20] The prelates had taught him that he had a greater power than 'the great Turk' who commanded his subjects to cast themselves into the fire for his entertainment; Charles could order his subjects 'to cast themselves into hell-fire' by following the idolatrous worship of the Service Book.[21] When they had refused he had sent a whole army, 'inspired with the spirit of antichrist, to destroy the whole land, if they should not submit, soul and conscience, to that wicked service'.[22] Not without reason did Rutherford feel he could introduce the example of Nero, 'wasting Rome, burning, crucifying Paul, and torturing Christians'.[23]

Moderate Covenanters were likely to find this genuinely shocking. Attacks on popery were thoroughly conventional, but direct acerbic attacks on the king were not. As Woodhouse observed, 'Unlike the Covenant, *Lex, Rex* makes little pretence of differentiating between the king and his advisers, but frankly asserts the will of the people as against the King himself.'[24] Something of the reaction to this can be gathered from a detailed refutation written after the Restoration by one of Rutherford's own colleagues at St Andrews, Andrew Honyman.[25] In his *Survey of Naphtali*,

---

[13] See, for example, *Lex, Rex*, pp. 324, 328, 342, 362 [158, 161, 168, 178].
[14] *Lex, Rex*, pp. 262–3 [142].　　[15] *Lex, Rex*, p. 373 [185].
[16] *Lex, Rex*, p. 64 [37].　　[17] *Lex, Rex*, pp. 267–8 [145].
[18] *Lex, Rex*, pp. 381–2 [189].　　[19] *Lex, Rex*, p. 46 [27].
[20] *Lex, Rex*, p. 200 [110].　　[21] *Lex, Rex*, p. 180 [100].
[22] *Lex, Rex*, p. 369 [182].　　[23] *Lex, Rex*, p. 274 [148].
[24] A. S. P. Woodhouse, ed., *Puritanism and Liberty* (London, 1992 edn), p. [62n].
[25] In the 1650s, Rutherford had bitterly attacked Honyman over his support for the

Honyman expressed his dismay at Rutherford's 'infinite inhumane bitterness against the late king'. *Lex, Rex* portrayed Charles I as a Nero, 'a great persecutor of Religion, intending the total ruine and destruction of the Protestant profession, and the total ruine and destruction of the whole people of the land', when the reality was 'that the king lived and died a Protestant . . . being exemplary devote'.[26]

The 'infinite inhumane bitterness' against Charles I expressed in *Lex, Rex* may have contributed to the intransigence of both royalists and their opponents, an intransigence that led to the eventual collapse of the negotiations at Uxbridge in January 1645. According to the Scottish moderate, Henry Guthry, every member of the 1645 General Assembly 'had in his hand that Book lately published by Mr Samuel Rutherford . . . [which was] so idolised that whereas Buchanan's treatise *De Jure Regni apud Scotos*, was looked upon as an oracle, this coming forth, it was slighted (as not antimonarchical enough) and Rutherford's *Lex, Rex* only thought authentic'.[27] Scottish Presbyterian ministers were not the only ones to read the book. John Livingstone, a close colleague of Rutherford, wrote of *Lex, Rex*: 'It is reported that when King Charles the First saw it, he said that book would hardly ever get ane answer.'[28] Although it is unlikely that the king was quite so impressed by Rutherford's argument, it may well be that he did read *Lex, Rex*. The fate of the book after the Restoration suggests that the Stuarts did not forget the damage Rutherford had done to the cause of reconciliation between the king and his subjects. A proclamation was issued in Scotland against 'two seditious books': *Lex, Rex* and Guthrie's *Causes of the Lord's Wrath against Scotland* (1653), a work which declared that Scotland was being punished for the sins of the house of Stuart.[29] They were burnt by the hangman and Rutherford was cited before parliament. Had he not died in March 1661, he would quite probably have been executed along with Guthrie, Wariston and Argyll.[30] This was the ultimate testimony to the effectiveness with which *Lex, Rex* had achieved its provocative purpose.

Resolutioner party in the kirk, and was said to have declared, 'Mr Honyman is a knave, and will prove soe!'. See Wodrow, *Analecta*, vol. II, p. 118. Honyman became Bishop of Orkney after the Restoration, and in 1666 he was wounded by a bullet intended for another of Rutherford's former colleagues, Archbishop James Sharp. The experience – quite understandably – led him to write a refutation of the Presbyterian case for violent resistance to established authority.
[26] [A. Honyman], *A Survey of the Insolent and Infamous Libel entituled 'Naphtali'* (1668), pp. 72, 20.
[27] Guthry, *Memoirs*, p. 139.
[28] W. K. Tweedie, ed., *Select Biographies*, I, p. 321. The same story is found in [J. Stewart], *Jus Populi Vindicatum* (1669), p. 381.
[29] The proclamation can be found in R. Wodrow, *The History of the Sufferings of the Church of Scotland from the Restoration to the Revolution*, I (Glasgow, 1828), p. 75n.
[30] See Baillie, *Letters and Journals*, III, p. 467.

Paradoxically, however, this inflammatory book was both intellectually demanding and convoluted in its arrangement. Its argument was set out in the form of answers to forty-four questions, and Rutherford's insistence upon this rigidly scholastic approach created a work of labyrinthine complexity. It can, nevertheless, be roughly subdivided into five main sections. Questions I to XIV dealt with the origins of government, and Questions XV to XXI with the relation between king and people, especially the institutions of parliament and the judiciary. The heart of the book is found in the answers to Questions XXII to XXVII, where Rutherford discussed the relationship between the king and the law, placing *rex* firmly under *lex*. Then in Questions XXVIII to XXXVII he defended the defensive wars of the Scots, and in Questions XXXVIII to XLIV he concluded by discussing a miscellaneous range of issues such as how his theory related to that of the Jesuits and how it fitted with the history of Scotland.

The exposition of the text that follows begins with a discussion of the relationship between nature and grace, reason and revelation in Rutherford's thought. Thereafter it takes a 'chronological' approach, moving from Rutherford's theory of the origins of government and the covenant that established it, to his theory of the nature of good government, his justification of the armed resistance that topples tyrannical rulers, and his use of Buchanan's ancient constitutionalism to underpin his natural-law argument.

NATURAL REASON AND BIBLICAL REVELATION

The reason for *Lex, Rex*'s intimate blend of secular and religious arguments is not hard to find. Although written by a Calvinist, it was in some ways a deeply Thomistic book.[31] In Questions I and II Rutherford quoted ten authors to support his case; one was Aristotle and the rest were Catholics, six of them being sixteenth-century Spanish neo-Thomists (Vitoria, de Soto, Suarez, Molina, Covarruvias and Ferdinand Vasquez).[32] In several places he

---

[31] It is often assumed that the Reformed stress on divine will and human depravity was incompatible with the Thomist insistence on human rationality and virtue. Carl Friedrich, for example, draws a sharp contrast between Richard Hooker's Thomistic optimism about human reason and Puritan denigration of it. See his *Transcendent Justice: The Religious Dimension of Constitutionalism* (Durham, NC, 1964), ch. 3. However, Reformed theologians never denied that a radically free God had created an ordered world, and their doctrine of depravity was intended to prove that man could not justify himself before God. It implied nothing about his ability to establish complex forms of human association. As Rutherford explained, the fact that men cannot be 'evangelically, or legally in God's court, good', did not mean that they cannot have 'a natural moral active power' to love their parents. See *Lex, Rex*, p. 51 [30]. On the readiness of Calvinists to think in Thomistic terms see J. P. Donnelly, 'Calvinist Thomism', *Viator*, 7 (1976), 441–51.

[32] For detailed analyses of the political thought of the Spanish Thomists see B. Hamilton, *Political Thought in Sixteenth Century Spain* (Oxford, 1963) and Q. Skinner, *The Foundations of Modern Political Thought*, II (Cambridge, 1978), chs. 5 and 6.

appealed to Aquinas's classic maxim, 'Grace does not destroy nature but perfects it.'[33] This maxim is perhaps the key to *Lex, Rex*, because Rutherford insisted throughout on the compatibility of natural reason's conclusions and God's revelation in Scripture.

It is important to understand the precise relationship between natural law and Scriptural prescription in Rutherford's thought.[34] *Lex, Rex* clearly assumed that there was considerable overlap between the two. The book was saturated in biblical references, and Rutherford regarded the Old Testament narratives as akin to a natural-law casebook, illustrating principles which could also be gathered from human reason. Since he believed that the God who inspired Scripture had also created man's conscience, it is no surprise that he stated that 'the Scripture's arguments may be drawn out of the school of nature'.[35] God had written the law of nature both on the consciences of men and on the pages of the Bible. A key passage in *A Free Disputation* explained this in detail:

in the inner Cabinet, the naturall habit of Morall principles lodgeth, the Register of the common notions left in us by nature, the Ancient Records and Chronicles which were in Adams time, the Law of Nature of two volumes, one of the first Table, that there is a God, that he createth and governeth all things, that there is but one God, infinitely good, most just rewarding the Evill and the Good; and of the second Table, as to love our parents, obey superiors, to hurt no man, the acts of humanity; All these are written in the soule in deep letters, yet the Inke is dimme and old, and therefore this light is like the moone swimming through watery clouds, often under shadow, and yet still in the firmament.[36]

The presence of both optimism and pessimism in this passage is worth noting. On the one hand, Rutherford declared that the whole of the Decalogue was 'written in the soule in deep letters'. If natural reason and

---

[33] *Lex, Rex*, pp. 122, 324, 327 [68, 158, 160].

[34] The political reading of the Bible in the early modern period is only beginning to be systematically explored. Christopher Hill, *The English Bible and the Seventeenth-Century Revolution* (Harmondsworth, 1993), has highlighted the importance of this theme, but by failing to examine the hermeneutical principles employed by Bible readers, Hill comes to the conclusion that the Bible was a ragbag and that its readers employed a slap-dash 'pick-and-mix' approach to its contents. Whilst this may have been true for some, most approached the Bible with far more rigour and reverence. Theologians like Rutherford were seriously engaged in the task of sorting out what was relative and temporary in the biblical text from what was absolute and permanently binding. The focus of future research should be on interpretative frameworks through which the Bible was viewed, rather than simply on how it was quoted in particular situations. In this respect, H. G. Reventlow, *The Authority of the Bible and the Rise of the Modern World* (London, 1984), is a study of early modern readings of the Bible superior to that of Hill.

[35] *Lex, Rex*, p. 5 [3]. In *Divine Right*, p. 656, Rutherford wrote that 'the Law of Nature, and right reason', was 'a deduction from Scripture'.

[36] *Free Disputation*, p. 7. This passage resembles very closely the comments of John Calvin, *Institutes of the Christian Religion*, trans. H. Beveridge (Grand Rapids, Mich., 1989), II. 8. 1.

conscience were functioning properly they could inform a person not only that adultery and murder were wrong, but that there was one God.[37] On the other hand, there was pessimism in Rutherford's account. Man's epistemic faculties had been seriously damaged by the Fall, and his original knowledge of morality and religion was now sadly dimmed. Hence the need for special revelation, for the Decalogue and the rest of Scripture. 'Had [man's] conscience been a faithful register', Rutherford had argued in an earlier sermon, 'there should have been no need of a written Bible. But now the Lord lippened [trusted] more to dead paper than to a living man's soul.' In his present fallen state, man was wise to cooperate with God's epistemological renovation project: 'make much of the written word, and pray to God to copy his Bible into your conscience, and write a new book of his doctrine in your hearts'.[38]

Scripture, therefore, may not have added much to what *ontologically* speaking was part of natural law, but it added immeasurably to what *epistemologically* speaking men could now know through natural reason. In particular, the nature and importance of true religion could only be known by those with access to special revelation; it could not be derived from natural reason. Although Scripture republished pre-lapsarian natural laws, it also provided an extensive supplement to what was known by post-lapsarian natural reason.[39]

Rutherford's view of natural reason was similar to that of other Calvinists. Calvin himself, for example, clearly believed that natural reason was capable of discerning numerous moral truths, and he even declared that the moral law of God was 'nothing else than the testimony of natural law and of the conscience which God has engraved on the minds of men' (*Institutes* IV.20.15). But Calvin was also insistent that natural reason was not independently adequate as a guide to morals or faith; it was unreliable, an inferior adjunct to the divine law. Although he agreed with Aquinas on the ontological status of natural law, Calvin differed over its epistemological status. Aquinas was ultimately quite sanguine over the powers of unaided human reason, whereas Calvin, with his heavy emphasis on the noetic effects of sin, believed that man was now dependent on special revelation for an adequate knowledge of natural law.[40]

---

[37] The Westminster Confession also taught this. It identified the covenant of works made between God and Adam as the moral law that was later delivered by God in ten commandments on Mount Sinai. See *The Westminster Confession of Faith*, XIX. i–ii.

[38] *Communion Sermons*, p. 232.

[39] The problem here is obviously over the use of the term 'natural'. If natural is used to refer to how God intended things to be, then Scripture merely republishes natural law known to natural (unfallen) reason. But if natural is taken to mean the way things actually are, then clearly Scripture adds a great deal to the amount of natural law known by natural reason.

[40] See H. Hopfl, *The Christian Polity of John Calvin* (Cambridge, 1982), pp. 179–84; and

Rutherford's close friend, George Gillespie, took a similar line. He distinguished between 'that law which God writeth and imprinteth in the nature of man in his first creation', and 'that law which, after the fall, God still writeth in the heart of every man'. The former included the whole of the Decalogue and the moral law, whereas the latter 'cometh far short, and wanteth much of that which was written in the heart of man before his fall'. Nature's light could teach man to seek the preservation of his own being, to propagate and conserve his kind, to know that there was a God who ought to be worshipped, to hold fast friendship and amity with his neighbour, and to live as a reasonable creature. Yet after the Fall it could not teach man the attributes of God, or the trinitarian nature of God, or 'what sort or manner of worship should be given unto God'. To know these things, it was necessary to look to 'the divine law, revealed from God'.[41]

Rutherford shared this conviction, and it is of considerable importance for understanding *Lex, Rex*. Any interpretation of *Lex, Rex* which focuses on its arguments from natural reason and misses its uniquely biblical arguments is incomplete.[42] Rutherford was not just using Scripture to corroborate his arguments from reason. As we shall see, he was also drawing from it something that fallen natural reason could never tell him – the covenant obligations of a godly nation.

Yet Rutherford was not foolish enough to think that every command and example in Scripture was still binding on Christians. He made a clear distinction between the moral laws of the Old Testament which were perpetually binding, and the typical laws which were only temporary.[43] The debate among Reformed theologians was over where to draw the line between the 'typical' and the moral. All orthodox divines agreed that the ceremonial laws of Moses (those that required animal sacrifices and temple rites) had been abrogated by the sacrifice of Christ. However, there was more controversy concerning the judicial laws of Moses, such as those that prescribed the death penalty for adultery and gathering firewood on the Sabbath. Calvin had contemptuously dismissed the idea that these laws might still be binding and argued that magistrates were free to set penalties that they saw as appropriate,[44] but John Cotton had drawn up laws for

---

P. Helm, 'Calvin and natural law', *Scottish Bulletin of Evangelical Theology*, 2 (1984), 5–22.

[41] G. Gillespie, 'A dispute against the English popish ceremonies', in *The Works of George Gillespie*, I (Edinburgh, 1846), pp. 184–8.

[42] This applies to almost every reading of the book so far. In concentrating on the natural-law constitutionalism of Rutherford, most commentators miss his passionate concern for true religion, which is derived not from natural reason, but from Scripture.

[43] In doing so he was, of course, following the example of Aquinas, among others. The same can be said of his traditional division of the Mosaic law into ceremonial, judicial and moral, with only the last of these being permanent.

[44] Calvin, *Institutes*, IV. xx. 14–16.

New England that followed the Mosaic judicial law closely.[45] In reality, the gulf between Calvin and Cotton may not have been as great as this suggests; Calvin's commentaries showed a greater respect for the Mosaic judicial law than his comments in the *Institutes* might lead one to suspect, and Cotton by no means disregarded existing English law.[46] As Rutherford's case illustrates, there were other options besides either affirming or denying the present validity of the entire judicial law. Rutherford argued that with the coming of Christ 'the whole bulk of the judiciall law, as judiciall, and as it concerned the Republick of the Jews only, is abolished', but he added that 'the morall equity of all those be not abolished'.[47] The judicial laws could not be dismissed as irrelevant by Christian magistrates; they contained elements of moral equity that were still binding.

The key problem, however, lay in discerning the moral and permanent element in particular judicial laws. Rutherford had fairly clear opinions on this. He was sure that the law commanding the Israelites to slaughter the Canaanites contained no element of moral equity. The genocide of the Canaanites was only justified because of a positive command of God. It was therefore 'typicall' and temporary, rather than moral and permanent.[48] Similarly, the type of punishment the law prescribed for a particular crime – for example, the death penalty for fornication – was not a moral absolute, but a 'mysterious' type of God's anger towards certain sins which was no longer binding on magistrates in the New Testament age (something for which Rutherford was no doubt personally grateful).[49] Yet, as we shall see shortly, Rutherford also believed that the Old Testament laws concerning national covenanting and the magistrate's duty to defend true religion were still binding on Christians, and it is likely that he regarded the biblical law 'thou shalt not suffer a witch to live' (Exodus 22.18) as a permanent, moral command.

Rutherford's attitude to the Mosaic law, therefore, was complex. Insofar as he maintained that the judicial law as judicial was no longer binding, he gave magistrates considerable leeway. He had no desire to see all the traditional institutions and laws of Scotland abolished and replaced by those of ancient Israel. A Christian magistrate was obliged to follow the moral equity of Old Testament law, but as long as he was doing that he was free to regulate his people in accordance with national custom.[50] But

[45] On this whole debate see the survey of P. D. L. Avis, 'Moses and the magistrate: a study in the rise of Protestant legalism', *Journal of Ecclesiastical History*, 26 (1975), 149–72.

[46] T. Bozeman, *To Live Ancient Lives: The Primitivist Dimension in Puritanism* (Chapel Hill, 1988), ch. 5, provides a nuanced interpretation of New England Puritan attitudes to the Mosaic judicial law.

[47] *Divine Right*, pp. 493–4.   [48] *Survey of Hooker*, p. 478.

[49] *Divine Right*, pp. 493–4.

[50] This was also the position of the *Westminster Confession of Faith* : 'To them [the Jews] also,

Rutherford's emphasis on the element of moral equity in Mosaic judicial law placed very heavy burdens on the magistrate. The Old Testament was to be the magistrate's most important political textbook, for it specified just how he should act when true religion was threatened.[51] As Michael Walzer has understood so well, Rutherford and the other radical Calvinist saints were 'judaisers' *par excellence*.[52] By arguing for the permanent validity of Israel's national covenant, Rutherford committed the magistrate to preserving true religion (that is, Reformed Protestantism) in all its purity. The slightest pollution of it was intolerable apostasy to be corrected by Old Testament-style revolts and purges.

Margaret Sampson – along with many other commentators – misses this element in *Lex, Rex* when she claims that in that book Rutherford moved from the 'rigorist' biblicism of his ecclesiological works to a 'laxist' casuistry which allowed him to justify rebellion against the king despite biblical texts to the contrary.[53] The latter is certainly prominent in *Lex, Rex*, but so is the former. Rutherford insisted on the binding authority of the Old Testament teaching that the magistrates of a covenanted nation must not permit the slightest deviation from the true religion, a religion whose parameters had now been precisely laid out in the New Testament. In the specific case of the Covenanters' war against Charles I, both secular constitutionalist arguments (drawn from reason but supported by Scripture) and Protestant covenant arguments (drawn from Scripture alone) pointed towards the same conclusion – the cause of the Covenanters was just. *Lex, Rex* was intended to demonstrate that both nature and grace corroborated the Covenanters' position.

---

as a body politick, he gave sundry judicial laws, which expired together with the state of that people, not obliging any other now, further than the general equity thereof may require.' *Westminster Confession*, XIX. iv. On the position of the Westminster Assembly, see S. Ferguson, 'An Assembly of theonomists? The teaching of the Westminster divines on the law of God', in W. S. Barker and W. R. Godfrey, eds., *Theonomy: A Reformed critique* (Grand Rapids, Mich., 1989), pp. 315–49.

51 This had been true for John Knox too. See R. Kyle, 'John Knox: a man of the Old Testament', *Westminster Theological Journal*, 54 (1992), 65–78.

52 M. Walzer, *Exodus and Revolution* (New York, 1985), p. 123. Intriguingly, Honyman argued against the Presbyterians' tendency to regard the Israelite experience as normative. Their customs suited them but not necessarily other nations, he suggested, and Christians should not 'force the particular example of that Nation [Israel] on all Nations . . . least we judaize too much'. *Survey of Naphtali*, pp. 96–7. This was probably part of the reason why both Mackenzie and Maxwell called the Presbyterian leaders 'Rabies' (see Maxwell, *Sacrosancta*, p. 16 and Mackenzie, *Jus Regium*, p. 98). Rutherford, of course, denied the charges that he was judaising, *Survey of Hooker*, pp. 480–2.

53 M. Sampson, 'Laxity and liberty in seventeenth-century English political thought', in E. Leites, ed., *Conscience and Casuistry in Early Modern Europe* (Cambridge, 1988), pp. 100n. and 110.

THE ORIGINS OF GOVERNMENT

Rutherford began the book with arguments about the origins of government, drawn largely from natural reason.[54] He devoted considerable attention to the subject because it had been the major focus of Maxwell's *Sacro-Sancta*. Maxwell had written that his targets were the Jesuits and Puritans, who, by arguing that supreme power originally and radically is seated in the people, made kings 'derivatives' of the people, and accountable to them, so that if kings failed in their duty they could be deposed. Maxwell pointed out that this heresy could be traced back through sixteenth-century writers like Goodman, Bouchier and Hotman to the conciliarists, Ockham, Gerson and Almain. The Puritans – whom Maxwell called 'our Rabies' – drew from these 'polluted cisterns'. Against them he argued that although men might designate individuals to the kingship, it was God who directly applied sovereign authority to the king. From this account of the origins of government, Maxwell concluded that divine prerogatives were inherent in the king and untransferable to the people, and that resistance by force of arms was always unlawful.

Rutherford's response to this was to reassert the radical scholastic theory that royal power was derived from the community. In doing so he was using what Johann Sommerville calls 'the leading mode of anti-absolutist argument current in Europe' since the late sixteenth century.[55] Richard Tuck has pointed out that, when compared with the strikingly original work of writers influenced by scepticism and *raison d'état* theory, the constitutionalist theorists of the seventeenth century added little to the work of their sixteenth-century predecessors.[56] We shall see that this was largely true with regard to Rutherford. He said little that had not been said before by the conciliarists, the Spanish Thomists and earlier Calvinist writers. However, he integrated their arguments in a unique manner, providing an unusually comprehensive statement of Calvinist political thought, and at times taking up more radical positions than were normal within the constitutionalist tradition.

The scholastics had claimed that all men were born free from subjection to magistrates, and Rutherford agreed. 'Every man by nature is a freeman born, that is, by nature no man cometh out of the womb under any civil

---

[54] The fullest treatment of these arguments is that of Ford, '*Lex, rex iusto posita*'.

[55] Sommerville, *Politics and Ideology in England*, p. 59. Chapter 2 of Sommerville's book provides a succinct summary of this mode of argument. The definitive account is to be found in Quentin Skinner's magisterial *The Foundations of Modern Political Thought, Volume II: The Reformation* (Cambridge, 1978). See also J. H. Burns and M. Goldie, eds., *The Cambridge History of Political Thought, 1450–1700* (Cambridge, 1991), chs. 5–9.

[56] R. Tuck, *Philosophy and Government, 1572–1651* (Cambridge, 1993), p. xii.

subjection to king, prince or judge.'[57] The corollary of this was that 'no man bringeth out of the womb with him a sceptre, and a crown upon his head'.[58] Captured in an aphorism, the plain truth was that 'King and beggar spring of one clay'.[59]

Rutherford balanced this with the Aristotelian idea that man was 'a social creature, and one who inclineth to be governed by man'. Since this was so, and since God and nature 'intendeth the policy and peace of mankind', it followed that mankind had been given 'a power to compass this end; and this must be a power of government'.[60] But how did this square with the claim that men were born free from subjection to magistrates? Rutherford explained at the beginning of Question II. 'As domestic society is by nature's instinct, so is civil society natural *in radice*, in the root, and voluntary *in modo*, in the manner of coalescing.'[61] This twofold distinction lay at the root of Rutherford's theory of the origins of government, and we need to examine it in detail.

By domestic society Rutherford meant the authority of fathers and husbands over their children and wives. This he believed to be a given, a primary law of nature. He did not accept Buchanan's Ciceronian picture of natural men living 'a wandering and solitary life' in huts and caves. Instead, he followed the more conventional Aristotelian portrayal of man's natural state as being one of community life under the heads of families. Yet this patriarchal authority was of an entirely different order to the authority of magistrates. Rutherford firmly repudiated the patriarchalist claim that kingly power originally derived from the power of fathers.[62] Apart from submission to fathers and husbands, Rutherford wrote, 'I conceive all jurisdiction over man to be as it were artificial and positive'.[63]

Yet not wholly artificial. Civil society was 'natural *in radice*, in the root, and voluntary *in modo*, in the manner of coalescing'. Rutherford attempted to clarify this throughout the early chapters of *Lex, Rex* by using a series of scholastic distinctions. He explained that the office of government (the 'powers' of Romans 13) was natural, but that the particular person who held the office and the form of government (monarchy, aristocracy, democracy) were appointed by the voluntary choice of the people.[64] The people naturally (and necessarily) held a power of government, a 'virtual' power, Rutherford called it; but they voluntarily chose to activate or formalise that power by creating magistrates who had the power to

[57] *Lex, Rex*, p. 91 [51].   [58] *Lex, Rex*, p. 75 [42]. See also pp. 10, 72 [6, 52].
[59] *Lex, Rex*, p. 3 [2].   [60] *Lex, Rex*, pp. 1–2 [1].
[61] *Lex, Rex*, p. 1 [2]. See also p. 93 [52]. Rutherford's employment of countless fine distinctions makes his argument very difficult to follow.
[62] *Lex, Rex*, Question XV.   [63] *Lex, Rex*, p. 3 [2].
[64] *Lex, Rex*, pp. 8, 53–4 [5, 31].

govern.[65] The people held sovereignty in the abstract but they used it to set up a concrete sovereign.[66]

Rutherford further clarified the point by showing that whilst natural instinct inclined men towards government (and towards subjection to fathers), it did not incline them to government by magistrates. The reason for this was obvious: 'no man, by the instinct of nature, giveth consent to penal laws as penal'. The natural instinct towards self-preservation caused men to shy away from establishing magistrates with the power to punish lawbreakers. The logic of magistrates was not seen by nature, but by 'reason in cold blood', which led man to submit to civil penalties by showing him the greater dangers of a state of anarchy. The analogy Rutherford used to illustrate this was that of a drastic medical operation; natural instinct led men to resist the amputation of a member of their body, but 'reason in cold blood' showed them that it was necessary if their lives were to be saved.[67]

The fundamental distinction between political society as 'natural *in radice* and voluntary *in modo*' was also to be seen as a distinction between the pre- and post-lapsarian states of man. Whereas the desire to preserve ourselves was 'a consequent of unbroken and sinless nature', the idea that we should devolve our power over into the hands of magistrates was a result of the Fall: 'if there had not been sin, there should not have been need of a king, more than there should have been need of . . . a physician to cure sickness where there is health . . . but because sin is entered into the world, God devised, as a remedy of violence and injustice, a living, rational, breathing law, called a king, a judge, a father'.[68] Indeed, after the Fall, 'it is not in men's free will that they have government or no government, because it is not in their free will to obey or not to obey the acts of the court of nature, which is God's court; and this court enacteth that societies suffer not mankind to perish, which must necessarily follow if they appoint no government'.[69]

---

[65] *Lex, Rex*, p. 50 [29].   [66] *Lex, Rex*, p. 156 [86].

[67] *Lex, Rex*, p. 4 [2]. R. Tuck, 'Power and authority in seventeenth century England', *Historical Journal*, 17 (1974), 43–61, argues that this demonstrates that radical Calvinists like Rutherford believed that the magistrate's authority depended on the consent of the individual citizen to each magisterial action. However, although we shall find such emphases elsewhere in *Lex, Rex*, Tuck is probably reading too much into this particular passage. Rutherford was not discussing the question of whether it is the individual or the body of the people as a whole that consents to the magistrate's every act or just to his tenure in office; when he did discuss it he generally took a more conservative line than Tuck suggests here. Rather, he was trying to illustrate a point he had found in Ferdinand Vasquez, that whilst the desire for government was part of the law of nature, the establishment of government *by magistrates* 'hath its rise from a positive and secondary law of nations, and not from the law of pure nature' (*Lex, Rex*, pp. 3, 92 [2, 52]).

[68] *Lex, Rex*, p. 213 [116].   [69] *Lex, Rex*, p. 8 [5]. See also p. 124 [69].

Despite writing this, Rutherford suggested elsewhere that mankind continued to live in familial groups for some time after the Fall. In this period, each family had its own government, but associations of families were without government. However, because of 'the numerous multiplication of mankind', the heads of families 'agreed to make either a king, or other governors, a head, or heads, over themselves'.[70] Kingly authority could only be dated to the biblical Nimrod (Genesis 10) who corresponded to the figure whom pagan historians called Belus, the father of Ninus who built Babylon.[71] (Classical histories and biblical narrative, like nature and grace, harmonised sweetly.)

At times, as Tuck has noted, Rutherford seems to explain the original establishment of government in terms of natural-rights theory. He wrote, for instance, that 'we defend ourselves by devolving our power over in the hands of one or more rulers', and that men 'put this power of warding off violence in the hands of one or more rulers'.[72] This might suggest that the *dominium* of the ruler was constituted by a transfer by individuals of their own natural rights of *dominium*. However, Rutherford explicitly distanced himself from this view. He agreed with Maxwell that individuals did not 'have in them formally any ray of royalty or magistratical authority', and argued that 'individual persons, in creating a magistrate, doth not properly surrender their right', since a power to do violence was not a right or a liberty, but 'servitude and bondage'.[73]

Magistrates were not, therefore, established by the transfer of individual rights, but through the use of the God-given power of government, which resided in the community. This power could only be found in men 'united in society',[74] in a 'joint political body'.[75] It did not belong to individuals. In response to Maxwell's jibe that Puritans made kings to be the derivatives of the irrational commonalty, Rutherford declared that 'We make not the multitude, but the three estates, including the nobles and gentry, to be as rational creatures', the source of royal authority.[76] To support this he pointed to the paradigmatic example of ancient Israel; though not one single man in Israel had political authority, 'yet it followeth not that Israel, parliamentarily convened' had not the authority to make Saul or David

---

[70] *Lex, Rex*, pp. 47–8, 93, 239 [27–8, 52, 130]. Rutherford was probably wavering between the accounts of the origins of government given by his principal sources: the Ockhamist pessimism of the Sorbonnists led them to see government as a result of the Fall, whilst the Thomist optimism of the Spanish suggested a rather less cataclysmic explanation. See Skinner, *Foundations*, II, pp. 116, 118 and 158.

[71] This fitted neatly with Rutherford's case. Nimrod was a notorious symbol of tyranny in seventeenth-century political literature. See C. Hill, *The English Bible and the Seventeenth Century Revolution*, pp. 217–22.

[72] *Lex, Rex*, pp. 2 [2] and 10 [6].   [73] *Lex, Rex*, pp. 43–4 [25].

[74] *Lex, Rex*, p. 10 [6].   [75] *Lex, Rex*, p. 44 [25].   [76] *Lex, Rex*, p. 38 [22].

king.[77] By stressing that it was the community rather than individuals who set up kings, Rutherford showed that the scholastic theory of the origins of government need not give authority to those whom Maxwell called the irrational multitude. This rejection of natural-rights theories and the concurrent stress on the community made Rutherford a much less populist and individualistic theorist than John Locke.

Besides demonstrating the origins of government in popular consent, Rutherford was deeply concerned to emphasise what Tuck calls 'the divine, non-natural character of political association'.[78] In Question I, he argued that 'the power of government in general' or 'civil power . . . in its root' was from God. He supported it first by appeal to Scriptures such as Romans 13 ('the powers that be are ordained of God') and I Peter 2 ('Submit yourselves to every ordinance of man').[79] He adamantly maintained that affirming the people's role in establishing governments did not rule out God's involvement. The distinction between government *in radice* and government *in modo* enabled him to do this; government *in radice* was instituted immediately by God, he explained, whilst government *in modo* was voluntarily constituted by the people. Yet this did not mean that God was uninvolved in the constitution of governments; he might not set them up immediately, but he was working mediately through the people.[80] God 'moveth and boweth the wills of a great multitude to promote such a man, who, by nature, cometh no more out of the womb a crowned king, than the poorest shepherd in the land'.[81] In this 'coronation covenant', God was acting through the free choice of the people. 'Here both the free gift of God, and the free consent of the people intervene.' God had freely given the kingly office by creating man with a natural inclination towards government, but

---

[77] *Lex, Rex*, p. 43 [25].

[78] Tuck, *Natural Rights Theories*, p. 144. Actually, 'non-artificial' would be better than 'non-natural', since Rutherford does see political association, *in radice*, as natural; he just thinks that none can deny 'the law of nature to be a divine law', since it was God who created human nature with an inclination towards government.

[79] *Lex, Rex*, pp. 1–2 [1].

[80] *Lex, Rex*, p. 5 [3]. Maxwell, Rutherford gleefully noticed, seemed to have an Antinomian view of how God operated; by arguing that God 'doth immediately create this man a king' the bishop seemed to be ignoring the way that God constantly used human means to accomplish his purposes. Although it was true that 'God in creation is the immediate author of all things', it was equally true that 'in the works of providence, for the most part in ordinary, God worketh by means'. In conversion, for instance, God worked supernaturally but also through the natural means of the human understanding and will. Maxwell, however, seemed to agree with the Anabaptist enthusiasts that man was still living in the biblical age of miracles where God did everything by 'extraordinary revelations'. Rutherford's accusations that Maxwell had an Antinomian political theology can be found at pp. 17, 21, 30–40, 57, 226 [10, 12, 17–23, 33, 123].

[81] *Lex, Rex*, p. 57 [33].

he now, 'by the intervening consent of the people, maketh David a king and not Eliab'.[82]

The fact that God immediately instituted and mediately constituted government underlined the God-given dignity of political office. The king, Rutherford declared, was not only created in the image of God as were other men, but he also reflected the glory of God's authority when he ruled: 'he hath a political resemblance of the King of heavens, being a little god, and so is above any one man'.[83] Yet this stress on the God-given dignity of royalty restrained the person of the king as much as it exalted his office. He was to rule in accordance with the commands of 'the King of heavens', otherwise he ceased to be 'a little god' and became a tyrant.

Rutherford's account of the origins of government, therefore, cautiously balanced divine sovereignty and human activity. On the one hand he avoided a natural-rights theory which would have suggested that the rule of magistrates was an artificial creation of human wills. He was concerned to emphasise that kings derived their authority – albeit indirectly – from God, who had created their office and expected them to obey his commands. On the other hand, he insisted that the immediate source of the king's power was popular consent. In this way, *Lex, Rex* steered between the conservative divine right of kings theory supported by Maxwell, and the radically individualistic theory which was to be promoted by Locke.

THE COVENANT

The precise mechanism by which governments were founded, Rutherford believed, was a covenant between king and people.[84] The accounts of Saul's coronation at Mizpah (I Samuel 10) and David's at Hebron (II Samuel 5 and I Chronicles 11) demonstrated that all legitimate royal government was grounded in a covenant between king and people.[85] This concept of the

---

[82] *Lex, Rex*, p. 67 [38]. Maxwell failed to understand this, Rutherford suggested, because being an Arminian he could not see that God was 'the first, eminent, principal, and efficacious pre-determinator of the creature' and its actions. *Lex, Rex*, p. 31 [18]. Any good Calvinist, Rutherford implied, would understand how God was at work even in the 'free consent' of the people.

[83] *Lex, Rex*, p. 139 [77].

[84] The origins of the Scottish covenant concept have been much discussed. Historians have pointed to several sources of the idea: the Scottish custom of 'banding' (signing agreements) for political, economic or religious purposes; the medieval notion of a contract of government; and the covenant theology which became popular in Scotland from the late sixteenth century. See D. Stevenson, *The Covenanters* (Edinburgh, 1988), pp. 28–34; and J. B. Torrance, 'The covenant concept in Scottish theology and politics and its legacy', *Scottish Journal of Theology*, 34 (1981), 232–8.

[85] *Lex, Rex*, p. 96 [54]. Honyman took exception to Rutherford's use of these texts to support the idea of a covenant that gave the people power to overthrow the king. The people did not swear: 'We shall obey you and be subject to you, if you rule us rightly; otherwise we will

covenant, which Rutherford defended in Question XIV, was of central importance in *Lex, Rex,* and to Calvinist political thought generally. It both set limits on the king's power and provided the basis for resistance to it. When the people transferred their virtual power of government to the king, thereby giving him a formal or active power of governing, 'they measure out, by ounce weights, so much royal power, and no more and no less. So as they may limit, moderate and set banks and marches to the exercise'. They gave it out 'upon this and that condition, that they may take again to themselves what they gave out upon this condition if the condition be violated'.[86] Moreover, they only resigned the power of executing laws, and they retained the 'fountain-power' of royalty, a power that they could use if the king became tyrannical.[87]

The covenant, however, was not merely civil but also religious. Rutherford wrote that the king 'is made by God and the people king, for the church and people of God's sake, that he may defend true religion for the salvation of all'.[88] Thus, religious obligations were welded onto the original secular obligations of the covenant. Charles I, as king of a Protestant nation, had a duty to preserve the Protestant constitution as well as to ensure the peace and safety of his people. The people made a man a king 'covenant-wise and conditionally, so he rule according to God's law, and the people resigning their power to him for their safety, and for a peaceable and godly life under him, and not to destroy them, and tyrannise over them'.[89] This double-barrelled covenant fused Knox's concern for true religion with Buchanan's more secular natural-law arguments.[90]

Rutherford was aware of the royalist objection that the covenant was all a convenient fiction, that no original covenant between the people and the king existed. His reply was that even if Scotland and England could not 'produce a written authentic covenant betwixt the first king and their

---

not, but use our co-active power upon you, to dethrone and destroy you and punish you.' *Survey of Naphtali,* pp. 93–7.

[86] *Lex, Rex,* p. 10 [6].

[87] *Lex, Rex,* p. 148–9 [82]. It could be that Rutherford was parting company with the Spanish Thomists at this point, and following the lead of the radical scholastics like Almain and the other conciliarists. Many writers, including Skinner, Tuck, Gough and Hamilton see Suarez and the other Spanish writers as arguing that the people alienate their authority to the king when they set up government, and can never reclaim it. However, Johann Sommerville has suggested that Suarez allows for the resistance of the original community whenever the ruler breaks the terms of the original contract. See Sommerville, 'From Suarez to Filmer: a reappraisal', *Historical Journal,* 25 (1982), 525–40. If so, Rutherford is siding with the majority opinion of his day and only taking issue with British patriarchalism advocated by James I and Maxwell.

[88] *Lex, Rex,* p. 100 [56].   [89] *Lex, Rex,* pp. 102–3 [57].

[90] On Knox and Buchanan see R. Mason, 'Covenant and commonweal: the language of politics in Reformation Scotland', in N. MacDougall, ed., *Church, Politics and Society: Scotland 1408–1929* (Edinburgh, 1983), pp. 97–126.

people', its factuality could still be demonstrated by appeal to three sources. First, natural-law principles showed that all government was founded on 'the general covenant of nature'. Secondly, the Old Testament laid down an immutable pattern for all Christian kings, and clearly taught that they should rule by covenant. In particular, Deuteronomy 17 – a passage to which Rutherford appealed again and again – described the definitive prototype (or 'first mould' as Rutherford put it) of the godly king ruling according to the divine law. Thirdly, 'the standing law and practice of many hundred acts of parliament, is equivalent to a written covenant'.[91] So natural law, Scripture and history all combined to prove that government must rest on a covenant between king and people.

Lex, Rex focused almost exclusively on this horizontal covenant between king and people. Charles I, it argued, had given his people just cause to resist him by violating both the secular and the religious principles of the Scottish constitution. But the Calvinist tradition had also commonly thought in terms of a vertical covenant or transcendent relationship between nations and God. The famous Huguenot tract, *Vindiciae Contra Tyrannos* (1579), for example, had argued that in the Old Testament 'there was a twofold covenant at the inauguration of kings: the first between the king and the people to the effect that the people should be the people of God; the second between king and people that while he commanded well he would be obeyed well'.[92] The first covenant radically altered the way in which the second covenant was to be understood. A nation that had made a covenant with God had placed itself in the same situation as Old Testament Israel, and this meant that for the king to 'command well' his commands had always to be in accord with the true religion. A king whose commands were damaging to the true religion was a king who had broken the covenant with God and the people, and thus given due cause for resistance to his rule.[93]

There can be no doubt that *Lex, Rex* – with its numerous references to Old Testament Israel – presupposed such a notion. In his letters, Rutherford frequently spoke of Scotland's covenant with the Lord. Yet the concept was a problematic one. Whilst it is often asserted that covenant theology inspired the idea of a national covenant, the precise relationship between the two is usually left vague.[94] The widespread popularity of federal

---

[91] *Lex, Rex*, pp. 106–7 [59].

[92] Stephanus Junius Brutus,*Vindiciae, Contra Tyrannos*, ed. G. Garnett (Cambridge, 1994), p. 21.

[93] None of this was 'incompatible' with the scholastic definition of the origins and purpose of government, as Skinner, *Foundations*, II, p. 325, asserts. The two covenants were complementary, the second being grafted on to the first when a nation converted to the worship of the true God. Yet in practice, as we shall see, they tended to come into conflict.

[94] This is true of the articles by G. D. Henderson, 'The Covenanters', in *Religious Life in Seventeenth-century Scotland* (Cambridge, 1937), ch. 8; 'The idea of the covenant in

theology obviously made it natural to think in terms of covenant relationships with God, but how did theologians move from the theological idea of
covenant to the political concept? How did they move from the covenant of
grace, which was made only with the elect, to the national covenant, which
was made with a whole people, both elect and reprobate? The radical
Puritan, Roger Williams, spotted the difficulty here. In the 1640s he poured
scorn on the Scottish idea of 'a Nationall holy Covenant'. 'Where find you',
he asked, 'evidence of a whole Nation or Kingdome converted to the Faith,
and of Christs appointing of a whole Nation or Kingdome to walk in one
way of Religion?' The whole concept was absurd, he thought, because those
who were 'visibly in a state of nature, dead in sinne, in a state of enmitie and
opposition against God', could never 'please God, be visibly maried to God,
fight for him under the Banners of Love'.[95]

The Covenanter leadership was certainly aware of this difficulty. As John
Ford has pointed out, the National Covenant itself urged subscribers to
renew their personal covenants with God. In 1640 Rutherford was
lamenting the fact that many who had signed the Covenant were not 'heart-
covenanters'; they were parties to the National Covenant but not to the
covenant of grace made with the elect.[96] Ford argues from this that 'what
mattered [to the Covenanter clergy] was not so much that subscribers
belonged to a godly nation as that the nation could be godly because elect
and covenanted people belonged to it'. He also claims that because the
Covenanters were concerned to re-establish God-given laws which had been
undermined by the ceremonial innovations, the Covenant 'had less to do
with asserting the particular heritage and destiny of the Scottish church and
nation than with retying the bonds of the universal law of God'.[97]

This account, however, fails to do justice to the theology of national
covenanting held by men like Rutherford. These godly Covenanters were
undoubtedly convinced of the *particular* importance of the elect, and of the
central place of the *universal* law of God, but they also had a clearly
worked out concept of the covenanted nation, which historians have so far

---

Scotland', in *The Burning Bush* (Edinburgh, 1957), ch. 4; S. A. Burrell, 'The covenant idea
as a revolutionary symbol: Scotland, 1596–1637', *Church History*, 27 (1958), 338–49; and
M. Steele, 'The "Politick Christian": the theological background to the National Covenant',
in J. S. Morrill, ed., *The Scottish National Covenant in its British Context, 1618–51*
(Edinburgh, 1990), pp. 46–50.

[95] Roger Williams, *Queries of the Highest Consideration* (London, 1644), pp. 24, 22.

[96] *Quaint Sermons*, pp. 61, 92–3.

[97] J. Ford, 'The lawful bonds of Scottish society: the Five Articles of Perth, the Negative
Confession and the National Covenant', *Historical Journal*, 37 (1994), 63–4. Similarly, in
his '*Lex, rex iusto posita*', p. 288, Ford claims that 'the point [about the covenanted nation]
was not so much that the Scots had been singled out for special favour as that they were
exemplifying a universal process'.

overlooked.[98] This concept was intimately connected to the justification of infant baptism provided by Reformed theologians, and it was fully expounded by Rutherford in three separate passages in his books.[99] Rutherford explained that Reformed theologians made a sharp distinction between national covenants and the covenant of grace. The covenant of grace, he argued, was a personal or 'internal' covenant. Those who were party to this covenant were the elect, the members of the invisible church. By contrast, national covenants were 'federal' or 'external', and included every baptised member of the visible national church. Just as God had shown mercy to a thousand generations of Abraham's descendants, and included them in the covenant their forefather had made, so he accepted infants into an external covenant with himself; even though they had no 'personal' holiness, they were partakers of a 'federal' holiness derived from their parents or godly forefathers. The National Covenant of 1638, therefore, was nothing new. Along with the 'covenants' of 1560, 1581, 1590 and 1596, it simply mended the 'external' covenant relationship between God and the nation which was first established at the time of Scotland's conversion to Christianity but had been repeatedly broken by apostasy.[100]

In response to the charge of Williams and other sectarians, that there was no trace of such national covenants or national churches in the New Testament, Rutherford maintained that the Old Testament had prophesied the existence of national churches in the new dispensation,[101] and that this made the Jewish practice of national covenanting part of the moral rather than the judicial law, and so perpetually binding on the church. So although

---

[98] The one partial exception is J. B. Torrance, 'Covenant or contract? A study of the theological background of worship in seventeenth-century Scotland', *Scottish Journal of Theology*, 23 (1970), 70. Torrance recognises that to understand the idea of the covenanted nation, one needs to grasp the distinction between the internal covenant to which the elect members of the invisible church are a party, and the external covenant to which all professors in the visible church belong. However, he mentions this only in passing, and David Stevenson misinterprets him as saying that Rutherford anticipated a fusion of the visible and invisible church in Scotland, 'The radical party in the kirk, 1637–45', *Journal of Ecclesiastical History*, 25 (1974), 140–2. This was not so; Rutherford never expected all Scots to be included in the covenant of grace and the invisible church. When he talked of a pure church, he meant a church pure in all its forms, not a church composed entirely of the elect.

[99] *Peaceable Plea*, pp. 164–83; *Covenant of Life*, pp. 72–117; *Survey of Hooker*, pp. 474–83.

[100] Rutherford's view of the history of the Scottish church since the nation's conversion is discussed below.

[101] He appealed to passages like Psalms 2, 72, 97 and 110, which were interpreted as prophecies of Christ's future reign over the nations and then argued from Revelation 11:15 that these prophecies were fulfilled in the era of the church: 'The kingdoms of this world are become the kingdoms of our Lord and of his Christ.' Radical sectarians, like Williams, would have argued that these prophecies would only be fulfilled at the second coming of Christ, and that Revelation was referring to that future day. The argument was ultimately an eschatological one.

Christian nations were not obliged to follow the Mosaic law, the Jewish state was in some respects still a model: 'what agrees to the Church of the Jews as a Religious society, to keep peace and Religion in purity, and to purge out offenders, and agreed to them in a moral, and no typical consideration, that agrees to us also'.[102]

This position had far-reaching consequences. As well as legitimating the idea of a national church and a national covenant, it provided the strongest argument for resistance to Charles I. As the king of a nation in covenant with God, Charles had been obliged to prosecute heresy and idolatry with the same zeal as Old Testament rulers. Yet he had done the opposite, encouraging Arminianism and popery. In doing so, he had not only violated Scotland's constitution, but had also severed the nation's covenant with the Lord, leaving it with no option but to renew the covenant and defend it against the king by force of arms. As Rutherford explained in 1658, in response to Thomas Hooker's misgivings over the legitimacy of national covenants under the New Testament, the Scottish imitation of Jewish precedent twenty years earlier had been wholly justified:

It is my prayer to God that our Brethren in New England, be not compelled to quit Christian Religion, as we in Scotland were thralled to embrace popery by the domineering power of the Prelates. And shall it be Judaisme for Protestant Nations to swear the like [covenant], if the man of sin should blow the trumpet, and raise all the Catholick Romans in Christendom, against the Lamb and his followers?[103]

The covenant, therefore, was of great significance, because it defined the purposes of government, purposes that the government of Charles I had hindered. As Glenn Burgess has pointed out, civil war broke out in Scotland and England not because of differences over the origins of government, but because of deeper disagreements over its purposes. Sommerville and Sanderson may have demonstrated a major rift between royalists and the parliamentarians over the origins of government (royalists arguing, like Maxwell, that the king's power came directly from God, and parliamentarians insisting, with Rutherford, that it derived from the people). But this rift over the efficient causes of government was less critical than that over its final causes.[104] What really motivated Rutherford was not his belief in the popular origins of royal authority but his passionate conviction that the king was obliged to defend true religion and purge the land of idolatry. As John Morrill has persuasively suggested, it was this passion rather than constitutionalist arguments that drove men to take up arms against the king.[105]

[102] *Survey of Hooker*, p. 477.   [103] *Survey of Hooker*, p. 480.
[104] G. Burgess, 'Revisionism, politics and political ideas in early Stuart England', *Historical Journal*, 34 (1992), 465–78.
[105] J. Morrill, *The Nature of the English Revolution* (London, 1993), chs. 2 and 3.

Andrew Honyman, recognising the immense destabilising potential of the notion of a religious covenant, was adamant in opposing the use of force against the king whenever his religious policy seemed unsatisfactory. God valued 'the keeping of humane societies in tolerable order' so much, he wrote, that 'he will not have the commonwealths, where justice between man and man is maintained for his glory, (although religion be not minded as it ought to be) casten loose'. The idea that the whole people, and not just the king, had a duty to ensure that the religious covenant was publicly maintained seemed to leave the commonwealth forever exposed to the danger of religious wars.[106] Rutherford, in contrast, had no time for such worldly considerations. In response to Maxwell's claim that 'the kingdom had peace and plenty in the prelates' time', he retorted: 'A belly-argument. We had plenty when we sacrificed to the queen of heaven.'[107] The Protestant covenant was to take precedence over the peace and order of the commonwealth.

THE NATURE OF GOOD GOVERNMENT

The terms of the dual covenant stipulated that the king's rule must be for the *salus populi*, the good of the people. 'The law hath one fundamental rule, *salus populi*', declared Rutherford. It was like 'the king of planets, the sun, which lendeth star-light to all laws, and by which they are exponed'.[108] This common good included both secular ends (justice, peace, safety, lives, liberties) and religious ends (the godly life, the salvation of souls). Rutherford's ecclesiological works defended at length the idea that whilst the church was primarily responsible for the religious ends and the civil magistrate for the secular, both institutions were to assist one another. The church had to denounce injustice, just as Elijah denounced King Ahab's seizure of Naboth's vineyard;[109] and the civil magistrate (Rutherford did not speak of the 'State') was obligated to aid the church by ensuring that she was well-financed and well staffed and by prosecuting heretics. We will deal with this in depth in Chapter 7, but it is important to remember here that in the polity Rutherford advocated, the church was an institution at least as influential in its own way as the civil power and the godly life was the chief end of national policy.

The king in Rutherford's ideal polity had severe constitutional limitations placed upon his authority. These were necessary because 'the goodness of the king, a sinful man, inclined from the womb to all sin, and so to tyranny, is no restraint'.[110] It was not enough to say with royalists that God's law

---

[106] [Honeyman] *Survey of Naphtali*, pp. 84–5.   [107] *Lex, Rex*, p. 432 [216].
[108] *Lex, Rex*, p. 252 [137].   [109] *Lex, Rex*, p. 175 [97].
[110] *Lex, Rex*, p. 215 [117].

was a 'moral restraint on kings'; there needed to be a restraint laid on him by 'man's law'.[111] Foremost amongst these was the stipulation, stated in his covenant with the people, that he must rule with the representatives of the original community, whom Rutherford called the 'states'. Famous nations had always had states, he assured his readers; among the Jews there were fathers of families and princes of tribes; among the Lacedaemonians the Ephori, amongst the Romans the senate, and in Scotland, England, France and Spain, parliaments. The king might be the head of the kingdom, but 'the states of the kingdom are as temples of the head'. The parliament was to be 'co-ordinate' with the king in making laws, but the king's authority was by derivation, whilst the estates – as the representatives of the community – were the original fountain of power, and thus superior to the king, as the effect was to the cause.[112] It was because the king 'doth improperly represent the people' that 'though the power for actual execution of laws be more in the king, yet a legislative power is more in the estates'.[113] Without the estates the king could do nothing, 'no more than a hand cut off from the body can write'. His authority was a 'royal power parliamentary'.[114]

The judiciary, those whom Rutherford called the 'inferior judges', were also to be independent of the king, even though they were originally created by him. They were answerable to God and not to the king. If God commanded inferior judges to execute his righteous judgement he did not say 'Respect not persons in judgement, except the king command you; crush not the poor, oppress not the fatherless, except the king command you.' The king had no right to stop an inferior judge executing judgement on a murderer. Judging was 'an act of conscience' and so the conscience of the inferior judge could not be deputy to that of the king.[115]

Rutherford's enthusiasm for the inferior judges was partly fired by a genuine passion for social justice. Without these judges, he argued, 'justice is physically impossible' in a kingdom. The king alone 'cannot minister justice to all'; he needed many judges to assist him. If judges did not live near the people, particularly the poor and the weak, they would be prey to violence and injustice. 'Justice should be at as easy a rate to the poor as a draught of water. Samuel went yearly through the land to Bethel, Gilgal, Mizpeh (I Samuel 7:16) and brought justice to the doors of the poor. So were our kings of Scotland obliged to do of old; but now justice is as dear as gold.'[116] Rutherford's private letters to noblemen urging them to help the

---

[111] *Lex, Rex*, pp. 181–2 [100].   [112] *Lex, Rex*, p. 210 [115].
[113] *Lex, Rex*, pp. 178–9 [99].   [114] *Lex, Rex*, p. 377 [186].
[115] *Lex, Rex*, p. 160 [88–9].
[116] *Lex, Rex*, pp. 171–2 [94–5]. Calvin also found support for the institution of circuit-judges in the books of Samuel. See Hopfl, *Christian Polity*, p. 182.

poor around them illustrate that this was not merely a convenient sentiment, but a real commitment.[117] He was equally enthusiastic about purging Scotland of idolatry and ensuring justice for the poor. The estates were to 'judge the cause of the poor' and 'crush the priests of Baal, and the idolatrous mass-prelates'.[118]

As well as insisting on judicial independence, Rutherford fiercely rejected the royal-command theory of law, which saw law as created by the command of the king. Only God's will and command could create law, he argued:

This is the difference between God's will and the will of the king, or any mortal creature. Things are good and just because God willeth them . . . and God doth not will things, because they are good and just; but the creature, be he king or any never so eminent, do will things, because they are good and just, and the kings willing of a thing maketh it not good and just.[119]

This argument was repeated several times in *Lex, Rex*, and it was one that John Lilburne later adopted in *The Freeman's Freedome Vindicated* (1646) and *Regall Tyrannie Discovered* (1647).[120] It occurred in the central section on the relationship between the king and the law (Questions XXII–XXVII). This section, which we might call 'Lex, rex', is really the heart of the book. Here Rutherford stated his theological voluntarism, his belief that law (that which defined good or evil) was constituted by the command of God. Since God's commands were clearly embedded in both natural law and Scripture, it followed that there was no need for the king to create law, since it already existed. 'There is intrinsecall worth in the law prior to the act of the will of lawgivers for which it meriteth to be enacted.' Positive law could be simply derived from entirely obvious principles of natural and divine law. The king merely 'putteth on it [the thing intrinsically lawful] this stamp of a politic law', adding the threat of punishment to 'a thing legally good in itself'.[121]

This contrasted sharply with James VI's understanding of human kingship. James also – as a good Calvinist – adopted the language of voluntarist theology, but he saw his own role as analogous to that of God. God had a

---

[117] *Letters*, p. 310.   [118] *Lex, Rex*, p. 175 [97].

[119] *Lex, Rex*, pp. 254–5 [138].

[120] See especially J. Lilburne, *The Freeman's Freedome Vindicated* (London, 1646), pp. 11–12. Theodore Pease, *The Leveller Movement: A Study in the History and Political Theory of the English Great Civil War* (London, 1916), p. 141 noted that the fundamental ideas in this passage 'are all to be traced to Rutherford', but he thought that the specific argument that God alone is sovereign reflected the theology of the Independents. Yet as we have seen, this argument too probably comes from *Lex, Rex*. According to Woodhouse, *Puritanism and Liberty*, p. [66], Rutherford forged 'in *Lex, Rex* almost every argument of revolution later to be employed by the Levellers'.

[121] *Lex, Rex*, pp. 207–8 [113–14]. This understanding of the nature of law applied to church ceremonies as much as to civil statutes, and as we shall see in Chapter 7, the Presbyterians used it to argue against the Articles of Perth.

potentia absoluta (an absolute power) by which he could do anything, but he chose to limit himself by his promise or covenant which explained his *potentia ordinata* (his ordained power). The king, argued James, is similar. In theory, he is absolute, but in practice he rules by established laws rather than by arbitrary will.[122] Thomas Hobbes also used the voluntarist language, but dropped James's emphasis on covenant, arguing that like the Almighty the earthly sovereign should rule by his own will and pleasure. To Rutherford this would have been blasphemous, for the king was a sinful man with a will as corrupt as that of anyone else. But Hobbes's point was that everyone else was as shortsighted as the king; no-one could penetrate the divine will. It was the height of presumption for anyone to think they knew God's will and then resist the king on the basis of this dubious knowledge – as the Scots and English Puritans had done in 1638 and 1642 – for God's commands were not as perspicuous as they imagined. When men realised this they would see that in order to have peace and freedom from bitter ideological conflict they must submit to the arbitrary will and commands of an earthly sovereign. They had to listen to the voice of law (the sovereign's voice) rather than the voice of Puritan preachers.[123]

Rutherford represented the two institutions that Hobbes hated most, the Puritan pulpit and the scholastic university. *Lex, Rex* fused the biblicism of the former and the natural-law theory of the latter and tried to show that both nature and grace were transparent. 'As the Scriptures in all fundamentals are clear, and expone themselves, and *actu primo* condemn heresies, so all laws of men in their fundamentals, which are the law of nature and nations, are clear.' The corollary of this was that 'Tyranny is more visible and intelligible than heresy and is soon discerned.' Moreover, it was the people who discerned tyranny, for they had 'a natural throne of policy in their conscience to give warning, and materially sentence against the king as a tyrant, and so by nature are to defend themselves'.[124] It was never right for the people to obey a law simply because the king had made it; they were obligated, in every instance, to discover if the command of a superior was in accordance with the will of God.[125] The king, therefore, was at the mercy of

---

[122] See F. Oakley, *Omnipotence, Covenant and Order: An Excursion in the History of Ideas from Abelard to Leibniz* (Ithaca, 1984), ch. 4.

[123] On Hobbes's voluntarist theology and its relation to his politics see M. Goldie, 'The reception of Hobbes', in Burns and Goldie, eds., *Cambridge History of Political Thought*, ch. 20; N. Malcolm, 'Thomas Hobbes and voluntarist theology', unpublished Ph.D. dissertation, University of Cambridge (1983). On the Hobbesian emphasis on ideological conflict see especially R. Tuck, *Hobbes* (Oxford, 1989), esp. pp. 51–66 and Hobbes's own complaint about the proliferation of biblical interpretations once the Scriptures were made generally available in *Behemoth, or the Long Parliament* in his *Complete Works*, ed. T. Molesworth, 11 vols. (1839–45), VI, pp. 190 ff.

[124] *Lex, Rex*, p. 214 [117].

[125] See *Due Right*, pp. 42–5. Although this would appear to give the individual conscience

the people and the '*conscientia humani generis*, the natural conscience of all men', for this was 'the last rule on earth for exponing of laws'.[126]

So what power was the king left with? Rutherford denied that he had turned the king into a mere 'delegate'; the people had 'irrevocably made over to the king their power of governing, defending, and protecting themselves', and in the executive power of the law, the king 'is really sovereign above the people'. However, considering that the legislative and judicial functions of government were in the hands of the estates and the inferior judges, this could be little comfort to the king. Rutherford, like Buchanan before him, seems to render monarchical government wholly ineffective by making the king an enforcer of laws that he himself had not created and had no power to interpret. Maxwell's jibe that if the parliamentarians were right, 'the king is in a poor case', had not really been answered.[127] Indeed, Rutherford confirmed Maxwell's suspicion by stating that 'the duke of Venice, to me, cometh nearest to the king moulded by God (Deuteronomy 17) in respect of power, *de jure*, of any king I know in Europe'.[128]

Furthermore, Rutherford took a strikingly agnostic stance over whether monarchy was even the best form of government. 'Nothing more unwillingly do I write than one word of this question', he confessed when he came to deal with the issue in Question XXXVIII. 'It is a dark way; circumstance in fallen nature may make things best to be, *hic et nunc*, evil, though to me it is probable, that monarchy in itself, monarchy *de jure*, that is, lawful and limited monarchy is best, even now, in a kingdom, under the fall of sin, if other circumstances be considered.'[129] Aristocracy was in fact the most natural form of government, growing out of fatherly government, and Rutherford was quick to defend its legitimacy with reference to the

---

great authority, we shall see in Chapter 7 that Rutherford's emphasis on a properly educated conscience actually placed the authority in the hands of the experts – like himself – who could discern the will of God. He was unremittingly hostile to those who demanded 'liberty of conscience'.

[126] *Lex, Rex*, Question XXVII, esp, p. 252 [137]. This would seem to constitute strong evidence for Tuck's claim – in his 'Power and authority' – that 'a significantly new political theory' was devised in the mid-1640s by men like Hunton and Rutherford. Whereas sixteenth-century Calvinist resistance theorists had argued that the body of the people as a whole had the right to assent or dissent from the magistrates' continued tenure in office, the new radicals seemed to be arguing that the magistrates' authority depended on the consent of the individual citizen to each magisterial action. This was clearly a much more individualistic theory than the earlier one, and Tuck suggests that it may have influenced Locke, who possessed copies of Hunton and Lawson. Ultimately, however, as Ford points out, 'In exhorting people to follow their own consciences the Presbyterians were in reality exhorting them to follow the guidance of the casuists who had the expertise to discern the determinations of divine providence' ('Lawful bonds', p. 62).

[127] *Lex, Rex*, p. 417 [208].   [128] *Lex, Rex*, p. 259 [140].

[129] *Lex, Rex*, p. 384 [190]. See also p. 67 [38].

Netherlands and Venice. His interest in doing so obviously arose from the fact that Scotland in 1644 was under an aristocratic form of rule. But he believed that God used the 'aptitude and temper' of each commonwealth 'to determine the wills and liberty of people to pitch upon' the right form of government for them, just as he guided people into either single or married life, though both were lawful ordinances.[130] But if, after a monarchy was chosen, the king degenerated into tyranny, 'we think the people have liberty to change monarchy to aristocracy'.[131] Ultimately, however, Rutherford favoured the Aristotelian option of 'a limited and mixed monarchy' in which parliaments ruled with the king. This combined the glory, order and unity of monarchy; the counsel, stability and strength of aristocracy; and the liberty, privileges, and promptitude of obedience found in democracies.[132]

The same hesitancy and lack of enthusiasm characterised Rutherford's views on hereditary succession in Questions X and XI. The 'first king of divine institution' (Deuteronomy 17) – who must necessarily be 'the rule, pattern, and measure of all the rest of kings' – was a king by election, not succession.[133] What gave a man the throne was not immediate designation by God, or conquest, or 'naked birth', but the people's election. For this reason 'no nation can bind their conscience, and the conscience of posterity, either to one royal line, or irrevocably to monarchy'.[134] They remained free to choose the best man for the job. But again Rutherford eventually held to the conservative Aristotelian position: 'the succession of kings by birth with good limitations' was the form of government most likely to ensure peace and prevent 'bloody tumults, which are the bane of human societies'.[135]

Still, Rutherford's half-hearted endorsement of monarchy and primogeniture must have enhanced the radical reputation of *Lex, Rex*. When the treatise was republished in 1648 is was significantly retitled, *The Pre-eminence of the Election of Kings*. The 1683 decree of the University of Oxford against 'Certaine pernicious books' included *Lex, Rex*, partly because it was seen to have argued that 'Birthright and proximity of blood give no title to rule or government, and it is lawful to preclude the next heir from his right of succession to the crown' (for obvious reasons a sensitive point in the 1680s).[136] If Charles I or those around him ever read *Lex, Rex*, its scepticism about hereditary monarchy must have worried them almost as much as its godly fury at idolatry.

---

[130] *Lex, Rex*, p. 8 [5] and p. 44 [25].   [131] *Lex, Rex*, p. 417 [208].
[132] *Lex, Rex*, p. 387 [192].   [133] *Lex, Rex*, p. 68 [39].
[134] *Lex, Rex*, p. 78 [44].   [135] *Lex, Rex*, p. 79 [45].
[136] Printed in Wootton, *Divine Right and Democracy*, pp. 120–6.

THE DUTY OF RESISTANCE

As we have already noted, Rutherford devoted about one-fifth of his book to the justification of 'defensive wars' (Questions XXVIII–XXXVII). The basic argument was taken from natural-law theory: 'God hath implanted in every creature natural inclinations and motions to preserve itself', and nature's law taught us to love ourselves 'more than our neighbour', for it said 'Thou shalt love thy neighbour as thyself'. Nature also guided men to the means of self-defence. The first means was the use of supplications and apologies, the second flight, and the third violence. 'Nature hath appointed innocent and offending violence, against unjust violence, as a means of self-preservation', Rutherford asserted. If I am attacked, and supplications and flight are of no use, my obligation is clear; because natural law tells me to love 'my own temporal life more than the life of any other . . . I am rather to kill than to be killed, the exigence of necessity so requiring'.[137]

The lawfulness of violent resistance to a tyrant was also confirmed by Roman law, a source to which Rutherford occasionally appealed throughout *Lex, Rex*. He quoted the famous phrase from Justinian's *Digest*, *Quia licet vim vi repellere* – it is justifiable to repel unjust force with force. This, suggested Rutherford, demonstrated that 'A tyrant, without title, may be resisted by a private man'.[138] This was doubtful, since the maxim was only intended to relate to private-law, but it had a long pedigree as a political argument, being employed by medieval canonists and conciliarists and then adopted by Lutheran and Calvinist theologians.[139]

The problem with these secular arguments, however, was that they seemed to conflict with the Scriptural doctrine of passive obedience. Aware of this, Rutherford devoted much of this section to the New Testament teaching. In Questions XXIX and XXXIII, he tackled Paul's admonition to be subject to the higher powers found in Romans 13. He argued that it must be interpreted by means of the distinction between the king *in abstracto*, the king 'as a king', and the king *in concreto*, the king 'as a man'. The 'higher powers' to which Christians must be subject referred to 'the power and office of the magistrate *in abstracto*, or, which is all one, to the person using the power lawfully'. The text was not urging subjection 'to the abused and tyrannical power of the king'. The magistrates of whom Paul spoke were a terror to evil-doers, not to good Protestant subjects!

---

[137] *Lex, Rex*, pp. 331–2 [162]. In one of the occasional flashes of sarcastic humour that light up *Lex, Rex*, Rutherford wrote, 'If the king send an Irish rebel to cast me over a bridge, and drown me in a water . . . nature and the law of self-defence warranteth me (if I know certainly his aim), to horse him first over the bridge, and then consult how to defend myself at my own leisure'. *Lex, Rex*, p. 338 [165].

[138] *Lex, Rex*, p. 260 [141]. See also p. 58 [33].

[139] See Skinner, *Foundations*, II, pp. 125–6, 197–204, 217–24.

Such an exegesis of Romans 13, however, hardly squared with the example set by Christ and the early Christian martyrs. But Rutherford was never without an answer. He called Christ's passive obedience 'this one merely extraordinary and rare example of Christ'. Christ had 'a very special commandment imposed on him by his Father' to lay down his life, and his case could not be regarded as normative. It was true that Christians were commanded to imitate Christ by patient suffering, but this command was written for those who had only two choices, suffering for their faith or denying Christ. When there was a third – defensive wars – it did not apply.[140] In Question XXXV, Rutherford worked hard to defuse the witness of the Fathers, Irenaeus, Tertullian and Cyprian. It was not an altogether convincing exercise, and Rutherford, knowing that he could not win was carrying out a damage-limitation exercise: 'Tertullian is neither ours nor theirs in this point; and we can cite Tertullian against them also.' Indeed, he was finally reduced at the end of this chapter to an appeal to Protestant witnesses – the divines in Luther's time, Calvin, Beza, Paraeus and Buchanan, and the practice of the Protestants in France and Holland.[141]

But Rutherford had weightier examples of violent resistance than these. He ransacked the Old Testament for cases of bloody revolutions, palace coups and armed resistance to royal authority. He cited the story of David, who defended himself against Saul by taking Goliath's sword; of Elisha who 'violently' kept the king's messenger from a house, 'as we did keep castles against king Charles' unlawfull messengers'; of the city of Libnah which revolted from under king Jehoram, 'because he had forsaken the Lord God of his fathers';[142] of Jehu who destroyed King Ahab's family in what Paul Johnson describes as 'one of the bloodiest coups in history';[143] and of Elijah and his followers, who slaughtered the 300 prophets of Baal.[144] Scripture, therefore, as much as natural law, supported armed resistance against tyranny.

But who could legitimately resist? On this point Rutherford was not altogether clear. At times he seemed willing to accept that in certain cases a private individual might have the duty to resist a king violently. An obvious case, he said, would occur when a king tried to force a young woman or man to commit adultery or sodomy with him. In such a situation, it would be absolutely necessary 'to violently oppose a king', for he was not the 'lord

---

[140] *Lex, Rex*, pp. 314–18 [153–5]. Honyman writes that the author of *Lex, Rex* 'jeers at passive obedience', but reasons 'very sophistically' when discussing the biblical teaching. *Survey of Naphtali*, pp. 32–3.

[141] *Lex, Rex*, pp. 371–2 [183–4].   [142] *Lex, Rex*, Question XXXII.

[143] P. Johnson, *A History of the Jews* (London, 1987), p. 68.

[144] *Lex, Rex*, pp. 364–5 [180].

of chastity'.[145] But Rutherford was emphatic that 'violent re-offending . . . against any man, far less against the servants of a king', was only legitimate 'in the exigence of the last and most inexorable necessity'.[146] And he admitted that 'a private man is to suffer the king to kill him rather than he kill the king, because he is to prefer the life of a private man to the life of a public man'.[147]

In less extreme situations, only the estates and the inferior judges had a legitimate power to resist. This was because Rutherford, quite unlike Locke, did not believe that tyranny dissolved the constitution and placed men back in the state of nature with a private right to resist violence. His view was that 'if the king turn tyrant, the estates are to use their fountain-power'.[148] This power allowed them to 'make kings, make laws, and raise armies'.[149] In keeping with the mainstream of Calvinist political thought, he believed that armed resistance to a tyrant must be led by the representatives of the people, not by the people themselves.

Later Covenanter theorists like James Stewart and Alexander Shields, having given up hope in the inferior magistrates after the Restoration, were to take a much more extreme line. In *Naphtali* (1667), Stewart marked the move away from Rutherford by appealing to the Old Testament example of Phineas, who had taken it upon himself to execute the judgement of God on evildoers.[150] Honyman's *Survey of Naphtali* (1668) pointed to the novelty of this position. Whereas Rutherford had endorsed resistance by the *Primores Regni*, Stewart was giving the right to resist to 'all meer private persons'.[151] In *Jus Populi Vindicatum* (1669), Stewart had to admit that Rutherford had said that a private man should rather suffer himself to be killed than to kill the king. However, Stewart could turn instead to the writings of John Knox, who in the 1550s had advocated a more populist theory of religious rebellion.[152] Alexander Shields, in *A Hind Let Loose*, followed the example of Stewart, and included a section in his book on 'The extraordinary execution of judgement by private men', which attempted to justify the terrorist tactics of the Covenanters who had assassinated Rutherford's old rival, James Sharp.[153]

---

[145] *Lex, Rex*, p. 331 [162].   [146] *Lex, Rex*, p. 328 [160].

[147] *Lex, Rex*, p. 335 [164]. Both George Mackenzie and Andrew Honyman seized on this admission. See Mackenzie, *Jus Regium*, p. 125 and [Honyman], *Survey of Naphtali*, p. 18.

[148] *Lex, Rex*, p. 210 [115].   [149] *Lex, Rex*, p. 377 [186].

[150] [J. Stewart], *Naphtali* (1667), pp. 20–5. Phineas was also praised in several of the Fast Sermons preached to the English parliament in the early 1640s. See Hill, *The English Bible*, pp. 90–1, 152–3.

[151] [Honyman], *Survey of Naphtali*, pp. 21, 70, 82–3, 99.

[152] [Stewart], *Jus Populi Vindicatum*, pp. 45, 173–215. On the populist theories of Knox and Goodman see Skinner, *Foundations*, II, ch. 7.

[153] Alexander Shields, *A Hind Let Loose* (1687), pp. 633–95. See also Smart, 'The political ideas of the Scottish Covenanters', pp. 183–92.

But if he always stressed the role of inferior magistrates, at times Rutherford came close to justifying king-killing. He wrote that 'the cutting off of a contagious member, that by a gangrene would corrupt the whole body, is well warranted by nature, because the safety of the whole is to be preferred to the safety of the part'. The commonwealth needed an immortal head, but this head was the office of the king, not the particular person of one who might be a tyrant.[154] However, Rutherford may only have been considering deposition of the king, for he clearly recoiled at the prospect of supporting the execution of Charles I. Charles was not 'a tyrant, void of all title'. He was rather a legitimate king acting tyrannically, and that was a very different matter. Rutherford wanted to make it clear that he was not 'pleading for the killing of kings; for lawful resistance is one thing, and killing of kings is another – the one defensive and lawful, the other offensive and unlawful, so long as he remaineth a king, and the Lord's anointed'.[155] Such a distinction was unlikely to impress royalists, who pointed out that the king had been in grave danger at Edgehill. Rutherford simply blamed the king's counsellors for his being there, but his protestations of innocence were unconvincing so long as he continued to uphold tyrannicide but not regicide. Since much of his argument hinged on the idea that Charles was a tyrant, it seemed that Rutherford was being inconsistent in denying that he favoured king-killing. After Charles's execution in 1649, Milton – who seems to have been familiar with *Lex, Rex* – chided the Scots for their hypocritical outcries against the regicide. The republicans were simply taking Presbyterian ideas to their logical conclusion.[156]

But if Rutherford baulked at regicide and at resistance by private individuals, he did make one strikingly radical point: parliament itself could be resisted by the original community. If parliament erred, he remarked at one point, 'the sounder part may resist'.[157] Honyman, drawing attention to this, claimed that in the end Rutherford 'placeth and fixeth the unpunishable sovereignty' in 'the rabble of the multitude, against King and all Nobles and Rulers'. The 'venome' which the writer of *Naphtali* had against the powers ordained of God, 'he hath sucked out of the breasts of *Lex, Rex*', 'his Magazine, whence he borrowes all his Stuffe'. However, this was an exaggeration, and Honyman immediately went on to point to the greater

[154] *Lex, Rex*, pp. 331–2 [162].   [155] *Lex, Rex*, p. 273 [148].

[156] See *The Tenure of Kings and Magistrates* in *Complete Prose Works of John Milton*, III, edited by M. Y. Hughes (New Haven, 1962), pp. 225–6. After pointing out that in many places Milton seems to be following *Lex, Rex*, Hughes comments 'It is strange that nowhere in *The Tenure* does Milton refer to Samuel Rutherford' (p. 126 n.128). Milton certainly had a copy of *Lex, Rex* in his library. See J. C. Boswell, *Milton's Library* (London, 1975), p. 214.

[157] *Lex, Rex*, p. 240 [131].

conservatism of the older work.[158] Rutherford never endorsed violent resistance by parties of private individuals, but he did believe that any magistratical authority, no matter how low, had the right and the duty to defend the covenant when it was being subverted.

Two further passages confirm this. In both cases Rutherford was responding to Maxwell's claim that a clear contrast could be found between the populism of Buchanan, and Parker's theory of parliamentary sovereignty. Rutherford argued that this was not the case, but in going on to defend Buchanan's populism, he does appear to have gone further than Parker and the other men of 1642 wished to go.

In Question IX Rutherford affirmed Buchanan's argument that if the people spoke against unjust acts of parliament, they were not laws at all. In some cases, the community as the 'subject' of royal power might resist the estates who were the 'receptacle' of that power. For instance, when the lords of the council in Scotland pressed the 'Mass Book' upon the kingdom of Scotland, 'the people did well to resist'.[159] This perhaps referred to the popular rioting against the Prayer Book in July 1637, rioting which two of Rutherford's closest colleagues – David Dickson and Alexander Henderson – had helped to organise. If so, Rutherford was returning to the radical populism of Knox and endorsing the godly Protestant mob. But it might refer, in a more conservative way, to the setting up of an alternative government, the Tables, by the disaffected members of the Scottish ruling class.[160]

In Question XIX, however, Rutherford did argue that corporations and shires had an authority that limited parliamentary sovereignty. Counties and corporations retained a 'fountain-power of making commissioners, and of self-preservation' analogous to the power the three estates retained for making the king. They elected the knights and burgesses of parliament on a 'fiduciary' basis, just as the king was elected by the estates, and retained the right to 'resist them, annul their commissions and rescind their acts', just as parliament itself could resist the king.[161] Rutherford used no examples to illustrate his case, but he was probably reflecting on his own experience in Scotland in the 1620s and 1630s, when the godly Presbyterians, ousted from positions of national authority, still kept control of local towns and counties. He himself had witnessed the struggle for the control of Edinburgh and Kirkcudbright, and he clearly felt that localities had the right to do all they could to maintain the Protestant constitution.

This aspect of Rutherford's thought brought him close to the celebrated

---

[158] *Survey of Naphtali*, pp. 72, 78–83.   [159] *Lex, Rex*, pp. 58–62 [33–5].
[160] See *Lex, Rex*, p. 153 [84] for a reference to 'the people' setting up the Tables.
[161] *Lex, Rex*, p. 152 [84].

federalism of Johann Althusius.[162] Edward Cowan has demonstrated that, at the beginning of the Covenanting revolution, key figures like Wariston were reading Althusius avidly.[163] The German theorist's *Politica Methodice Digesta* (1604) had argued that each successive level of political association was formed by a federal union of the entities on the level below; villages were created by the federal union of families, provinces by the federal union of villages and towns, and so on. Carl Friedrich believed that of all the writings of the Interregnum period in Britain, Rutherford's *Lex, Rex* came 'perhaps closest to the Althusian position'.[164] Rutherford certainly referred to Althusius on a number of occasions, and his ideal polity clearly had a federalist structure: authority ascended from shire and corporation to parliament, and from parliament to the king, with the lower level always retaining its 'fountain-power'. Moreover, as Friedrich noted, Presbyterianism provided an ecclesiastical analogue to political federalism. In Presbyterianism, self-contained congregations are federated in a universal church, and representatives are elected at each level of ecclesiastical authority to be sent on to the higher body; from kirk session to presbytery to regional synod to national general assembly and then to international synod.

The federalism of Rutherford's political theory was recognised by his critic, Honyman, who made the Bodinian point that 'supreme power is indivisible and incommunicable to distinct subjects in any one political society'. Rutherford, claimed Honyman, by setting up 'a multitude of Supreme Powers in one humane Civil Society, destroyes the divine order set by God himself'. He had made 'idle distinctions' between the royal power in the king and the fountain-head of royalty in the people, talking nonsense about coordinate and collateral sovereigns in one kingdom, and about courts of necessity and nature as well as ordinary royal courts. All of which made Rutherford one of the 'late masters of confusion'.[165]

Yet, as Friedrich recognised, *Lex, Rex* 'lacked the systematic foundation' of Althusius's federalist theory and addressed more fully the concrete problems of parliamentary institutions.[166] Rutherford made no attempt to build up a comprehensive theory of political association starting from the family and moving up through villages, guilds, cities and provinces to the state. He mentioned corporations and shires only briefly, devoted almost all his attention to the estates, and was, in the end, very hesitant about an

---

[162] See T. Hueglin, 'Have we studied the wrong authors? On the relevance of Johannes Althusius', *Studies in Political Thought*, 1 (1992), 75–93.

[163] E. J. Cowan, 'The making of the National Covenant', in J. Morrill, ed., *The Scottish National Covenant*, pp. 78–82.

[164] In his preface to *The Politics of Johannes Althusius*, trans. F. Carney (London, 1964), p. xii.

[165] *Survey of Naphtali*, p. 73.

[166] C. Friedrich, *The Age of Baroque, 1610–60* (New York, 1952), p. 31.

individual's right of resistance. As Wootton puts it, Rutherford 'did not envisage the possibility of an appeal from the electorate to the people as a whole, or a revolutionary transformation of the constitution. By insisting that kings could be deposed and parliaments could err, he adopted the most radical position which could be reconciled with the claim that people as individuals could not reassume authority.'[167]

The fact that Rutherford was consciously defending Buchanan in these passages is significant. It demonstrates that Skinner is right in noting the populism of Buchanan's thought, but suggests also that he is wrong to see Buchanan as Locke's real predecessor.[168] As Richard Mouw has observed, Skinner's 'progressive descent' model, in which Calvinist political thought gets steadily more radical until it culminates in the 'almost anarchic' ideas of Buchanan, is hard to square with the fact that the seventeenth-century Scots who followed him (chronologically and intellectually) maintained that political authority resided in the inferior magistrates, not in individuals. Although Buchanan's theory of the origins of government was clearly individualistic, he also wrote that it was the *maior pars* who called the king to book, and insisted that citizens should be valued 'not by their number, but by their worth'.[169] The most we can say, therefore, is that Buchanan – and Rutherford in the two passages referred to – was prepared to concede that the original, corporated community as well as the parliament held political power. Neither Buchanan nor Rutherford disprove Mouw's claim that all Calvinist political theorists located political authority in 'the middle range', between the individual citizen and the king.[170] If we see Lockeian individualism as one of the two vital characteristics of a modern political theory, as Skinner does, then Rutherford does not qualify as a modern. Nonetheless, he provided a relatively radical theory of popular sovereignty.

By contrast, he was nowhere near meeting Skinner's second criterion of modern political thought – secularity. Rather than presenting an argument for the secular right to resist, *Lex, Rex* concentrated on the religious duty to resist. The cause of true religion was always preeminent in Rutherford's mind, and, in comparison with it, other concerns paled into insignificance. He hinted, for instance, that the grievance over Ship Money was not a good enough pretext for resistance to a king. Christ, 'no doubt to teach us the like', had told his followers to pay taxes to Caesar 'where it was not due', rather than be accused of being a disloyal subject to lawful emperors and

---

[167] Wootton, *Divine Right and Democracy*, p. 50.
[168] For Skinner's exposition of Buchanan see his *Foundations*, II, pp. 339–48.
[169] On Buchanan see J. H. Burns, 'The political ideas of George Buchanan', *Scottish Historical Review*, 30 (1951), 64; Wootton, *Divine Right and Democracy*, pp. 49–50; F. Oakley, 'On the road from Constance to 1688: the political thought of John Major and George Buchanan', *Journal of British Studies*, 1 (1962), 24–6.
[170] See R. Mouw, *The God Who Commands* (Notre Dame, 1990), pp. 106–8.

kings.[171] The king did not become a tyrant the moment he committed a single tyrannical act, and 'the people are to suffer much before they will resume their power'.[172]

Charles I had become a tyrant for a very simple reason: his idolatry constituted a flagrant violation of the religious terms of the covenant. The Scottish revolution had started as a rebellion against a brazenly 'popish' Prayer Book. Not only had Charles tried to impose this idolatrous service on them, he had also sent an army against them when they refused it. If this was not sufficient ground for armed resistance, Rutherford asked, what was? Where in the Old Testament, he demanded, could one find an example of a king of Israel or Judah raising 'an army of malignants, of Philistines, Sidonians, or Ammonites' against his own people with the purpose of setting up Dagon or tolerating the worship of Sidonian gods? Yet this was precisely what Charles I had done, for by obtruding upon Scotland 'a worshipping of bread and the mass' he had introduced something 'as abominable as the worshipping of Dagon or the Sidonian gods'.[173]

The thought of this treacherous betrayal of the true religion set Rutherford's blood boiling and his invective flowing:

a king may command an idolatrous and superstitious worship – send an army of cut-throats against them, because they refuse that worship, and may reward papists, prelates, and other corrupt men, and may advance them to places of state and honour because they kneel to a tree altar – pray to the east – adore the letters and sound of the word Jesus – teach and write Arminianism, and may imprison, deprive, confine, cut the ears, slit the noses and burn the faces of those who speak and preach and write the truth of God; and may send armies of cut-throats, Irish rebels, and other papists and malignant atheists, to destroy and murder the judges of the land, and innocent defenders of the reformed religion.[174]

These explicit references to the Laudian policies of the 1630s, to the punishment of Burton, Bastwick and Prynne, to Rutherford's own confinement at Aberdeen, and to the king's pact with the Catholic Irish, bring us to the emotional heart of *Lex, Rex*. Now we are listening to Rutherford the apocalyptic preacher, rather than the cold scholastic professor.

Again, this was in keeping with the mainstream of Calvinist political thought. However much some Calvinists – like Knox and the later Covenanters – broke through to a populist theory of revolution, they never considered a secular theory. It is true that they used 'secular' constitutionalist arguments, but religion was never far from the surface and often proved to be the real driving force. Richard Kyle has argued that Knox's crusade against idolatry was 'the great motivation of his career' and 'the

---

[171] *Lex, Rex*, p. 322 [157].   [172] *Lex, Rex*, pp. 63, 266–7 [36, 144].
[173] *Lex, Rex*, p. 369 [182].   [174] *Lex, Rex*, pp. 267–8 [145].

primary motivation for Knox's notions of resistance to idolatrous men'.[175] Even George Buchanan, whom Skinner sees as prefiguring Locke's secular argument as much as his individualism, declared that the Decalogue is the foundation of all law. It is true that, as Skinner writes, 'Buchanan makes no mention of the religious covenant at all' – and this is surely a striking omission. But Skinner is quite wrong to say the same about Althusius, who explicitly states that the people make a covenant with God. It is going too far to portray these writers as 'talking exclusively about politics, not theology, and about the concept of rights, not religious duties'.[176] Skinner has secularised Calvinist political thought, making it seem prematurely modern.[177]

Nevertheless, the fact remains that Rutherford did employ secular arguments. But why devote so much of a book to natural-law arguments when the real problem is idolatry? Why bother with the cumbersome scholastic constitutionalism? Since natural law does not by definition tell men about revealed religion, why not simply stick to biblical evidence? There are two answers. The first is that whilst the king's tyranny might have been specifically religious and not secular, armed resistance to it could be legitimised by appeal to both 'nature's law of self-preservation' and 'God's law of defending religion against papists in arms'.[178] Secondly, true religion could be incorporated into a natural-law definition of human welfare. Since men were by the law of nature 'to care for their own souls', argued Rutherford, it followed that they were 'to defend in their way true religion, which so nearly concerneth them and their eternal happiness'.[179] Grace did not destroy nature, but perfected it.

TWO NARRATIVES

Rutherford's arguments from both nature and grace were undergirded by two narratives. As Michael Lynch has observed, the Scottish Covenanters 'depended on two historical myths: a determinedly one-eyed reading of the history of the Kirk since the Reformation of 1560 and historians such as Calderwood and Row rushed into print to secure its foundations; and the right, already established by George Buchanan in his *History of Scotland*, of

---

[175] Kyle, 'John Knox: a man of the Old Testament', pp. 71–2; 'John Knox and the purification of religion: the intellectual aspects of his crusade against idolatry', *Archiv fur Reformationsgeschichte*, 77 (1986), 265–80.

[176] Skinner, *Foundations*, II, pp. 341–2. Cf. *The Politics of Johannes Althusius*, pp. 157–60.

[177] On this point see D. Wootton, 'The fear of God in early modern political theory', *Historical Papers* (1983), 56–80; P. Marshall, 'Quentin Skinner and the secularization of political thought', *Studies in Political Theory*, 1 (1992), 85–104.

[178] *Lex, Rex*, p. 383 [179].   [179] *Lex, Rex*, p.100 [56].

the nobles over nineteen centuries to censure their kings.'[180] Rutherford employed both of these myths to substantiate his more abstract claims. Scotland, he believed, was both a nation with a constitution modelled on natural-law principles and a nation in covenant with God.[181] It provided, therefore, an excellent illustration of how grace did not destroy nature but perfected it.

In the penultimate chapter of *Lex, Rex*, Question XLIII, Rutherford dealt with the story of the Scottish constitution. He aimed to provide a third layer of corroborating evidence to add to the biblical and classical data to which he had appealed throughout. His principal source for this chapter was George Buchanan's *History of Scotland* (1582). Rutherford used Buchanan to show that historically 'a parliament must be before the king'.[182] He began with Fergus, the first of Scotland's 107 kings. Fergus – just like Saul and David – had been 'freely elected' to his throne by the estates of the kingdom, and had not attained it by conquest, as Buchanan's pupil, James VI, maintained in *Basilikon Doron*.[183] The implication, though it was not one that Rutherford chose to draw out, was that Scotland was originally an aristocracy. After Fergus's death, he explained, 'the estates convened without any king, and made that fundamental law *regni elective*, that when the king's children were minors, any of the Fergusian race might be chosen to reign'. Thus 'it is clear that parliaments were *consortes imperii*, and had authority with and above the king'. Faced with two rival versions of Scottish history, Rutherford had no problem deciding which to choose; King James VI could not compete with his tutor.

Rutherford went on to demonstrate, still following Buchanan, how the principle established at the outset of Scottish royal history had been maintained ever since. Corbredus II, the twenty-first king, had sworn at his coronation 'that he should be ruled by parliament'. Conarus, the twenty-fourth king, was cast into prison by parliament because he tried to rule 'by private advice, without the judicial ordinance of parliament'. Eugenius VIII, the sixty-second king, 'a wicked prince, was put to death by the parliament'. Kenneth III, the eightieth king, almost succeeded in changing 'the elective kings into hereditary'; 'observe the power of parliaments', wrote

---

[180] M. Lynch, *Scotland: A New History* (London, 1991), p. 264.

[181] There is an intriguing comparison to be made with the Ayatollah Khomeini. In 1963 the Iranian cleric made a speech – while holding the Koran in one hand and a copy of the nation's Constitution in the other – in which he accused the Shah of violating his oath to defend Islam and the Constitution. See S. A. Arjomand, *The Turban for the Crown: The Islamic Revolution in Iran* (Oxford, 1988), p. 85.

[182] *Lex, Rex*, p. 449 [224].

[183] Andrew Honyman noted that not even Buchanan claimed that Fergus had to swear an oath at his coronation. The reality was, argued Honyman, that the covenant was a recent innovation, first introduced in the reign of James VI. *Survey of Naphtali*, p. 90.

Rutherford. Macbeth, the eighty-fifth king, was rebuked for governing by private counsel. When Malcolm I, the ninety-second king, tried to make a treaty 'to the hurt of the kingdom, the nobles said, *Non jus esse regi*, the king had no right to take anything from the kingdom'.[184]

The limited nature of royal authority and the fact of parliamentary sovereignty had also been acknowledged under the Stuart monarchs. In June 1560 the estates had suspended the government of Mary because she had violated her duty by declaring that 'Faith of promise should not be sought from princes.' The acts of the 1560 parliament which had been 'conceived only in the name of the states, without the king and queen', had been confirmed by the parliaments of 1567, 1572, 1581, 1587, 1592 and even of 1633. Similarly, a host of legislation in James VI's reign was used to demonstrate that 'the absolute prerogative of the king above law, equity, and justice, was never ratified in any parliament of Scotland to this day'.[185] Charles I had not been crowned 'till one of every one of the three estates came and offered to him the crown, with an express condition of his duty, before he be crowned'.[186] Monarchs were, therefore, bound by their coronation oaths 'to govern by law', and could have 'no prerogative above the law'.[187] Parliament was 'the highest court of the kingdom'.[188]

Rutherford's *Lex, Rex* therefore incorporated the Scottish Whig historiography whose rise and fall has been carefully chronicled by Colin Kidd. He added nothing new to this tradition of historical writing, contenting himself with bringing Buchanan's story up to date, but it was an important element of his worldview. Buchanan's royal genealogy – itself a reworking of those constructed by John Fordun, Hector Boece and John Major – produced a sense of a Scoto-Celtic community stretching back to antiquity and stressed the contractual nature of the relationship between the Scottish people and their kings.[189] This Scottish equivalent of the English idea of an 'ancient constitution' enabled the Covenanters to present an historical justification for their revolution, and helped them attract the support of the disaffected nobility.

However, Buchanan's secular narrative of the ancient constitution was not the only Scottish history Rutherford had to relate. Alongside it we should place the vision of the history of the kirk which Rutherford outlined elsewhere, a vision which he inherited from his pastor, David Calderwood. Essentially, it was a story of a covenant broken. The king and nobility of

---

[184] *Lex, Rex*, pp. 448–51 [224–6].   [185] *Lex, Rex*, p. 435 [217].
[186] *Lex, Rex*, p. 454 [227].   [187] *Lex, Rex*, p. 434 [217].
[188] *Lex, Rex*, p. 453 [227].
[189] C. Kidd, *Subverting Scotland's Past: Scottish Whig Historians and the Creation of an Anglo-British Identity, 1689–c.1830* (Cambridge, 1993). On the Scottish Calvinist historiographical tradition see also D. Allan, *Virtue, Learning and the Scottish Enlightenment: Ideas of Scholarship in Early Modern History* (Edinburgh, 1993).

Scotland had received the Christian gospel around AD 205, and 'in a short time the whole nation became Christians'. At this time, we may assume, a religious covenant (one of those predicted in the Old Testament prophecies) was welded onto the secular covenant established at Fergus's coronation in BC 330. The Scottish people were godly and pious for many generations after this, but then they fell into bondage to popish superstition and idolatry. Only at the Reformation in 1560 had the original purity of their religion been restored. Christ visited the people of Scotland and entered into covenant with them, a covenant renewed by the king and the people in the Negative Confession of 1581. 'Then was the Church of Scotland for doctrine sound and lively; for worship, pure and spiritual; for discipline, powerful and impartial; and for government, and unity, and order, beautiful and comely.' Yet this golden age was all too brief. King James VI and his son Charles, desirous to please English prelates, corrupted the kirk by 'reducing' it, 'in its worship and government, unto a conformity with the church of England'.[190] The Scottish nobility, who ought to have defended the Reformed kirk, betrayed it by allowing it to be corrupted by the introduction of idolatrous ceremonies and bastard prelates.

Rutherford summarised this Presbyterian story in a letter to Marion McNaught:

Wearied Jesus, after He had travelled from Geneva, by the ministry of worthy Mr Knox, and was laid in His bed, and reformation begun, and the curtains drawn, had not gotten His dear eyes well together, when irreverent bishops came in, and with the din and noise of ceremonies, holy days, and other Romish corruptions, they awake our Beloved. Others came to His bedside, and drew the curtains, and put hands on His servants, banished, deprived, and confined them; and for the pulpit they got a stool and a cold fire in the Blackness [castle]; and the nobility drew the covering off Him, and have made Him a poor, naked Christ, spoiling His servants of the tithes and kirk rents. And now there is such a noise of crying sins in the land, as the want of the knowledge of God, of mercy, and truth; such swearing, whoring,

<hr>

[190] *A Testimony to the Truth of Jesus Christ ... by the ministers of Perth and Fife* (Kilmarnock, 1783; original edition, Edinburgh, 1660), pp. 93–5. As Rutherford is the first signatory to this testimony it is reasonable to suppose that he was the author; he certainly subscribed to its content.

A fuller version of this Presbyterian view of Scottish church history can be found in a manuscript history of the Church of Scotland, which David Laing ascribed to John Brown of Wamphray, a student of Rutherford's at St Andrews. It begins with the story of the earliest Scottish Christians, the Culdees, who had no bishops, and then proceeds to describe the gradual corruption of the kirk in the centuries following. First bishops were introduced, then the keeping of Yule (AD 500), then popish corruptions (AD 697), then the anointing of the king with oil at his coronation (1098), until around AD 1200 the Culdees were totally extinguished. See 'MS History of the Church of Scotland till 1639', Hornel Library, Kirkcudbright, MS 4/24a, ff. 1–22. This mythical reconstruction of Scottish ecclesiastical history was common among Scottish Presbyterians. See Kidd, *Subverting Scotland's Past*, pp. 22–4, 63–9. For an Irish example see Trevor-Roper's essay on Archbishop Ussher in his *Catholics, Anglicans and Puritans* (London, 1987), pp. 144–9.

lying, and blood touching blood; that Christ is putting on His clothes, and making Him, like an ill-handled stranger, to go to other lands.[191]

Here was a provocative and emotive tale of an abused Saviour told in intoxicating prose that fused the erotic language of the Song of Songs with the declamations of the Hebrew prophets. It was one far more likely to arouse popular passion than Buchanan's dry narrative of a marginalised institution. Yet both stories were essential to the success of the covenanting revolution and to the alliance of noble and cleric which made it possible. They had been fused in 1638, because the reassertion of the authority of the three estates over the king went hand in hand with the renewal of the national covenant with God. Natural law and true religion seemed eminently compatible. In 1644, when Rutherford wrote *Lex, Rex*, this was still the case, despite the defection of some of the nobility from the Covenants. The book was born out of the confidence that nature and grace were reinforcing one another, a confidence that is evident in its interweaving of secular and religious arguments. Government was said to originate in both the sovereign ordinance of God and in the will of the people; the covenant on which Christian governments were founded contained both secular and religious obligations; the purpose of government was to secure the ends of both peace and godliness; and resistance was legitimated by royal support for injustice and idolatry.

However, the two forms of discourse in *Lex, Rex* – natural-law constitutionalism and religious covenantalism – remained in tension, and make it an ambiguous book for modern readers. On the one hand, Rutherford's arguments for popular sovereignty, the rule of law, and the right of resistance to tyranny, remind us of Locke, and can lead to the impression that the author of *Lex, Rex* was something of a modern liberal. On the other hand, his desire for a covenanted nation purged of heresy, idolatry and unbelief, makes him appear thoroughly reactionary, utterly committed to the ideals of Christendom. Ultimately, it was Rutherford's 'reactionary' side that was to win out, for it was the Old Testament concept of a nation in covenant with God that lay closest to his heart. The quest for a godly nation was destined to undermine the advice of natural reason. But that is a story for our final chapter.

---

[191] *Letters*, p. 56.

━━━━━━━━━━━━━━━━ ⟪ *7* ⟫ ━━━━━━━━━━━━━━━━

The ecclesiastical statesman

As well as being famed as a defender of Reformed theology and Covenanter politics, Rutherford distinguished himself as one of the foremost champions of divine-right Presbyterianism. Indeed, so convinced was he of the value and necessity of correct ecclesiastical forms that he published almost three thousand pages on the doctrine of the church and its relationship to the state.[1] In addition, for four years in the mid-1640s he was an active participant in the Westminster Assembly debates on church government, discipline and liturgy.

Rutherford's zeal for ecclesiastical form has puzzled many of his admirers. Generations of Evangelical pietists could hardly comprehend how someone who wrote the warmest of devotional prose could also engage in bitter and labyrinthine polemics against other Protestant believers. What they failed to recognise was Rutherford's conviction that true religion was not simply a matter of passionate subjectivity. For him, it also involved following biblically prescribed forms of church government. This belief set him apart from those like Hooker, who felt that ecclesiastical forms were largely *adiaphora* – things that were 'indifferent' because not prescribed by Scripture, and hence capable of being determined by the magistrate. It also distinguished him from antiformalists like Cromwell, who believed that ecclesiastical and, to some extent, even doctrinal forms were unimportant and that what mattered was the 'spirit', the religion of the heart.[2]

Cromwell's attitude prefigured that of many later Evangelicals, but

---

[1] The works we shall examine in this chapter are: *A Peaceable and Temperate Plea for Paul's Presbytery in Scotland* (1642); *The Due Right of Presbyteries* (1644); *The Divine Right of Church Government and Excommunication* (1646); *A Free Disputation against Pretended Liberty of Conscience* (1649); and *A Survey of . . . Thomas Hooker* (1658). In addition, *A Survey of Spiritual Antichrist* (1648), though more focused on theological issues, attacked ecclesiastical antiformalists like William Dell.

[2] On antiformalism see J. C. Davis, 'Cromwell's religion', in J. Morrill, ed., *Oliver Cromwell and the English Revolution* (London, 1990), pp. 198–208; 'Against formality: one aspect of the English Revolution', *Transactions of the Royal Historical Society*, 6th series, 3 (1993), 265–88.

Rutherford would have no truck with it.[3] He believed that orthodox Calvinism, Presbyterianism and Covenanter constitutionalism provided the essential framework within which God could reveal himself to the individual and the nation, the channels through which true spiritual experience would freely flow. In employing two quite different prose styles – the enthusiastic Hebraism of his letters and sermons and the argumentative scholasticism of his polemics – Rutherford was attempting to hold together substance and form. In his devotional works he could stir up affection for Christ, whilst in his polemics he could argue for the kind of theology, church government and constitution that would most effectively foster the religion of the heart.

Rutherford's polemical writings on ecclesiastical matters are so voluminous that it is impossible to cover in detail his opinions on every aspect of church government and worship. What we shall seek to do instead is to focus on the fundamental tension in Rutherford's ecclesiastical thought between the idea of the church as a pure gathering of the godly and the idea of the church as a comprehensive national institution. This tension can be said to parallel the tension we have seen in *Lex, Rex* between the politics of natural reason and the politics of true religion. In Chapter 8 we shall see how Rutherford chose the particular cause of true religion when it came into conflict with certain universal principles of natural law. In this chapter we shall discuss the way in which his desire for ecclesiastical purity eventually led him into a deeply exclusive and almost schismatic position in the 1650s. This should serve to correct the assumption, particularly widespread among English historians, that Rutherford was simply an uncompromisingly conservative defender of a monolithic Scottish Presbyterianism. In the mid-1640s, it is true, he did close ranks with other Scottish Presbyterians against the threats of Independency and toleration, and appeared to be utterly unyielding towards anything slightly sectarian. Yet this disguised an uneasy relationship with the mainstream of the Scottish church, a relationship that was to disintegrate rather spectacularly in the critical years of 1650–51.

SCOTTISH ECCLESIASTICAL CONTROVERSIES (1560–1618)

In order to understand Rutherford's ecclesiological ideas, it is necessary to gain an overview of ecclesiastical developments in Scotland since the Reformation in 1560. As far as church government is concerned, Scottish historians have long debated the distance that Knox and the first generation of Reformers travelled on the road to Presbyterianism. Donaldson has

---

[3] Rutherford explicitly attacks Cromwell's antiformalism in *Survey of Spiritual Antichrist*, pp. 250ff.

claimed that the superintendents provided for by the *First Book of Discipline* (1560) were bishops, whereas Kirk maintains that they were introduced to meet a temporary emergency, and were subordinate to the rest of the ministry.[4] Certainly, the Reformers took pains to ensure that the church had a system of representative conciliar government, exercised through a graded series of courts (kirk sessions, provincial assemblies, and general assemblies). However, only in the 1570s did an unambiguously anti-episcopal movement emerge in Scotland. Led by Andrew Melville,[5] this movement codified its principles in the *Second Book of Discipline* (1578), which is generally regarded as the classic statement of Presbyterian principles.[6] Diocesan episcopacy was to be abolished and replaced by a system of visitation by ministers appointed by the General Assembly. Although James VI got the 1584 parliament to restore the power of bishops and assert his authority over all estates, temporal and spiritual, the Presbyterians quickly regained the upper hand, and in the 'Golden Act' of 1592, parliament approved the Presbyterian government of the church.

Liturgical matters were much less controversial in the late sixteenth century. The Book of Common Order had been used by Knox among the Protestant exiles in Geneva in the 1550s, and it was the official Scottish service book from 1562 to 1644. It was neither the mere directory favoured by radicals, nor the fixed liturgy preferred by conservatives. Consequently, it created space for divergent liturgical practices. Because of their hostility to set prayers, the radicals (who were nearly all Presbyterian) tended to regard the prayers in the book simply as samples. They encouraged extempory prayer, and some even abandoned the recitation of the Creed. Conservatives on the other hand (including the vast majority of Episcopalians and some moderate Presbyterians) believed that the prayers had been set down in order to be read, and they emphasised the traditional elements in the book such as its use of the Lord's Prayer, the Doxology and the Apostles' Creed. Some ministers even used the English Book of Common Prayer alongside the Book of Common Order.[7]

James VI was very definitely on the Episcopalian side on issues of both church government and liturgy. 'Presbyterianism agreeth as much with monarchy as God with the Devil', he had once declared. He began his decisive move against the Presbyterians in 1596, and over the next twenty

[4] See G. Donaldson, *The Scottish Reformation* (Cambridge, 1960); J. Kirk, *Patterns of Reform: Continuity and Change in the Reformation Kirk* (Edinburgh, 1989).
[5] There is no modern academic study of Melville. The most useful biography remains that of Thomas McCrie, *The Life of Andrew Melville* (Edinburgh, 1899).
[6] See *The Second Book of Discipline*, ed. J. Kirk (Edinburgh, 1980).
[7] Gordon Donaldson provides an excellent summary of the liturgical developments in 'Reformation to covenant', in D. Forrester and D. Murray, eds., *Studies in the History of Worship in Scotland* (Edinburgh, 1984), ch. 3.

years he consolidated his control over the church by imprisoning and exiling major Presbyterian leaders and gradually reintroducing an Erastian diocesan episcopacy, which was ratified by parliament in 1612. Once this was achieved, he turned his attention to liturgical reform. His campaign began in 1614 with the order that communion be celebrated on Easter Day, and that colleges observe the main Holy Days and use the Book of Common Prayer for certain services. This was anathema to Presbyterian opinion, which regarded Holy Days and the English Prayer Book as little short of popish. James pressed ahead, however, and the 1616 General Assembly called for 'a common form of service' to be drafted. Ultimately, however, the attempt to draft a Scottish prayer book was shelved because of the controversy aroused by the passing of the Five Articles at the Perth General Assembly in 1618. These included private baptism and communion, which many believed should only be administered in the presence of the congregation; the celebration of Holy Days, which Puritans tended to see as unscriptural; episcopal confirmation; and, by far the most controversial article, kneeling at communion, widely regarded by advanced Protestants as tantamount to idolatrous worship of the sacrament. Although parliament ratified the Five Articles in 1621, James wisely refrained from enforcing them too strenuously once the scale of the opposition became clear.[8]

FORMATIVE INFLUENCES ON RUTHERFORD (1600–1628)

The most vociferous opponent of James's reforms in church government and liturgy was none other than Rutherford's pastor, David Calderwood. We have already seen in Chapter 2 how Calderwood confronted James in 1617 to protest against the king's attempt to establish royal control over the church. This had led to Calderwood's banishment to Holland, but it did not stop his protests. Indeed, Calderwood was more of a threat in exile than at home. He published a monumental attack on episcopacy, *The Altar of Damascus* in 1621, and criticised the Perth Articles in a number of smaller works. Like Knox before him, Calderwood was obsessed by the theme of idolatry; the altar of Damascus to which the title of his book

---

[8] For summaries of the struggle between the Presbyterians and James VI, see G. Donaldson, *Scotland: James V–James VII* (Edinburgh, 1965), ch. 11; J. Wormald, *Court, Kirk and Community: Scotland, 1470–1625* (Edinburgh, 1981), ch. 8; and J. Morrill, 'A British patriarchy: ecclesiastical imperialism under the early Stuarts', in A. Fletcher and P. Roberts, eds., *Religion, Culture and Society in Early Modern Britain: Essays in Honour of Patrick Collinson* (Cambridge, 1994), pp. 209–37. D. G. Mullan, *Episcopacy in Scotland: The History of an Idea, 1560–1638* (Edinburgh, 1986), deals with the ideological debates between Episcopalian and Presbyterian. See also J. MacPherson, *The Doctrine of the Church in Scottish Theology* (Edinburgh, 1903).

referred was the foreign altar which King Ahaz had copied for the temple in Jerusalem.[9] This theme was to be equally important to Rutherford. As we have seen in *Lex, Rex*, Charles I's unconstitutional actions were less offensive to Rutherford than was his idolatry.

The influence of Calderwood on the young Rutherford was consolidated whilst he was at university by the Edinburgh conventicles. The godly merchants with whom Rutherford came into contact were utterly opposed to the Five Articles of Perth, particularly to kneeling at communion and the observance of Holy Days. Not only did they refuse to obey the Five Articles, they also began to foster an alternative form of worship for the godly by establishing private conventicles. In January 1619, one of the Edinburgh clergy complained that country ministers were coming to the town and staying for a month or more: ' they go about feasting from house to house, seducing the people, speaking against Bishops, and they themselves are Popes: For they have an Anabaptistical spirit'.[10] In 1624, a proclamation against private meetings in Edinburgh claimed that they were being held at the same time as ordinary parish services, and that those who went to them 'have assumed to these their seditious conventicles the name of Congregation'. The proclamation also recalled that 'such pernicious seeds of separation, & singularitie of blind and fained zeal, have brought forth damned Sects of Anabaptists, Families of Love, Brounists, Arminians, Illuminats, and many such Pests, enemies to Religion, Authoritie and Peace'.[11]

This attempt to brand conventiclers as Anabaptists was not unusual in the early seventeenth century, and although one historian has described the Edinburgh conventicles as virtually separatist,[12] and others have seen them as the first shoots of congregationalism in Scotland,[13] the reality was probably different. Calderwood flatly denied that the Edinburgh conventicles were held at the same time as ordinary services or that they assumed the name of congregations. In England, some conventicles did tend to turn into gathered churches, but as Patrick Collinson has reminded us, clandestine gatherings of the godly were usually intended to complement rather than rival the services of the parish church. Conventiclers saw the church as imperfectly reformed and corrupt in some points, but they did not deny that

[9] The most detailed discussion of Calderwood's ideas is to be found in Mullan, *Episcopacy in Scotland*, and in J. D. Ford, 'Conformity in conscience: the structure of the Perth Articles debate in Scotland, 1618–38', *Journal of Ecclesiastical History*, 46 (1995), 256–77.

[10] D. Calderwood, *The True History of the Church of Scotland* (1678), p. 719.

[11] Calderwood, *History*, pp. 809–10.

[12] M. Lynch, 'Calvinism in Scotland, 1559–1638', in M. Prestwich, ed., *International Calvinism, 1541–1715* (Oxford, 1985), p. 241.

[13] For example, H. Escott, *A History of Scottish Congregationalism* (Glasgow, 1960), pp. 6–7.

it was still a true church. Schism was not on their minds.[14] Like the English Puritans, the Scots Presbyterians aimed to create a church within a church so that the dissatisfied would feel no need to separate. As one Edinburgh conventicler put it in the 1620s: 'I never separated myself from the kirk and never thinks [*sic*] to do. I know there is no man nor woman but they are sinful, nor any Kirk so pure but there are some faults in it. As for myself, I had rather live in the kirk of Scotland than in any other kirk.'[15]

However, this did not satisfy critics of conventicling like Calderwood. As we shall see later, Calderwood was to protest against private meetings and the liturgical innovations associated with them in the 1640s, whilst Rutherford was to leap to their defence. The combined influence of Calderwood and the Edinburgh radicals may have ensured that Rutherford was implacably opposed to Episcopacy, Erastianism and any liturgical practices that carried the slightest whiff of popery. But the Edinburgh experience had also added elements to Rutherford's ecclesiology that were later to set him at odds with the moderate Presbyterian majority in the Covenanting kirk.

RUTHERFORD'S NONCONFORMITY (1627–1638)

Shaped by his experiences in Edinburgh, it was not long before the young minister at Anwoth gained a reputation for nonconformity. With the accession to the throne of Charles I, the ceremonial innovations of James's reign were taken a step further. Some historians have described the new movement of reform as 'Arminianism',[16] and Rutherford was certainly concerned about the threats to theological orthodoxy in the Reformed churches. However, the most controversial changes were probably liturgical rather than theological. Kenneth Fincham neatly summarises the innovators' position: 'anti-Calvinists advocated a vision of decorous public worship based around a strict observance of the prayer book and canons, in which divine grace through prayer and sacraments were available, to the entire Christian community, participating in an inclusive national church, primarily defined by its unbroken episcopal succession through the ages'.[17]

Rutherford was deeply antagonistic towards this new sacramentalism. He preached against the Articles of Perth, and feared as early as 1631 that 'the

---

[14] P. Collinson, 'The English conventicle', in W. J. Sheils and D. Wood, eds., *Voluntary Religion* (Oxford, 1986), pp. 223–59; 'Sects and the evolution of Puritanism', in F. J. Bremer, ed., *Puritanism: Transatlantic Perspectives on a Seventeenth-Century Anglo-American Faith* (Boston, 1993), pp. 147–66.

[15] Quoted in G. Donaldson, 'The emergence of schism in seventeenth-century Scotland', in his *Scottish Church History* (Edinburgh, 1985), p. 209.

[16] Most prominently N. Tyacke, *Anti-Calvinists: The Rise of English Arminianism, c. 1560–1640* (Oxford, 1987).

[17] K. Fincham, ed., *The Early Stuart Church, 1603–42* (London, 1993), p. 10.

English service, and the organs, and King James Psalms, are to be imposed upon our kirk'.[18] As far as Rutherford was concerned these innovations were nothing less than 'anti-Christian'. In his letters he raged against the 'bastard porters'[19] – the bishops – who had allowed the church to become corrupted in 'doctrine, sacrament and discipline'. The 'multitude' was 'ready to receive any religion that shall be enjoined by authority'.[20] Erastianism, episcopacy and popish ceremonies had turned the church into a 'whorish mother'.[21]

Two sources provide us with a reliable guide to the arguments Rutherford used against Laudian innovations in this period. The first is a manuscript record of a debate between Rutherford and the Bishop of Galloway, Thomas Sydserff.[22] The second is Rutherford's *Divine Right of Church Government*, which although published in 1646, included two lengthy sections directed against Richard Hooker, who presented the first coherent expression of the sacramentalist position, and the Aberdeen Doctors. In these writings Rutherford presented essentially the same argument as that found in the works of his colleagues, David Calderwood and George Gillespie.[23] His objection to Hooker was that he 'will have Christs kingdom altogether spirituall, mysticall, and invisible', because he regarded most external forms in church government and worship as *adiaphora*, things indifferent, which could be determined by the magistrate.[24] Rutherford disagreed profoundly with this. Along with other radical Presbyterians, he believed that 'everything was necessarily right or wrong when it came to the particular act'.[25] For example, riding ten miles with a friend might seem to be an indifferent action, but when each individual case was examined it would be either right or wrong; if the excursion was an idle action, it was undeniably wrong, because Scripture commanded Christians to redeem the time.[26] The same was true with church ceremonies; every one of them could

[18] *Letters*, p. 60.   [19] *Letters*, p. 53.   [20] *Letters*, p. 93.

[21] *Letters*, p. 216. For other references to the kirk as a 'harlot-mother' see pp. 87, 103, 191, 204, 213, 290.

[22] 'Ane discussing of some arguments agt cannons & ceremonies in Gods worship', National Library of Scotland, MSS 15948, pp. 322–44. The debate probably took place at the time of Rutherford's trial before the High Commission in 1636.

[23] Besides Calderwood's *The Altar of Damascus* (1621), the other great Scottish work against ceremonies was *A Dispute against the English Popish Ceremonies, Obtruded upon the Church of Scotland* (1637), published by Rutherford's close friend, Gillespie, when he was only twenty-four. See G. Gillespie, *The Works of George Gillespie*, 2 vols. (Edinburgh, 1846).

[24] *Divine Right*, p. 13.

[25] J. Ford, 'The lawful bonds of Scottish society: the Five Articles of Perth, the Negative Confession, and the National Covenant', *Historical Journal*, 37 (1994), p. 46. Ford's 'Conformity in conscience' provides the clearest account of the radical Presbyterian position on ceremonies.

[26] *Divine Right*, p. 107.

be determined to be lawful or unlawful by appeal to Scripture. Christ Jesus had 'established a perfect Plat-forme of Church-Government' in the Scriptures, which left 'no liberty or latitude to Magistrates or Churches whatsoever'.[27] Christ's was 'an externall Politick mission', and hence it was virtually blasphemous to suggest that anyone else could specify the exact forms of government and worship that his church should follow.[28] Moses could not make even one pin of the tabernacle but according to God's pattern,[29] and 'there is nothing so small in either Doctrinals or Policie, so as men may alter, omit, and leave off these smallest Positive things that God hath commanded'.[30] In both civil and ecclesiastical matters, rulers found things that were 'intrinsecally good' because they were commanded in the law of nature or the Word of God, and then simply rubber-stamped them. Nothing could be made lawful by the authority and will of men alone. If a ceremony originated in man's will, then 'man's lust made it', and the will of man 'shall be a Pope and God'.[31]

This defence of a rigid regulative principle did not, of course, entail that absolutely everything in divine worship had to be determined by Scripture. Rutherford was willing to admit that some things were not intrinsically 'moral' but 'meere circumstantials' – the materials used to make the pulpit or the communion cup, and the clothes worn by the congregation, for example, were not specified by Scripture. However, symbolical ceremonies were different. The use of oil, bells, surplice and salt, and the gestures of bowing towards the east and kneeling to receive communion were 'toyes of the Masse'.[32] As for Hooker's claim that ceremonies 'leave a more deep and strong impression then the Word', Rutherford retorted: 'What blasphemy? that crossing and surplice leave a deeper impression in the soul, then Gods Word, the power of God to salvation.'[33] As Julian Davies points out, the replacement of the altar by the pulpit at the centre of the church had been one of the chief symbols of the Reformation; the reversal of this seemed tantamount to a counter-Reformation.[34]

On the most controversial of the Five Articles, kneeling to receive communion, Rutherford was unbending. To invent a worship not commanded in Scripture was sheer idolatry. Bowing signified religious honouring, and it was simply 'impossible to adore God, in and through an Image, and give no Religious reverence to the Image at all'. The Israelites

---

[27] *Divine Right*, p. 1.   [28] *Divine Right*, pp. 14–17.   [29] *Divine Right*, p. 26.

[30] *Divine Right*, p. 19.

[31] *Divine Right*, pp. 25, 204, 115–25, 647–9. For Rutherford's belief that civil laws simply add a sanction to 'a thing legally good in itself' see Chapter 6 and *Lex, Rex*, pp. 207–8 [113–14].

[32] *Divine Right*, pp. 1–4.   [33] *Divine Right*, pp. 129–31.

[34] J. Davies, *The Caroline Captivity of the Church: Charles I and the Remoulding of Anglicanism* (Oxford, 1992), p. 205.

had committed idolatry although they had no intention of worshipping the calf, because God could not be represented by any 'invention of man'.[35] The distinction between external bowing to an image and internal worship of God could be just as easily used to justify the action of a woman who gave her (external) body to a stranger with the (internal) intention of having children for her husband.[36] Instead of kneeling, communicants should sit, for this followed the practice of Christ and his disciples at the Last Supper, including the divine precept, 'Do this in remembrance of me.' It also avoided the idolatry of kneeling, and signified our 'Table-Fellowship' with Christ.[37]

In an appendix to *Divine Right* – 'A Dispute touching scandal and Christian liberty' – and in his debate with Sydserff, Rutherford laid out another argument against the Laudian ceremonies, one which he claimed to have used 'while I was confined in Aberdeene, with one of their chief Doctors'.[38] He appealed to Romans 14, in which Paul had written that Christians should avoid behaviour that scandalises 'weaker brethren'. Rutherford argued that even if the ceremonies were indifferent – and he thought they were not – they would still be sinful, because they caused great scandal within the church.[39] Many within the church were saddened because they believed that rulers 'love Popish toyes better than the simplicitie of the Gospel'.[40] To persist in causing scandal to these brethren was like running 'a horse in a street amongst bairns' and amounted to 'spirituall murther'.[41] The Service Book had to be removed, because even if its content was good – and again Rutherford thought it was not – its 'structure, frame, style, grammar, methode, and forme is popish'.[42] Knox and the Reformers were absolutely right to embark on their iconoclastic crusade.[43]

However, despite his revulsion at the corruption of the church, Rutherford was not willing to contemplate schism. In his dispute with Sydserff he used a particularly gruesome metaphor to make a distinction between separation from the church and separation from its faults. He argued that though the godly 'ly in one God with our mother kirk and touch her wholl skin, yet it is a sinfull societie to lay our skinne to her boyles and

[35] *Divine Right*, pp. 148–54. The same example is found in MSS 15948, p. 337. The example of the three young Jewish men who refused to bow to Nebuchadnezzar's statue in Daniel 3 is also used in both sources.
[36] *Divine Right*, p. 169.   [37] *Divine Right*, pp. 192–200.
[38] 'A Dispute', p. 1. The Doctor was almost certainly Robert Baron, of whom Rutherford writes: 'Dr Barron hath often disputed with me, especially about Arminian controversies, and for the ceremonies. Three yokings laid him by; and I have not been troubled with him since.' See *Letters*, pp. 189, 239.
[39] 'A Dispute', p. 13.   [40] 'A Dispute', p. 27.
[41] MSS 15948, pp. 326–7. See also 'A Dispute', p. 38.
[42] 'A Dispute', p. 88.   [43] 'A Dispute', p. 77.

scabb'.[44] With schism rejected, Presbyterians were left with three options. In the first place, they could (and did) continue to protest against the corruption of the church. 'I dare not for my soul be silent', he declared, 'to see my Lord's house burning, and not cry, "Fire, fire!" '[45] Although we only possess his letters and notes on his sermons from the early 1630s, we know that Rutherford wrote manuscript treatises 'anent the corruptions of this time'.[46] In 1629, he met with other nonconforming ministers to draw up 'Greivances and Petitions concerning the disordered state of the Reformed Church of Scotland'.

The second option open to the Presbyterian militants had, like the first, been explored in Edinburgh in the 1620s – namely, holding conventicles. Writing from Aberdeen to the parishioners of Kilmalcolm, who complained of a 'dead ministry' in their area, Rutherford urged 'conference and prayer at private meetings'.[47] He himself, together with 'the best affected of the ministry', arranged days of prayer and fasting for the state of the church.[48] According to Robert Baillie, Rutherford circulated manuscripts that encouraged the meeting of conventicles 'in greater numbers and for moe purposes than yet we have heard practised'.[49] One such manuscript discussed 'private men's libertie in publick praying and exponing of Scripture'.[50] In a sermon preached at Anwoth in the 1630s, Rutherford pointed out that the New Testament character, Philemon, 'had a kirk at his house'. 'The Word's working and the Spirit's working', he argued, 'are not always confined to the hour of the sand-glass, neither is the Spirit tied to a pulpit, and a gown and a minister's tongue.' Yet this did not justify 'the conventicles and unwarrantable meetings of Separatists and Brownists, who despise public meetings, and make a kirk in private homes of their own'.[51]

Rutherford's apparent willingness to endorse private meetings in which popular participation was encouraged is interesting, for it fits with evidence that shows the nonconformists to have been liturgical innovators. Although much of their energy was directed in protest against 'High Church' innovations, they themselves were quite willing to innovate in the opposite direction. Rutherford argued that it would be good if read prayers 'were out of the service of God'. 'For such prayers are meditations set down in paper and ink, and cannot be his heart-meditations who useth them.' The point here was twofold: God in Scripture had not commanded read prayers, so they seemed like a human invention; and worship was to be affectionate,

---

[44] MSS 15948, p. 343. In a later work, *Peaceable Plea* (1642), p. 94b, Rutherford suggested that a church could be both 'an whoore', *de facto* in respect of deserving judgement, and 'the Spouse and Bride of Christ', *de jure* as regards God's calling.
[45] *Letters*, p. 94.   [46] *Letters*, p. 105.   [47] *Letters*, pp. 561, 564.
[48] *Letters*, pp. 92–3.
[49] R. Baillie, *Letters and Journals*, 3 vols., ed. D. Laing (Edinburgh, 1841–2), I, p. 252.
[50] Baillie, *Letters and Journals*, I, p. 8.   [51] *Quaint Sermons*, p. 125.

'the pouring out of the soul to God'.[52] A premium was to be placed on extemporary prayer, though it was banned in the 1636 Book of Canons. Almost universal customs, such as the minister kneeling in the pulpit before preaching, were also rejected as unscriptural, since they involved private prayer at a time of public worship.[53] Many zealous Presbyterians even went so far as to give up saying the Creed, the Lord's Prayer, the confession, and the Doxology.[54]

Rutherford's support for conventicles suggests that at this stage he was in a strikingly similar position to that of the English semi-separatists with whom he was to argue bitterly in the 1640s. This is confirmed by the autobiography of John Livingstone, the colleague of Rutherford who preached in the north of Ireland. In 1634 Livingstone travelled to London to enquire about the third option open to nonconformists – emigration. Some of the Ulster Presbyterians were seriously contemplating the possibility of emigration to New England, and they were visited by John Winthrop, junior, who told them about the New England colony. In London, Livingstone made contact with a number of men who were deeply involved in the plan to emigrate to New England and were part of 'the developing Independent wing of puritanism'.[55] These included three Puritan members of the Yorkshire gentry (Sir Matthew Boynton, Sir Richard Saltonstall, Sir William Constable); Sir Nathaniel Rich, a kinsman of the Earl of Warwick and later a Fifth Monarchist; and two ministers, Thomas Goodwin and Philip Nye.[56] Both Goodwin and Nye were to emigrate to the Netherlands in the late 1630s, where they were to develop their semi-separatist ecclesiology. In the early 1640s they returned to England, established self-governing congregations in London, and defended the Independent cause at the Westminster Assembly against the Scots commissioners, including Rutherford. In the mid-1630s, however, the differences between them were not so clear.

It is intriguing to speculate on what Rutherford and his fellow nonconformists in Scotland would have done had the Laudian bishops continued to rule the roost. Would they have emigrated to New England, and if so would they have co-operated with the congregationalism of Massachusetts or tried to establish a Presbyterian system of church government? Or would they have stayed in Scotland and eventually separated from the Church of Scotland altogether, forming gathered congregations of the godly? These

---

[52] *Letters*, p. 611.   [53] *Letters*, pp. 578–9.
[54] See D. Stevenson, 'The radical party in the kirk, 1637–45', *Journal of Ecclesiastical History*, 25 (1974), 140–2.
[55] See M. Tolmie, *The Triumph of the Saints: The Separate Churches of London, 1616–49* (Cambridge, 1977), pp. 44–5.
[56] Livingstone's 'Memoirs', in *Historical Collections of Accounts of Revival*, ed. J. Gillies (Kelso, 1845), p. 172.

possibilities are rarely contemplated by historians because we know from hindsight that though the Protestant sects were to flourish in England, in Scotland separatism was to be a late, weak, and mainly Presbyterian development. Yet in the early seventeenth century this divergence would not have seemed inevitable, because there were many obvious similarities between the two countries. In both Scotland and England, the national church was controlled by the same king through bishops whom he appointed, and was tainted in the eyes of Puritans by ceremonies that they considered popish. In this period, widespread sectarianism looked no more likely in England than in Scotland, for Puritans in both countries had a strong aversion to schism. They preferred to foster a church within a church by means of conventicles. Or to put this another way, the growth of sectarianism would have been just as likely in Scotland as in England had the episcopal attack on Puritanism continued. Bishops were notoriously the most effective sect-makers of all; their persecution of non-separatist Puritans drove many into schism.

However, there was one vital difference between the ecclesiastical situations in England and Scotland. In England, from 1590 to 1640, Presbyterianism was nearly extinct. The English had never had a Presbyterian system of church government, and Archbishop Whitgift had crushed the campaign to establish one in the early 1590s. In Scotland, by contrast, a Presbyterian system had been established in the late sixteenth century, and although James VI set about dismantling it, Scottish Puritans never lost their vision of its restoration. Men like Rutherford, raised on the memories of the Presbyterian successes of the 1570s and 1580s, were far less likely to adopt semi-separatism than were English Puritans in a similar position. Nevertheless, had the Scottish Presbyterians been kept out of power for many more years, it is quite possible that Presbyterianism would have declined in Scotland as it did in England. To establish a system of presbyteries, synods and general assemblies, one needed the support of the state, and when that was not given, the tendency was to resort to separatist or semi-separatist gathered churches.[57]

In 1636, the chances of Presbyterianism being re-established seemed slim indeed. Rutherford was talking of Christ leaving Scotland, and in July he was banished to Aberdeen for his nonconformity. Yet just one year later, the Prayer Book riot was to transform the political and ecclesiastical face of the land. When, after the signing of the National Covenant, a General Assembly of the church was called for the first time since 1618, Rutherford knew that the great opportunity for ecclesiastical reform had arrived.

[57] See Watts, *The Dissenters: From the Reformation to the French Revolution* (Oxford, 1978), pp. 56–62.

TRIUMPH AND CONTROVERSY WITHIN THE SCOTTISH CHURCH
(1638–1643)

In June 1638, Rutherford preached in Edinburgh. Baillie recorded that he 'felles all the fourteen Bishops and hoghes the ceremonies'. Baillie himself was of a much more cautious temperament: 'As for Bishops and Ceremonies, I melled [meddled] not with them.'[58] In the General Assembly held at Glasgow in 1638, moderate opinion like that of Baillie was swept aside. Not only were the Service Book, the Book of Canons and the Five Articles of Perth condemned, but episcopacy was abolished too. It was a remarkable triumph for the Presbyterians.

Yet Rutherford regarded this as only the first step on the road of continuing reformation.[59] The popish innovations had been cleared away, but godly practices needed to be introduced. Over the next months, the radical party in the kirk continued to foster the private meetings and liturgical changes that they had been practising in the 1620s and 1630s. Their actions began to arouse opposition from within the covenanting movement, and in the General Assembly of 1639, the conservative minister, Henry Guthry, complained bitterly of the conventicles being held in his parish. A gulf began to open up within the church over this issue. Critics of private meetings believed they could discern Brownist tendencies at work among the radicals. Two of Rutherford's former mentors were amongst the fiercest critics of private meetings. Andrew Ramsay, professor of divinity in Edinburgh in the 1620s, spoke often against the radicals, as did David Calderwood, whose experience of sectarians in the Netherlands had left him deeply suspicious of anything that smelt of Brownism. However, together with his colleagues from the south-west – Blair, Dickson and Livingstone – Rutherford leapt to the defence of the conventicles. The 1640 Assembly, which met in conservative Aberdeen, proved thoroughly antagonistic towards the radical party, and an act was passed that limited family meetings to the members of one family, allowed set prayers and ruled that only ministers or prospective ministers could expound Scripture. In the Assembly of 1641, however, the radicals were able to replace the previous year's act with one that gave tacit approval to private meetings. In the following years, little was heard of the subject. The church accepted the existence of coventicles, for to do otherwise would have been to cause disunity and risk offending the English Puritans, many of whom were highly favourable to private meetings.

However, the controversy over liturgical innovations would not die down

---

[58] Baillie, *Letters and Journals*, I, p. 79.
[59] The following paragraphs rely heavily on Stevenson, 'The radical party'.

so easily. Prominent ministers, like Andrew Cant of Aberdeen, had given up the Lord's Prayer in favour of extemporary prayer, and instead of reading evening prayer gave lectures expounding the Scriptures. In the south-west, in particular, a number of ministers close to Rutherford refused to counte-nance practices such as bowing in the pulpit, and saying the Doxology. In this instance, Rutherford, together with fellow radicals, Dickson and Blair, tried to bring the dissenters into line. It is probable that he assumed that the forthcoming alliance with the English Puritans would lead to the removal of these ceremonies in due time. In the meantime, unity had to be preserved within the kirk.

The behaviour of the radical party in the years after 1638 aroused the suspicion that they had decidedly Brownist tendencies. In 1641, a letter was received by the General Assembly from some ministers in England who had heard a rumour that some well-known Scottish ministers (Dickson and Cant) favoured Independency. Among the clergy there was talk that the kirk was 'burning with schisme', and that men like Dickson were friendly towards the sects in Amsterdam and England. This was hardly fair, as there were almost no separatists in Scotland at this time, and the radicals in the kirk were not even semi-separatists like Goodwin and Nye, who formed congregations outside the parish system whilst still holding the established church to be a true church. Rutherford was categorical in a letter written around 1640: 'As for separation from worship for some errors of a church, the independency of single congregations, a church of visible saints, and other tenets of Brownists, they are contrary to God's word.' Indeed, he had at that moment a treatise in the press at London, 'against these conceits'.[60] Private meetings among the radicals were avowedly non-separatist in intent.

Nevertheless, these internal kirk disputes provide an indication that the Scottish kirk was not the monolithic bloc that contemporary Englishmen and later historians have too often assumed it to be. The Scots are usually seen to have alienated opinion south of the border by their arrogant attempt to impose their ecclesiastical system, and their hatred of toleration and Independency. But as David Stevenson has pointed out in his survey of these controversies within the kirk, Scottish Presbyterianism was itself divided, with some of the Scots – including Rutherford – inclining towards the English Puritan position on conventicles and towards an Independent position on liturgical matters. Indeed, in his *Peaceable and Temperate Plea for Paul's Presbyterie in Scotland* (1642), Rutherford used the 1641 General Assembly Act to reassure English Puritans that the kirk allowed private meetings and did not insist on set prayers.[61] Not only were the Scots

---

[60] *Letters*, p. 611. The treatise was *A Peaceable Plea for Pauls Presbyterie*, published in 1642 and directed against the Independents.

[61] *Peaceable Plea*, pp. 325–6.

commissioners prepared to make concessions in non-essential matters; some of them were actually expecting to see some positive changes in Scottish worship as a result of the alliance with the English parliament.

They were not to be disappointed. The *Directory for Public Worship*, drawn up by the Westminster Assembly, was approved by the Scottish General Assembly in January 1645. Although Baillie opposed some of its changes to traditional worship, Rutherford and Gillespie persuaded Henderson to accept them. The *Directory* recommended lectures expounding Scripture to be established, and urged that bowing in the pulpit be laid aside. The Doxology and set prayers were not banned, but neither were they encouraged, and in practice they were allowed to fall into disuse. This was just what Rutherford and his friends had desired. Not only had their private meetings been tacitly allowed by the 1641 General Assembly, but now the 1645 Assembly had been forced to accept their liturgical innovations. As Stevenson explains, 'The radicals in the kirk had triumphed.'[62]

THE CHALLENGES IN ENGLAND (1643–1647)

The vast majority of Rutherford's published work on the doctrine of the church was written not for a Scottish audience, but for an English one. It is natural, therefore, that he should be remembered as a staunch defender of the Scottish kirk, a man bitterly opposed to the major alternative available to the English in the 1640s – Independency and, with it, toleration. Yet in many ways, this is the exceptional period in Rutherford's life. As we have seen, his relationship with the Scottish kirk, whose polity he advocated so vigorously, was not always a happy one. He was classed among the radical innovators who veered towards Brownism. Yet to the English, Rutherford was the arch-conservative, one of the most prominent apologists for the tyranny of the Presbyterian hierarchy. At the Westminster Assembly, faced by common enemies, Rutherford and Gillespie plastered over their differences with Baillie, who waxed lyrical about his 'sweet colleagues' and testified that there was not 'the smallest eyelist betwixt any of us'.[63] Yet this was simply untrue. In the following pages we will examine Rutherford's contribution to English debates on church government in the 1640s, and argue that even when he got to England, he showed some sympathy towards the Independent position.[64]

[62] Stevenson, 'The radical party', p. 160.
[63] Baillie, *Letters and Journals*, II, p. 159.
[64] The fullest study of the Westminster Assembly is R. S. Paul, *The Assembly of the Lord: Politics and Religion in the Westminster Assembly and the 'Grand Debate'* (Edinburgh, 1985). On the role of Scottish commissioners at the Assembly see W. Spear, 'Covenanted uniformity in religion: the influence of the Scottish commissioners upon the ecclesiology of the Westminster Assembly', unpublished Ph.D. dissertation, University of Pittsburgh (1976),

Independency

In January 1644, only two months after Rutherford's arrival in London, five members of the Assembly published a pamphlet, *An Apologeticall Narration*, which revealed their differences with the Presbyterian majority. Up until this time they had closed ranks with the Presbyterians against the sects, but now they had declared their own dissent. Among the authors were Thomas Goodwin and Philip Nye, whom Livingstone had met ten years before on his visit to London. In the late 1630s, Goodwin and Nye had moved to the Netherlands, that haven of sects, where they had joined an Independent congregation at Arnhem. In their pamphlet they announced that they sought 'a middle way betwixt that which is falsely charged on us, Brownism, and that which is the contention of the times, the authoritative Presbyterial government'.[65]

The origins of their position can be traced to the congregationalism of Henry Jacob, who had established an Independent church in London in 1616, whose members continued to associate with their parish churches. They differed from Presbyterians in arguing that congregations should be self-governing and not subject to the ruling of higher ecclesiastical courts. However, unlike strict separatists, they did not deny that parish churches could be true churches, or dissociate themselves completely from the state church. After the collapse of the Presbyterian attempt to reform the English church on a national level in the 1590s, this belief that the concept of the gathered church could be reconciled with communion with the national church became attractive.[66] So when Goodwin and Nye emigrated to the Netherlands, they formed and joined congregations that were self-governing yet not opposed to the idea of a national established church. Because their stance was so ambiguous, the Independents are difficult to classify. For a while they tried to identify themselves with the New England ecclesiology of Cotton and Hooker, but whereas the New England Puritans had a system of parochial congregationalism that tolerated no dissent, the English Independents supported the idea of the gathered church and a limited toleration for orthodox separatists.[67]

---

and I. Murray, 'The Scots at the Westminster Assembly', *The Banner of Truth* (August–September, 1994), pp. 6–40. For a very detailed study of the ecclesiology of Gillespie, see W. D. J. MacKay, 'The nature of church government in the writings of George Gillespie (1613–48)', unpublished Ph.D. dissertation, Queen's University, Belfast (1992). Some of the minutes of the Assembly's debates were transcribed and published by A. Mitchell and J. Struthers, eds., *Minutes of the Sessions of the Westminster Assembly of Divines* (Edinburgh, 1874).

[65] *An Apologeticall Narration* is discussed in Watts, *Dissenters*, pp. 101–3.
[66] See Watts, *Dissenters*, pp. 50–66.
[67] Tolmie suggests that, in practice, the Independents were actually much closer to the sects than to the parish churches. See *Triumph of the Saints*, chs. 5–6.

Rutherford had conflicting feelings about these Independents. He had great respect for them as fellow sufferers for the Puritan cause under Episcopacy, and as defenders of orthodox Reformed theology. His *Peaceable and Temperate Plea*, as its title suggests, adopted a conciliatory tone towards the non-separating congregationalism of the New England Puritans, referring to them throughout as 'our brethren'. He considered the Independents to be 'friends, even gracious men', 'the best of the people'.[68] In a debate in the Assembly in February 1645, Rutherford declared that when he first read John Cotton's *Keys of the Kingdome*, published by the Independents, 'I thought it an easy labour for an universal pacification, he comes so near to us.'[69]

It should not surprise us, therefore, that in the Assembly debates, Rutherford and Gillespie sided with the English Independents on several points where they disagreed with the English Presbyterians. As far as liturgical practice was concerned, the Scottish radicals agreed with the Independents on the value of extemporary prayer, and the dangers of a fixed liturgy.[70] Rutherford also opposed those who favoured a system of rigidly fixed congregations, with no freedom to seek fellowship outside the parish. He argued that being in the vicinity of a church was not an adequate basis for determining church membership, but that the consent of the people was also necessary. Although he thought that a church covenant was not needed at a local level, he did favour a 'voluntary agreement' on the part of the church members in order to form a congregation. Spear suggests that Rutherford's views may have had something to do with the mildness with which the Assembly treated the gathering of churches.[71] The Scottish commissioners also submitted a paper to the Assembly recommending that governing power rest with the elders of a congregation, rather than with the classical presbyteries, as the *Second Book of Discipline* had suggested. Calderwood was deeply disturbed by this, and wrote to them saying that it constituted 'a great stepp to Independencie'. The two more conservative commissioners, Baillie and Henderson, came to agree with this verdict. Rutherford and Gillespie, on the other hand, did not deny that suspension, excommunication and ordination had to be carried out by higher courts, but they wanted a power of general oversight to reside in the congregation.[72]

Furthermore, Rutherford was happy to stand closer to the Independents

[68] *Letters*, pp. 618–19. See also p. 616.   [69] See Paul, *Assembly of the Lord*, p. 435.
[70] See above. See also Paul, *Assembly of the Lord*, p. 445.
[71] Spear, 'Covenanted uniformity', pp. 214–17. Paul argues that the Scots ecclesiology 'in some ways was closer to the Independents' than to that of the English Presbyterians, who pressed for a simplified form of the traditional English parish. *Assembly of the Lord*, p. 345. See also p. 209.
[72] On this see Spear, 'Covenanted uniformity', pp. 249–50; Paul, *Assembly of the Lord*, pp. 342–3.

than to the English Presbyterians on the role of the congregation in electing a minister.[73] Whereas most English Presbyterians were only willing to give the congregation a power of veto, Rutherford defended their power to elect: 'The Scriptures constantly give the choice of the pastor to the people. The act of electing is in the people; and the regulating and correcting of their choice is in the presbytery.'[74] By acknowledging the role of the presbytery, and its power to ordain, Rutherford distanced himself from the position which said that the power of ordination lay wholly with the local congregation. However, his emphasis on 'election' went beyond even the *Second Book of Discipline*, which spoke only of the eldership electing and the congregation consenting.[75] All of this should again remind us that Scottish Presbyterians were not a monolithic bloc united in implacable opposition to anything that smelled of Independency.[76] As Spear says, the experience of the 1620s and 1630s seems to have given Rutherford and Gillespie a heightened sense of the authority of the local congregation.[77]

However, Rutherford knew that for all their virtues, the Independents were 'mighty opposites to presbyterial government',[78] and most of his energies in the Assembly debates and in his books were directed against their position. Despite making room for the role of the congregation in electing a minister, Rutherford was adamant that the power of the keys mentioned in Matthew 16 – the power to ordain, suspend, excommunicate – belonged not to 'the multitude of believers' but to 'Church guides' or elders. For Presbyterians, the government of God's house was not 'Democraticall and popular'; if the power of the keys were given to all believers, then women and children would have authority over the congregation (a quite unthinkable state of affairs).[79]

Rutherford also took issue with the Independents' criterion for church membership. Following the New England Congregationalists, the Independents argued that only those who were perceived, according to Christian charity, to be among the elect, could be received into membership. They aimed at a church made up of 'visible saints'.[80] To Rutherford, this was a repetition of the old Donatist confusion of the pure invisible church of the

---

[73] See Paul, *Assembly of the Lord*, pp. 315–31.
[74] John Lightfoot, *Journal of the Proceedings of the Assembly of Divines* in *Complete Works*, XII, ed. J. R. Pitman (London, 1824), p. 231.
[75] *Second Book of Discipline*, ed. J. Kirk, p. 179.
[76] Baillie, *Letters and Journals*, III, p. 94, records that in a 1649 debate, Rutherford and James Wood defended the congregation's right to elect a minister, whereas the other ministers present followed Gillespie's *Miscellanies* in arguing that the presbytery directed, the kirk session ordained, and the people consented.
[77] Spear, 'Covenanted uniformity', p. 216.
[78] *Letters*, p. 618.   [79] *Peaceable Plea*, chs. 1–8.
[80] The classic discussion of their position is E. S. Morgan, *Visible Saints: The History of a Puritan Idea* (Ithaca, 1963).

elect, and the mixed visible church of professors.[81] Their position amounted to 'downe right Anabaptisme',[82] and assumed that one could read men's hearts. Yet the example of hypocrites in the New Testament church – Ananias and Sapphira, Judas and Simon Magus – showed that even the apostles could not do this.[83] Augustine and his followers had been right when they asserted that the 'Visible Church is a draw net, wherein are good and bad fishes, a barne-floore, wherein are chaffe and good wheat'.[84] All that was required to constitute a true church was 'The pure Word of God purely preached, and the sacraments duely administred, with discipline according to God's Word, and withall a people externally professing the fore-said faith.'[85] A church that fulfilled these requirements was a true church even if all its members were hypocrites, and its pastor was himself unsaved.[86] The Donatists were entirely wrong to suggest that the effectiveness of the ordinances depended upon the holiness of the minister.[87] Although Rutherford denied the Roman Catholic doctrine of the 'character *indelibilis*' of the priest, he insisted on an apostolic succession of pastors (though not on an unbroken succession), and even on the validity of ordination and baptism performed by papists and bishops.[88] Against the charisma-oriented ecclesiology of the Independents, he was determined to assert the importance of formal office.

This emphasis on office and form as well as personal virtue was connected to the Presbyterian belief that the church was to be a national institution that embraced the whole population, and not just a congregation of the saints. Rutherford had no objection to private meetings of the godly within this church, but he wanted to avoid the exclusivism of the sects. He could not agree with the New England policy of restricting baptism to the children of visible saints, nor with the Baptists' complete rejection of infant baptism. 'All infants borne within the visible church', he argued, 'whatever the wickednesse of their neerest parents are to be received within the church by Baptisme.'[89] The visible church was to be a truly comprehensive, national church. Rutherford also wanted it to be a pure church, of course, but by this he meant a church pure in its doctrine and forms, not one composed entirely of the elect.

---

[81] For comparisons of the Independents to the Donatists, see *Peaceable Plea*, p. 147; *Survey of Hooker*, pp. 40, 45, 64.
[82] *Due Right*, p. 268.
[83] *Peaceable Plea*, p. 106; *Survey of Hooker*, pp. 13, 53–6.
[84] *Peaceable Plea*, p. 94. In his *Due Right*, p. 255, Rutherford listed the names of sixty-one Fathers and Reformers who supported this Augustinian ecclesiology.
[85] *Peaceable Plea*, pp. 97–8.   [86] *Peaceable Plea*, p. 31.   [87] *Due Right*, p. 41.
[88] *Due Right*, pp. 186–9. See also pp. 237–41.
[89] *Peaceable Plea*, pp. 164–83. Rutherford justified this by appeal to the external or 'federal' covenant which was discussed in Chapter 6.

Besides differing with the Independents over the breadth of the church's membership, Rutherford also crossed swords with them over its jurisdiction. Goodwin and his colleagues came into conflict with the other Westminster divines largely because they were unwilling to accept that local congregations had to submit to synodical judgements. The Presbyterians believed that this was contrary to the example of the early church, where controversies had been settled by the decisions of synods, such as the council of Jerusalem recorded in Acts 15.[90] They argued for a system of ascending courts, ranging from individual kirk sessions, through presbyteries, provincial synods, general assemblies, to ecumenical synods like the one that had taken place at Dort some twenty-five years before.[91] Christ, argued Rutherford, had promised that his Spirit would lead the church into all truth, and this promise held good for ecumenical councils.[92] Although the word of synods was only to be believed 'in so farre as it is agreeable to the Word of God', this was not to say 'that Pastors and Synods have no power and authoritie at all to determine, but onely to counsell, advise and perswade'.[93]

Erastianism

If the Independents feared the tyranny of synods over local congregations, another minority group within the Assembly feared that the Scottish model would result in a clerical tyranny over the civil magistrates. This group became known as the Erastians, after the Swiss theologian Thomas Erastus (1524–83), who argued against Beza that the civil authorities in a state with one religion have the right to exercise jurisdiction over ecclesiastical matters. Whereas the Scots, following Andrew Melville, saw good discipline (such as excommunication and suspension from communion) as an essential mark of the church to be administered *jure divino* by elders, the Erastians believed that it was too great a power to be left wholly in the hands of the clergy. 'A Christian magistrate as a Christian magistrate is a Governor in the church', declared one of their number, Thomas Coleman, in a controversial sermon to the House of Commons in July 1645. This was a message with an obvious appeal to MPs like the erudite John Selden, himself a member of the Assembly. Selden fits the Scottish stereotype of the Erastians as cynical men who merely wanted to increase the power of the civil magistrate. However, as William Lamont has explained, Erastus and his seventeenth-century successors like Coleman and Prynne, were actually deeply concerned about the reform of the church, but believed that if the clergy were able to excommunicate sinners *en masse*, the result would be a

---

[90] See *Peaceable Plea*, ch. 14; *Due Right*, pp. 355ff.
[91] *Due Right*, p. 332.   [92] *Due Right*, pp. 374, 332b.   [93] *Due Right*, p. 345.

loss of the church's influence rather than a moral reformation. They agreed with the Presbyterians about the end, but not the means.[94]

The debate between the Melvillian and the Erastian factions in the Westminster Assembly and the City of London raged for a year after Coleman's sermon.[95] The major Scottish critic of the Erastians was Rutherford's fellow commissioner, George Gillespie. Yet Rutherford himself produced a major work on the controversy, *The Divine Right of Church Government and Excommunication*, published in March 1646. In it, he defended Melville's two kingdom theory as laid out in the *Second Book of Discipline*. According to the theory, church and state were distinct, with different sources, means and ends. The church was concerned with the internal, spiritual part of man, his soul and conscience, and could only use persuasive, non-violent corrective punishments, most notably excommunication. Christ, in Matthew 18, had given the church the authority to preach and the 'keys of the kingdom' to discipline its members. However, he 'hinteth not, in any sort, at any word of blood, wrath, vengeance, the sword . . . the proceeding here is with much lenity, patience and long suffering to gain an offender'.[96] The magistrate, on the other hand, was concerned with the external part of man, and he could add co-active, compulsive and penal punishments to the gentle censures of the church, a case which Rutherford argued at length elsewhere. The two powers were intended to be 'co-ordinate', 'two parallel supreme powers on earth',[97] each operating in their own sphere and complementing each other.

The Melvillian concern to distinguish the spheres of church and state entailed a rejection of theocracy, if by that we mean rule by clerics. Although Rutherford talked often of the reign of 'King Jesus', he did not envisage a wholesale destruction of Scotland's traditional constitution or a replacement of secular rulers by godly ministers.[98] In a letter to the Scottish parliament in 1648, he wrote that 'we professe our detestation of yt Episcopal disease of authoritative meddling with civil affaires'.[99] The prelates were like frogs, moving in two elements, church and state.[100] The

---

[94] W. Lamont, *Godly Rule: Politics and Religion, 1603–60* (London, 1969), ch. 5; 'Pamphleteering, the Protestant consensus and the English Revolution', in R. C. Richardson and G. M. Ridden, eds., *Freedom and the English Revolution* (Manchester, 1986), pp. 78–80.

[95] For a helpful summary see G. Yule, *Puritans in Politics: The Religious Legislation of the Long Parliament, 1640–47* (Appleford, 1981), ch. 7.

[96] *Divine Right*, pp. 227–8.   [97] *Due Right*, p. 407.

[98] This distinguishes the Covenanter clergy quite sharply from theocrats like the Shi'ite clerics in Iran, who after their revolution quickly established a hierocracy run according to sacred law. See S. A. Arjomand, *The Turban for the Crown: The Islamic Revolution in Iran* (Oxford, 1988).

[99] Minutes of the Presbytery of St Andrews, 1641–1656, St Andrews University Library, deposit 23, p. 131.

[100] *Lex, Rex*, p. 432 [216].

Scottish Presbyterian clergy, by contrast, did not usurp both swords, but had excluded themselves from civil office in 1638, and condemned the prelates, 'because they, being pastors, would be also lords of parliament, of session, of secret council, of exchequer, judges, barons, and in their lawless high commission, would fine, imprison, and use the sword'.[101] The Presbyterians, unlike even Catholic conciliarists, claimed no authority to wield 'coercive temporal power' and to fine or imprison heretics. In theory, at least, they did not aim at clerical tyranny or priestly government.

Nevertheless, Rutherford's writings failed to calm troubled English minds. The Scottish clergy may not have held civil office, but they certainly tried to be the unofficial power behind the throne, exerting immense psychological pressure on politicians in order to persuade them to implement their policies and impose civil penalties on their enemies. The Presbyterian ideal seemed to be one of the church prescribing and the magistrate executing (sometimes literally). The power of excommunication alone was a great weapon in a society in which everyone belonged to one church. Rutherford was adamant that even a ruler could be excommunicated from the fellowship of the church. He pointed to the example of Ambrose, who had demanded penance from the Emperor Theodosius after the latter had ordered the massacre of the Thessalonians.[102] If magistrates 'crush the poore and needy, and turne tyrant, as heretick and an apostate', he warned, 'the Pastors may not only denounce wrath from the Lord against them, but also judge them dogs and swine, and not dispense to them the pearls of the Gospel'.[103]

Besides threatening the magistrate with excommunication if he did not toe their line, the Presbyterians also greatly reduced his legislative power. As John Ford has shown, the Episcopalians argued that the king could determine things indifferent and that the people were obliged to follow his ruling. The Presbyterians, however, claimed that nothing was in practice indifferent and that the morality of every action was determined by divine authority. By doing so they 'were not so much subverting public authority as elevating the private authority of right-minded ministers'. Since everything was regulated by divine law, the people were obliged to examine every law in their consciences before obeying it, so that they could be sure that it was consonant with the Word of God.[104] Almost inevitably this meant that they had to rely on the guidance of the clerical casuists who were experts in the divine law of Scripture.[105] Ultimately, therefore, despite their refusal to occupy civil office, the Presbyterians advocated a radical redistribution of moral authority from the civil magistrate to the clergy.

[101] *Lex, Rex*, sig. a2v.   [102] *Divine Right*, pp. 437–47.   [103] *Divine Right*, p. 537.
[104] See *Divine Right*, pp. 42–5.
[105] Ford, 'Lawful bonds of Scottish society', pp. 61–2.

Another aspect of Presbyterian practice was equally worrying to godly Erastians. By talking freely of suspension from communion, the Presbyterians were keeping away from the sacrament the very people who needed it the most – ungodly Christians. Rutherford insisted that only children, the ignorant, the mad and the scandalous would be excluded,[106] but elsewhere he spoke of 'multitudes' of 'hearers' and 'knowne unbeleevers' not being admitted to the sacrament.[107] The Erastians realised that in practice the Presbyterians often admitted very few parishioners to communion. As Rutherford said, the preaching of the Word was the converting ordinance, not the partaking of the sacrament.[108] For this reason, although preaching was open to everyone, and baptism available to all those born into the church, communion was to be severely restricted. The Independents might complain that the Scottish church was too comprehensive, but for the Erastians it was too exclusive.

In the end, it was the Erastians who understood Rutherford and Gillespie best. Although both men supported the ideal of a national church, they had always encouraged the formation of a church within a church through special gatherings of the truly godly. In the 1650s, as we shall see, Rutherford's desire for a pure church was to undermine his support for a comprehensive church. William Campbell maintained that this purism and the plentitude of suspensions and excommunications after the Engagement could be traced to the idea of excommunication formulated by Rutherford, Wariston and Gillespie at the Westminster Assembly.[109] Rutherford was adamant in the *Divine Right*, that a verbal profession of repentance was not enough for those who wished to be readmitted to the sacrament. Those who advocated tolerant admission policies, he suggested, were prepared to accept those who had 'come but an houre before out of the Bordell-house, and have hands and sword hot and smoking with innocent blood'.[110] This was the line he was to take after the Engagement and the defeat at Dunbar, and it was intransigence on this point that ultimately divided the Church of Scotland in the 1650s.

English Presbyterians

In the mid-1640s, however, the challenges of Independency and Erastianism did not prevent the triumph of Presbyterianism in the Westminster Assembly. Indeed, as George Yule reminds us, the voices of Independent and

---

[106] *Peaceable Plea*, pp. 184–6.   [107] *Peaceable Plea*, p. 187.
[108] *Divine Right*, pp. 523–4.
[109] W. Campbell, 'Samuel Rutherford: propagandist and exponent of Scottish Presbyterianism', unpublished Ph.D. dissertation, University of Edinburgh (1937), p. 215.
[110] *Divine Right*, pp. 489–90.

Erastian ministers were actually rarely heard in sermons to parliament, and the documents that the Assembly produced – the *Directory of Worship*, the *Larger and Shorter Catechisms*, the *Confession of Faith* and the *Form of Presbyteriall Church Government* (FPCG) – were all more or less satisfactory to the Scots.[111] The FPCG endorsed many of the ecclesiastical offices and practices that the Scots had advocated: the office of deacon, the congregation's right to veto the appointment of an unsuitable pastor, a plurality of officers at congregational level, ordination by presbyteries, ruling elders, and a hierarchy of assemblies. Altogether, thirteen out of the fourteen points in the FPCG were in conformity with the Scottish pattern. Only the claim that those in the office of teacher had the right to administer the sacrament was contrary to the *Books of Discipline*.[112]

However, we have already seen that the Scots differed from their English Presbyterian allies on a number of points, and the FPCG did not meet all their requirements. The Scots did not succeed in converting the English divines to fully fledged Melvillianism as some historians have asserted.[113] Many of the elements that they wished to be recognised as 'by divine right' (prescribed as obligatory by Scripture) were simply 'recommended' or said to be 'permissible'. This was true of the power of assemblies to call members before them and dispense church censures, the governing of several congregations by one presbytery, and the existence of several kinds of synodical assemblies.

Yet although it was inferior to the *Second Book of Discipline* in their estimation, the Scots accepted the FPCG. They had covenanted to do so, and they were determined not to break their covenant. As a number of historians have pointed out, this is clear evidence of the good faith in which the Scots engaged in the Westminster Assembly debates. They had sent their commissioners to an Assembly where they were greatly outnumbered, and agreed to abide by its findings. When a document was produced that was not entirely satisfactory, they nevertheless willingly accepted it as the new constitution for the Church of Scotland.[114]

Sectarianism and toleration

If the Scots were pleased about persuading the English to accept their model of church government, however diluted, they were to be disappointed by the outcome. A Presbyterian system was never effectively established, except in London and a few other areas. In the rest of the country, as John Morrill has demonstrated, much of the population and many of the clergy retained

---

[111] Yule, *Puritans in Politics*, pp. 163–71.   [112] Spear, 'Covenanted uniformity', p. 342.
[113] Especially Yule, *Puritans in Politics*, p. 157.
[114] See Spear, 'Covenanted uniformity', pp. 18, 331–49.

a strong attachment to Prayer Book Anglicanism.[115] Moreover, although parliament was predominantly in favour of a Presbyterian form of church government, real power now lay with the New Model Army, which was favourably disposed not only towards the clerical semi-separatists, but also towards much more radical sects like the Baptists. In the late 1640s, as power shifted to the Independents in the army, Rutherford realised that what was being advocated by them went far beyond the New England Way. John Cotton's *Keys of the Kingdome*, he claimed, 'is well sound in our way, if he had given some more power to assemblies'. But now the Independents opposed 'that Godly and learned Divine' and pleaded for toleration of the sects.[116] The talk was now of toleration for all godly Protestants, and many sectarian preachers were openly hostile to all set forms of church government. The sects, rather than the respectable clerical Independents, were to be Rutherford's target in the late 1640s.[117]

Rutherford had been aware of the sects since he arrived in London. His first experience of the city must have been comparable to that of a 'Wee Free' from the Western Isles dropped into the religious jungle that is contemporary California. We can detect his disorientation and consternation in his early letters home. He had been aware of the phenomenon of gathered churches since the 1630s at least, but he had probably never encountered out-and-out separatists before he went to London. He was discovering that in the crowded alleyways of the capital, 'Multitudes of Anabaptists, Antinomians, Familists, Separatists' had begun to gather.[118] The varieties of these sects were soon enumerated by the English Presbyterian, Thomas Edwards, in his major work, *Gangraena*, published in three parts in 1646. Edwards counted sixteen types of sectaries and as many as 271 different errors, including Socinianism and even atheism.[119]

Rutherford did not publish a major treatise on the sects until November 1648, after he had been back in Scotland for a whole year. Before this time he had been preoccupied with events within the Assembly, and with refuting respectable Puritan clergymen who supported Independency and Erastianism. In his *Survey of Spiritual Antichrist*, however, he declared: 'I have long been silent . . . silence may be a washing of the hands with Pilate,

---

[115] J. Morrill, 'The Church in England, 1642–49', in his *The Nature of the English Revolution* (Harlow, 1993), ch. 7.

[116] *Survey of Antichrist*, p. 177.

[117] On the growth of religious radicalism and ideas of religious toleration during the 1640s see J. F. McGregor and B. Reay, eds., *Radical Religion in the English Revolution* (Oxford, 1984); Tolmie, *Triumph of the Saints*; Watts, *Dissenters*, Pt. II; Yule, *Puritans in Politics*, ch. 8.

[118] *Letters*, p. 619. On the sectarian underground in 1640s London, see P. F. Gura, *A Glimpse of Sion's Glory: Puritan Radicalism in New England, 1620–60* (Middleton, Conn., 1984), ch. 10.

[119] A brief summary of Edwards's book is to be found in Watts, *Dissenters*, pp. 111–15.

saying, I am innocent of the blood of lost souls.' He paid tribute to Thomas Edwards, who was one of the few to protest against the rising tide of heresy in the land, and lamented the fact that Scottish Presbyterians were reviled in England, though they had stood up to Charles I and popery when 'not one sect durst face the field against Antichrist'.[120]

The *Survey* has been described as 'the first substantial analysis in the English tongue of Enthusiasm', predating by a decade those of Henry More and Meric Causabon.[121] One of its major concerns was to add some historical depth to Edwards's contemporary portrait, by tracing the origins of the present heresies back to the Anabaptist and Spiritualist teachers of the early Reformation period. Almost every error of the present time, Rutherford argued, had been maintained by men like Thomas Muntzer, Caspar Swenckfeld, Balthasar Hubmaier, Melchoir Hoffman and Menno Simons. The idea that the moral law had been abolished by Christ, that the Christian was perfect and divine, that wars were unlawful, that property should be held in common, that human learning was sinful, that Scripture should be interpreted allegorically, that the magistrate should not prosecute heretics – all these beliefs, Rutherford demonstrated, had been found among the Anabaptists.[122] They had also been promoted in England by the sect known as the Family of Love, which had been founded by the sixteenth-century German Roman Catholic, Henry Nicholas. Nicholas had spent some time in England, and though the Familists survived underground, their ideas had recently resurfaced in New England and now in England itself.[123]

The re-emergence of these old ideas in England in the 1640s had led to a proliferation of Protestant sects, the like of which had only been seen before in the early days of the Reformation in Switzerland and Germany and in that hotbed of the sects, Amsterdam. Rutherford was horrified by this fragmentation, and believed that it could be attributed to the Antinomian tendency to play down the value of the external forms, ordinances and offices that traditionally held the church together. Many of the sects were 'enthusiasts' whose emphasis on the inner promptings of the Spirit led to every man setting up his own conscience as his pope and turning Scripture into a 'nose of wax' which could be twisted to fit with subjective

---

[120] *Survey of Spiritual Antichrist*, preface.
[121] E. C. Walker, *William Dell: Master Puritan* (Cambridge, 1970), p. 92.
[122] See Part I, chs. 2–5,
[123] Rutherford discusses Henry Nicholas in Part I, pp. 56–68, and thereafter indiscriminately labels many of the heretics he describes as 'Familists'. He reproduces the 1604 petition of the Familists to James I on pp. 343–53. C. Marsh, *The Family of Love in English Society, 1550–1630* (Cambridge, 1994), provides the fullest study of the Familists. He suggests (p. 241), that Rutherford's claim about an underground Familist movement resurfacing in the 1640s in the form of numerous sects is less likely than a continuity of hostile stereotype.

whims.[124] Some, like John Saltmarsh, had gone so far as to denounce all formal ministry and taught that all believers could preach, because in Christ all had the same office.[125] William Dell, another New Model Army chaplain, also denigrated outward reformation of church and state as 'carnall', and wrought by flesh and blood. What mattered, he claimed, was not the letter of the Word, or the work of the magistrate, or reformation of church government, but the work of the Spirit in the heart.[126] Rutherford discerned this antiformalism in the commander of the New Model Army, Oliver Cromwell. In his 'scandalous and unsound' letter to the House of Commons in 1645, Cromwell had written that what really mattered was that 'Presbyterians, Independents, all have the same Spirit of Faith and Prayer'. Real union was not external, but inward, and the sword could not be used to interfere with religious beliefs, which were 'things of the minde'.[127] Conscience was inviolable.

Rutherford believed that by exalting the role of conscience and the concept of 'new light', men like Cromwell were encouraging a subjectivist approach to religion and opening the floodgates to a fissiparous pluralism. 'Conscience is hereby made every mans Rule, Umpire, Judge, Bible and his God',[128] and with as many opinions as individual consciences and no objective criteria by which to judge them, faith was turned into a 'whirly-gigge'.[129] Subjectivism bred pluralism which engendered scepticism.[130] Rutherford summarised the end result in one of his wittiest pieces of satire, an Independent prayer:

> Lord open my eyes, and increase my knowledge, grant that thy holy Spirit may bestow upon my dark soule more scepticall, conjecturall, and fluctuating knowledge to know and beleeve things with a reserve, and with a leaving of roome to beleeve the contrary tomorrow of that which I beleeve today, and the contradicent of that the third day which I shall beleeve tomorrow, and so till I dye; let me Lord, have the grace of a circular faith, running like the wheel of a wind-mill.[131]

Rutherford's response to this situation can be found in the *Survey of Antichrist* and *A Free Disputation against Pretended Liberty of Conscience* (1649). Religion, he maintained, could not be purely internal; it had to be embodied in actions and institutions that were far from being simply

---

[124] Rutherford uses the 'nose of wax' image in *Survey of Antichrist* and *Free Disputation*. On the history of its use see H. C. Porter, 'The nose of wax: Scripture and the Spirit from Erasmus to Milton', *Transactions of the Royal Historical Society*, 14 (1964), 155–74.

[125] *Survey of Antichrist*, I, p. 214.   [126] *Survey of Antichrist*, II, pp. 187–217.

[127] *Survey of Antichrist*, I, pp. 250–61. On Cromwell's antiformalism, see Davis, 'Cromwell's religion', pp. 201–8.

[128] *Free Disputation*, sig. A3v.   [129] *Free Disputation*, p. 77.

[130] For a classic sociological exposition of the corrosive effects of pluralism on religious belief see P. Berger, *The Social Reality of Religion* (Harmondsworth, 1973).

[131] *Free Disputation*, p. 81.

indifferent. 'External and spiritual are not opposed', he declared in 1646, 'nor are politicall and spirituall opposed.'[132] Rutherford did not deny the importance of the 'internal' in religion, of course. We have seen in Chapter 4 that he placed great stress on the work of the Spirit, and on the experiences of the heart. But as a good Presbyterian, he also believed that forms of church government and worship had been biblically prescribed, and were of immense value as the framework within which spiritual life could flourish. As he explained, Presbyterians believed that true union consisted in union 'in the true Doctrine, and substantial practices of faith, worship, government of the Church in fundamentals'.[133]

Rutherford began his reassertion of the objective by challenging the new notion of conscience. Traditionally, a good conscience had been seen as one that combined good will and right understanding.[134] However, Cromwell seemed to think that as long as a man had good intentions, he could not be said to have failed against religion. The implication of this view, according to Rutherford, was that religion was 'fettered within the circle of the mind', and its consequences were far reaching. If one denied that true religion was intimately bound up with certain practices and forms, one could have nothing to say to the man who sincerely believed it was his religious right to take fifteen wives, or sacrifice his child to God.[135] In order to avoid this dire situation, one had to reassert the traditional teaching that 'A conscience void of knowledge is void of goodnesse.'[136] Conscience was 'not a free borne absolute Princesse' which could 'no more incur guiltinesse in its operations about an infinite Sovereigne God, and his revealed will . . . then can fire in burning'.[137] As we saw in the last chapter, Rutherford believed that although conscience had once been a reliable guide for man, the Fall had seriously damaged it, erasing much of the knowledge of religion and morality that Adam had possessed.[138] Because conscience was no longer like Scripture, nor 'God nor Pope, but can reele, and totter and dream', it was not to be considered as 'an Absolute and independent Soveraigne, whose voice is a law', but as 'an under-Judge onely', subordinate to God's will revealed in the law of nature written in the hearts of all, and in the

---

[132] *Divine Right*, p. 422.   [133] *Survey of Antichrist*, I, p. 257.

[134] Two recent articles illuminate the differences between the traditional and the modern ideas of conscience, and argue that this period was one of transition from one to the other. See M. Goldie, 'The theory of religious intolerance in Restoration England', in O. P. Grell, J. I. Israel and N. Tyacke, eds., *From Persecution to Toleration: The Glorious Revolution and Religion in England* (Oxford, 1991), ch. 13; K. Thomas, 'Cases of conscience in seventeenth-century England', in J. Morrill, P. Slack and D. Woolf, eds., *Public Duty and Private Conscience in Seventeenth Century England: Essays Presented to G. E. Aylmer* (Oxford, 1993), pp. 29–56.

[135] *Survey of Antichrist*, I, p. 261.   [136] *Free Disputation*, p. 5.

[137] *Free Disputation*, sig. A3.   [138] *Free Disputation*, p. 7.

Scriptures which had republished and clarified that law.[139] The focus had to be on the objective material on which conscience worked.[140]

Of course, the difficulty with appealing to objective Scripture was that there were many different interpretations of that most complex of texts. Indeed, the situation in England in the late 1640s amounted to hermeneutical anarchy. Christopher Hill, one of the historians most familiar with this period, has asserted that the Bible lost its universal power in these years because 'it had been demonstrated that you could prove anything from it, and that there was no means of deciding [between interpretations] once the authority of the church could not be enforced. (How right Rome had been!)'[141] Rutherford wanted to show that Rome had not been right. He argued that Scripture was – despite appearances to the contrary – perfectly perspicuous, if interpreted according to the grammatical-historical method. To follow the allegorical and typological hermeneutic of Origen – which sought to uncover esoteric symbolism in the Bible – was 'lying wrestling of Scripture from the literall and native sense of the Spirit',[142] and made it impossible for Scripture to be a 'certain rule of faith'. Only 'by setting letter to letter, Scripture to Scripture (understood according to the naturall, and genuine grammaticall sense, which the words yeeld with constraint)' could the Bible become a book with objective, identifiably univocal meanings and so become 'the judge of controversies'.[143] This was not to say that 'Christians should adore and fall downe before an Inke-Divinity, and meere paper-godlinesse, as if the Spirit were frozen into inke',[144] but it was to rescue religion from pure subjectivism and to provide it with a stable and authoritative reference point.

[139] *Free Disputation*, pp. 10, 8.

[140] For this reason it would be a mistake to drive a wedge between Rutherford's Thomistic faith in 'right reason' in *Lex, Rex* (1644), and his Calvinian sense of the fallenness of human reason in *A Free Disputation* (1649). As we saw in Chapter 6, Rutherford always balanced a Thomistic belief in natural law with a Calvinian sense that, because of the Fall, unaided reason was inadequate and the mind was not necessarily a vehicle of rationality. In order to function properly, reason had to depend on divine revelation, which re-equipped it with the knowledge about God and morality that man had possessed before the Fall. Heretics were irrational because they trusted their own fallen minds without checking them against the objective revelation given by God. Richard Tuck, 'Power and authority in seventeenth-century England', *Historical Journal*, 17 (1974), 60, rightly sees that Rutherford attached high importance to the idea of rationality in both politics and ecclesiastical matters, but fails to note that Rutherford saw rationality as only attainable through the aid of revelation. His attitude was summed up in his reminder to the subjectivist sectarians (*Survey of Antichrist*, I, p. 315) that 'all the Scripture is a masse and booke of discoursive refined reason, unbeleevers are absurd, unreasonable men, going against sense and sound reason'.

[141] C. Hill, *The English Bible and the Seventeenth-Century Revolution* (Harmondsworth, 1993), p. 428.

[142] *Survey of Antichrist*, I, p. 296. See also p. 229.

[143] *Survey of Antichrist*, I, p. 272.   [144] *Survey of Antichrist*, I, p. 304.

Elevating the grammatical-historical method of interpretation to such a level inevitably put a considerable amount of authority in the hands of those trained to read Scripture according to this method. Rutherford acknowledged this, and although he wanted all Christians to read Scripture he was clearly worried by the tendency of 'mechanick' preachers to think that the direct inspiration of the Spirit made them as qualified to teach as educated ministers. He had no time for the anti-intellectualism of William Dell, and maintained that those who 'goe from weaving, sowing, carpentarie, shoo-making to the pulpit . . . being voyd of all learning, tongues, logick, arts, sciences, and the literal knowledge of the Scripture' had not been sent by the Lord. Christ, after all, knew Hebrew and used logical consequences, and human learning when sanctified by the Spirit, could help men to understand the Scriptures and solve disputes.[145]

In cases where there was conflict over Christian doctrine and practice, therefore, a solution could be found in the authoritative decision of properly trained ministers, meeting in a synod and interpreting Scripture according to the grammatical-historical method. If this approach was not followed, and 'if interpretations be left free to every man', the inevitable result would be 'millions of faiths with millions of senses, and so no faith at all'.[146] Rutherford did not claim for Protestant synods the infallibility that had been claimed for Roman Catholic councils, because only Scripture could be regarded as infallible, and the judgements of synods were binding only insofar as they were 'agreeable to the Word of God'.[147] Nevertheless, he believed that a synodical pronouncement had to be taken very seriously, and could 'burie [heresies] by the power of the Word'.[148]

Besides the authority of an objective Scripture interpreted by a synod, there was one more formal authority to which Rutherford pointed – that of the magistrate.[149] To the definitions, teachings and prescriptions of the church, the magistrate could add 'a civill sanction', 'an accumulate and auxiliary supplement'.[150] Rutherford's support for this use of the sword in religious matters was linked to his formalism. He knew that the sword 'cannot reach soule, minde, will, conscience and affections', and that it was not 'a meanes of converting soules to Christ'. Yet because he considered

[145] *Survey of Antichrist*, I, pp. 45–55.   [146] *Free Disputation*, p. 28.
[147] *Survey of Antichrist*, sig. b2. He insisted strongly on this point, claiming that Henry Burton had deliberately misrepresented the Scottish view on the matter.
[148] *Free Disputation*, p. 32.
[149] On Rutherford's argument against toleration see W. Campbell, 'The Scottish Westminster Commissioners and toleration', *Records of the Scottish Church History Society*, 9 (1947), 1–18; J. Cameron, 'Scottish Calvinism and the principle of intolerance', in B. Gerrish, ed., *Reformatio Perennis* (Pittsburg, Pa., 1981), pp. 113–28; J. Hunt, *Religious Thought in England from the Reformation to the End of the Last Century*, I (London, 1870), pp. 353–8.
[150] *Free Disputation*, pp. 61b–62b.

external circumstances to be of considerable importance, he believed that the 'externall' sword could be used to 'hinder wolves and greivous foxes', so that the external environment in which souls dwelt would not be dangerously polluted with heresy.[151]

Like Bullinger in the sixteenth century and the Anglican divines of the Restoration period, Rutherford appealed to the authority of St Augustine's writings against the Donatists to support his doctrine of persecution.[152] But of even greater importance was the example of the Old Testament magistrates who had punished idolaters and apostates, and the commands in passages like Deuteronomy 13 that false prophets should be killed.[153]

Rutherford did set some limits on the state's intolerance, limits ironically very similar to those set by Johannes Althusius, who is often regarded as one of the most tolerant of orthodox Calvinists.[154] Christians were not to use the sword to compel pagans or Jews to convert to Christianity; only apostates from the visible church were to be punished, and then only because they were actively propagating their blasphemies.[155] Moreover, the state could not interfere with the 'internal liberty . . . to think, understand, judge, conclude'.[156]

However, despite these riders, the overall message of Rutherford's work in the late 1640s was that objectivity had to be restored if the disintegration of Reformed Protestantism was to be avoided. Scripture interpreted according to its literal sense by trained ministers meeting in a synod and backed up by the sanction of the civil magistrate was the only solution to the crisis of Protestant coherence in the English revolution. The English disease could only be cured by the adoption of the Melvillian Presbyterianism which the English had already rejected. This was not a solution likely to appeal to those in power in England in the late 1640s, and it turned out that Rutherford was protesting in vain – the Protestant sects had come to stay. Yet Rutherford's critique of the sects takes us close to the heart of the antiformalism that made the English revolution genuinely revolutionary and the religious pluralism that made it genuinely modern. The careful balance that the magisterial Reformers sought to maintain between pure forms and the religion of the heart was broken down in the late 1640s by a search for millennial fluity, which enabled the leaders of the New Model

---

[151] *Survey of Antichrist*, I, p. 261.
[152] See P. Biel, 'Bullinger against the Donatists: St Augustine to the defence of the Zurich reformed church', *Journal of Religious History*, 16 (1991), 237–46; Goldie, 'Theory of religious intolerance', pp. 335–45.
[153] See *Due Right*, pp. 356–7.
[154] See *The Politics of Johannes Althusius*, trans. F. Carney (London, 1964), pp. 155–69. Althusius's tolerance is highlighted by H. Kamen, *The Rise of Toleration* (London, 1967), pp. 217–20.
[155] *Free Disputation*, pp. 51–3.   [156] *Free Disputation*, p. 46.

Army to take the momentous step of dissolving the old constitution without replacing it with a new one.[157]

DIVISION WITHIN THE KIRK (1648–1661)

If Rutherford was distressed by the course of the Puritan revolution in England, he was to find the situation in Scotland equally demoralising. The Engagement between the majority of the Covenanters and the king in December 1647 seemed to the kirk to be a betrayal of the Solemn League and Covenant, since it only allowed for a three-year trial period for Presbyterianism in England. Yet things were to swing the kirk's way after the defeat of the Engagers by Cromwell in August 1648. The militants, led by Rutherford and his close friend, George Gillespie, saw their opportunity. On his deathbed, in September 1648, Gillespie issued statements warning against association and compliance with 'malignant enemies of truth and godliness'. 'The Lord', he wrote, 'is about to purge his churches. I have often comforted myself, and still do, with the hopes of the Lord purging this polluted land . . . I know there will always be a mixture of hypocrites, but that cannot excuse the conniving at gross and scandalous sins.'[158]

Gillespie's statement, which was fully endorsed by Rutherford, held the key to the developments in the years to come. The hardliners within the kirk – inspired by the Old Testament concept of the covenanted nation – were to be guided by belief in the necessity of purging malignants, both in church and state. The irony of this was that in England, Gillespie and Rutherford had been at the forefront of Presbyterian efforts to defend a comprehensive national church against sectarian purism; back in Scotland, they themselves were the purgers. Gillespie was well aware of the irony. He once told John Livingstone that 'he was hardly a moneth [in London] before he was in danger to turn a malignant, and hardly again a month in Scotland, but he was in danger to turn a sectary'.[159]

In the next chapter we shall see how the desire for purity in the state undermined the synthesis of natural-law and true-religion arguments that we found in *Lex, Rex*. Here, however, we will concentrate on how Rutherford's desire for ecclesiastical purity got the better of his belief in a comprehensive, authoritative Presbyterian national church, in practice at least, if not in theory.

The two years of the kirk party's rule allowed the radicals to begin the purge of the church. Among the 'corrupt and scandalous ministers' censured

[157] Davis, 'Against formality'.
[158] Gillespie, 'The testimony of Mr George Gillespie', in *Works*, II (Edinburgh, 1844).
[159] Livingstone, 'Memorable Characteristics', in W. K. Tweedie, ed., *Select Biographies*, I (Edinburgh, 1845), p. 331.

were Henry Guthry, who had opposed private meetings in the early 1640s, and Andrew Ramsay, Rutherford's theology tutor at Edinburgh University. Among those who were elected to the Committee of Estates for the first time was John Mein, the merchant who had led conventicles in Edinburgh when Rutherford was a student.[160] When the radicals looked back on these days in 1653, they wrote: 'this church was in a fair way of purgeing out ignorant corrupt and scandalous ministers and Elders, and in a way of more tenderness and circumspection and care in admitting of persons to the sacrament of the Lord's Supper'.[161]

While the kirk party was in control in Scotland, this strategy of purging, though not as thorough as the militants wished, did succeed in appeasing them. However, after Cromwell's defeat of the Scots at Dunbar in September 1650, the moderate majority in the kirk changed direction dramatically and began to readmit repentant Engagers into the army, the state and the church. Those who opposed this new policy became known as the Remonstrants, because of their support for the Western Remonstrance of October 1650, which had condemned the hasty admission of the king to the covenants when he had not shown clear evidence of a change of heart. The crowning of Charles II in January 1651 widened the gulf between the two sides, and the breach was finalised at the General Assembly in July. Here Rutherford handed in a Protestation against the lawfulness of an Assembly from which the Remonstrants had been excluded. They declared that they would consider all its proceedings null and void.[162]

The rift in the kirk was not to be healed within Rutherford's lifetime. Following the 1651 Assembly, the Protesters and the Resolutioners began to hold separate presbyteries and synods. In 1653 separate General Assemblies were planned, and in some cases, rival ministers were ordained in the same parish. The Resolutioners wrote to John Livingstone in the mid-1650s to protest against his moves to admit a minister to a kirk in the presbytery of Dunce, 'which is already planted, with the consent of the farre greatest part of the Parish, by the whole Presbytery unanimously'. This action, they pointed out, was 'a grosse violation of our discipline' and 'a violent overturning of all Presbyteriall Government'.[163] Livingstone, Rutherford

---

[160] D. Stevenson, 'The deposition of ministers in the Church of Scotland under the Covenanters, 1638–51', *Church History*, 44 (1975), 329–32; 'The radical party', pp. 161–2.

[161] 'Protesters Declaration or Testimonie to English Actings among us', in *Register of the Consultations of the Ministers of Edinburgh and some other Brethren in the Ministry*, ed. W. Stephen (Edinburgh, 1921), I, p. 22.

[162] On the Protester/Resolutioner schism see J. D. Ogilvie, 'A bibliography of the Resolutioner–Protester controversy, 1650–59', *Transactions of the Edinburgh Bibliographical Society*, 14 (1930), 57–86; Donaldson, 'The emergence of schism'; F. N. McCoy, *Robert Baillie and the Second Scots Reformation* (Berkeley, 1974), chs. 7–9.

[163] *Register of the Consultations*, ed. Stephen, pp. 87–8.

and the other Protesters denied that they were overturning Presbyterianism, but their protests were deeply unconvincing. They certainly avoided the Brownist assertion that the parish churches were not true churches at all and must be completely abandoned. But by refusing to submit to the hierarchy of courts that lay at the heart of the Presbyterian system, and by establishing what amounted to gathered congregations of the godly as alternatives to the parish church, they seemed to have adopted – in practice, though not in theory – the semi-separatist position advocated by the Independents. Philip Nye, after all, had been happy to be a parish minister and the minister of a gathered church at the same time. Livingstone, by the 1650s, had arrived at the same position as his old acquaintance.

A number of Protesters were unhappy with this halfway house, and actually went the whole way to separatism. Two of the Protester commanders in the army, Gilbert Ker and Archibald Strachan, were known to be sympathetic towards the English Independents. Ker was in close contact with Rutherford, who wrote letters to him supporting the idea of a purged army. The minister's zeal for purity in church and state was sufficient to keep Ker within the Presbyterian fold. Strachan, however, had been with Cromwell at Preston in 1648, and his sectarian impulses were clearly stronger. Even so, he was said to have been heartbroken when the kirk excommunicated him for his sympathy towards the English Independents.[164]

Another Protester who moved on to Independency was Alexander Jaffray. Captured by the English at Dunbar, Jaffray was persuaded to abandon Presbyterianism after conversations with Cromwell and John Owen. In May 1652 Jaffray and several other Aberdeen Protesters issued a letter in which they advocated Congregationalism and unmixed churches.[165] The response of the Protesters to this development is revealing, for it highlights the ambiguity of their ecclesiological thought at this time. On the one hand, they condemned 'separation from this Church'. 'The Lord's indulgence', which was granted to those who separated from a corrupt English church, would not be granted to those who separated from a church as reformed as that of Scotland. On the other hand, the Protesters recognised that the separation arose because of a laudable desire to see the church purged. The Aberdeen Independents, they believed, had left the church when they 'apprehended the work of purgeing of Elderships and communions to be altogether impossible'. The Protesters fully shared this

---

[164] D. Stevenson, 'The Western Association, 1648–50', *Ayrshire Collections*, 13 (1982), 152–73.
[165] On Jaffray and the Scottish Independents see G. D. Henderson, 'Some early Scottish Independents', in his *Religious Life in Seventeenth-Century Scotland* (Cambridge, 1937), pp. 107–16; W. I. Hoy, 'The entry of the sects into Scotland', in D. Shaw, ed., *Reformation and Revolution* (Edinburgh, 1967), pp. 181–7.

frustration, but believing that things would improve if they steadfastly resisted the temptation to separate. Even in mixed communions, they testified, the Lord had 'manifested himself'.[166]

There can be little doubt that the Protesters were sincere in their rejection of separatism. They did not abandon the Church of Scotland in practice, and they certainly clung to the ideal of a national Presbyterian church. In St Andrews, Rutherford was surrounded by Resolutioner colleagues, and although Protesters elsewhere established rival church structures, he himself made no attempt to set up an alternative kirk. Throughout the 1650s, he continued to attend meetings of the presbytery, though he quarrelled acrimoniously with Resolutioners like Blair and Wood. He may have been, in Gordon Donaldson's words, 'close to a schismatic point of view', but he could never bring himself to secede.[167] He chided the Aberdeen Independents for doing so, and explained that he regarded 'this visible church [of Scotland], though black and spotted, as the hospital and guest-house of sick, halt, maimed and withered . . . and we would wait upon those that are not yet in Christ, as our Lord waited upon us and you both'.[168] In keeping with his actions in the 1640s, he continued to protest against the Erastianism of the English government and against the policy of toleration that it had introduced to Scotland.[169]

In his *Survey of Hooker*, published in London in 1658, he reiterated the critique of Independency that he had presented in *A Peaceable Plea* and *The Due Right of Presbyteries*. He rejected the claim that the church should be composed of visible saints, that authority in the congregation rested with the people and not with the elders, and that each local congregation could be self-governing and not subject to the rulings of higher courts. He was still – in theory – a *Second Book of Discipline* Presbyterian. However, the theory seemed to be contradicted by the practice, and by the sectarian tone of the *Survey*'s preface, in which Rutherford launched a bitter attack on the Resolutioners. While criticising Thomas Hooker and the New England Congregationalists for denying the authority of Reformed synods, Ruther-

---

[166] 'Protesters Declaration to Separatists in Aberdeen, 17 March 1653', in Stephen, ed., *Register of the Consultations*, pp. 37–43.

[167] Donaldson, 'The emergence of schism', p. 218.   [168] *Letters*, pp. 704–7.

[169] A series of Protester documents – most signed by Rutherford – attacked Erastian control of the church and the toleration of heresy: 'Letter from the Protesters to Lieutenant General Cromwell, January 1652', in *Register of the Consultations*, ed. Stephen, pp. 1–12; 'Protesters Declaration or Testimonie to English Actings amongst us, 17 March 1653', in *Register of the Consultations*, ed. Stephen, pp. 13–36; 'Another Declaration or Testimonie of the Protesters, March 1654', in *Register of the Consultations*, ed. Stephen, pp. 44–56; 'Protestation and Testimony given to General Monk, October 1658', in J. C. Johnston, ed., *Treasury of the Scottish Covenant* (Edinburgh, 1887); 'A Testimony to the Truth of Jesus Christ by the ministers of Perth and Fife, 1660', in *A Collection* (Kilmarnock, 1783), pp. 71–116.

ford himself claimed that the Resolutioner synods were like a 'popish Councel'. 'No authority of a Judicature', he declared, 'can make that to be the Word of God, and obedience to God'. There seemed to be a double standard; others had to accept majority rule, but not Rutherford.[170]

Robert Baillie certainly believed that his colleague was denying two major planks of the Presbyterian platform that they had together defended in the 1640s: subordination to ecclesiastical authority and the concept of a mixed church. By refusing to submit to the jurisdiction of synods and assemblies which all Presbyterians had accepted between 1638 and 1648, Rutherford was opening the way for 'anarchie and confusion; that every particular person may and must follow the judgement of his own braine, without controll of any judge or judicatorie upon earth, whether civill or ecclesiastick'. Moreover, by challenging the Resolutioners for readmitting the Engagers to church fellowship, Rutherford was following the example of the Novationists and Donatists, who would not accept those who had compromised under persecution back into their churches even when they had repented. Rutherford wanted an even stricter policy of admission to the Lord's Supper, despite the fact that the current Scottish practice was more stringent than that of any of the continental Reformed churches. This was to strengthen 'the arme of calumniating Sectaries', wrote Baillie, 'whose professed aime long has been the dissolution of all the standing congregations in the Reformed churches, that a new gathering of churches in their way may be set a foot'. It was hardly surprising then, that after their failure to gain the support of the London Presbyterian ministers, the Protesters had sought 'the help of their better friends the Independents, Anabaptists, and Erastians, their only intime [intimate] familiars and confidents, with whom they keeped frequent fastings and prayers in their conventicles'.[171]

This last point may have been exaggerated, for Rutherford never had any time for Anabaptists (though Baillie was probably referring to Patrick Gillespie, who was much more favourably inclined towards the Independents and Cromwell). Moreover, Rutherford could claim that he was being consistent with his earlier position. He had always insisted that Protestant synods did not have the infallible authority of popish councils, and that their decision was only binding if agreeable with the Word of God. More significantly, he could claim abiding loyalty to the covenants of 1638 and 1643. As far as he was concerned, the willingness of the General Assembly to endorse the Estates' decision to readmit covenant-breakers to the covenants, was the surest way to destroy them. Neither the king nor the Engagers had any real passion for the covenants; their oaths were manifestly

---

[170] The phrase is from Donaldson, 'Emergence of schism', p. 215.
[171] Baillie, *Letters and Journals*, III, pp. 375–81.

hypocritical, and it was the height of naïvety to accept them. If the choice was to be between the integrity of the covenants and the authority of a Presbyterian synod, then the former had to take precedence. In any case, the Protesters claimed that the 1651 General Assembly was not a properly constituted synod at all, since elections to it had been rigged in order to exclude them. This legal loophole enabled them to argue that – despite appearances to the contrary – they were upholding both the covenants and the authority of the Presbyterian system.

However, against these claims to consistency, Baillie had been able to turn upon the Protesters the very arguments that Rutherford himself had used in *A Free Disputation* almost a decade previously. Rutherford was now the Donatist sectarian, unwilling to put up with a mixed church and the authority of synods, though these were the very things his own ecclesiological works had contended for. Whereas in the 1640s it had seemed possible to hold together the ideal of a pure church and that of a comprehensive, national church, the corruption of the nation after 1650 drove these two further apart. The choice was between submitting to the authority of a Presbyterian hierarchy that was prepared to tolerate malig-nants, and dissenting from that authority and forming small gatherings of the godly. Rutherford pursued the latter course, and though he never let go of the theory of a national, mixed, Presbyterian church, in practice he could tolerate it no longer. One of the greatest seventeenth-century defenders of divine-right Presbyterianism finished his days a rebel against the church polity he had fought so hard to establish.[172]

---

[172] In the words of W. L. Mathieson, the Protesters 'revolted against a system of ecclesiastical government which they still asserted to be divine'. Quoted in Donaldson, 'Emergence of Schism', p. 215.

8

The national prophet

PROVIDENCE

Early modern Europeans believed in a God who was active in the world he had created. Not only did he uphold the natural processes of his earth, he also intervened directly to display his pleasure and displeasure to men through specific events. Books like Thomas Beard's *The Theatre of God's Judgements* (1631) related tales which illustrated the principle that God frequently made his opinions on human actions manifestly clear. Such providentialism rested on a belief in the all-pervasiveness of divine intervention and in 'the decipherability of particular providences'.[1]

Both of these convictions were firmly held by Samuel Rutherford. He believed that all that happens in the world happens because of God's 'influences'. God determined the number of stars, the length of our lives, and he determined that Jehoash should smite the ground three times and not six.[2] That this was so was enough to produce 'precious thoughts' in the mind of the believer, for he saw 'millions and numberless numbers of influences with all the drops of rain, hail, dew falling between the creation and the dissolving of the world'. It was sheer atheism to think that 'all the stirrings in Nature, Societies and Kingdoms, were set on work by the sway of Nature, and blind Fortune without God, as a wheel rolling about with the mighty violence of a strong arm, moves a long time, after the arm of the mover is removed'.[3]

Rutherford also believed in the perspicuity of divine activity in the world. Just as having a divinely inspired sacred text was not much help if its message was hopelessly obscure, so knowing that God was active in all earthly events was of little use if the purpose and meaning of his action was

---

[1] See B. Donagan, 'Providence, chance and explanation: some paradoxical aspects of Puritan views of causation', *Journal of Religious History*, 11 (1991), 385–403. See also K. Thomas, *Religion and the Decline of Magic* (Harmondsworth, 1971), ch. 4; B. Worden, 'Providence and politics in Cromwellian England', *Past and Present*, 109 (1985), 55–99.
[2] *Influences*, sig. A3. [3] *Influences*, pp. 7–8.

not clear. Rutherford concluded that, with some exceptions, the process of reading the Bible and of reading the book of providence was a relatively straightforward one.

It is this conviction that explains the readiness of Puritans 'to detect the hand of God in daily events'.[4] Robert Blair recorded in his autobiography that when he planned to visit Rutherford at Anwoth and Marion McNaught at Kirkcudbright in 1632, he came to the parting of the ways and simply 'laid the bridle on the horse's neck, entreating the Lord to direct the horse as he saw meet'. The horse took him to Kirkcudbright where he found both the people he wanted to meet.[5] Rutherford himself had a similar experience when leaving Stirling after speaking to the Marquis of Argyll there in the 1650s. His horse came to a standstill, and Rutherford – probably with the story of Balaam's donkey in mind – knew that God was telling him to turn back. The result was a much more profitable conversation with Argyll.[6]

To take a further example, Rutherford believed that God's will could be determined by lots 'that seem to be ruled by fortune and chance'.[7] He took this seriously even when the result was not to his liking. When Alexander Jameson applied for the vacant regent's position at St Mary's College, he found himself competing for the place with one of Rutherford's protégés. Since they were so equal, lots were cast after Rutherford had prayed for guidance. The lot fell on Jameson, and Rutherford 'was extremely stormy'. He called for the lot to be cast again, but again it fell on Jameson. 'This perfectly confounded Mr Rutherford, and no doubt lett him see his rashness and errour.' He turned to Jameson and said, 'Sir, put on your gown, you have a better right to it then I have to mine!' After this, Rutherford and Jameson 'wer extraordinarily intimate and bigg'.[8]

However, as well as believing that providence was decipherable on a personal level, Rutherford was also sure that it could be discerned on a national scale. God's anger and distress at the apostasy of Scotland expressed itself in quite unmistakeable ways. At the Edinburgh parliament of August 1621 which was held to ratify the Articles of Perth, for example, a series of remarkable events had taken place. David Calderwood later recorded that on the night before the Articles were accepted, a fire swept through city streets; in the morning, as the nobles prepared for the final session of parliament, a swan flew overhead, 'flaffing with her wings, &

---

[4] Thomas, *Religion and the Decline of Magic*, p. 109.
[5] *The Life of Robert Blair*, ed. T. McCrie (Edinburgh, 1848), p. 96.
[6] R. Wodrow, *Analecta*, II (Edinburgh, 1842), p. 163.   [7] *Influences*, pp. 6–7.
[8] R. Wodrow, *Analecta*, I (Edinburgh, 1842), pp. 140–1. For another example of Rutherford's faith in lots as a guide to the divine will see *Wodrow's Biographical Collections*, ed. R. Lippe (Aberdeen, 1840), pp. 243–4.

muttering her natural song'; and at the precise moment at which the Articles were ratified, three terrible bolts of lightning came in quick succession from the heavens, followed by 'an Extraordinary great Darkness', and a spectacular thunderstorm. Calderwood had no doubt that these were omens that revealed God's perspective on the Articles of Perth. Although Rutherford had graduated several weeks before the events described took place, and may have gone home to his family near Jedburgh, he would certainly have heard about the fire, the swan and the great storm from the Presbyterians in Edinburgh or even from Calderwood himself, and its impact on him was undoubtedly significant. Throughout the 1620s and 1630s Rutherford interpreted national events through this providential framework. The success of the bishops was not a sign of God's approbation, but evidence of his anger at the nation. God was abandoning Scotland, leaving her to her own sinful devices.[9]

Rutherford's treatment of Scotland's history was modelled on the way the Hebrew prophets treated the history of Israel. As we have already seen, he believed that Scotland had entered into a covenant with God, in much the same way as ancient Israel had. The future of Scotland was conditional on her response to God. If she obeyed the terms of the covenant, she could expect blessing; if she disobeyed, curses and desertion would follow. Yet there was another mode of thinking about history that Rutherford also borrowed from the Hebrew prophets – the apocalyptic. Whereas prophets like Hosea were committed to delivering ultimatums from the Lord (forthtelling), apocalyptic preachers like Daniel engaged in the explicit prediction of the future (foretelling). The 'prophetic' genre emphasised human agency and the conditionality of the covenant, whereas the 'apocalyptic' form stressed divine initiative and the inevitability of God's victory.[10]

In the rest of this chapter, we shall describe Rutherford's prophetic and apocalyptic ideas in turn, and then show how they developed between 1638 and 1661, forcing him into a denial of the Scottish constitutionalism and natural-law theory that he had advocated in the mid-1640s.

---

[9] As Donagan notes, the great advantage of providentialism was that no event could disprove God's care, for mishaps were seen as warnings or useful trials, rather than as signs of God's disapproval of a cause. See Donagan, 'Providence, chance and explanation', p. 387.

[10] See J. F. Wilson, *Pulpit in Parliament: Puritanism during the English Civil Wars, 1640–48* (Princeton, 1969), ch. 7. Wilson suggests that the Puritan movement was divided between 'prophetic' and 'apocalyptic' preachers. However, as this study of Rutherford will show, the two styles were seen by most Puritans as complementary and not at odds. The future was open in the short term and dependent on the church's response to God's covenantal terms, but in the long term it was closed, because the final outcome was guaranteed, and God would work irresistibly through his church to achieve it.

COVENANTED NATION

Rutherford's preaching and writing in the 1630s provides us with a classic example of 'the Scottish jeremiad tradition'. At the root of this tradition lay the assumption that a covenant existed between God and his chosen people, one which made analogies between Scotland and Israel wholly appropriate.[11] Rutherford held firmly to this assumption, believing that God was not simply calling the elect out from among the nations, but was in the business of calling nations too. In a 1634 sermon, he appealed to Isaiah 49, which, according to Christians, predicted that with the Jewish nation's rejection of Christ, he would go to the Gentiles. What excited Rutherford was that the chapter mentioned the 'isles'. Christ was saying, 'Listen, O isles, and hear, O Scotland and England. Ye who lie far out in an isle of the sea, listen unto Me, and ye shall be My land and heritage.' The Father had promised his Son, 'I will make the nations your inheritance, the ends of the earth your possession' (Psalm 2: 8). This was 'Scotland's Charter', declared Rutherford, and good grounds for exultation: 'Now, O Scotland, God be thanked, thy name is in the Bible!'[12]

Historians have usually taken this statement to be a classic example of Scottish national pride. S. A. Burrell referred to the Covenanters' 'insular sense of national self-confidence' and declared that 'Scotland, to Rutherford, was more than a covenanted nation; its people were the Christian successors of the Israelites specially chosen for the fulfillment of prophecy.'[13] Yet nothing could be further from the truth. The discovery that Scotland's name was in the Bible excited Rutherford not because it confirmed his patriotic self-confidence, but because he had been driven to deep despair over the state of his nation. The two great historical myths about Scotland in which someone like Rutherford could take pride, lay in tatters by the 1630s. The nobility, which had so often stood up to tyrannical kings, was now supinely subservient to royal wishes. And the kirk, once so pure in her government, doctrine and worship, was now being corrupted by bishops, Arminianism and popish ceremonies. So to discover that Scotland's name was in the

[11] See R. Sher, 'Witherspoon's "Dominion of Providence" and the Scottish jeremiad tradition', in R. Sher and J. Smitten, eds., *Scotland and America in the Age of Enlightenment* (Edinburgh, 1990), p. 50.

[12] *Communion Sermons*, pp. 115–16.

[13] Burrell, 'The apocalyptic vision of the early Covenanters', *Scottish Historical Review*, 43 (1964), 2, 16. Burrell's interpretation of this phrase has misled other historians. Jenny Wormald, though arguing that Rutherford's statement does not reveal an extreme chauvinism, nevertheless believes that it illustrates 'that the more universalist attitudes of the late sixteenth and early seventeenth centuries changed, as the fears and strains of the mid-seventeenth century focused Scottish minds on their Scottish God'. See her 'The union of 1603', in R. Mason, ed., *Scots and Britons: Scottish Political Thought and the Union of 1603* (Cambridge, 1994), p. 28.

Bible, that the ends of the earth and the isles of the sea were part of Christ's inheritance, was a tremendous reassurance, far sweeter than the general knowledge that God was sovereign over the world. However culturally inferior Scotland might seem, and however corrupt she had become, here was a promise to cling to.

None of this made Rutherford a little Scotlander. He was not 'insular' in his view of the world, despite not having lived abroad, and he did not believe that Scotland was *the* New Israel. Like all early modern Protestants, Rutherford drew analogies between his land and Israel, but he was not putting Scotland on a par with Israel in terms of historical significance. In the past the Jews had been the vehicle of God's revelation to the world in the Bible; but the canon of Scripture was now closed and no other nation would ever perform a similar role. In the future, the conversion of the Jews to Christ would be one of the features of the last days; other nations might play important parts, but the Jews would still be unique. The Old Testament passages to which Rutherford appealed were general prophecies of the conversion of all the Gentile nations. What enthralled him was the knowledge that England and Scotland (as isles of the sea at the ends of the earth) were clearly included in these promises. In an unpublished sermon preached in the 1650s, Rutherford explained that Scotland was just one part of Christ's inheritance:

Christ's geographie is through all the parts of the world; east and west, south and north; all those are in Christ's charter . . . Goe where ye will ye are in Christ's bounds, he maketh all the world the holy land; Scotland is a part of the aikers of Immanuels land; is ther any holding lyk this?[14]

In keeping with this internationalist theology, Rutherford himself continually thought in terms of 'the three kingdoms'. The community of the godly was spread throughout the three kingdoms, but so was apostasy; 'some of all ranks in the three kingdoms are posting to hell on idolatry and masses'.[15] Rutherford yearned for religious revival throughout these lands: 'Oh, if all three kingdoms had part of my love feast, and of the comfort of a dawted prisoner!'[16] Britain, after all, was included among the isles in Christ's Charter in Psalm 2, and Rutherford – like Knox – expected a British reformation. 'Be not discouraged', he told Marion McNaught, 'Christ will not want [lose] the Isles-men.'[17] He was kept informed about ecclesiastical developments in England, particularly regarding the persecution of Puritans and the emigration of 'worthy preachers' to New England.[18] Although the

---

[14] Unpublished manuscript sermon on Genesis 28 in Edinburgh University Library, Dc. 5. 30, n. p.
[15] *Communion Sermons*, p. 100. [16] *Letters*, p. 301. [17] *Letters*, p. 126.
[18] *Letters*, pp. 56, 60, 64.

precise nature of his contacts with the English Puritans is not clear, he was obviously an avid reader of their works; his first book drew heavily on William Twisse's attack on Arminianism, and the reason he gave for not drawing up a Christian Directory was that the English divines, Rogers, Greenham and Perkins, had already done it 'more judiciously than I can'.[19] As far as Ireland was concerned, several of Rutherford's closest allies in the kirk – Robert Blair, John Livingstone and John McLelland – were ministers in the north, and he knew from their brushes with episcopal authority that 'the world barketh at Christ's strangers, both in Ireland and in this land'.[20]

But the Calvinist international extended beyond British shores to the European continent. Rutherford's first book was published in Amsterdam and although there is no evidence that he ever visited the Netherlands, he was obviously in contact with Dutchmen of a similar ecclesiastical persuasion. East of the Netherlands, in Germany, the Thirty Years War was raging during the 1630s and it loomed large in Rutherford's consciousness, forming the apocalyptic backdrop against which he understood his own troubles. His struggles with episcopal authority were part of a larger war between Christ's kirk and the Antichrist. He referred to 'the distresses of the Reformed churches abroad',[21] God's kirk in France, Germany and Bohemia,[22] and the death of the Protestant champion, Gustavus Adolphus, on the battlefield in 1632.[23]

Added to this feeling of solidarity with Protestants in other lands was an Augustinian sense of alienation from the world, a conviction that the godly were strangers passing through on their journey to the homeland. The image of the Christian as a traveller staying overnight in a smoky inn is one that recurs throughout his letters and sermons. 'The silly stranger, in an uncouth country, must take with a smoky inn and coarse cheer, a hard bed, and a barking, ill-tongued host.'[24] 'The instinct of nature maketh a man love his mother-country above all countries', Rutherford wrote in 1637, but supernatural grace and the renewed nature led men 'to love [their] country above'. With a pilgrim's eye they looked on this world with discontent and disdain, saying 'Fy, fy, this is not like my country.'[25] The belief that God would accomplish his purpose in time was always balanced by the knowledge that the Christian's home was in eternity.

However, Rutherford did believe that in the unravelling of salvation history, Scotland had a special role. Considering the purity of the

---

[19] *Letters*, pp. 292–3.
[20] *Letters*, p. 83. While Rutherford was confined to Aberdeen, Baillie suggested to his cousin, Spang, that a place be found for him in a Dutch university. See Robert Baillie, *Letters and Journals*, 3 vols., ed. D. Laing (Edinburgh, 1841–2), I, p. 9.
[21] *Letters*, p. 93.   [22] *Letters*, p. 94.   [23] *Letters*, p. 118.
[24] *Letters*, pp. 83–4.   [25] *Letters*, p. 392.

Reformation with which God had blessed Scotland, this seemed to be a justified conclusion. England was not so fortunate. When Lady Kenmure was preparing to move south, Rutherford wrote to her 'Ye are going to a country where the Sun of righteousness, in the Gospel, shineth not so clearly as in this kingdom.'[26] Scotland, by contrast, had feasted at Christ's table and drunk deep at his well for seventy years. It was a land with an impeccable spiritual pedigree, and with a potentially glorious spiritual future. Moreover, as Rutherford later explained in *Lex, Rex*, God's promise to give the isles of the sea to Christ as his eternal possession, obliged the Protestants of England and Scotland to defend their lands against false religion and never abandon them to Antichrist. Providence reinforced the lessons of natural law, for the Protestants of Britain and Ireland were obliged to defend their countries 'both by the law of nature and grace'.[27]

Again, it would be a mistake to assume that this was an exercise in complacent patriotism, a religious endorsement of a jingoistic *status quo*. As Patrick Collinson explains, the belief that England was a new Israel, an elect nation, did not necessarily undermine internationalism or foster chauvinism. John Foxe – so often seen as the architect of English Protestant nationalism – was actually more concerned about national backsliding than about national celebration, and his focus was primarily on the universal Church rather than on England. English Protestants were very conscious of belonging to a Calvinist international. Their sense that God was on the side of the nation could heighten ethnocentric enthusiasm, but it could also produce an awareness that his support was conditional, that the nation could forfeit his favour, that he had 'a controversy with the inhabitants of the land', as the prophet Hosea had put it.[28] John Downame made precisely this point in his *Lectures upon . . . Hosea* (1608). England may have been God's most favoured nation, but if it continued to sin like Israel, it would share Israel's fate, and become known as Lo-Ammi ('not my people').[29]

Rutherford had absorbed this teaching only too well. In March 1637, he wrote to his fellow minister, David Dickson, 'I purpose, God willing, to set

---

[26] *Letters*, p. 42.   [27] *Lex Rex*, p. 328 [160–1].

[28] P. Collinson, 'The Protestant nation', in *The Birthpangs of Protestant England: Religion and Cultural Change in the Sixteenth and Seventeenth Centuries* (London, 1988), pp. 14–20. For the case of the Netherlands, it has been argued that Dutch Calvinists did see their land as the elect nation. See G. Groenhuis, 'Calvinism and national consciousness: the Dutch Republic as the New Israel', in A. C. Duke and C. A. Tamse, eds., *Britain and the Netherlands*, VII (The Hague, 1981), pp. 118–33. However, one suspects that Groenhuis – like many English historians – reads far too much into the common analogy drawn between Christian nations and Israel.

[29] See M. McGiffert, 'God's controversy with Jacobean England', *American Historical Review*, 88 (1983), 1151–74.

about Hosea, and to try if I can get it to the press here.'[30] Though this project was never realised, Rutherford's letters and sermons in this period form one long Hosead, a lament over the spiritual adultery of the Church of Scotland. God's favour towards Scotland was not an excuse for pride and complacency, but a reason for humility and repentance. 'Christ Jesus', he warned his listeners in a sermon in the early 1630s, 'is an abiding heritage to no people'.[31] After telling his congregation that Scotland's name was in the Bible, he gave them a warning: 'Now be not high-minded, but fear. Learn a lesson of the Jews, and be not spoilt bairns.'[32]

Yet all the evidence pointed to the conclusion that the Scots were indeed spoilt bairns. Christ's 'fair face' was 'spitted upon by dogs', and 'loons [rogues] were pulling the crown off my royal King's head'.[33] He was:

banished, silenced, and treated worse than Barrabus. He gets no justice in our Parliaments; Papists, Arminians, and Atheists, get favour, honour, and court preferment; but an honest professor is counted an ill subject, a seditious man, and an enemy to authority. But see how God has met us, He has broken His staff, Beauty: the purity, power, and life of doctrine is away. The word of God is not sharp from preachers' mouths: it draws no blood in men's consciences . . . We see the sheep devoured and poisoned with Popery and false doctrine in colleges and pulpits . . . Think ye that a pair of organs, and an ill said mass (as King James VI termed it), and a busking of dirty ceremonies, the whore's abominations, which we once spued out, think ye that ever this staff will draw blood of a man's conscience?[34]

The kirk, once married to Christ, had now – like Hosea's adulterous wife Gomer – 'played the harlot, and hath left her first husband'.[35] The whole of Scottish society was riddled with corruption. There was 'mickle [much] vanity and pride in apparel, extortion, no justice, but many false laws, incest, and adulteries; many unrevenged bloods, a wicked and windy profession'.[36] Like the woman in Ezekiel's graphic and explicit prophecy, 'false and declining Scotland, whom our Lord took off the dunghill and out of hell, and made a fair bride to Himself, hath broken her faith to her sweet Husband, and hath put on the forehead of a whore'.[37]

Who was to blame for this sorry state of affairs? The guiltiest party was the bishops, whom Rutherford regarded as 'bastard porters' who had stolen the keys of the Lord's house. They had built 'their house and nests upon the ashes of mourning Jerusalem', and had 'drawn our King upon hard and dangerous conclusions against such as are termed Puritans, for the rooting of them out'.[38]

Yet not everything could be blamed on the bishops. Rutherford realised

---

[30] *Letters*, p. 226.   [31] *Communion Sermons*, p. 340.
[32] *Communion Sermons*, p. 134.   [33] *Letters*, p. 297.
[34] *Communion Sermons*, pp. 153–4.   [35] *Letters*, p. 103.
[36] *Communion Sermons*, pp. 167–8.
[37] *Letters*, p. 87. The prophecy is found in Ezekiel 16.   [38] *Letters*, p. 53.

that the problem was actually much wider: 'authority, king, court, and churchmen oppose the truth'.[39] In his letters he avoided attacking the king directly, but his attacks on those who tried to curry favour with the court made it clear that he had little respect for Charles I or his policies. The best the radical ministers could do was to urge that the king's heart be 'recommended to God'.[40] Rutherford referred to 'the King' in many of his letters, but he was speaking of King Jesus not King Charles. Indeed, his letters implied that a choice must be made between them. He wrote to Lord Boyd in 1637 that he should be prepared to hazard 'the favour of men (suppose kings with three crowns)' in order to stand for 'the Prince of your salvation'. 'Winning court with the Prince of the kings of the earth' should be his aim, for blessed were the hands 'that shall help to put the crown upon the head of Christ again in Scotland!'[41]

Here Rutherford's apocalyptic view of history joined with his history of the ancient Scottish constitution. Both suggested that the monarch was very much a secondary figure, subordinate to King Jesus or to parliament. The experience of the Scottish Melvillians since the 1590s reinforced this belief. Whereas the English Puritans had followed Foxe in placing their hopes in a godly emperor, hopes that were also shared by some Scots,[42] the Melvillians had been thoroughly disillusioned with their kings for forty years by the mid-1630s. Rutherford had grown up listening to David Calderwood, the man who was to write the official Presbyterian history of the post-Reformation kirk. Calderwood had doubtless explained to his promising young parishioner how the purity of the Scottish Reformation had been compromised by King James's reintroduction of bishops and popish ceremonies. Rutherford probably grew up with tales of the king's treacherous imprisonment of Andrew Melville in the Tower of London, and he had seen Calderwood himself exiled from Scotland by this same king. The distrust of monarchy, which reached its full extent in *Lex, Rex*, had been planted in Rutherford at a very young age. Not for him the godly prince.

Instead, Rutherford put his trust in nobles. He had learned from Buchanan how they were the traditional check on royal power, and Knox and Calderwood had taught him that they had supported the cause of reformation in the past. The conclusion was clear; Scotland's apostasy had happened because the nobility had abdicated its religious and constitutional responsibilities. As Rutherford explained to Lord Loudon, the nobles 'stand looking on with their hands folded behind their back when louns [louts, rogues] are running with the spoil of Zion on their back, and the boards of

[39] *Letters*, p. 93. [40] *Letters*, p. 93. [41] *Letters*, pp. 165–6.
[42] See A. H. Williamson, *Scottish National Consciousness in the Age of James VI: The Apocalypse, the Union and the Shaping of Scotland's Public Culture* (Edinburgh, 1979), esp. pp. 91–6, 102–5.

the Son of God's tabernacle'.[43] It could all have been so different: 'Oh, if the nobles had done their part, and been zealous for the Lord! it had not been as it is now', he exclaimed in a letter to the Earl of Cassillis.[44]

The reason for the nobility's failure to protect Christ was quite simply worldliness. 'For what has overturned Christ and religion but men's love of the world, court, honour?' The worldlings, like Judas, the Scribes and the Pharisees, had bought and sold Christ for thirty pieces of silver. Their hearts were upon 'policy, state, benefices, honour, and court', and so they tried to remake religion, and the truth, 'as a wide shoe to suit their foot'.[45] These men wanted 'a kirk, conscience, and religion made of gold, silks, and velvets, and foot-mantles, and high horses, and much court'. Indeed, 'the poor of the flock are the only on-waiters on Christ'.[46]

Such praise of the poor and condemnation of the rich and powerful foreshadowed the social radicalism that was to be a key component of the Covenanting movement in the later seventeenth century. However, at this stage, Rutherford had not given up on the nobility. Rather, he was calling them back to what he saw as their traditional historical role, that of checking the power of a tyrannical king.[47] The Scottish nobility was not performing this function because it had been corrupted by the court, and Rutherford makes this clear in no uncertain terms. Indeed, when one considers that his own patron, Sir John Gordon, had withdrawn from the controversial 1633 parliament on the pretext of feeling unwell, shortly after he had been made a viscount, Rutherford's preaching at this time seems genuinely courageous. He castigated those who tried to climb to heaven with the clay of the world on their backs. They were treating Christ like a 'pack-horse', who would carry their clay, their lusts, and their 'baronies'.[48] This, like the reference to Judas in the 1634 Anwoth sermon quoted above, was a none too subtle condemnation of Kenmure's betrayal of the Presbyterian cause in the previous year. In the light of the ferocity of his attacks on the nobility it is perhaps surprising that Rutherford survived in his parish as long as he did.

However, condemnation went hand in hand with appeal. Rutherford and his fellow militants among the clergy had to persuade the nobility of the necessity and efficacy of action on behalf of the cause. Just as Lenin had to persuade the 'vanguard' to take positive action instead of passively waiting for great historical forces to do their work, so these ministers had to

---

[43] *Letters*, p. 235.   [44] *Letters*, p. 253.   [45] *Communion Sermons*, pp. 168–9.
[46] *Communion Sermons*, p. 160.
[47] On the key role traditionally assigned to the nobility in Scottish political thought, see E. J. Cowan, 'The political ideas of a covenanting leader: Archibald Campbell, Marquis of Argyll, 1607–61', in R. Mason, ed., *Scots and Britons* (Cambridge, 1994), pp. 243–9.
[48] *Communion Sermons*, p. 94.

convince potential supporters that God's providence left room for genuine human agency. The 'ordinary logic' that action was useless until the Lord himself began to work was 'not (with reverence to your Lordship's learning) worth a straw'. 'Let us do [act], and not plead against God's office.'[49] Providence ought not to be used as an excuse for inaction. As Rutherford was fond of saying, 'Duties are ours, events are the Lord's.'[50]

Moreover, when confronted with the thought of death, judgement and eternity, the nobles could be taught the futility of worldly success and prosperity, and the necessity of godly action. In focusing on Puritan notions of time, we should not forget that the conviction that 'time shall be no more' was a powerful weapon in the Puritan armoury. Rutherford reminded the aging John Gordon of Cardoness: 'Ye are now upon the very border of the other life.' 'Look beyond time: things here are but moonshine. They have but children's wit who are delighted with shadows, and deluded with feathers flying in the air.' The aim here was not to inculcate a detached other-worldliness, but to encourage godly activism and the vigorous effort to transform the world: 'Awake, awake to do righteously', Rutherford urged Cardoness.[51]

He made similar appeals to Lord Loudon, Lord Balmerino, and the earl of Cassillis, obviously believing that the nobility could be persuaded to act decisively for Christ in time by being confronted with the thought of meeting Christ in eternity. Perhaps this was naive; perhaps cynical and worldly-wise aristocrats were swayed by more mundane considerations. Yet in an age when belief in judgement, hell and eternal damnation was almost universal, Rutherford's spiritual threats may have had a powerful impact on those tempted to be what he disparagingly dismissed as 'middoway man'.[52] The fact that Loudon, Balmerino and Cassillis – along with Argyll with whom Rutherford had indirect contact in the 1630s – were among the only nobles who supported the radical kirk party regime in 1648, suggests that their Presbyterian faith was more than just a nominal affair.[53]

At times Rutherford wrote as if the nobility was being given a final chance. Christ, his head 'wet and frozen' like the Beloved in the Song of Songs, was already leaving the house because his spouse had not let him in. But he could be prevailed upon to tarry:

If we could but weep upon Him, and say, 'We will not let Thee go', it may be that then, He, who is easy to be intreated, would yet, notwithstanding of our high

[49] *Letters*, p. 238.   [50] *Letters*, pp. 238, 226, 235.
[51] *Letters*, pp. 310–11. In this case the pastor's words seem to have had their desired effect; in 1638 Cardoness's name headed the list of Anwoth parishioners petitioning to keep Rutherford in their parish. See T. Murray, *Life of Rutherford* (Edinburgh, 1828), p. 356.
[52] *Quaint Sermons*, p. 137.
[53] On their support for the kirk party see D. Stevenson, *Revolution and Counter-Revolution in Scotland, 1644–51* (London, 1977), p. 131.

provocations, condescend to stay and feed among the lilies, till that fair and desirable day break, and the shadows flee away.[54]

Yet at other times Rutherford seems to be have been convinced that it was too late to persuade Christ to stay in Scotland. He had already been 'banished', and although he would one day return to reign, in the immediate future Scotland was destined to be the victim of God's wrath and the ravages of the Dragon. Here apocalyptic language took over, for only through the books of biblical prophecy could one understand the future. It is to Rutherford's understanding of these biblical prophecies that we shall now turn.

GLOBAL APOCALYPSE

The way in which mainstream Christian theologians traditionally read biblical prophecies – particularly the Book of Revelation – had been profoundly influenced by Augustine, who had poured a great deal of cold water on apocalyptic speculation. In contrast to those who attempted to connect the various beasts, vials and trumpets of Revelation with particular events and individuals, Augustine encouraged a dehistoricised and spiritualised approach to the Book. Rather than seeing it as providing an outline of past or future history, he read most of it as a symbolic representation of the perpetual struggle between the city of God and the city of Man. In contrast to many of the early Fathers, who had argued that the millennium of Revelation 20 was a period of material peace and prosperity at the end of history, Augustine suggested that it represented the rule of Christ over the church throughout history. To those fired up by dreams of a future millennium, Augustine in effect retorted: 'It's already here, it's just that you haven't noticed.'[55]

Augustine's influence on Protestant theologians was very great, and can be seen in the rejection of millenarian ideas by both Lutherans and Calvinists in the sixteenth century.[56] However, many Protestants felt

---

[54] *Letters*, p. 88.

[55] Augustine, *Concerning the City of God against the Pagans*, trans. H. Bettenson (London, 1984 edn), Bk 20.

[56] There is now a substantial literature on early modern Protestant eschatology: W. Lamont, *Godly Rule: Politics and Religion, 1603–60* (London, 1969); Wilson, *Pulpit in Parliament*; P. Toon, ed., *Puritans, the Millennium and the Future of Israel: Puritan Eschatology, 1600–1660* (Cambridge, 1970); C. Hill, *Antichrist in Seventeenth-Century England* (Oxford, 1971); I. Murray, *The Puritan Hope: Revival and the Interpretation of Prophecy* (Edinburgh, 1971); B. W. Ball, *A Great Expectation: Eschatological Thought in English Protestantism to 1660* (Leiden, 1975); R. Bauckham, *Tudor Apocalypse* (Appleford, 1978); P. Christianson, *Reformers and Babylon: English Apocalyptic Visions from the Reformation to the Eve of the Civil War* (Toronto, 1978); K. Firth, *The Apocalyptic Tradition in Reformation Britain, 1530–1645* (Oxford, 1979); Williamson, *Scottish*

unhappy about Augustine's dehistoricised 'symbolic' reading of Revelation. Instead, they took an 'historicist' view of Revelation, seeing it as containing prophecies about particular events throughout the history of the Church, including the Reformation itself.[57] Moreover, they also believed that some of Revelation's predictions about the fall of Babylon (the Roman papacy) were to be fulfilled in the near future. An increasing number followed Beza and Perkins in the belief that the conversion of the Jews predicted in Romans 11 was also imminent, and some came to believe that this would usher in a period of 'latter-day glory' for the church.[58]

For all these new views, however, most Protestants continued to believe that the millennium described in Revelation 20:1–6 was either a symbolic representation of the whole of church history or of a thousand-year period in the church's past. Expectation of a future millennium did not take off until the first half of the seventeenth century when it was encouraged by the books of Thomas Brightman, Johannes Alsted and Joseph Mede. Although its early popularity may have been exaggerated by historians, there can be little doubt that by the time of the British civil wars millenarian ideas had become widespread, particularly among the Protestant sects.[59]

Even among those who retained Augustine's amillennialism there was intense apocalyptic expectation. The fall of the Antichrist, the conversion of the Jews, and the worldwide triumph of the Reformed faith were all thought to be imminent. John Napier (the Scottish inventor of logarithms) placed the end-time events in the period from 1688 to 1700. Millenarian English Puritans opted for similar dates: Brightman suggested 1650 to 1695, Thomas Goodwin attached great significance to the year 1666, and John Cotton believed that in 1655 a great blow would be given to the Antichrist.[60] Such men, we do well to remember, were highly educated intellectuals; as William Lamont once wrote, in the seventeenth century apocalyptic belief was far from being a 'creed for cranks'.[61]

Rutherford frequently spoke in apocalyptic language, but his own

---

National Consciousness; D. Katz, *Philo-Semitism and the Readmission of the Jews to England, 1603–55* (Oxford, 1982); P. Lake, 'William Bradshaw, antichrist and the community of the godly', *Journal of Ecclesiastical History*, 36 (1985), 570–89; A. Zakai, *Exile and Kingdom: History and Apocalypse in the Puritan Migration to America* (Cambridge, 1992). Of these, Ball and Toon are the most theologically precise, but Lamont's must still be credited as the most politically perceptive. Williamson and Murray deal specifically with Scottish ideas.

[57] According to Ball, *A Great Expectation*, p. 71, the overwhelming majority of Protestant interpreters of Daniel and Revelation agreed that most of these prophecies had already been fulfilled.

[58] Murray, *The Puritan Hope*, pp. 41–5.

[59] T. Bozeman, *To Live Ancient Lives: The Primitivist Dimension in Puritanism* (Chapel Hill, NC, 1988), ch. 6, argues that millenarianism was a late development among Puritans and that it only really took hold after 1637.

[60] Ball, *A Great Expectation*, pp. 115–21.   [61] Lamont, *Godly Rule*, p. 13.

eschatological position is difficult to ascertain with any precision. He only made reference to the prophecies of Revelation in passing and never systematically expounded his views. Throughout his works he made no reference to the famous commentaries on Revelation by Napier, Alsted and Mede, and he referred to Brightman only as a defender of Presbyterianism. However, we can get some idea of the options open to him and of the eschatological views he was likely to hold by looking at those held by three of his ministerial colleagues in Scotland: Robert Baillie, George Gillespie and James Durham.

Baillie wrote from the Westminster Assembly complaining that many of its members were millenarians.[62] In the final chapter of *A Dissuasive from the Errors of our Time* (1645), he attacked the millenarian beliefs of the Independents and especially the notion that Christ would reign personally on the earth. Whether Baillie anticipated a period of latter-day glory is unclear; he was certainly at pains to stress that as long as it existed on earth the church would be a mixed company of the elect and the reprobate. He seems, therefore, to have reasserted a traditional Augustinian position against the millenarian innovations of Alsted and Mede.

Gillespie and Durham were less traditional. In a sermon to the House of Commons in March 1644, Gillespie was bold enough to date the 1,260 years of the reign of the Beast from the Pope's ascendancy in AD 383 to the year 1643, in which the Westminster Assembly had begun to meet![63] Although he rejected the idea that the Jews would build the Temple again in Jerusalem, Gillespie clearly looked forward to a period of latter-day glory in which the spiritual Temple predicted in Ezekiel 40–8 would be built, the Jews would be converted, and the earth would be filled 'with the knowledge of the glory of the Lord as the waters cover the sea' (Habakkuk 2:14).[64] Gillespie did not explain his views on the millennium, but James Durham argued that the thousand years – though not necessarily to be taken literally – may well have begun in 1560, 'being in part past, but in their vigour still to come'. The final three vials of Revelation 16 were still to be poured out; the fifth was the collapse of the city of Rome, the sixth the fall of the Antichrist and the conversion of the Jews (though not necessarily their restoration to Palestine), and the seventh the final destruction of Christ's enemies. The period that saw these vials poured out would be a glorious millennium for the Reformed churches.[65]

[62] Baillie, *Letters and Journals*, II, p. 313.
[63] Gillespie, 'A Sermon preached before the Honourable House of Commons at their Late Solemn Fast, Wednesday, March 27, 1644', in *The Works of George Gillespie*, 2 vols. (Edinburgh, 1846), I, pp. 23–4.
[64] Gillespie, 'Sermon before the House of Commons', pp. 20–2.
[65] On Durham see J. K. Cameron, 'The commentary on the Book of Revelation by James

Rutherford joined Baillie, Gillespie and Durham in repudiating the chiliastic notion that Christ would rule in person on the earth; when he spoke on his deathbed of the rule of Christ he made it clear that he did not mean 'any such visible Reign of Christ on Earth as the Millenaries fancy'.[66] Yet Rutherford did expect the final era of history to be characterised by great apocalyptic events – the fall of the popish Antichrist, the conversion of the Jews, and the triumph of Reformed Protestantism. Whether he expected such events to occupy only a short time-span before the return of Christ, or whether he agreed with Durham that a long millennial rule of the saints lay ahead is not altogether clear. But his belief that he was living in the last days described in the apocalypse is quite unmistakable.

At the beginning of the 1630s, as the Swedish king, Gustavus Adolphus, won a series of great Protestant victories in Germany, Rutherford had rejoiced that Christ was 'daily posting upon this horse', spattering 'dirt upon the Beasts face and the false Prophet'.[67] In a letter to Marion McNaught, Rutherford urged her to pray for this latter-day Gideon, through whom 'the Lord hath begun to loose some of Babylon's corner stones'. 'The victory is certain', he wrote, 'for when Christ and Babel wrestle, then the angels and saints may prepare themselves to sing, "Babylon the great is fallen, is fallen".'[68] But the call for a celestial choir practice seemed sadly premature when Gustavus died on the battlefield of Lutzen on 6 November 1632. Christ, whom Rutherford so often imagined on his great white horse, had been almost personified by the dashing Scandinavian warrior. Rutherford was not slow in drawing the lesson: Gustavus's death taught the godly to 'reverence our Lord, who doth not ordinarily hold Zion on her rock by the sword, and arm of flesh and blood, but by His own mighty and outstretched arm'.[69]

Yet though the fall of the Antichrist had been delayed, it would still surely come. 'Those who are with the beast and the dragon, must make war with the Lamb', Rutherford told McNaught in 1635, ' "but the Lamb shall overcome them: for he is Lord of lords and King of kings" . . . (Rev. 17:14).'[70] The Lamb would be victorious in Scotland too. 'I know that Christ shall yet win the day, and gain the battle in Scotland', Rutherford wrote from Aberdeen in 1637.[71]

If the Antichrist's fall was the negative side of apocalyptic expectation, a great revival of true religion among Jews and Gentiles was its positive face. Belief in the imminent conversion of the Jews to Christianity was wide-

Durham', in M. Wilks, ed., *Prophecy and Eschatology* (Oxford, 1994), pp. 123–9; Ball, *A Great Expectation*, pp. 161–4; and Toon, *Puritans*, pp. 39–41.
[66] Rutherford, *A Testimony to the Work of Reformation* (Lanark, 1739), p. 4.
[67] *Communion Sermons*, p. 10.   [68] *Letters*, p. 62.   [69] *Letters*, p. 118.
[70] *Letters*, p. 121.   [71] *Letters*, p. 222.

spread in Britain and the Netherlands, so yet again Rutherford reflected a facet of international Calvinism. In a good deal of Catholic apocalyptic thought, the Antichrist was expected to be a Jew, but seventeenth-century Calvinists generally believed that the Jews would turn to Christ and play a key role in the destruction of the Antichrist and the establishment of the Kingdom of God.[72] In Scotland, Rutherford's great Presbyterian predecessor in the Kirkcudbright area, John Welsh, firmly believed in the coming conversion of the Jews.[73]

Rutherford himself wrote often and exuberantly about Israel's salvation:

Oh to see the sight, next to Christ's Coming the most joyful! our elder brethren, the Jews, and Christ fall upon one another's necks and kiss each other! They have been so long asunder, they will be kind to one another when they meet: O longed for and lovely day, dawn! O sweet Jesus, let me see that sight that will be as life from the dead, thee and thy ancient people in mutual embraces![74]

The return of the Jews to Christ would lead to their full reconciliation to the Gentiles. In an extraordinarily intimate metaphor drawn from the Song of Songs, Rutherford pictured Christ's 'ancient widow wife, our dear sister, the Church of the Jews' coming to 'suck the breasts of their little sister' the church of the Gentiles, and so 'renewing their old love with their first Husband'.[75]

The restoration of the Jews and the fall of the Antichrist would be accompanied by the spread of Christ's glory throughout the world. Christ would embrace the younger sister, the church of the Gentiles, along with the elder sister, the church of the Jews.[76] Scotland too would experience spiritual resurrection. 'In the name of the Son of God', Rutherford urged McNaught, 'believe that buried Scotland, dead and buried with her dear Bridegroom, shall rise the third day again, and there shall be a new growth after the old timber is cut down.'[77] Scotland might now be in 'Rome's brothel-house' but the day would come when 'there shall be a fair after-growth for Christ in Scotland' and when 'this church shall sing again the Bridegroom's welcome again to His own house'.[78]

Such apocalyptic ideas, as John Pocock has demonstrated, were a vital

---

[72] See Y. Kaplan et al., eds., *Menasseh Ben Israel and His World* (Leiden, 1989). This fascinating volume amply illustrates the great interest in the prophetic Scriptures shared by Jews and Christians in Britain, America and the Netherlands. Of particular relevance is Arthur Williamson's chapter, 'The Jewish dimension of the Scottish apocalypse: climate, covenant and world renewal', pp. 7–30, which discusses Rutherford's views in some detail. See also his 'Latter day Judah, latter day Israel: the millennium, the Jews, and the British future', *Pietismus und Neuzeit*, 14 (1988), 149–65. On the English ideas about the Jews' prophetic role see Katz, *Philo-Semitism*.

[73] Williamson, 'The Jewish dimension', pp. 15–16.   [74] *Letters*, pp. 122–3.

[75] *Letters*, pp. 570–1. This use of the Song of Songs in an apocalyptic context was very common in the seventeenth century. Cf Ball, *A Great Expectation*, pp. 239–42.

[76] *Letters*, p. 88.   [77] *Letters*, p. 121.   [78] *Letters*, p. 410.

aspect of 'the time dimension of political thought'. Along with historical narratives, they played a critical role in shaping early modern people's sense of national identity and political agency.[79] This was certainly true for Rutherford. We have already seen that his understanding of the Scottish past was moulded by two narratives: Buchanan's myth of the ancient constitution, and Calderwood's tale of the covenanted and apostate kirk. The apocalyptic story was the metanarrative into which these particular narratives could be fitted. Scotland's story made greatest sense when it was placed within the context of God's redemptive plan for the consummation of history.

Yet Rutherford's faith that Christ would reclaim Scotland as his possession was (at least until mid-1637) mixed with a belief that terrible days lay ahead for the land. Like Protestants all over Europe, Rutherford was fascinated by the grotesque images of the Beast and the whore of Babylon in Revelation and identified both with the Roman papacy.[80] But he believed that the Antichrist was not just a foreign power; he was also the enemy within. Scotland's apostasy was due to 'the power of Antichrist working in this land'.[81] The bishops – and the Aberdeen Doctors who provided intellectual justification for their idolatry – were 'the friends and lovers of Babel among us'.[82] They were weaving a web for the Antichrist, bringing 'the Popes foul tail first upon us (their wretched and beggarly ceremonies)' in order that they might 'thrust in after them the Antichrist's legs and thighs, and his belly, head and shoulders'.[83]

These enemies of Christ were playing a foolhardy game, for as well as subjecting the nation to the Antichrist's rage they also exposed it to the wrath of the Lamb. They were 'like a child thrusting up a stick in the nose of a sleeping lion, and pulling his beard; which is no wise play'. With 'one stroke of His paw', the Lion of the tribe of Judah would smite them down; fire from his mouth would 'devour and burn all His enemies'.[84] Rutherford reiterated this message in a letter to one of his parishioners in June 1637: 'I told you often of wrath, wrath from the Lord, to come upon Scotland; and yet I bide by my Master's word. It is quickly coming! desolation for Scotland, because of the quarrel of a broken covenant.'[85] In June 1637, around the time when his closest friends were meeting in Edinburgh to plan the Prayer Book riots, Rutherford broke into one of his bitterest jeremiads:

---

[79] J. G. A. Pocock, 'Time, history and eschatology in the thought of Thomas Hobbes', in his *Politics, Language and Time* (London, 1972), pp. 148–201; and 'England', in O. Ranum, ed., *National Consciousness, History and Political Culture in Early Modern Europe* (London, 1975), pp. 98–117.

[80] For evidence of the widespread belief that the Antichrist equalled the papacy, see Hill, *Antichrist*, ch. 1; Christianson, *Reformers and Babylon*.

[81] *Letters*, p. 333.   [82] *Letters*, p. 300.   [83] *Letters*, p. 544.

[84] *Communion Sermons*, p. 15.   [85] *Letters*, p. 348.

Woe, woe, woe be to apostate Scotland! There is wrath, and a cup of the red wine of the wrath of God Almighty in the Lord's hand, that they shall drink and spue, and fall and not rise again. The star called 'Wormwood and gall' is fallen into the fountains and rivers, and hath made them bitter. The sword of the Lord is furbished against the idol-shepherds of the land. Women shall bless the barren womb and the miscarrying breast; all hearts shall be faint, and all knees shall tremble. An end is coming; the leopard and the lion shall watch over our cities; houses great and fair shall be desolate without an inhabitant. The Lord hath said, 'Pray not for this people, for I have taken My peace from them.'[86]

Christ appeared to be abandoning Britain, and many Puritans in the 1630s came to believe that it was too late to prevent him from leaving. Shortly before he emigrated to New England, Thomas Hooker told his congregation at Chelmsford that 'as sure as God is God, God is going from England'.[87] Rutherford also came to believe that God was going from Scotland. In the early days of the Reformation,

At the beginning of this Supper, one sermon or a Communion was sweet; people ran to it like hungry banqueters; now it is disregarded. One sermon in the day of the Lord's banquet is now thought sufficient . . . I fear, beloved, I fear (think of it as ye please) the word shall be taken from you, the board drawn, and the plague of the Lord follow it.

The seventy years of feasting were drawing to a close,[88] and Christ was going elsewhere. 'Our Blessed Lord Jesus, who cannot get leave to sleep with his spouse in this land, is going to seek an inn where He will be better entertained.'[89]

This sense of impending doom in no way contradicted Rutherford's expectation of the imminent reign of Christ. Indeed, it was precisely because the end was near that Satan was raging so fiercely. The 'prince of the bottomless pit' knew that 'it is near the time when he shall be tormented; and now in his evening he has gathered his armies, to win one battle or two, in the edge of the evening, at the sun going down'.[90] It was this that accounted for the Thirty Years War in Germany, the persecution of the Puritans in the three kingdoms, and their emigration to New England. The woman was being chased by the Dragon into the wilderness just as had been predicted in Revelation 12.[91] God was allowing the 'whore of Rome' to 'smite Scotland, and make it a den of dragons'.[92]

Because of the Antichrist's rage and the Lamb's wrath the immediate future for the church would be bleak. After telling McNaught of his confidence that 'Zion shall be well', Rutherford went on to explain that he foresaw a time of purging ahead, by which God intended to 'bring out a fair

---

[86] *Letters*, p. 333.   [87] Quoted in Collinson, 'Protestant nation', p. 20.
[88] *Communion Sermons*, p. 63.   [89] *Letters*, p. 56.   [90] *Letters*, p. 94.
[91] *Communion Sermons*, pp. 10, 52.   [92] *Communion Sermons*, p. 32.

beautiful bride out of the furnace'. During this time, the bride would 'be hidden for a time from the dragon that pursueth the woman with child'. God would be with his kirk at this time, but Rutherford feared that the Lord would 'cast down the shepherd's tents, and feed his own in a secret place'.[93]

If Christ was to leave Scotland to the ravages of the Dragon and the Whore of Babylon, perhaps the best thing for the godly to do was to follow the example of Thomas Hooker and emigrate to New England. This was an option that Rutherford considered with the utmost earnestness in the 1630s. After telling Marion McNaught in 1634 that the bridegroom was on the verge of leaving Scotland, Rutherford said, 'Pray Him to tarry, or then to take us with Him.'[94] In April 1635 he told McNaught that the Dragon may so prevail as to chase the woman and her man-child over the sea. Then he asked her to see if her husband 'can be induced to think upon going to America'.[95] The underlying message was clear; the bride and bridegroom were being hounded across the sea to the American 'wilderness'. Rutherford's colleagues – Blair, Livingstone and McLelland – having been deprived of their livings in Ireland, felt compelled to sail to New England in 1636 but were blown back by the wind. In 1637, Rutherford wrote to one of those who tried to emigrate with them, telling him, 'Let me hear from you, for I am anxious what to do. If I saw a call for New England, I would follow it.'[96]

None of this suggests a man who expected a dramatic breakthrough for the Puritan cause in Scotland. On the contrary, it reveals someone who believed that he could do little in his own land in the near future. The attraction of breaking away from the cultural constraints of the old European world, and establishing a new sacred space in the wilderness appealed to Rutherford as much as it did to the English Congregationalists who set out to create a city on a hill.[97]

DEVELOPMENT (1637–1661)

The success of the revolution in 1637–8, therefore, came as a great surprise to Rutherford.[98] Yet once the rebellion got under way, the apocalyptic

---

[93] *Letters*, p. 94. The feeding in a secret place seems to hint at conventicles.

[94] *Letters*, p. 115.   [95] *Letters*, p. 122.   [96] *Letters*, p. 301.

[97] On the ideological motivation behind the Puritan colonisation of New England see Zakai, *Exile and Kingdom*. Had Rutherford emigrated, of course, I would probably not be writing this now. American historians would doubtless have written several major studies of Rutherford the New England Puritan.

[98] Burrell has argued that 'had the rebellion against the Service Book not occurred, there is no reason for believing that the apocalyptic vision of the dissenting ministry could have carried on for more than another generation', 'Apocalyptic vision', p. 16.

outlook that had been fostered by the Presbyterian preachers gave it great momentum.[99] On 28 February 1638, the National Covenant was signed in Greyfriars kirk, Edinburgh, and Wariston was moved to declare that this was 'the glorious marriage day of the Kingdom with God'.[100] 'They call us now no more "Forsaken" nor "Desolate" ', boasted Rutherford in 1639, 'but our land is called "Hephzibah" and "Beulah" (Isaiah 35:10). For the Lord delighteth in us, and this land is married to Himself.'[101] Christ was once again on horseback, just as in the early 1630s, 'hunting and persuing the Beast'.[102] He was 'fetching a blow upon the Beast, and the scarlet-coloured Whore', and the day was not far off when 'The kings of Tarshish, and of the isles, must bring presents to our Lord Jesus (Psalm 72:10).' Rutherford now saw Britain as 'one of the chiefest isles',[103] prepared by God for a great providential purpose.

This was written in 1639, but Rutherford's sense of the British significance of the Scottish Revolution pre-dated this. At the beginning of February 1638, he wrote of his longing to see the glory of Christ 'advanced in all the world, and especially in these three kingdoms'.[104] Morrill's assertion that until 1639 the Covenanters regarded the Covenant as 'non-exportable' does not seem to apply to Rutherford. Seeing current events through an apocalyptic framework he could not help thinking that what was happening in Scotland was part of God's global plan for the last days. Nevertheless, Morrill's claim that up to 1639 the Scots did not regard their problem as stemming from England, does fit Rutherford.[105] Indeed, it is striking that he portrayed the enemies of Christ as Scottish and not English. His letters contained no reference to Laud whatsoever, but many to the 'fourteen prelates' and the nobles who failed to defend Christ. Scotland had been corrupted just as much as England. The Antichrist, like the Lord, sought the whole of Britain, not just a part. The problem for Rutherford was not one of anglicisation, but of anti-Christianisation; he perceived the crisis in apocalyptic rather than nationalistic terms.

By August 1640, on the eve of the Second Bishops' War, Rutherford's apocalyptic sense was at its most acute:

[99] See Burrell, 'Apocalyptic vision', pp. 16ff.; Williamson, *Scottish National Consciousness*, pp. 143–5. Apocalypticism was also a vital force in the Iranian revolution of 1979. Khomeini encouraged speculation that he was the Twelfth Imam who, according to Shi'ite eschatology, was to come as the Mahdi to redeem the world. On the eve of the revolution, in 1978, such speculation was rife and messianic longings were very strong. See S. A. Arjomand, *The Turban for the Crown: the Islamic Revolution in Iran* (Oxford, 1988), pp. 100, 208–9.

[100] Archibald Johnston of Wariston, *Diary*, I, ed. G. M. Paul (Edinburgh, 1911), pp. 321–2.

[101] *Letters*, p. 570.   [102] *Letters*, p. 577.   [103] *Letters*, pp. 570–1.

[104] *Letters*, p. 554.

[105] Morrill, *The Nature of the English Revolution* (Harlow, 1993), pp. 108–14.

Who knows but this great work which is begun in Scotland now when it is going into England, and it has tane some footing there, but the Lord He will make it to go over the sea? Who knows but the Lord will make Scotland, who is a worm indeed in comparison of other nations, to be a sharp threshing instrument, to thresh the mountains and to beat the hills to pieces?

An awesome thought had occurred to Rutherford: the Scottish National Covenant might just be the trigger to set off a series of events culminating in the fall of the Antichrist, the conversion of the Jews and the establishment of Christ's earthly rule.[106] And how beautifully appropriate this would be, for God – who refused to share his glory with another and chose the weak and despised things of this world to shame the powerful – would be taking up Scotland, a 'worm' of a nation at the ends of the earth, to accomplish his purpose! Only at this point, after the unexpected triumph of the Covenanting movement, could Rutherford dare to contemplate Scotland's world-historical importance. And even at this point he was tentative: he 'hopes', he 'desires', he asks 'Who knows'.[107] To suggest that he was swaggering with national self-confidence is far wide of the mark.

Indeed, for all his enthusiasm, Rutherford was always capable of a level-headed assessment of political possibilities. He recognised that not everyone in the Covenanting movement shared his ambitions. Many had taken the Covenant but were not real 'heart-covenanters',[108] and only 'the letter of religion' had been reformed.[109] God might be at work, but God used means. Was Scotland really up to the great task it had been set? In 1639 Rutherford was far from certain. 'Alas! I fear that Scotland be undone and slain with this great mercy of reformation, because there is not here that life of religion, answerable to the huge greatness of the work that dazzleth our eyes.'[110] A year later his doubts were if anything even greater. God had made Scotland 'a favoured people in the sight of the nations',[111] but 'It is universally complained of that there is a strange deadness upon the land, and on the hearts of His people.'[112] Rutherford was painfully aware that most Scots were not particularly godly, and he knew that this would prove the greatest obstacle to attempts to establish a holy commonwealth.

However, as the possibility of a British reformation beckoned, Rutherford temporarily forgot the sins of his homeland. In the preface to his *Peaceable and Temperate Plea for Paul's Presbyterie in Scotland* (1642) he tried to explain the internationalism of his vision. Primary loyalty must be given to one's religion and not one's nation, because it was 'a weaknesse to overlove

---

[106] *Quaint Sermons*, p. 36. [107] See *Letters*, p. 596.
[108] *Quaint Sermons*, p. 61. [109] *Letters*, p. 596. [110] *Letters*, p. 570.
[111] *Letters*, p. 611. See Chapter 4 for more evidence of the ungodliness of the majority of Scots in Rutherford's eyes.
[112] *Letters*, p. 614.

a Nationall faith because Nationall, and not because it's faith'. He described his eschatological dream of the two sisters, 'Britaines Israel and Judah, England and Scotland comming together, weeping and asking the way to Sion'. But Christ's glory was not to be 'confined within this narrow Isle of Britaine'. Rutherford wanted to live to be one of the 'eye-witnesses of his last Marriage-glory on earth', when all the nations would be reconciled to their Lord.[113]

With his appointment to the Westminster Assembly, Rutherford had the chance to play his part in the fulfillment of these apocalyptic dreams. He was awed by 'the honour of being a mason to lay the foundation for many generations, and to build the waste places of Zion in another kingdom' and of having 'a hand or a finger in that carved work in the cedar and almug trees in that new temple'.[114] The allusion here was to Solomon's temple, but as Gillespie's sermon to the Commons showed, the Scots also saw themselves as helping to build the temple described in Ezekiel's apocalyptic prophecy, a spiritual temple only to be constructed 'about the time of the destruction of Antichrist and the conversion of the Jews'.[115]

After his arrival in England, Rutherford continued to entertain apocalyptic ambitions. Preaching to the House of Commons in January 1644, he declared that 'the rise of the Gospel-sun' was like a comet warning of 'woe to the Pope, king of the Bottomlesse Pit, and his bloody lady Babel'. The English parliament had 'the power and opportunitie to send the Glory of Christ over sea, to all Europe'.[116] Even in 1646 Rutherford could write that 'Christ hath a great design of free grace to these lands'. But his European vision had dimmed and he began to repeat the jeremiads of the 1630s: 'I can write nothing for the present concerning these times (whatever others may think), but that which speaketh wrath and judgement to these kingdoms.'[117]

Such spiritual depression was easily accounted for. Zion was being built 'with carcasses of men, in two kingdoms, fallen as dung in the open field'.[118] Thousands of Protestants had been slaughtered in Ireland, fierce wars were being fought all over Britain, and the Covenanter army had seen little success. In November 1645, Rutherford wrote to a Scottish woman whose son-in-law had been killed in battle, telling her that 'If Zion be builded with your son-in-laws blood, the Lord (deep in counsel) can glue together the stones of Zion with blood, and with that blood which is precious in his sight.' He reminded her of what Job had learned, that 'we cannot teach the Almighty knowledge'.[119] The Lord's ultimate purpose was

[113] *Peaceable Plea*, sigs. av–a2.   [114] *Letters*, p. 615.
[115] Gillespie, *Sermon to the Commons*, in *Works*, I, pp. 7–9.
[116] *Sermon to the Commons*, sig. A2v, p. 7.   [117] *Letters*, pp. 640–1.
[118] *Sermon to Commons*, sig. A2.   [119] *Letters*, p. 628.

still clear, but he was moving in mysterious ways, hiding himself behind a mask. With divine providence looking so painfully 'darke', it was important to look on the 'faire and smiling side of God's providence'. But the darkness had a lesson for the godly too, for it showed them that the earth was 'their Inne, not their home, their Pilgrimage, not their Countrey'.[120] The pendulum was swinging away from the revelation of God to the hiddenness of God, from his apocalyptic purpose in time to the Christian's home in eternity.

Even more disconcerting than the violence of the war was the spiritual state of the English. Although Rutherford had hitherto had little to say against the English, he was soon deeply disillusioned. The Scottish commissioners found themselves fighting against Erastians, Independents, a recalcitrant parliament and a plethora of dangerous sects. In May 1644 Rutherford told Lady Boyd that 'for my part, I often despair of the reformation of this land, which saw never anything but the high places of their fathers, and the remnants of Babylon's pollutions'. He even went so far as to admit that he sometimes thought that he was no more likely to find 'a sound Christian' in London than in Spain.[121]

In his public pronouncements, however, Rutherford sounded very different. In a treatise devoted to demonstrating that the Antichrist was alive and well in England, he declared, 'I judge that in England the Lord hath many names . . . and that in that renowed Nation, there be men of all rankes, wise, valourous, generous, noble, heroick, faithfull, religious, gracious, learned.'[122] Those who prevented 'National ruptures' between England and Scotland would be blessed by the Lord, said Rutherford, for 'Christ Jesus is a uniting Saviour' and it was right that one religion should be like 'Chains of Gold to tie these two Nations and Churches together in *uno tertio*, that they may be concentred and united in one Lord Jesus'.[123] So despite his disillusionment with the English, Rutherford had not lost the vision of 'sister churches' and 'Britaines Israel and Judah'.

Nevertheless, the tide of apocalyptic internationalism, which seemed to have been coming in so quickly, was now receding, and the retreat towards 'Presbyterianism in one country' had already begun. The last books Rutherford addressed to England were *A Survey of Spiritual Antichrist* (1648) and *A Free Disputation Against Pretended Liberty of Conscience* (1649), angry works denouncing English heresies and revealing the depth of Rutherford's bitterness and sense of betrayal. Scottish Presbyterians, who had taken the field against the Antichrist when the sects were cowering 'like

---

[120] *Sermon to Commons*, pp. 9–10. [121] *Letters*, p. 618.
[122] *Survey of Spiritual Antichrist*, sig. a3. [123] *Divine Right*, sigs. A4v, A3.

silly Doves and fainting Does', were now being reviled as 'worse than Egypt or Babylon'.[124]

In November 1647, Rutherford left England, with his work in the Westminster Assembly completed, and the establishment of Presbyterianism in severe jeopardy. As the Independents gained control over English government, his attention turned to Scotland. The movement of reformation, which had once seemed destined to travel all over Europe, was now in danger in the land of its birth. The signing of the Engagement in December was followed by clerical attacks on malignants who had betrayed the covenants. One of the most influential was that of George Gillespie, who, on Rutherford's recommendation, denounced the Engagers from his deathbed. The need to purge the nation in order to avert God's wrath was put firmly on the national agenda by Gillespie. In his final testimony he declared, 'I have often comforted myself, and still do, with the hopes of the Lord's purging this polluted land.'[125]

The language of pollution and purging was to form a vital part of Rutherford's vocabulary over the next decade, as indeed it had in the 1630s. The Protestant covenant and the apocalyptic future undermined the natural-law contractualism and the constitutionalist history found in _Lex, Rex_.[126] Up to this point they had co-existed in creative tension, because reformation could be furthered through the traditional constitutional mechanisms. But when with the Engagement it became clear that the bulk of the political nation was willing to betray the covenants by forming an alliance with popish malignants, the militants were forced to face up to the fact that secular constitutionalism could conflict with religious goals. Like the Hebrew prophets, they had to warn the people to repent or face God's wrath for breaking their national covenant.

Alongside abandoning his careful synthesis of traditional constitutionalism and Protestant covenantalism, Rutherford also began to shift his hopes from the shoulders of the nobility to the shoulders of the godly alone.[127] In his Epistle Dedicatory to the _Last Speeches of Viscount_

---

[124] _Survey of Spiritual Antichrist_, sig. A3v.

[125] 'The Testimony of Mr George Gillespie', in _Works_, II, p. 2. Rutherford had written (_Letters_, p. 645), 'If ye leave any testimony to the Lord's work, against both Malignants and Sectaries (which I suppose may be needful), let it be under your hand, and subscribed before faithful witnesses.'

[126] The tension between these modes of political discourse was common in the seventeenth century. Oliver Cromwell, for example, used natural-law contractualist arguments, but was also obsessed with discerning God's providence, and following where it led. See J. Sommerville, 'Oliver Cromwell and English political thought', in J. Morrill, ed., _Oliver Cromwell and the English Revolution_ (London, 1990), ch. 9.

[127] W. H. Makey, _The Church of the Covenant, 1637–51: Revolution and Social Change in Scotland_ (Edinburgh, 1979), argues that the Scottish revolution saw the predominance of the nobility threatened by the rising middling classes, of whom Rutherford was typical. The

Kenmuir, dedicated to 'the whole nobility of Scotland', he reminded them that 'It's not the antiquity of your families, nor the long descent of an ancient pedigree through many noble or princely branches, that can make you noble. True nobility consists in that adoption by which you are made the sons of God.' Nevertheless, even at this point Rutherford did not give up on the Buchananite idea of the nobility as the defenders of Scottish liberty: 'God hath set you (noblemen) as stars in the firmament of honour; upon your influence depends the whole course of the inferior world.'[128]

Yet despite these reservations, Rutherford and his colleagues did want to see a purge, and their opportunity came after the defeat of the Engagers at Preston in August 1648. The Act of Classes (January 1649) excluded Engagers and all other 'malignants' from civil office, and in August 1650 several thousand officers and men were expelled from the army because they fell short of the standard of godliness required.[129] Lying behind these purges was the example of Gideon, who, after ruthlessly reducing his army to a force of three hundred men, was given a great victory by the Lord. In August 1650, less than a month before the battle of Dunbar, Rutherford explained the logic of this position to Colonel Gilbert Ker, telling him that all the swords in Britain were but 'cyphers making no number' to God, who had put all his influence in 'Gideon's sword'. Rutherford's British ambitions were once again apparent: 'a throne shall be set up for Christ in this island of Britain (which is, and shall be, a garden more fruitful of trees of righteousness, and which payeth and shall pay more thousands to the Lord of the vineyard than is paid in thrice the bounds of Great Britain upon earth)'.[130]

Yet Rutherford's hopes were to be cruelly dashed. On 3 September 1650, Cromwell's army inflicted a devastating defeat on the Scots, killing 3,000 men and wounding 10,000. For Cromwell, this was an enormously important victory; for the first time in his military career he had had to confront another godly army, and the Lord had given him the victory. This was the ultimate evidence of divine approbation. Rutherford, by contrast, was devastated by Dunbar. It threw into confusion all his firm convictions about God's providential purpose. 'Oh, how little of God do we see, and how mysterious is He!', he wrote to Colonel Gilbert Ker.[131] To a fellow minister, William Guthrie, he confessed,

---

replacement of the nobility by poorer but more godly men is described in Stevenson, *Revolution and Counter-Revolution*, pp. 134–9.

[128] *The Last and Heavenly Speeches of John, Viscount Kenmuir*, p. 381.
[129] Stevenson, *Revolution and Counter-Revolution*, pp. 130, 174–5.
[130] *Letters*, p. 650.
[131] *Letters*, p. 655. Lamont's comment about Hobbes and the Erastians in the 1640s applies equally well to Rutherford: 'The Book of Job had conquered the Book of Revelation', *Godly Rule*, p. 131.

I have suffered much, but this is the thickest darkness, and the straitest step of the way I have yet trodden . . . Alas, alas! poor I am utterly lost, my share of heaven is gone, and my hope is poor; I am perished, and I am cut off from the Lord . . . I profess that I am almost broken and a little sleepy, and would fain put off this body.[132]

Cromwell was eventually to experience emotional trauma like this himself when the English expedition to Hispaniola was defeated in July 1655. When he heard the news, the Lord Protector retired to his room for a whole day. According to Blair Worden, he may have 'never fully recovered' from the demoralisation of this experience. Providence seemed to have deserted him. In order to make sense of this bewildering event, Cromwell turned to the story of Achan, whose sin brought a heavy military defeat upon the people of Israel. He needed to discover the 'accursed thing' that had provoked the Lord's wrath.[133]

In September 1650, Rutherford also sought to identify the source of provocation. He concluded that Scotland had been defeated at Dunbar because of her unfaithfulness to the covenants, her easy acceptance of malignants, not least Charles II.[134] 'I am abundantly satisfied, that our army, through the sinful miscarriage of men, hath fallen', he told Colonel Ker on 5 September. Dunbar signalled not God's favour towards the sectaries, but his displeasure at the Scots for tolerating those who had broken the covenant. The army was not 'Gideon's three hundred, by whom He is to save us; we must have one of our Lord's carving'.[135] What was needed, therefore, was further purging. Covenantal logic eschewed the 'Trust in God and keep your powder dry' approach. Rutherford, who had so often explained how God worked through 'second causes' and called upon men to make use of 'means', now claimed that the obvious means – a large army – must be thrown aside, because it inhibited reliance on God. Gideon and Samson had achieved their victories not because of natural strength but because 'the breathings of the Spirit of the Lord' came upon them. Rutherford hinted strongly that Ker would be given a similar empowerment. 'If I conceive aright, the Lord hath called you to act against that enemy . . . Ye are, Sir, to lay hold on opportunities of Providence, and to wait for Him.'[136]

---

[132] *Letters*, p. 653.

[133] See B. Worden, 'Oliver Cromwell and the sin of Achan', in D. Beales and G. Best, eds., *History, Society and the Churches: Essays in Honour of Owen Chadwick* (Cambridge, 1985), pp. 125–45.

[134] The post-Restoration Covenanter, Alexander Shields, was to refer to Joshua 7 when describing the defeat of the Scots at Dunbar and Worcester. He notes that Charles II, 'the Achan, the cause of the overthrow, was forced to hide himself in the Oak', and then escape into exile. See *A Hind Let Loose, or an Historical Representation of the Testimonies of the Church of Scotland* (1687), p. 75.

[135] *Letters*, pp. 651–2.   [136] *Letters*, p. 654.

Ker was the sort of man to take Rutherford and his advice very seriously indeed. He had strongly supported the Western Remonstrance of October, which condemned the Covenanters for signing a treaty with the untrustworthy Charles II, and rejected any co-operation with malignants or sectaries. Ker declared that he would serve the king, but only on condition that 'the King himselfe be a servant to the King of Kings'. When he refused to follow orders from the committee of estates on the grounds that he could not see how they would benefit the Lord's work, the government quickly dispatched another commander to replace him. Ker now believed that providence's opportunity had arrived. Early on 1 December, he launched an attack on the English forces at Hamilton. The result, as at Dunbar, was disastrous. The forces of the Western Association were routed, with a hundred men killed and a hundred captured, including Ker, who had suffered a head wound and a shattered right hand. The English, who laid the blame for the colonel's action squarely at the feet of Rutherford, believed that this defeat was even more demoralising for the militant Covenanters than Dunbar.[137] They may well have been right. In January Rutherford wrote to Ker saying that he knew a man who, on receiving news of the battle, had 'longed to have the weather-beaten and crazy bark safely landed in that harbour of eternal quietness'. The sun would rise upon Scotland again, but Rutherford was pessimistic for the short-term prospects of the land: 'I see the nobles and the state falling off from Christ, and the night coming upon the prophets.'[138]

The majority of Rutherford's ministerial colleagues, however, had little sympathy for his complaints. Ever since Dunbar they had been convinced that what was needed was not more purging, but less.[139] With the defeat of the Western Association they were able to put their ideas into practice. On 1 January 1651, Charles II was crowned at Scone, and in June the Acts of Classes were repealed. Royalists and Engagers flooded back in to public office. The moderate ministers even justified the policy from *Lex, Rex*. Recognising the conflict between Rutherford's religious covenantalism and his natural-law contractualism, they argued that the inclusion of malignants in the army could be defended by appeal to the law of nature and nations, on which Rutherford had written at such length; the people had a natural obligation to defend their lives, liberties and estates against invasion, and a

---

[137] See *Mercurius Politicus*, 12–19 December 1650, p. 471. For Cromwell's view see W. C. Abbott, *The Writings and Speeches of Oliver Cromwell*, 4 vols. (Oxford, 1937–47), II, pp. 364–5.

[138] Stevenson, *Revolution and Counter-Revolution*, pp. 186–93.

[139] Stevenson, *Revolution and Counter-Revolution*, p. 181.

government had the right to call all those under its protection to its defence.[140]

Rutherford, of course, was no longer operating according to such worldly logic. He rejected the safety in numbers argument as 'carnal confidence', and rejoiced instead that 'the most wonderful works of God have been done with fewest men'. 'O what strength is there in Christ's little finger', he declared.[141] The crisis had to be interpreted in terms of the religious covenant, not natural law. Where there was a conflict between the principles of natural reason and the logic of true religion, religion took precedence. When asked how it could be legitimate to prevent men defending their liberties, lives and estates against an invader, Rutherford was emphatic: 'Light of nature is no rule for a Christian man; he has something dearer to him than these. When religion and the people of God could not be preserved but with the loss of men's natural interests, the one must give place to the other; otherwise excommunicate men, and papists and idolaters could not be debarred.'[142] The synthesis of nature and grace worked out in *Lex, Rex* had been shattered. The obligation of grace (to defend the religious covenant) had subverted the obligation of nature (for every man to defend his homeland against attack). The demands of the external covenant of grace had taken precedence over the natural-law demands of the covenant of works.[143] Grace could not only perfect nature, but also destroy it. The rule of the saints, it seemed, was necessary in order to defend true religion.

The more moderate Presbyterians eschewed this line, but their policy of readmitting the Engagers was unable to prevent the Cromwellian conquest of Scotland. For the rest of the 1650s Rutherford identified himself with the radical Protesters, the heirs of those who supported the Western Remonstrance in 1650. They attacked the moderate Resolutioners for their lax attitude towards malignants and produced periodic condemnations of Scotland's apostasy, the most famous of which was Guthrie's *The Causes of the Lord's Wrath against Scotland* (1653). However, as a party they were increasingly marginalised, despite attracting a large popular following. In the 1650s, Rutherford returned to his role of the 1630s, a prophet preaching his jeremiads in the wilderness. Disoriented though he was, he held on to the belief that reformation had only been delayed, that God was storing up

---

[140] See *Register of the Consultations of the Ministers of Edinburgh and Some other Brethren in the Ministry*, ed. W. Stephen, I (Edinburgh, 1921), p. 307.
[141] Unpublished manuscript sermon on Genesis 28, Edinburgh University Library, Dc. 5. 30, n. p.
[142] *The Diary of Alexander Brodie, 1652–80*, ed. D. Laing (Aberdeen, 1863), p. 48.
[143] According to Rutherford (*Covenant of Life*, p. 214), the covenant of works, given to all mankind, incorporated the natural law. The nature–grace conflict, therefore, can be seen as a conflict between the requirements of the covenant of works and those of the external covenant of grace.

wrath for his enemies, especially the English. 'Wo is me for England!' he intoned in 1651. 'That land shall be soaked with blood, and their dust made fat with fatness; that pleasant land shall be a wilderness, and the dust of their land pitch.'[144] Yet the Scots were not to rebel against Cromwell, Rutherford insisted, for they were meant 'to stande under him as the first punishment of our inquitie'. He recommended two mottoes for his fellow countrymen: 'I will bear the Indignation of the Lord becaus I have sinned' (Micah 7: 9), and 'I was dumb and opened not my mouth, because you did it' (Psalm 39: 9).[145]

As Job had discovered, submission to providence was the only response to the revelation of one's ignorance. Rutherford still clung on to the promises about Christ's future kingdom, but he was now agnostic about the timing: '*when* this shall be in Scotland (and it must be) is better to believe than prophesy; and quietly to hope and sit still (for that is yet our strength), than to quarrel with Him, that the wheels of this chariot move leisurely'.[146] Rutherford was no longer so sure that he understood providence or even the Bible: 'The book of holy providence is good marginal notes on His revealed will, in His word, and speaks much to us, could we read and understand what He writes, both in the one and the other.'[147] As the Quaker, George Keith, noted, the letters Rutherford wrote in his later years show that he 'was become exceeding dark, and barren'.[148] Yet even as he lay dying with the knowledge that all the Covenanters' legislation was being repealed, Rutherford was unrepentant: 'Yet we are to believe Christ will not so depart from the land, but a remnant shall be saved; and he shall reign a victorious conquering king, to the ends of the earth.'[149]

---

[144] *Letters*, p. 660.
[145] 'The Power of the Civil Magistrate in matters of Religion', Laing Manuscript III. 69 no. 5, Edinburgh University Library, f. 9.
[146] *Letters*, p. 676. [147] *Letters*, p. 678.
[148] G. Keith, *The Way cast Up* (n.p., 1677), p. 17. [149] *Testimony*, p. 10.

Conclusion: The failure of godly rule

For all his single-minded devotion to the rule of Christ, Samuel Rutherford was a highly complex individual. We have seen that he was a scholastic humanist, and a cerebral enthusiast, a professor and ecclesiastical statesman who toiled in committees and assemblies with other men, and a pastor who cultivated intimate friendships with godly women. We have also learnt that though he is famed as an uncompromising defender of Scottish Presbyterianism, he fostered practices that are more often associated with English Independency and ended his days estranged from the majority within the kirk.

This complexity is also reflected in Rutherford's political thought, which is marked by its use of several different topoi. In *Lex, Rex*, Rutherford tried to balance the language of natural law with a biblical insistence on the need to preserve national religious covenants. He also employed the ancient constitutionalism and the apocalypticism that Arthur Williamson has seen as merging to produce 'Scotland's heroic moment' in 1638.[1] If Rutherford's political theory is to be properly understood, each of these four modes of discourse must be taken into account. They came together from 1638 to 1648 to create a multi-faceted and powerful vision, one which gave the Scottish Covenanters a clear sense of their place in history and succeeded in balancing aristocratic and clerical interests.

However, there were always tensions between the two modes of political argument deriving from secular classical sources that stressed the role of the aristocracy (natural-law theory and ancient constitutionalism), and the two deriving from the Hebrew Scriptures which emphasised the importance of the people of God (religious covenantalism and apocalypticism). In 1648, and finally in 1650, these tensions became too great to maintain. As the nobility betrayed the covenants, the radical Covenanters abandoned the secular languages that they had earlier employed, in favour of exclusively

---

[1] A. Williamson, 'A patriot nobility? Calvinism, kin-ties and civic humanism', *Scottish Historical Review*, 72 (1993), 1–21.

biblical discourse. The religious covenant and God's apocalyptic plan had to take precedence over the traditional prominence of the nobility and the natural right of all men to defend their land when it was attacked. To allow the Engagers to reassume control of the nation was to betray the national covenants with God. When the kirk gave its blessing to the state's policy of readmitting the Engagers, Rutherford had no choice but to move into an increasingly isolated and sectarian position.

Ultimately, therefore, for all his classical learning, Rutherford's political thought was governed by biblical categories. The cause of true religion was his great obsession, and all else was subordinate to it. Back in the 1630s he had preached that 'kingdoms and kings that stand by policy, and not on Christ and his Word, they stand on rotten tree-legs [wooden legs]'.[2] His greatest yearning was to see Scotland become a land of 'heart-covenanters' truly committed to God. In his most ecstatic moments he believed that such a covenanted Scotland might spearhead the apocalyptic movement that would see the conversion of the Jews, the overthrow of the popish Antichrist, and the establishment of Christ's rule in all the nations of the earth.

The supreme irony of Rutherford's life was that he had misread the times. He lived not at the end of history, but at the end of an era in which religion had formed a sacred canopy covering every area of life, and in which the principle of 'one realm, one religion' had been taken for granted. There lay ahead not the kingdom of God on earth but a world in which religious plurality and tolerance would gradually expand, and in which religion would eventually be pushed to the margins of political life. Rutherford saw the beginning of this trend in England in the 1640s, and he resisted it with all the arguments that he could muster. His books against toleration perhaps entitle him to be described as one of the last full-blooded defenders of the medieval *respublica christiana*. But he was trying to save a sinking ship. The fragmentation of Protestantism was too far advanced, the demands of intolerance too onerous, the attractions of pluralism too great.

It is important not to exaggerate the suddenness of this shift.[3] Recent work on the late seventeenth century has reminded us of the persistence of millenarian expectations, popish plot scares and theories of persecution.[4] Moreover, in different ways both Linda Colley and Jonathan Clark remind

---

[2] *Communion Sermons*, p. 16.
[3] For an undeniably eloquent example of such exaggeration see the contrast drawn between the Puritan 'Titans' of the seventeenth century and the 'Augustan calm' of the eighteenth in R. H. Tawney, *Religion and the Rise of Capitalism* (Harmondsworth, 1964), esp. pp. 197–8.
[4] See W. Lamont, *Richard Baxter and the Millennium* (Brighton, 1979), ch. 4, which revises his earlier claim that 1660 marked a sharp dividing line between a religious and a secularised politics; T. Harris et al., eds., *The Politics of Religion in Restoration England* (Oxford, 1990); C. Rose, 'Providence, protestant union and godly reformation in the 1690s', *Transactions of the Royal Historical Society*, 6th Series, 3 (1993), 151–69.

us of the importance of religion in eighteenth-century Britain.[5] Their work casts doubt on the assumption that 1660 was the watershed that ushered in a new world and suggests that historians have tended to read twentieth-century secularism back into earlier eras.

Yet it remains true that the theocratic vision of authoritarian Puritanism was dealt a devastating blow by the failures of the Interregnum.[6] The late seventeenth and eighteenth centuries saw the two traditions of Erasmian humanism and Evangelical pietism flourish at the expense of Puritan ambitions for godly rule.[7] After the Restoration there was a powerful reaction against the enthusiasm of the Interregnum. Ironically, the aggression of orthodox zealots like Rutherford was one of the major factors in the growth of the rationalist heterodoxy that they would have deplored.[8] In 1663 the Scot, George Mackenzie, poured scorn on 'the mad-cap Zealots of this bigot Age, intending to mount heaven, Elias-like, in Zeals fiery Chariot'. Wearied by the religious fanaticism of the Covenanters, Mackenzie advocated a new Stoicism; his hero was not 'Jehu, who drove furiously', but the 'unconcerned Gallio', a Roman official in the Book of Acts whose indifference to religious matters made him a byword among the Covenanters.[9] Mackenzie was offering a powerful apologia for the tolerant, sceptical and latitudinarian tradition which Trevor-Roper has seen as the major source of the eighteenth-century European Enlightenment.[10]

Yet, contrary to what Trevor-Roper suggests, this was not the only route to the more tolerant attitudes characteristic of modernity.[11] For those who still wanted their religion hot, there remained the option of pietism, a religious style that was zealous and purist, but ultimately far less politicised than Puritanism had become. It is revealing that a number of Rutherford's friends, deeply committed to the Protester vision of a pure church but

[5] See L. Colley, *Britons: Forging the Nation, 1707–1837* (London, 1992), ch. 1; and J. C. D. Clark, *English Society, 1688–1832: Ideology, Social Structure and Political Practice during the Ancien Regime* (Cambridge, 1985).
[6] It is for this reason that John Morrill has spoken of the English Revolution as a 'revolution in the consciousness of those who lived through it'. See his *Nature of the English Revolution* (London, 1993), p. 284 and also pp. 29, 393–7, 443–6.
[7] W. Lamont, *Godly Rule: Politics and Religion, 1603–60* (London, 1969), chs. 6 and 7.
[8] See W. L. Craig's analysis of the rise of Deism in *The Historical Argument for the Resurrection of Jesus during the Deist Controversy* (Lewiston, NY, 1985), pp. 169–75.
[9] Mackenzie, *Religio Stoici* (Edinburgh, 1663), pp. 1–2. Rutherford had once declared that Aberdeen was full of men of 'Gallio's naughty faith', *Letters*, p. 163.
[10] H. Trevor-Roper, 'The religious origins of the Enlightenment', in his *Religion, the Reformation and Religious Change* (London, 1967), ch. 4.
[11] By contrasting the enlightened Erasmian tradition to 'Catholic authoritarianism' and to the 'Protestant fundamentalism' of Rutherford, Voetius and Perkins, Trevor-Roper fails to do justice to the contribution of the Protestant sects to the rise of religious toleration and ideological pluralism. The same could be said of B. Worden, 'Toleration and the Cromwellian Protectorate', in W. J. Sheils, ed., *Persecution and Toleration* (Oxford, 1984), pp. 199–233.

disillusioned with the political struggles and persecution used to establish it on a national scale, gravitated towards Independency and Quakerism.[12] Roger Williams – in his anti-Constantinian tract, *The Bloudy Tenent of Persecution* (1644) – had pointed the way out from the *respublica christiana* just as surely as John Locke was to do. The rationalist intelligentsia and the enthusiastic sectarians both made significant contributions to the collapse of the old 'confessional orthodoxy' and the emergence of a world characterised by toleration, greater individualism and voluntaristic associations.[13]

The course of Rutherford's own life, in fact, was indicative of these broader cultural transformations. Contrary to what most of his biographers have implied, it was more of a tragedy than a romance. After trumpeting the imminent rule of King Jesus in the 1640s, Rutherford was sidelined in the 1650s, ignored by his former allies and incapable of preserving ideological purity even in his own theological college. Conscious of the defeat of many of his greatest ambitions, he began to show signs of regret. In his belated reply to Thomas Hooker's attack on Presbyterianism, he admitted to the demoralising effect of years of intellectual combat: 'when the head is filled with topicks, and none of the flamings of Christ's love in the heart, how dry are all disputes? For too often, fervour of dispute in the head weakens love in the heart. And what can our Paper-industry adde to the spotless truth of our Lord Jesus?'[14] On his deathbed, as the acts of the Covenanters were being swept away by the Restoration parliament, Rutherford admitted that his party had mistakenly tried to set up 'a state opposite a state', when 'We might have driven gently, as our Master Christ, who loves not to overdrive; but carries the Lambs in his Bosom.'[15]

Rutherford's poignant confessions anticipated the attitudes of those who in future years were to revere his memory. These Evangelicals had little time for his Reformed scholasticism or his intolerance – it was his piety that entranced them. In Britain, America and the Netherlands, they devoured scores of editions of the devotional letters and sermons that Rutherford himself had never intended for publication, while at the same time neglecting his polemical works. The one exception to this rule was his

[12] Alexander Jaffray, who became an Independent in the 1650s later joined the Quakers. See *The Diary of Alexander Jaffray* (London, 1833), *passim.* G. D. Henderson tells the story in 'Some early Scottish Independents', in his *Religious Life in Seventeenth Century Scotland* (Cambridge, 1937), ch. 5. For further evidence of the move towards quietism see the Quaker George Keith's charge of 'blood-guiltiness' against the Presbyterians and his criticisms of Rutherford in *The Way cast Up* (1677).

[13] On the combined contribution of sceptics and sectarians to the development of toleration see Henry Kamen, *The Rise of Toleration* (London, 1967). For a discussion of the affinities of pietism and the Enlightenment, particularly their common opposition to confessional orthodoxy, see W. R. Ward, 'Orthodoxy, Enlightenment and religious revival', in K. Robbins, ed., *Religion and Humanism* (Oxford, 1981), pp. 275–96.

[14] *Survey of Thomas Hooker*, sig. A2.   [15] *Testimony*, pp. 6–7.

political treatise, *Lex, Rex*, which, though seldom read, was much praised. Yet what attracted Evangelicals to it was not Rutherford's passionate desire for a godly magistrate who would stamp out idolatry and advance the cause of true religion. Instead, eighteenth- and nineteenth-century writers warmed to Rutherford's natural-law arguments for a mixed constitution and the liberties of subjects. *Lex, Rex* was interpreted as an apology for Victorian liberalism, though Rutherford would have been appalled at the tolerance of popish idolatry, heresy and unbelief that characterised nineteenth-century Britain. His admirers had now abandoned the bellicosity of the Puritan drive towards godly rule. Thomas Chalmers may still have longed for Scotland to be a model Christian commonwealth,[16] but his was the kinder, gentler Presbyterianism which the dying Rutherford regretted having done so little to promote.

[16] See S. J. Brown, *Thomas Chalmers and the Godly Commonwealth in Scotland* (Oxford, 1982).

BIBLIOGRAPHIES

BIBLIOGRAPHY OF
SAMUEL RUTHERFORD

This is the most complete bibliography of Rutherford to be compiled to date. Besides listing all of Rutherford's works and their numerous posthumous editions, it also catalogues works written in response to him, his own unpublished manuscripts and secondary literature written about him. The aim is to illustrate both the volume of his output and the extent of his popularity.

In compiling the bibliography I have relied heavily on library catalogues for details of posthumous editions of Rutherford's works, particularly his letters and sermons. Besides checking the catalogues in the Scottish National Library (Edinburgh), New College Library (Edinburgh), Edinburgh University Library, St Andrews University Library and Cambridge University Library, I have consulted the following printed volumes: *The National Union Catalogue pre-1956 imprints*, vol. 512 (London, 1977), pp. 115–20; *The British Library General Catalogue of Printed Books to 1975*, vol. 286 (London, 1985), pp. 45–7; *Dictionary Catalogue of Research Libraries*, vol. 635 (New York, 1979), pp. 287–9; *The English Catalogue of Books, 1801–1968*, 28 vols. (London, 1914–69); *The Eighteenth Century Short-Title Catalogue; Eighteenth-Century British Books: An Author Title Catalogue*, vol. 4 (Newcastle, 1981), p. 711; *The Nineteenth-Century Short-Title Catalogue*, series I, vol. 4 (Newcastle, 1985), p. 85; series II, vol. 34 (Newcastle, 1993), pp. 555–6. For Dutch editions of Rutherford's works I have consulted *Brinkman's Catalogus der Boeken*, 1850–1990, J. van der Haar, *From Abbadie to Young: A Bibliography of English Puritan Works Translated into Dutch Language* (Veenendaal, 1980), pp. 116–17 and C. Schoneveld, *Intertraffic of the Mind: Studies in the Seventeenth Century Anglo–Dutch Translation* (Leiden, 1983). For German editions, I have relied on *Gesamtverzeichnis des Deutschsprachigen Schrisfttums, 1700–1910*, vol. 121 (Munchen, 1984), p. 139.

WORKS PUBLISHED IN RUTHERFORD'S LIFETIME

Exercitationes Apologeticae pro Divina Gratia. *In quibus vindicatur doctrina orthodoxa de divinis decretis, et Dei tum aeterni decreti tum gratiae efficacis operationis, cum hominis libertae consociatione et subordinatione amica. Adversus Jacobum Arminium ejusque asseclas, et Jesuitas imprimis vero Fran. Suarezium, Gabri. Vasquezium, Lodiv. Molinum, Leonard Lessium, Pet. Fonsecum et Robert Bellarminium* (Amsterdam, 1636). 8°; 529 pages.
2. Franeker, 1651.

A Peaceable and Temperate Plea for Paul's Presbytery in Scotland, *a modest and brotherly dispute of the government of the Church of Scotland, wherein our principle is demonstrated to be the true apostolick way of divine truth and the Arguments on* *the contrary are friendly dissolved, the grounds of Separation and Independencie of particular Congregations, in defence of Ecclesiasticall Presbyteries, Synods and Assemblies, are examined and tryed* (London, 1642). 4°; 326 pages. WING R2389. Printed for John Bartlett.

A Sermon Preached before the honourable House of Commons, January 31, 1644 (London, 1644). Thomason: 31 Jan. 1644. 4°; 64 pages. WING R2391.
2. Edinburgh, 1644.
3. Edinburgh, 1709.
4. Cheltenham, 1879.
5. London, 1971. In *The English Revolution I: Fast Sermons to Parliament*, vol. 9, pp. 267–334.

The Due Right of Presbyteries, or a Peaceable Plea for the government of the Church of Scotland. *Wherein examined*
1. *The way of the Church of Christ in New England, in Brotherly equality, and independency, or co-ordination, without subjection of one Church to another.*
2. *Their apology for the said Government, their answers to thirty and two questions are considered.*
3. *A treatise for a Church Covenant is discussed.*
4. *The Arguments of Mr. Robinson in his justification of seperation are discovered.*
5. *His Treatise, called "The people's Plea for the exercise of prophecy" is tryed.*
6. *Diverse late arguments against presbyteriall government, and the power of synods are discussed, the power of the Prince in matters ecclesiastical is modestly considered, and divers incident contraversies resolved* (London, 1644). Baillie (I: 175): April 1644. 4°; 768 pages. WING R2378. Richard Whittaker and Andrew Crook.

Lex Rex, or The Law and the Prince. *A dispute for the just prerogative of King and People containing the Reasons and causes of the most necessary Defensive wars of the Kingdom of Scotland, and of their expedition for the ayd and help of their dear Brethren of England. In which their Innocency is asserted and a full Answer is given to a Seditious Pamphlet, Intituled "Sacro-sanctum Regum Majestas or The Sacred and Royall Prerogative of Christian Kings" Under the Name of J.A. but penned by Jo: Maxwell the excommunicate P. Prelate. With a Scripturall Confutation of the ruinous Grounds of W. Barclay, H. Grotius, H. Arnisaeus, Ant. de Domi. P. Bishop of Spalato and of other late Anti-Magistratical Royalists; as the author of Ossorianium, D. Fern, E. Symmons, the Doctors of Aberdeen. In XLIV Questions.* Published by authority (London, 1644). Thomason: 7 October, 1644. 4°; 467 pages. WING R2386. John Field.
2. London, 1648. Published as *The Pre-eminence of the Election of Kings*. For Lawrence Chapman. WING R 2390
3. London, 1657. Published as *A Treatise of Civil Policy*. Printed and are to be sold by Simon Miller. WING R 2396.
4. Edinburgh, 1843. Reprinted with Buchanan's *De Jure Regni* .
5. Edinburgh, 1846. Reprint of the 1843 edition.
6. Harrisburg, Virginia, 1982. Reprint of the 1843 edition. Wing also lists a 1686 edition (R2388), but tells us that the only known copy, in Oxford, was 'not found'.

A Sermon Preached before the Honourable House of Lords, June 25, 1645 (London, 1645). Thomason: 25 June, 1645. 4°; 62 pages. WING R2393.

2. Edinburgh, 1709.
3. Groningen, 1848. *De slapende Christus, outwaakt door gebeden.* A translation into Dutch.
4. Cheltenham, 1879.
5. Veenendaal, 1976. Reprint of the 1848 Dutch edition.
6. London, 1971. In *The English Revolution*, I: *Fast Sermons to Parliament*, vol. XVII, pp. 199–270.

The Tryal and Triumph of Faith Or *an exposition of the history of Christs dispossessing of the daughter of the woman of Canaan. Delivered in 27 sermons; in which are opened, The victory of Faith; the condition of those that are tempted; the excellency of Jesus Christ and Free grace . . . and some speciall Grounds and Principles of Libertinisme and Antinomian Errors* (London, 1645). 4°; 336 pages. WING R2397.
2. London, 1652. WING R2397A.
3. Edinburgh, 1721.
4. Edinburgh, 1727.
5. Glasgow, 1743.
6. Edinburgh, 1827.
7. Edinburgh, 1845.
8. Edinburgh, 1854.
9. Wheeling, VA, 1890.
10. Leiden, 1915. *De beproeving en zegepraal des geloofs.* Translation into Dutch by I. J. Doornveldt and C. B. van Woorden.
11. Leiden, 1916. Reprint of the 1915 translation.
12. Veenendaal, 1974. New edition of the 1915 translation.
13. Keyser, West VA, n.d. 1980s American reprint of the 1845 edition.

The Divine Right of Church Government and Excommunication Or *a peaceable dispute for the perfection of the holy Scripture in point of Ceremonies and Church Government: In which The removal of the service Book is justified, The six books of Tho: Erastus against Excommunication are briefly examined; with a vindication of that eminent Divine Theod: Beza against the Assertions of Erastus, the Arguments of Mr. Pryn, in so far as they side with Erastus, are modestly discussed. To which is added, A Brief Tractate on Scandal; with an answer to the new Doctrine of The Doctors of Aberdeen, touching Scandal* (London, 1646). 4°; 759 pages. WING R2377. Printed by John Field for Christopher Meredith.

Christ Dying and Drawing Sinners to Himself Or *A Survey of our Saviour in his soul-suffering, his loveliness in his death and the efficacie thereof. In which Some Cases of Soul-trouble in weake beleevers, grounds of submission under the absence of Christ, with the flowings and heightnings of Free grace, are opened. Delivered in Sermons on the Evangel according to S. John Chap. XII. vers 27–33. Where are also interjected some necessary Digressions, for the times, touching divers Errors of Antinomians; and a short vindication of the Doctrine of Protestants, from the Arminian pretended universality of Christ's dying for all, and every one of mankind; the Moral and fained way of resistible conversion of sinners; and what faith is required of all within the visible Church, for the want whereof, many are condemned* (London, 1647). 4°; 598 pages. WING R2373.
2. Edinburgh, 1727.
3. Glasgow, 1803.

4. Leiden, 1919. *Christus stervende en zondaren tot zich trekkende.* Translation into Dutch by C. B. van Woorden.
5. Veenendaal, 1979. New edition of the 1919 translation into Dutch.

A Survey of Spiritual Antichrist, *opening the Secrets of Familisme and Antinomianisme in the Antichristian Doctrine of John Saltmarsh, and Will. Del., the present preachers of the Army now in England, and of Robert Toun, Tob. Crisp, H. Denne, Eaton and others. In which is revealed the rise and spring of Antinomians, Familists, Libertines, Swenckfeldians, Enthysiasts. The minde of Luther a most professed opposer of Antinomians, is cleared, and diverse considerable points of the Law and the Gospel, of the Spirit and the Letter, of the two Covenants, of the nature of free grace, exercise under temptationes, mortification, justification, sanctification are discovered. In two parts* (London, 1648). Thomason: Nov. 1648. 4°; 618 pages. WING R2394. Andrew Crooke.

A Free Disputation against Pretended Liberty of Conscience *tending to Resolve Doubts moved by Mr. John Goodwin, John Baptist, Dr. Jer. Taylor, the Belgick Arminians, Socinians and other Authors contending for the lawlesse Liberty of licentious Toleration of Sects and Heresies* (London, 1649). Thomason: 6 August 1649. 4°; 410 pages. WING R2379. Printed by R.I. for Andrew Crook.
2. 1651. WING R2379A.

The Last and Heavenly Speeches and Glorious Departure of John Gordoun, Viscount Kenmuir (Edinburgh, 1649). Printed by Evan Tyler, printer to the King's most Excellent Majesty.
2. Edinburgh, 1703.
3. Edinburgh, 1712.
4. Edinburgh, 1749.
5. Edinburgh, 1774.
6. Also printed in J. Howie, *Scots Worthies* (Edinburgh, 1775); and W. K. Tweedie, *Select Biographies,* vol. 1. [34 pages].
7. London/Edinburgh, 1827.

Disputatio Scholastica de Divina Providentia. *Variis Praelectionibus, quod attinet ad summa rerum capita, tradita S. Theologiae Adolescentibus Candidatis in Inclyta Academia Andreapolitana in qua adversus Jesuitas, Arminianos, Socinianos, de Dominio DEI, actione ipsius operosa circa peccatum, concursu primae causae, praedeterminatione & contenditur & decertatur. Adjectae sunt Disquisitiones Metaphysicae de Ente, Possibli, Dominio DEI in entia et non entia, et variae Quaestiones quae ad uberiorem et exquisitiorem cognitionem Doctrinae de Providentia Divina imprimis conducunt* (Edinburgh, 1649). 4°; 620 pages. WING R2375.
2. Edinburgh, 1650. WING R2376.

The Covenant of Life Opened *Or, A Treatise of the Covenant of Grace containing something of The Nature of the Covenant of Works, The Sovereignty of God, The extent of the death of Christ, The nature and properties of Grace, And Especially of The Covenant of Suretyship or Redemption between the Lord, and the Sonne Jesus Christ, Infant rights to Jesus Christ, and the Scale of Baptisme. With some Practicall Questions and Observationes* (Edinburgh, 1655). Thomason: 20 February, 1655. 4°; 368 pages. WING R2374. Robert Broun.

A Survey of the Survey of that Summe of Church Discipline penned by Mr. Thomas Hooker *Late Pastor of the Church at Hartford upon Connecticut in New England* *wherein The Way of the Churches of N. England is now re-examined; arguments in favour thereof winnowed; The Principles of that Way discussed; and the reasons of most seeming strength and nerves removed* (London, 1658). 4°; 521 pages. WING R2395. Andrew Crook.

Influences of the Life of Grace *Or a Practical Treatise concerning The way, manner and means of having and improving of Spiritual Dispositions, and quickning influences from Christ the Resurrection and the Life* (London, 1659). 2 March 1659. 4°; 438 pages. WING R2380. Andrew Crook.

POSTHUMOUSLY PUBLISHED WORKS

LETTERS

Joshua Redivivus or Mr. Rutherfoord's Letters, *Divided into two parts.*
The first containing these which were written from Aberdeen, where he was confined by a sentence of the High Commission, drawn forth against him, partly upon the account of his declining them, partly upon the account of his Non-conformitie.
The second containing some which were written from Anwoth before he was by the Prelates persecution thrust from his Ministery; and others upon diverse occasions afterward, from St Andrews, London.
Now published for the use of all the people of God; but more particularly, for these who now are, or afterward may be put to suffering for Christ and his cause: By a wellwisher to the work, and people of God (Rotterdam?,1664). 8°; 576 pp. WING R2381. Contained 286 letters. Collected and edited with a preface by Robert McWard, Rutherford's student and amanuensis at the Westminster Assembly.

Numerous editions of these letters have been printed since 1664. A list of over thirty editions was compiled by Andrew Bonar in his *Letters of Samuel Rutherford* (Edinburgh, 1891), pp. 736–40. My own bibliography updates and expands on Bonar's. Over sixty British editions and reprints are listed below, along with fifteen American editions, fifteen Dutch and four German. Some are complete, others only selections. A few – such as Wesley's *Christian Library* - are anthologies which contain substantial material from Rutherford's letters. Modern anthologies which only include brief extracts from the letters are mentioned separately below. In addition, there may well be other editions not listed in any of the catalogues that I have consulted.

British editions
2. 1671.
3. 1675. This included a third part which added 68 additional letters. Subsequent editors followed this edition.
4. London, 1692.
5. Edinburgh, 1709.
6. Edinburgh, 1724.
7. Edinburgh, 1738.
8. Bristol, 1753. Extracts from Rutherford's Letters appear in vol. XXVIII of John Wesley's *Christian Library: Consisting of Extracts from and Abridgements of*

the Choicest Pieces of Practical Divinity which have been published in the English Tongue, pp. 43–265.

9. Edinburgh, 1761.
10. Glasgow, 1765.
11. Glasgow, 1783.
12. Glasgow, 1796.
13. Aberdeen, 1802.
14. Edinburgh, 1809. Marked 'Thirteenth edition', which is correct if Wesley's extracts are not included.
15. Glasgow, 1818. 152 letters.
16. Glasgow, 1821.
17. London, 1823. Extracts from Rutherford's letters appear in vol. 16 of the second edition of John Wesley's *Christian Library*.
18. London, 1824. Selection of sixty letters published by the Religious Tract Society.
19. Glasgow, 1824.
20. Glasgow, 1825. Includes doctrinal preface by Thomas Erskine, and one half of the letters.
21. Glasgow, 1827. Reprint of Erskine's edition.
22. Glasgow, 1830.
23. Glasgow, 1834.
24. London, 1836. A two-volume edition which added explanatory notes, arranged the letters chronologically, and improved on former editions which had followed the three part structure established in 1675. Edited by Charles Thomson.
25. 1839.
26. Aberdeen, 1846. This edition is in double columns.
27. Edinburgh, 1848. Added 10 new letters. Edited by James Anderson, with a sketch of Rutherford's life by Andrew Bonar.
28. London, 1848. *Letters of Rutherford during Persecution.*
29. Edinburgh, 1854. *Gleanings from Rutherford.*
30. London, 1854. *Prison Sayings of Samuel Rutherford*. Extracts from his Aberdeen letters.
31. Birmingham, 1855? *Christ's Cross.*
32. Bonmahon, Co. Waterford and London, 1857. Edited by D. A. Doudney.
33. Edinburgh, 1859. *Gleanings from Rutherford* reprinted as part six of the *Christian Graces* series.
34. London, 1859. *A Memoir of Leighton, with selections from his works; also extracts from the letters of Rutherford.*
35. 1862.
36. Edinburgh, 1863. Added 2 new letters. Andrew Bonar's complete edition in two volumes contained 365 letters.
37. Edinburgh, 1867. Edited by J. McEwan.
38. 1869. Another edition of McEwan.
39. 1875. Edited by Thomas Smith. Preface by Alexander Duff.
40. London, 1875. *The Refiners Fire: Thoughts on Affliction selected from the works of Archbishop Leighton, Rutherford, Hooker, Newton, Cecil and other eminent writers.* Pages 104–62 contain material from Rutherford's letters on the loss of children and affliction.
41. 1876.
42. Edinburgh, 1878. *One Hundred Choice Letters.*

43. Edinburgh, 1881. A reprint of Thomas Smith's 1875 edition.
44. London, 1884. Select Letters in *Devotional Manuals* series.
45. Edinburgh, 1884. Extracts published in Andrew Thomson's *Life of Samuel Rutherford*, pp. 143–200.
45. Edinburgh and London, 1891. A new, complete edition by Bonar, containing 365 letters. (4; 744 pages).
46. Edinburgh, 1892. *Rubies from Rutherford*, ed. Walter J. Mathams.
47. 1893. *The Loveliness of Christ*, ed. Ellen S. Lister. Preface by the Bishop of Durham.
48. London and Edinburgh, 1894. Bonar's complete edition republished by Oliphants.
49. London, 1894. *Select Letters*.
50. Edinburgh, 1897. *Daily Thoughts for a year from Samuel Rutherford*, ed. Eva S. Sandeman.
51. Edinburgh, 1899. Selected letters from the Bonar edition.
52. London, 1902. *Christ and his Cross*, ed. L. H. M. Soulsby.
53. London, 1903. *The Upward Way*, ed. Eleanor C. Gregory.
54. 1906.
55. 1906. Matham's extracts reprinted.
56. London, 1908. Gregory's extracts reprinted.
57. London, 1909. Lister's extracts reprinted.
58. London, 1920. A complete edition, rearranged and revised for the use of modern readers by James Stephen.
59. London, 1925. Bonar's edition.
60. 1930. Lister's extracts reprinted.
61. London, 1955. *The King in his Beauty*, ed J. Cyril Downes. Extracts from Rutherford's letters and sermons.
62. London, 1957. *Selected Letters of Samuel Rutherford*, ed. H. Martin.
63. London, 1973. *The Letters of Samuel Rutherford: a Selection*.
64. Edinburgh, 1984. Reprint of Bonar's complete edition of 1891. 744 pages.
65. Edinburgh, 1989. Faith Cook, *Grace in Winter*. A selection of verse based upon the letters.

The following modern anthologies also contain brief extracts from Rutherford's letters:

Dunn, D., ed., *Scotland: An Anthology* (London, 1992), pp. 189–90.
Freemantle, A., ed., *The Protestant Mystics* (London, 1964), pp. 58–62.
Jack, R. D. S., ed., *Scottish Prose: 1550–1700* (London, 1971), pp. 173–181.
Reid, D., ed., *The Party-Coloured Mind: Selected Prose relating to the Conflict between Church and State in Seventeenth-Century Scotland* (Edinburgh, 1982), pp. 44–52.
Tileston, M., ed., *Daily Strength for Daily Needs* (Boston, 1920).
Toon, P., ed., *Spiritual Companions: An Introduction to the Christian Classics* (London, 1990), pp. 151–2.
Wirt, S. E., ed., *Exploring the Spiritual Life* (Tring, Herts., 1985), pp. 106–20.

American editions

1. New York, 1826. First American edition.
2. New York, 1850. Anderson's 1848 edition.

3. New York, 1851. Anderson's edition.
4. New York, 1856. Anderson's edition.
5. New York, 1858. Anderson's edition.
6. New York, 1861. Anderson's edition.
7. New York, 1863. An American version of Bonar's new edition.
8. Philadelphia, 1865. *Manna : Crumbs for hungry souls*, ed. W. P. Breed.
9. Cincinnati, 1869. *A Garden of Spices: Extracts from the Religious Letters of Samuel Rutherford*, ed. L. R. Dunn.
10. New York, 1875. Bonar's edition.
11. New York, 1875. Smith's edition.
12. New York, 1881. Bonar's edition.
13. Cincinnati, 1913. *A New Epistle, being the wise and beautiful counsel of that saintly man, Samuel Rutherford*, ed. G. H. Westley.
14. Chicago, 1951. Edited by F. Gaebelein.
15. Chicago, 1980. Reprint of Gaebelein edition.

Dutch editions

1. Amsterdam, 1672. *De Brieven van Samuel Rhetorfort* are translated into Dutch by the pietist pastor Jacobus Koelman. All subsequent Dutch editions use Koelman's translation.
2. Vlissingen, 1673.
3. Vlissingen, 1674.
4. Vlissingen, 1679.
5. Amsterdam, 1679.
6. Amsterdam, 1687.
7. Groningen, 1720.
8. Groningen, 1740.
9. Groningen, 1754.
10. Amsterdam, 1840.
11. Groningen, 1845.
12. Gravenh, 1855.
13. Rotterdam, 1870.
14. Leiden, 1886.
15. Leiden, 1887.
16. Gorinchem, 1929.
17. Veenendaal, 1973.
18. Veenendaal, 1981.
19. Houten, 1990.

German editions

1. Berlin, 1834–5. *Briefe; nebst einem kurzen abriss seines lebens aus dem English-chen.*
2. Basel, 1863. *Briefe von S. Rutherford.* Mit einer Biographie desselbun von C. F. Ledderhose. Auf's neue herausgegeben zum besten der Pilgermissions Ansalt St Chrischona.
3. Berlin, 1873.
4. Karlsruhe, 1879.

French editions

Paris, 1848. *Lettres aux Chretiens persecutes ou afflige ecrites en 1630 . . . par Samuel Rutherford.* Traduitee de l'anglais, et precedees d'une notice sur Rutherford et son epoque par G. Masson.

Gaelic editions

Glasgow, 1851. Nine letters, translated by J. Gillies.

Manuscript copies

1. National Library of Scotland, Edinburgh.
   (i) MS 15950 ff. 1–55. This volume contains copies of 109 letters which Rutherford wrote from Aberdeen. The ink is badly faded and they are very difficult to read in places. However, all appear to be included in Bonar's edition.
   (ii) Copies of nine letters also appear in the Wodrow papers: Fol. XXVII nos. 42 and 43; Fol. LIV no. 9; Fol. LIX no. 5; Quarto XXIV nos 13, 21, 66, 88; Quarto XXXI no. 6.
2. Edinburgh University Library. Copies of letters in a history of the affairs of the Church of Scotland 1638: Dc. 4. 57.
3. St Andrews University Library. MS BX. 8915, R. 8. L. 4. C. 37. This volume contains copies of sixty-one letters written from Aberdeen in 1637. All of them are to be found in Bonar's edition, which in wording is usually fairly close to them, though the spelling is somewhat modernised.
4. Sutton Courtenay Press, Abingdon. The proprieter of the press claims to own a manuscript copy of Rutherford's letters dating to 1655.
5. Bodleian Library, Oxford. Letter from Samuel Rutherford to Simeon Ashe in 1656. No. 346 in Bonar's edition. Rawlinson MSS. A. 44. 343.

SERMONS

Single sermons

Christ and the Doves Heavenly Salutations, *with pleasant conference together: or a sermon on Canticles 2: 14–17, preached before the Communion in Anwoth, anno 1630* (n.p., n.d.). Although this is listed in Wing (R2372A), and dated c. 1660, other catalogues suggest a later date, probably in the early eighteenth century.
2. 1725.
3. Edinburgh, 1729.
4. Glasgow, 1778. Reprinted as *Heavenly Salutations with pleasant conferences between Christ and His People.*
5. Glasgow, 1781.
6. Glasgow, 1876. Sermon 11 in *Communion Sermons*, ed. A. Bonar.

Christ's Napkin, *or a sermon on Revelation 21: 4–8, preached in Kirkcudbright at the Communion, May 12, 1633.* (n.p., n.d.). As with *Christ and the Doves,* this is listed in Wing (R2373A), but an early eighteenth century date seems more likely. The *Eighteenth Century Short Title Catalogue* tentatively suggests Edinburgh, 1710.

2. Bolsward, 1668. Translation by Samuel van Haringhouk.
3. Edinburgh, 1734.
4. Edinburgh, 1739.
5. Glasgow, 1739.
6. Glasgow, 1778. Reprinted as *Glad Tidings to the people of God.*
7. Glasgow, 1779.
8. Falkirk, 1784.
9. Glasgow, 1789.
10. Glasgow, 1796.
11. Falkirk, 1801.
12. Kilmarnock, 1817
13. Groningen, 1848.
14. Glasgow, 1876. Sermon 10 in *Communion Sermons*, ed. A. Bonar.
15. Woudrichem, n.d.
16. Ouddorp, n.d.

An Exhortation at a Communion to a Scots Congregation in London (Glasgow, 1718).
2. Edinburgh, 1719.
3. Edinburgh, 1728.
4. Edinburgh, 1729.
5. Glasgow, 1730.
6. Edinburgh, 1731.
7. Edinburgh, 1741.
8. 1746.
9. 1747.
10. Edinburgh, 1749.
11. Glasgow, 1765. Published as *A Cry from the dead, from the flower of the Church of Scotland, or an exhortation to a Scots congregation in London.*
12. 1773.
13. Falkirk, 1775.
14. 1804.
15. Glasgow, 1876. Sermon 12 in *Communion Sermons*, ed. A. Bonar.
16. Part of this sermon is reproduced in M. Lindsay, ed., *Scotland: an Anthology* (London, 1974), pp. 340–1.

The Cruel Watchmen: *a sermon on Song 5: 7,8,9,10* (Edinburgh, 1728).
2. Glasgow, 1738.
3. 1885. Sermon 6 in *Quaint Sermons.*

The Lamb's Marriage Supper Proclaimed, *an action sermon, preached before the celebration of the Lord's Supper at Kirkcudbright, 1634, on Revelation 19* (Glasgow, 1775).
2. Glasgow, 1776.
3. Glasgow, 1779.
4. Glasgow, 1781.
5. Falkirk, 1822.
6. Glasgow, 1877. Sermon 13 in *Communion Sermons*, ed. A. Bonar.

Christ's Love to His Church, *a sermon preached upon a sacramental occasion* (Glasgow, 1775).

2. Glasgow, 1798.
3. Glasgow, 1877. Sermon 14 in *Communion Sermons*, ed. A. Bonar.

Collected sermons

A Collection of valuable Sermons (Glasgow, 1802). Nine sermons never previously published.
2. Glasgow, 1876. *Communion Sermons*. Ed. A. Bonar. A reprint of the 1802 edition with three additional sermons: *Christ's Napkin, Christ and the Doves* and *An Exhortation to a Scots Congregation in London*.
3. Glasgow, 1877. *Fourteen Communion Sermons*. Ed. A. Bonar. Reprint of the 1876 edition with two additional sermons: *The Lamb's Marriage Supper* and *Christ's Love to His Church*.
4. Edinburgh, 1986. Reprint of the 1877 edition. 8°; 362 pages.

Quaint Sermons. Transcribed by J. Thomson, with a preface by A. Bonar. (1885). 8°384 pages. All 18 sermons in this collection, with the exception of *The Cruel Watchmen*, had never before been published.
2. Gorinchem, 1931. *Het bedrukt en verdrukte wormke Jacobs: De Weenende Maria: De Slaperige Bruid: De Verloren zoon*. Translations by C. B. van Woerden of sermons 1, 2, 4, 5, 6 and 9–15.
3. Houten, 1987.

Manuscript copies of Rutherford's published sermons

1. St Andrews University Library. MS 30386. This volume contains nearly all of the sermons published in *Quaint Sermons*, and all but two of those published in *Communion Sermons* (only nos. 9 and 12 from that collection are not found in this manuscript).
2. New College Library, Edinburgh. W 13 b 1/3. Sermons on Isaiah 49 and Hebrews 12, preached by Rutherford and written in a contemporary hand. The first is *Communion Sermon* no. 6, and the second *Communion Sermon* no. 5.

The only sermons listed above that lack manuscript attestation are *Communion Sermons* 9 and 12. However, this does not disprove their authenticity. Internal evidence strongly supports their attribution to Rutherford. Sermon 9 is based on the Song of Songs, Rutherford's favourite biblical book, and it contains images which are found elsewhere in his works: the big print of children's books, Christ as the lover standing outside the door with a cold, wet head, and the 'harlot lovers' in the kirk. Sermon 12 is said to have been preached to a Scots congregation in London, and it dwells on the characteristic Rutherford theme of Christ's Cross; the image of Christ as the apple on the tree of the Cross is one which can also be found in *Christ Dying*. The style of both sermons is unmistakeably Rutherford's.
     The only sermon attributed to Rutherford which Bonar did not include in his collections, and which is certainly inauthentic, is 'The Door of Salvation Opened'. This is an old-fashioned hell-fire sermon which contains nothing uniquely Rutherfordian. The *Eighteenth Century Short-Title Catalogue* says that it is 'Not in fact by Samuel Rutherford, but an anonymous text first printed in 1665, attributed to "T. P.", and reprinted many times with various authorship attributions.'
     In addition to the thirty-two sermons of Rutherford published posthumously, unpublished contemporary notes on forty of his sermons survive in Scottish libraries.

They are to be found in the National Library of Scotland (24), Edinburgh University Library (9), New College Library, Edinburgh (1), and St Andrews University Library (6). They are listed under Unpublished manuscript works, below.

OTHER WORKS

Examen Arminianismi, *conscriptum et discipulis dictatum a doctissimo clarissimoque viro.* Edited by M. Nethenus, professor of theology at Utrecht, with a preface by Gisbertus Voetius and a short biography of Rutherford by Nethenus (Utrecht, 1668). 8°; 761 pp.

The Power and Prevalency of Prayer *evidenced in a practical discourse upon Matthew 9: 27,31* (Edinburgh?, 1713). 111 pages.
2.   Stornaway, 1991.

A Testimony to the Work of Reformation in Britaine and Ireland (Glasgow, 1719). 12°; 15 pp.
2.   Edinburgh, 1726,
3.   1738
4.   Lanark, 1739.
5.   1740.
6.   Glasgow, 1784.
7.   Glasgow, 1788.
8.   1790.
9.   Stirling, 1802.
10. Hull, 1860. *The Last Words of Samuel Rutherford.* Verses based on them. The *Testimony* and *Last Words* of Rutherford are also appended to some editions of Rutherford's *Letters.*

Ane Catechisme conteining the Soume of Christian Religion. Published in A. F. Mitchell, ed., *Catechisms of the Second Reformation* (London, 1886), pp. 161–242. A manuscript copy of this catechism can be found in Edinburgh University Library: Dc. 4. 57.

PROTESTER DOCUMENTS DRAFTED OR SIGNED BY RUTHER-FORD

The Representation, Propositions and Protestation of divers Ministers, Elders and Professors, &c. Presented by Lord Warriston, Mr. Andrew Cant, Mr. John Livingstone, Mr. Samuel Rutherford and diverse others (Leith, 1652).

Protester Declaration or Testimonie to English Actings amongst us, 17 March 1653. Printed in W. Stephens, ed., *Register of the Consultations of the Ministers of Edinburgh and Some other Brethren in the Ministry,* I (Edinburgh, 1921), pp. 13–36.

Protesters Declaration to Separatists in Aberdeen, 17 March 1653. Printed in Stephens, ed., *Consultations,* pp. 37–43.

Protesters Address to Colonel Lilburne, April 1653
In *Scotland and the Commonwealth: Letters and Papers relating to the Military Government of Scotland from August 1651 to December 1653,* ed. C. H. Firth (Edinburgh, 1895), pp. 108–9.

Another Declaration or Testimonie of the Protesters, March 1654. Printed in Stephens, ed., *Consultations*, pp. 44–56.

The Supplication of the ministers, elders and professors, who are for the Protestation, March 1655. Printed in *A Collection of the State Papers of John Thurloe, Esq*, ed. T. Birch (London, 1742), pp. 255–7.

A Testimony to the Truth of Jesus Christ, or, to the Doctrine, Worship, Discipline and Government of the Church of Scotland by the ministers of Perth and Fife (Edinburgh, 1660).

UNPUBLISHED MANUSCRIPT WORKS OF RUTHERFORD

1. A copy of notes on a debate between Rutherford and Sydserff, Bishop of Galloway in 1636. National Library of Scotland, Edinburgh: 15948 p. 322.
2. Latin notes of lectures given by Rutherford in 1654. National Library: 16475 ff. 2–26.
3. Notes on 24 sermons of Rutherford, preached at St Andrews, c. 1658. National Library: Acc. 9270 no. 3. None of these sermon notes have ever been published. However, there are usually only two or three sides of notes on each sermon. There are ten sermons on Psalm 88, and others on passages from Isaiah, Ezekiel, Mark, Luke and Hebrews.
4. Treatise on the nature of obedience to a usurped power and on the power of the civil magistrate in matters of religion. Edinburgh University Library: La. III. 69/5.
5. Portions of a discourse on Ephesians 1:4 signed by Samuel Rutherford. 18 pp. Edinburgh University Library: La. II. 394. This contains a defence of supralapsarianism.
6. Notes on nine sermons of Rutherford in two volumes of notes on Covenanter sermons. Edinburgh University Library: Dc. 5. 30–31. This volume also includes sermons by Blair, Wood, Douglas and Cant. Rutherford's sermons all seem to have been preached in the mid to late 1650s. There are detailed notes on sermons on Genesis 28 (3), Hebrews 4 (2), and Revelation 3:20 (1), and brief notes on three sermons on Isaiah. The manuscript is quite easy to read.
7. A passage with which a manuscript copy of 'The Last Speeches and Departure of John Viscount Kenmuir' begins. 1 p. Edinburgh University Library: La. III. 263/3.
8. Sermon on Galatians 2:20. New College Library, Edinburgh: B. b. b. 12.
9. Latin notes taken by William Tullidelph of Rutherford's 'Dictates on Holy Scripture'. St Andrews University Library: BS 540 R8. 10.
10. Notes of Rutherford sermons preached between c. 1630 and 1647. 332 pp. St Andrews University Library: MS 30386. Only six of these twenty-five sermons have never been published. Three are on Revelation 3, two on Canticles 5, (both of these were favourite passages for Rutherford), and another on Hebrews 13.

WORKS WRITTEN IN RESPONSE TO RUTHERFORD

Many works mention Rutherford briefly, but the following include substantial sections criticising his arguments:

Baxter, Richard, *Catholick Theologie: Plaine, Pure, Peaceable, for pacification of the*

Dogmaticall Word-warriors (London, 1675). Pages 106–14 are a critique of Rutherford's *De Providentia*.

Cotton, John, *The Way of the Congregational Churches Cleared . . . from some misconstructions of learned Mr. Rutherford in his book intituled, The Due Right of Presbyteries* (Boston, 1648). One of four treatises written by the New England clergy to defend their model of church government against Rutherford's attacks.

Cotton, John, *Of the Holinesse of Church Members* (1650). Another reply to *Peaceable Plea* and *Due Right*.

Hagen, J. F., *Dissertatio academica, qua sententia communis . . . de concursu Dei generali a oxuapinis S. Retorfortis . . . Liberatur* (1674). A reply to Rutherford's Latin works on metaphysics and theology.

[Honyman, Andrew], *A Survey of the Insolent and Infamous Libel entituled 'Naphtali'* (1668). The only contemporary pamphlet to attack *Lex, Rex* in any detail.

Hooker, Thomas, *Survey of the Summe of Church Discipline.* (London, 1648). A reply to *The Due Right of Presbyteries*.

Keith, George, *The Way cast Up . . . containing answere to a postscript printed at the end of Samuel Rutherford's Letters, 3rd edition* (1677). A Quaker response to Presbyterian hero-worship of Rutherford and his *Letters*.

Mather, Richard, *A Reply to Mr Rutherford's The Due Right of Presbyteries.* (Boston, 1647).

Owen, John, *A Dissertation on Divine Justice,* in *Works,* X, ed. W.H. Goold (1850–53). Chapter 17 is a reply to *De Providentia* similar to that of Baxter.

Strang, John, *De Voluntate Dei et Actionibus circa Peccatum* (1657). Another attack on the necessitarianism of Rutherford's Latin works by a fellow Scot.

Tombes, John, *Anti-Paedobaptism, or the third part* (London, 1657). Section 86 refutes Rutherford's defence of infant baptism in *The Covenant of Life Opened*.

Towne, Robert, *A Reassertion of Grace . . . in a reply to Mr. Rutherford's 'Tryal and Triumph of Faith'* (1654).

Towne, Robert, *Monomachia, or a single reply to Mr. Rutherford's 'Christ Dying and Drawing Sinners'*

SECONDARY LITERATURE ON RUTHERFORD

PUBLISHED BOOKS AND ARTICLES

Baxter, J. H., 'Tercentenary of Samuel Rutherford: commemoration service', *St Andrews Citizen,* 1 April 1961.

Brentnall, J. M., *Samuel Rutherford in Aberdeen* (Inverness, c. 1981).

Cameron, J. K., 'The piety of Samuel Rutherford (c. 1600–61): a neglected feature of seventeenth-century Scottish Calvinism', *Nederlands Archief voor Kerkgeschiedenis,* 65 (1985), 153–9.

Campbell, W. M., '*Lex, Rex* and its author', *RSCHS,* 7 (1941), 204–28.

Chambers, R., ed., *A Biographical Dictionary of Eminent Scotsmen,* revised by T. Thomson, III (London, 1875), pp. 318–19.

Clark, J., *The Life and Works of Samuel Rutherford* (Edinburgh, 1986).

Collins, G. N. M., *Samuel Rutherford: Saint and Statesman* (London, 1961).

Cook, F., *Samuel Rutherford and his Friends* (Edinburgh, 1992).

Flinn, R. 'Samuel Rutherford and Puritan political theory', *Journal of Christian Reconstruction,* 5 (1978–9), 49–74.

Ford, J. D., '*Lex, rex iusto posita*: Samuel Rutherford on the origins of government', in R. Mason, ed., *Scots and Britons: Scottish Political Thought and the Union of 1603* (Cambridge, 1994), pp. 262–90.

Gilmour, R., *Samuel Rutherford: A Study Biographical and Somewhat Critical* (Edinburgh, 1904).

Grosart, A. B., 'Samuel Rutherford', in his *Representative Nonconformists* (London, 1874), pp. 197–262.

Howie, J., *The Scots Worthies* (Glasgow, 1846 edn), pp. 217–25.

Innes, A. T., 'Samuel Rutherfurd', in his *Studies in Scottish History, Chiefly Ecclesiastical* (London, 1892), pp. 3–60.

Isbell, S., 'Samuel Rutherford', in N. Cameron, ed., *Dictionary of Scottish Church History and Theology* (Edinburgh, 1993), pp. 735–6.

Knox, R. B., 'The Presbyterianism of Samuel Rutherford', *Irish Biblical Studies* (July 1986), 143–53.

Lamb, J. A., 'Samuel Rutherford, 1600–61', in R. S. Wright, ed., *Fathers of the Kirk: Some Leaders of the Church of Scotland from the Reformation to the Revolution* (London, 1960), pp. 73–84.

Lilley, P., 'Samuel Rutherford, 1600–61', *Transactions of the Hawick Archaeological Society* (1935), 11–15.

Loane, M., 'Samuel Rutherford', in his *Makers of Religious Freedom in the Seventeenth Century* (London, 1960), ch. 3.

Louden, R. S., 'Samuel Rutherford', in G. Wakefield, ed., *The Westminster Dictionary of Christian Spirituality* (Philadelphia, 1983), p. 345.

Machar, A. M., 'A Scottish Mystic', *The Andover Review*, 6 (1986), 379–95.

Maclear, J. F., 'Samuel Rutherford: the law and the king', in G. L. Hunt and J. T. McNeill, eds., *Calvinism and the Political Order* (Philadelphia, 1965), pp. 65–87.

Martin, H., *Great Christian Books* (London, 1945). Chapter 3 is on Rutherford's *Letters*.

Meier, H., 'Love, law, and lucre: images in Rutherfurd's letters', in M.-J. Arn and H. Wirtjes, eds., *Historical and Editorial Essays in Medieval and Early Modern English for Johan Gerritsen* (Groningen, 1985), pp. 77–96.

Morrison, N. B., *They Need no Candle: The Men who built the Scottish Kirk* (London, 1957), ch. 4.

Morton, A. S., 'Samuel Rutherford', in his *Galloway and the Covenanters, or the Struggle for Religious Liberty in the South-west of Scotland* (Paisley, 1914), ch. 31.

Muir, P. M., 'Samuel Rutherford', in *Scottish Divines, 1505–1872* (Edinburgh, 1883), pp. 73–108.

Murray, T., *The Literary History of Galloway* (Edinburgh, 1822), ch. 7.

Murray, T., *Life of Rutherford* (Edinburgh, 1828).

Philip, A., 'The golden book of love', in his *The Devotional Literature of Scotland* (London, 1920), pp. 116–25.

Roberts, M., 'Samuel Rutherford: the comings and goings of the heavenly bridegroom', in *The Trials of Puritanism: papers read at the 1993 Westminster Conference* (privately published, 1994), pp. 119–134.

Ross, J. M., 'Post-Reformation spirituality 3: Samuel Rutherford', *The Month* (July 1975), 207–11.

Scott, H., *Fasti Ecclesiae Scoticanae: The Succession of Ministers in the Parish Churches of Scotland from the Reformation, A. D. 1560, to the Present Time*, VII (London, 1867), pp. 418–19.

Smellie, A., *Men of the Covenant* (London, 1905 edition), ch. 3.

Sturrock, J. B., 'Samuel Rutherford', in his *Representative Men of the Covenant* (Stirling, 1913).

Thomson, A., *The Life of Samuel Rutherford* (Edinburgh, 1884).

Whyte, A., *Samuel Rutherford and Some of his Correspondents* (Edinburgh, 1894).

UNPUBLISHED DISSERTATIONS

Burgess, J. P., 'The problem of Scripture and political affairs as reflected in the Puritan Revolution: Samuel Rutherford, Thomas Goodwin, John Goodwin, and Gerard Winstanley', unpublished Ph.D. dissertation, University of Chicago (1986).

Button, C. N., 'Scottish mysticism in the seventeenth century, with special reference to Samuel Rutherford', unpublished Ph.D. dissertation, University of Edinburgh (1927).

Campbell, W., 'Samuel Rutherford: propagandist and exponent of Scottish Presbyterianism', unpublished Ph.D. dissertation, University of Edinburgh (1937).

Coffey, J., 'Samuel Rutherford (c. 1600–61) and the British Revolutions', unpublished Ph.D dissertation, Cambridge (1991).

Hall, T., 'Rutherford, Locke and the Declaration', unpublished M.Th. dissertation, Dallas Theological Seminary (1984).

Marshall, J. L., 'Natural law and the covenant: the place of natural law in the covenantal framework of Samuel Rutherford's *Lex Rex*', unpublished Ph.D. dissertation, Westminster Theological Seminary (1995).

Rae, C., 'The political thought of Samuel Rutherford', unpublished MA dissertation, University of Guelph (1991).

Rendell, K. G., 'Samuel Rutherford: the man and his ministry', unpublished MA dissertation, University of Durham (1987).

Strickland, D. R., 'Union with Christ in the theology of Samuel Rutherford', unpublished Ph.D. dissertation, University of Edinburgh (1972).

Webb, O. K., 'The political thought of Samuel Rutherford', unpublished Ph.D. dissertation, Duke University (1964).

GENERAL BIBLIOGRAPHY

PRIMARY SOURCES

MANUSCRIPTS

This bibliography refers to all manuscript sources quoted in the text. In addition, the bibliography of Rutherford contains a complete list of manuscripts of his letters, sermons and other works, whether published or unpublished. Despite extensive searches, I have been unable to locate manuscripts which shed much light on Rutherford's biography.

1. National Library of Scotland, Edinburgh. MSS 15948: record of debate between Rutherford and Bishop Sydserff of Galloway concerning ceremonies in 1636. Acc. 9270 no. 3: 'St Andrews Sermons, 1658'.
2. Edinburgh University Library. Dc.5. 30–31: 'Sermons by Covenanters'. La. III. 69/5: 'Treatise on the Nature of Obedience to a Usurped Power'.
3. St Andrews University Library. MS BX 8915. R. 8. L. 4. C. 37. A book containing copies of sixty-one letters written by Rutherford from Aberdeen in 1637, transcribed in a contemporary hand.
4. Hornel Library, Kirkcudbright. MS 4/24a. A History of the Church of Scotland till 1639 believed to be by Brown of Wamphray, author of The Apologeticall Relation, c. 1660–70.

PRINTED

This list does not include works written by or directly in response to Rutherford. They can be found in the bibliography of Rutherford.

Abbott, W., *The Writings and Speeches of Oliver Cromwell*, 4 vols. (Oxford, 1937–47).

Althusius, Johannes, *The Politics of Johannes Althusius*, trans. F. S. Carney (London, 1964).

Augustine, *Concerning the City of God Against the Pagans*, trans. H. Bettenson (London, 1984 edn).

Baillie, Robert, *Letters and Journals*, 3 vols., ed. D. Laing (Edinburgh, 1841–2, 2nd edn).

Baillie, Robert, *Dissuasive from the Errours of our Time* (London, 1645).

[Balcanquhall, Walter], *A Large Declaration concerning the Late Tumults in Scotland* (1639).

Balfour, Sir James, *The Historical Works*, 4 vols. (London, 1824–5).

Brodie, Alexander, *The Diary of Alex. Brodie, 1652–80, and of his son, James Brodie of Brodie, 1680–85*, ed. D. Laing (Aberdeen, 1863).

Brutus, Stephanus Junius, *Vindiciae, Contra Tyrannos*, ed. G. Garnett (Cambridge, 1994).

Burnet, Gilbert, *The History of my own Time*, I, ed. O. Airy (Oxford, 1897).

Calderwood, David, *The True History of the Church of Scotland: from the Beginning of the Reformation unto the End of the Reigne of King James VI* (n.p., 1678).

Calvin, John, *Institutes of the Christian Religion*, trans. H. Beveridge (Grand Rapids, Mich., 1989 edn).

The Covenants and the Covenanters: Covenants, Sermons and Documents of the Covenanted Reformation, ed. J. Kerr (Edinburgh, 1895).

Crauford, Thomas, *History of the University of Edinburgh from 1580 to 1646* (Edinburgh, 1808).

Curate, Jacob, *Scotch Presbyterian Eloquence Display'd, or the Teaching of their Folly Discover'd from their Books, Sermons and Prayers* (Rotterdam, 1738 edn).

Extracts from the Council Register of the Burgh of Aberdeen, 1643–1747 (Edinburgh, 1872).

Extracts from the Records of the Burgh of Edinburgh, 1604–1626, ed. M. Wood (Edinburgh, 1931).

Gillespie, George, *The Works of George Gillespie*, 2 vols. (Edinburgh, 1846).

Gordon of Rothiemay, James, *History of Scots Affairs from 1637 to 1641* (Aberdeen, 1841).

Guthry, Henry, *Memoirs of Henry Guthry, late Bishop of Dunkel in Scotland* (London, 1702).

Halyburton, Thomas, *Memoirs of the Life of the Reverend, Learned and Pious Mr Thomas Halyburton* (3rd edn: Edinburgh, 1733).

Historical Collections of Accounts of Revival, ed. J. Gillies (Kelso, 1845).

Historical Manuscripts Commission, *Report on the Laing Manuscripts*, I (London, 1914).

Historical Manuscripts Commission, *Supplementary Report on the Manuscripts of his Grace the Duke of Hamilton*, ed. J. H. McMaster and M. Wood (London, 1932).

Hobbes, Thomas, *Behemoth, or the Long Parliament* in his *Complete Works*, ed. T. Molesworth, 11 vols. (1839–45), VI.

Jaffray, Alexander, *The Diary of Alexander Jaffray* (London, 1833).

Kirkcudbright Town Council Records, 1606–58, ed. John, 4th Marquis of Bute and C. M. Armet (Edinburgh, 1958).

Lamont of Newton, John, *The Diary of Mr John Lamont of Newton, 1649–71*, ed. G. R. Kinloch (Edinburgh, 1830).

Leslie, Henrie, *A Treatise of the Authoritie of the Church* (Dublin, 1637).

The Life of Robert Blair, containing his Autobiography, 1593–1636, with Supplement to his Life and Continuation of the History of the Times to 1680 by his Son-in-law William Row, ed. T. McCrie (Edinburgh, 1848).

Lightfoot, John, *The Journal of the Proceedings of the Assembly of Divines from January 1st 1643 to December 31st 1644*, in *Complete Works*, XIII, ed. J. R. Pitman (London, 1824).

Lilburne, John, *The Freeman's Freedome Vindicated* (London, 1646).

Lilburne, John, *Regall Tyrannie Discovered* (London, 1647).

Livingstone, John, 'Life by himself' and 'Memorable characteristics', in W. K. Tweedie, ed., *Select Biographies*, I (Edinburgh, 1845).

Mackenzie, George, *Religio Stoici* (Edinburgh, 1663).

Mackenzie, George, *Jus Regium; or the Just and Solid Foundations of Monarchy* (London, 1684).

Mather, Cotton, *Student and Preacher: Or Directions for a Candidate of the Ministry* (London, 1789).

Maxwell, John, *Sacro-sancta Regum Majestas: or the Sacred and Royall Prerogative of Christian Kings* (Oxford, 1644).

Milton, John, *Complete Prose Works*, 8 vols. (New Haven, 1952–83).

John Milton, ed. S. Orgel and J. Goldberg (Oxford, 1990).

Minutes of the Westminster Assembly of Divines, ed. A. F. Mitchell and J. Struthers (London, 1874).

Owen, John, *The Works of John Owen*, ed. W. H. Goold (London, 1967).

Prynne, William, *The Soveraigne Power of Parliaments* (1643).

Records of the Commissions of the General Assemblies of the Church of Scotland, ed. A. F. Mitchell and J. Christie, 3 vols. (Edinburgh, 1892–1909).

Records of the Kirk of Scotland, 1638–51, ed. A. Peterkin (Edinburgh, 1838).

Register of the Consultations of the Ministers of Edinburgh and some other Brethren in the Ministry, ed. W. Stephen, 2 vols. (Edinburgh, 1921, 1930).

[Ridpath, George], *An Answer to the Scotch Presbyterian Eloquence* (London, 1693).

Row, John, *The History of the Kirk of Scotland, From the Year 1558 to 1637* (Edinburgh, 1842).

[Rule, Gilbert], *A Just and Modest Reproof of a Pamphlet called the Scotch Presbyterian Eloquence* (Edinburgh, 1693).

Second Book of Discipline, ed. J. Kirk (Edinburgh, 1980).

Selections from the Minutes of the Presbyteries of St Andrews and Cupar, 1641–98, ed. G. R. Kinloch (Edinburgh, 1837).

Selections from the Minutes of the Synod of Fife, 1611–87, ed. G. R. Kinloch (Edinburgh, 1837).

Shields, Alexander, *A Hind let Loose, or an Historical Representation of the Testimonies of the Church of Scotland* (1687).

Spalding, John, *Memorials of the Trubles in Scotland and in England, 1624–45*, 2 vols. (Aberdeen, 1850–1).

[Stewart, James and Stirling, James], *Naphtali, or the Wrestlings of the Church of Scotland for the Kingdom of Christ* (1667).

[Stewart, James], *Jus Populi Vindicatum, or the Peoples Right to Defend Themselves and their Covenanted Religion Vindicated* (1669).

Tweedie, W. K., ed., *Select Biographies*, I (Edinburgh, 1845).

University of Edinburgh: Charters, Statutes, and Acts of the Town Council and the Senatus, 1583–1858, ed. A. Morgan (Edinburgh, 1937).

Walker, Sir Edward, *Historical Discourses upon Several Occasions* (London, 1705).

Wariston, Archibald Johnston of, *Diary*, I, ed. G. M. Paul (Edinburgh, 1911); II, ed. D. H. Fleming (Edinburgh, 1919); III, ed. J. D. Ogilvie (Edinburgh, 1940).

Wilkins, John, *Ecclesiastes, or the Gift of Preaching* (London, 1693).

Williams, Roger, *Queries of the Highest Consideration* (London, 1644).

Wodrow, Robert, *Analecta, or Materials for a History of Remarkable Providences mostly relating to Scotch Ministers and Christians*, 4 vols. (Edinburgh, 1842–3).

Wodrow, Robert, *The History of the Sufferings of the Church of Scotland from the Restoration to the Revolution*, I (Glasgow, 1828).

Wodrow's Biographical Collections, ed. R. Lippe (Aberdeen, 1840).

SECONDARY SOURCES

BOOKS AND ARTICLES

Adams, R. M., 'Middle knowledge and the problem of evil', in R. M. Adams and M. M. Adams, eds., *The Problem of Evil* (Oxford, 1990), pp. 110–25.

Allan, D., *Virtue, Learning and the Scottish Enlightenment: Ideas of Scholarship in Early Modern History* (Edinburgh, 1993).

Allen, J. W., *English Political Thought, 1603–44* (London, 1938).

Altholz, J., 'The warfare of conscience with theology', in G. Parsons, ed., *Religion in Victorian Britain*, IV: *Interpretations* (Manchester, 1988), pp. 150–69.

Arjomand, S. A., *The Turban for the Crown: The Islamic Revolution in Iran* (Oxford, 1988).

Armstrong, B., *Calvinism and the Amyraut Heresy: Protestant Scholasticism and Humanism in Seventeenth Century France* (Madison, Wis., 1969).

Armstrong, B., 'Puritan spirituality: the tension of Bible and experience', in E. R. Elder, ed., *The Roots of the Modern Christian Tradition* (Kalamazoo, Mich., 1984), pp. 229–48.

Avis, P. D. L., 'Moses and the magistrate: a study in the rise of Protestant legalism', *Journal of Ecclesiastical History*, 26 (1975), 149–72.

Baker, J. W., *Heinrich Bullinger and the Covenant* (Athens, Ohio, 1980).

Ball, B. W., *A Great Expectation: Eschatological Thought in English Protestantism to 1660* (Leiden, 1975).

Barbour, G. F., *The Life of Alexander Whyte* (London, 1923).

Barkley, J. M., 'Some Scottish bishops and ministers in the Irish Church, 1605–35', in D. Shaw, ed., *Reformation and Revolution* (Edinburgh, 1967), pp. 141–59.

Barth, K., *Church Dogmatics*, I/1–IV/4 (Edinburgh, 1936–81).

Bauckham, R., *Tudor Apocalypse* (Appleford, 1978).

Beeke, J., *Assurance of Faith: Calvin, English Puritanism and the Dutch Second Reformation* (New York, 1991).

Beeke, J., 'Personal assurance of faith: the Puritans and chapter 18.2 of the Westminster Confession', *Westminster Theological Journal*, 55 (1993), 1–30.

Bell, M. C., *Calvin and Scottish Theology: The Doctrine of Assurance* (Edinburgh, 1985).

Bellah, R. N., *Beyond Belief: Essays on Religion in a Post-traditional World* (New York, 1970).

Berger, P., *The Social Reality of Religion* (Harmondsworth, 1973).

Bettenson, H., *Documents of the Christian Church* (Oxford, 1943).

Biel, P., 'Bullinger against the Donatists: St Augustine to the defence of the Zurich Reformed Church', *Journal of Religious History*, 16 (1991), 237–46.

Black, G. F., *A Calendar of Cases of Witchcraft in Scotland, 1510–1727* (New York, 1938).

Blaisdell, C. J., 'Calvin's letters to women: the courting of ladies in high places', *Sixteenth Century Journal*, 13 (1982), 67–84.

Blaisdell, C. J., 'Calvin and Loyola's letters to women: politics and spiritual counsel in the sixteenth century', in R. V. Schnucker, ed., *Calviniana: Ideas and Influence of Jean Calvin* (Kirksville, Mo, 1988), pp. 235–53.

Boswell, J. C., *Milton's Library* (London, 1975).

Boughton, L. C., 'Supralapsarianism and the role of metaphysics in sixteenth-century Reformed theology', *Westminster Theological Journal*, 48 (1986), 63–96.

Bouswma, W., *John Calvin: A Sixteenth-Century Portrait* (Oxford, 1988).
Bouyer, L., *Orthodox Spirituality and Protestant and Anglican Spirituality* (London, 1969).
Bower, A., *The History of the University of Edinburgh*, I (Edinburgh, 1917).
Bozeman, T., *To Live Ancient Lives: The Primitivist Dimension in Puritanism* (Chapel Hill, NC, 1988).
Bray, J. S., *Theodore Beza's Doctrine of Predestination* (Nieuwkoop, 1975).
Bremer, F. J., ed., *Puritanism: Transatlantic Perspectives on a Seventeenth-Century Anglo-American Faith* (Boston, 1993).
Bremer, F. and Rydell, E., 'Performance art? Puritans in the pulpit', *History Today*, 45 (September 1995), 50–4.
Brodrick, J., *Robert Bellarmine: Saint and Scholar* (London, 1961).
Brown, C., *Christianity and Western Thought*, I (Leicester, 1990).
Brown, K., 'Aristocratic finances and the origins of the Scottish revolution', *English Historical Review*, 54 (1989), 46–87.
Brown, S. J., *Thomas Chalmers and the Godly Commonwealth in Scotland* (Oxford, 1982).
Bruce, S., *A House Divided: Protestantism, Schism and Secularisation* (London, 1990).
Buckle, H. T., *On Scotland and the Scotch Intellect*, ed. H. J. Hanham (Chicago, 1970).
Burgess, G., 'Revisionism, politics and political ideas in early Stuart England', *Historical Journal*, 34 (1992), 465–78.
Burns, J. H., 'The political ideas of George Buchanan', *Scottish Historical Review*, 30 (1951), 60–8.
Burns, J. H., and Goldie, M., eds., *The Cambridge History of Political Thought, 1450–1700* (Cambridge, 1991).
Burrell, S. A., 'The covenant idea as a revolutionary symbol: Scotland, 1596–1637', *Church History*, 27 (1958), 338–49.
Burrell, S. A., 'The apocalyptic vision of the early Covenanters', *Scottish Historical Review*, 43 (1964), 1–24.
Bush, S., *The Writings of Thomas Hooker* (London, 1980).
Bynum, C. W., *Jesus as Mother: Studies in the Spirituality of the High Middle Ages* (London, 1982).
Bynum, C. W., *Holy Feast and Holy Fast: The Religious Significance of Food to Medieval Women* (London, 1987).
Cameron, E., 'The late Renaissance and the unfolding Reformation in Europe', in J. Kirk, ed., *Humanism and Reform: The Church of Scotland in Europe, England and Scotland, 1400–1643* (Oxford, 1991), pp. 15–36.
Cameron, J. K., 'Scottish Calvinism and the principle of intolerance', in B. Gerrish, ed., *Reformatio Perennis* (Pittsburg, 1981), pp. 113–28.
Cameron, J. K., 'The commentary on the Book of Revelation by James Durham', in M. Wilks, ed., *Prophecy and Eschatology* (Oxford, 1994), pp. 123–9.
Cameron, N., ed., *Dictionary of Scottish Church History and Theology* (Edinburgh, 1993).
Camp, L. R., *Roger Williams: God's Apostle of Advocacy* (Lewiston, 1989).
Campbell, W. M., 'The Scottish Westminster commissioners and toleration', *Records of the Scottish Church History Society*, 9 (1947), 1–18.
Casey, M., *Athirst for God: Spiritual Desire in Bernard of Clairvaux's Sermons on the Song of Songs* (Kalamazoo, Mich., 1988).

Chadwick, O., *The Reformation* (Harmondsworth, 1964).
Christianson, P., *Reformers and Babylon: English Apocalyptic Visions from the Reformation to the Eve of the Civil War* (Toronto, 1978).
Clark, J. C. D., *English Society, 1688–1832: Ideology, Social Structure and Political Practice during the Ancien Regime* (Cambridge, 1985).
Clifford, A. C., *Atonement and Justification: English Evangelical Theology 1640–1790: An Evaluation* (Oxford, 1990).
Cohen, C. L., *God's Caress: The Psychology of Puritan Religious Experience* (Oxford, 1986).
Colley, L., *Britons: Forging the Nation, 1707–1837* (London, 1992).
Collinson, P., *The Elizabethan Puritan Movement* (Oxford, 1967).
Collinson, P., *The Religion of Protestants: The Church in English Society, 1559–1625* (Oxford, 1982).
Collinson, P., *Godly People: Essays on English Protestantism and Puritanism* (London, 1983).
Collinson, P., 'The English conventicle', in W. J. Sheils and D. Wood, eds., *Voluntary Religion* (Oxford, 1986), pp. 223–59.
Collinson, P., *The Birthpangs of Protestant England: Religion and Cultural Change in the Sixteenth and Seventeenth Centuries* (London, 1988).
Collinson, P., 'Sects and the evolution of Puritanism', in F. J. Bremer, ed., *Puritanism: Transatlantic Perspectives on a Seventeenth-Century Anglo-American Faith* (Boston, 1993), pp. 147–66.
Collinson, P., 'Elizabethan and Jacobean Puritanism as forms of popular religious culture', in C. Durston and J. Eales, eds., *The Culture of English Puritanism* (London, 1996), pp. 32–57.
Costello, W. T., *The Scholastic Curriculum at Early Seventeenth Century Cambridge* (Cambridge, Mass., 1958).
Cowan, E., 'The making of the National Covenant', in John Morrill, ed., *The Scottish National Covenant in its British Context* (Edinburgh, 1990), pp. 68–89.
Cowan, E. J., 'The political ideas of a covenanting leader: Archibald Campbell, Marquis of Argyll, 1607–61', in R. Mason, ed., *Scots and Britons* (Cambridge, 1994), pp. 241–61.
Cowan, I. B., 'The five articles of Perth', in D. Shaw, ed., *Reformation and Revolution* (Edinburgh, 1967), pp. 160–77.
Craig, W. L., *The Historical Argument for the Resurrection of Jesus during the Deist Controversy* (Lewiston, NY, 1985).
Craig, W. L., *The Problem of Divine Foreknowledge and Future Contingents from Aristotle to Suarez* (Leiden, 1988).
Cunningham, W., *The Reformers and the Theology of the Reformation* ([1862] Edinburgh, 1989).
Curtis, M. H., *Oxford and Cambridge in Transition, 1558–1642: An Essay on Changing Relations between the English Universities and English Society* (Oxford, 1959).
Dalzel, A., *History of the University of Edinburgh from its Foundations*, II (Edinburgh, 1862).
Davies, J., *The Caroline Captivity of the Church: Charles I and the Remoulding of Anglicanism* (Oxford, 1992).
Davies, K. M., 'The sacred condition of equality: how unique were Puritan doctrines of marriage?', *Social History*, 5 (1977), 563–78.

Davis, J. C., 'Puritanism and revolution: themes, categories, methods and conclusions', *Historical Journal*, 33 (1990), 693–704.

Davis, J. C., 'Cromwell's religion', in J. S. Morrill, ed., *Oliver Cromwell and the English Revolution* (London, 1990), pp. 181–208.

Davis, J. C., 'Religion and the struggle for freedom in the English revolution', *Historical Journal*, 35 (1992), 507–30.

Davis, J. C., 'Against formality: one aspect of the English Revolution', *Transactions of the Royal Historical Society*, 6th series, 3 (1993), 265–88.

Davis, K. R., *The Rutherfords in Britain: A Guide and a History* (Gloucester, 1987).

Donagan, B., 'Providence, chance and explanation: some paradoxical aspects of Puritan views of causation', *Journal of Religious History*, 11 (1991), 385–403.

Donald, P., *An Uncounselled King: Charles I and the Scottish Troubles, 1637–41* (Cambridge, 1991).

Donaldson, G., *The Making of the Scottish Prayer Book of 1637* (Edinburgh, 1954).

Donaldson, G., *The Scottish Reformation* (Cambridge, 1960).

Donaldson, G., *Scotland: James V–James VII* (Edinburgh, 1965)

Donaldson, G., ed., *Four Centuries: Edinburgh University Life, 1583–1963* (Edinburgh, 1983).

Donaldson, G., 'Reformation to covenant' and 'Covenant to Revolution', in D. Forrester and D. M. Murray, eds., *Studies in the History of Worship in Scotland* (Edinburgh, 1984), chs. 3 and 4.

Donaldson, G., *Scottish Church History* (Edinburgh, 1985).

Donnelly, J. P., *Calvinism and Scholasticism in Vermigli's Doctrine of Man and Grace* (Leiden, 1976).

Donnelly, J. P., 'Calvinist Thomism', *Viator*, 7 (1976), 441–51.

Dunn, J., 'The identity of the history of ideas', in P. Laslett, Q. Skinner and W. G. Runciman, eds., *Philosophy, Politics and Society*, Fourth series (Oxford, 1982), pp. 158–73.

Durston, C. and Eales, J., eds., *The Culture of English Puritanism, 1560–1700* (London, 1996).

Dworkin, R., *Life's Dominion: An Argument about Abortion and Euthanasia* (London, 1993).

Escott, H., *A History of Scottish Congregationalism* (Glasgow, 1960).

Faludi, S., *Backlash: the Undeclared War against Women* (London, 1992).

Ferguson, S. B., 'An Assembly of theonomists? The teaching of the Westminster divines on the law of God', in W. S. Barker and W. R. Godfrey, eds., *Theonomy: a Reformed critique* (Grand Rapids, Mich., 1989), pp. 315–49.

Fincham, K., ed., *The Early Stuart Church, 1603–42* (London, 1993).

Finlayson, C. and Simpson, S., 'The history of the library, 1580–1710', in J. R. Guild and A. Law, eds., *Edinburgh University Library, 1580–1982* (Edinburgh, 1982), pp. 43–54.

Firth, K., *The Apocalyptic Tradition in Reformation Britain, 1530–1645* (Oxford, 1979).

Fletcher, A., *The Outbreak of the English Civil War* (London, 1981).

Fletcher, A. and Roberts, P., *Religion, Culture and Society in Early Modern Britain: Essays in Honour of Patrick Collinson* (Cambridge, 1994).

Ford, J. D., 'The lawful bonds of Scottish society: the Five Articles of Perth, the Negative Confession and the National Covenant', *Historical Journal*, 37 (1994), 45–64.

Ford, J., 'Conformity in conscience: the structure of the Perth Articles debate in Scotland, 1618–38', *Journal of Ecclesiastical History*, 46 (1995), 256–77.

Forrester, D., and Murray, D. M., eds., *Studies in the History of Worship in Scotland* (Edinburgh, 1984).

Foster, W. R., *The Church before the Covenants* (Edinburgh, 1975).

Freddeso, A. J., ed., *Luis de Molina's 'On Divine Foreknowledge'* (Ithaca, 1988).

Freemantle, A., ed., *The Protestant Mystics* (London, 1964).

Friedrich, C. J., *The Age of Baroque, 1610–60* (New York, 1952).

Friedrich, C. J., *Transcendent Justice: The Religious Dimension of Constitutionalism* (Durham, NC, 1964).

Garvey, J., 'Fundamentalism and American law', in M. Marty and R. S. Appleby, eds., *Fundamentalisms and the State: Remaking Polities, Economies, and Militance* (Chicago, 1993), ch. 3.

Gatter, F. T., 'On the literary value of some Scottish Presbyterian writings in the context of the Scottish Enlightenment', in D. Strauss and H. W. Drescher, eds., *Scottish Language and Literature, Medieval and Renaissance* (Frankfurt, 1986), pp. 175–92.

Geertz, C., *The Interpretation of Cultures* (New York, 1973).

George, C. H., 'Puritanism as history and historiography', *Past and Present*, 41 (1968), 77–104.

Ginsburg, F., 'Saving America's souls: Operation Rescue's Crusade against abortion', in M. Marty and R. S. Appleby, eds., *Fundamentalisms and the State* (Chicago, 1993), ch. 23.

Gleason, R. C., *John Calvin and John Owen on Mortification: A Comparative Study in Reformed Spirituality* (New York, 1995).

Godfrey, W. R., 'Reformed thought on the extent of the atonement', *Westminster Theological Journal*, 37 (1975), 133–71.

Goldie, M. A., 'Obligations, utopias and their historical context', *Historical Journal*, 26 (1983), 727–46.

Goldie, M. A., 'The theory of religious intolerance in Restoration England', in O. P. Grell, J. I. Israel and N. Tyacke, eds., *From Persecution to Toleration: The Glorious Revolution and Religion in England* (Oxford, 1991), ch. 13.

Gooch, G.P., *English Democratic Ideas in the Seventeenth Century* (New York, 1959 edn).

Gough, J. W., *The Social Contract: A Critical Study of its Development* (Oxford, 1936).

Grant, A., *The Story of the University of Edinburgh During its First Three Hundred Years* (London, 1884).

Greaves, R., 'John Bunyan and the covenant tradition in the seventeenth century', *Church History*, 36 (1967), 151–69.

Grell, O. P., Israel, J. I., and Tyacke, N., eds., *From Persecution to Toleration: The Glorious Revolution and Religion in England* (Oxford, 1991).

Groenhuis, G., 'Calvinism and national consciousness: the Dutch Republic as the new Israel', in A. C. Duke and C. A. Tamse, eds., *Britain and the Netherlands, VII: Church and State since the Reformation* (The Hague, 1981), pp. 118–33.

Groome, F. H., ed., *Ordnance Gazetteer of Scotland*, 6 vols. (London, 1894–5).

Guild, J. R. and Law, A., eds., *Edinburgh University Library, 1580–1980: A Collection of Historical Essays* (Edinburgh, 1982).

Gura, P. F., *A Glimpse of Sion's Glory: Puritan Radicalism in New England, 1620–60* (Middleton, Conn., 1984).

Hall, B., 'Calvin and the Calvinists', in G. E. Duffield, ed., *John Calvin* (Abingdon, 1966).

Haller, W., *The Rise of Puritanism* (New York, 1938).

Hambrick-Stowe, C. E., *The Practice of Piety: Puritan Devotional Disciplines in Seventeenth-Century New England* (Chapel Hill, 1982).

Hambrick-Stowe, C. E., 'Loss and hope in Reformed spirituality: the example of Anne Bradstreet', in B. C. Hanson, ed., *Modern Christian Spirituality* (Atlanta, Ga., 1990), pp. 85–112.

Hamilton, B., *Political Thought in Sixteenth Century Spain: A Study of the Political Ideas of Vitoria, de Soto, Suarez, and Molina* (Oxford, 1963).

Hanna, W., ed., *Memoirs of Thomas Chalmers*, III (Edinburgh, 1851).

Hanson, B. C., *Modern Christian Spirituality: Methodological and Historical Essays* (Atlanta, 1990).

Harris, T., Seaward, P. and Goldie, M., eds., *The Politics of Religion in Restoration England* (Oxford, 1990).

Harrison, J., *The Library of Isaac Newton* (Cambridge, 1978).

Helm, P., *Calvin and the Calvinists* (Edinburgh, 1982).

Helm, P., 'Calvin and natural law', *Scottish Bulletin Evangelical Theology*, 2 (1984), 5–22.

Hempton, D., and Hill, M., eds., *Evangelical Protestantism in Ulster Society, 1740–1890* (London, 1992).

Henderson, G. D., *The Scottish Ruling Elder* (London, 1935).

Henderson, G. D., *Religious Life in Seventeenth-Century Scotland* (Cambridge, 1937).

Henderson, G. D., *The Claims of the Church of Scotland* (London, 1951).

Henderson, G. D., *Presbyterianism* (Aberdeen, 1957).

Henderson, G.D., *The Burning Bush* (Edinburgh, 1957).

Henderson, J. M., 'An advertisement about the Service Book 1637', *Scottish Historical Review*, 23 (1925–6), 199–204.

Hibbard, C., *Charles I and the Popish Plot* (Chapel Hill, NC, 1983).

Hill, C., *The Intellectual Origins of the English Revolution* (Oxford, 1965).

Hill, C., *Antichrist in Seventeenth-Century England* (London, 1971).

Hill, C., *The Collected Essays of Christopher Hill*, III (Brighton, 1986).

Hill, C., *The English Bible and the Seventeenth-Century Revolution* (Harmondsworth, 1993).

Hoekema, A., 'The covenant of grace in Calvin's teaching', *Calvin Theological Journal*, 2 (1967), 133–61.

Hopfl, H., *The Christian Polity of John Calvin* (Cambridge, 1982).

Howe, D. W. 'Religion and politics in the antebellum North', in M. Noll, ed., *Religion and American Politics: From the Colonial Period to the 1980s* (Oxford, 1990), ch. 6.

Hoy, W. I., 'The entry of the sects into Scotland', in D. Shaw, ed., *Reformation and Revolution* (Edinburgh, 1967), pp. 174–211.

Hueglin, T., 'Have we studied the wrong authors? On the relevance of Johannes Althusius', *Studies in Political Thought*, 1 (1992), 75–93.

Hughes, A., 'Thomas Dugard and his circle in the 1630s: a parliamentary-puritan connexion?', *Historical Journal*, 29 (1986), 771–93.

Hunt, J., *Religious Thought in England from the Reformation to the End of the Last Century*, I (London, 1870).
Hunt, W., *The Puritan Moment: The Coming of Revolution in an English County* (Cambridge, Mass., 1983).
Hutton, R. *The Rise and Fall of Merry England: The Ritual Year 1400–1700* (Oxford, 1994).
Jack, R. D. S., ed., *Scottish prose 1550–1700* (London, 1971).
Jack, R. D. S., ed., *The History of Scottish Literature, Volume I: Origins to 1660* (Aberdeen, 1988).
Johnson, P., *A History of the Jews* (London, 1987).
Jordan, W. K., *The Development of Religious Toleration in England*, 4 vols. (London, 1932–40).
Kamen, H., *The Rise of Toleration* (London, 1967).
Kaplan, Y., Mechoulan, H., and Popkin, R. H., eds., *Menasseh ben Israel and his World* (Leiden, 1989).
Katz, D., *Philo-Semitism and the Readmission of the Jews to England, 1603–55* (Oxford, 1982).
Kearney, H. F., 'Puritanism, capitalism and the scientific revolution', *Past and Present*, 28 (1964), 81–101.
Kearney, H. F., *Scholars and Gentlemen: Universities and Society in Pre-industrial Britain, 1500–1700* (London, 1970).
Keeble, N. H., and Nuttall, G., eds., *Calendar of the Correspondence of Richard Baxter*, 2 vols. (Oxford, 1991).
Kendall, R. T., *Calvin and English Calvinism to 1649* (Oxford, 1979).
Kevan, E., *The Grace of Law: A Study in Puritan Theology* (London, 1964).
Kidd, C., *Subverting Scotland's Past: Scottish Whig Historians and the Creation of an Anglo-British Identity, 1689–c.1830* (Cambridge, 1993).
Kinloch, M. G. J., *Studies in Scottish Ecclesiastical History* (London, 1898).
Kirk, J., 'Clement Little's library', in J. R. Guild and A. Law, eds., *Edinburgh University Library 1580–1980* (Edinburgh, 1982), pp. 1–42.
Kirk, J., *Patterns of Reform: Continuity and Change in the Reformation Kirk* (Edinburgh, 1989).
Kirk, J., ed., *Humanism and Reform: The Church of Scotland in Europe, England and Scotland, 1400–1643* (Oxford, 1991).
Kolakowski, L., *God Owes Us Nothing: A Brief Remark on Pascal's Religion and on the Spirit of Jansenism* (Chicago, 1995).
Kyle, R., 'John Knox and the purification of religion: the intellectual aspects of his crusade against idolatry', *Archiv fur Reformationsgeschichte*, 77 (1986), 265–80.
Kyle, R., 'John Knox: a man of the Old Testament', *Westminster Theological Journal*, 54 (1992), 65–78.
Lachman, D., *The Marrow Controversy, 1718–23* (Edinburgh, 1988).
Lake, P., 'Puritan identities', *Journal of Ecclesiastical History*, 35 (1984), 112–23.
Lake, P., 'William Bradshaw, antichrist and the community of the godly', *Journal of Ecclesiastical History*, 36 (1985), 570–89.
Lake, P., 'Feminine piety and personal potency: the "emancipation" of Mrs Jane Ratcliffe', *The Seventeenth Century*, 2 (1987), 143–65.
Lake, P. 'Anti-popery: the structure of a prejudice', in R. Cust and A. Hughes, eds., *Conflict in Early Modern England* (London, 1989).
Lake, P., ' "A charitable Christian hatred": the godly and their enemies in the

1630s', in C. Durston and J. Eales, eds., *The Culture of English Puritanism 1560–1700* (London, 1996), pp. 144–83.

Lamont, W., *Marginal Prynne, 1600–69* (London, 1963).

Lamont, W., 'Puritanism as history and historiography: some further thoughts', *Past and Present*, 44 (1969), 133–46.

Lamont, W., *Godly Rule: Politics and Religion, 1603–60* (London, 1969).

Lamont, W., *Richard Baxter and the Millennium* (Brighton, 1979).

Lamont, W., 'Pamphleteering, the Protestant consensus and the English revolution', in R. C. Richardson and G. M. Ridden, eds., *Freedom and the English Revolution* (Manchester, 1986), pp.72–92.

Lamont, W., 'The Puritan revolution: a historiographical essay', in J. G. A. Pocock, ed., *The Varieties of British Political Thought 1500–1800* (Cambridge, 1993), 119–45.

Lamont, W., 'The two "national churches" of 1691 and 1829', in A. Fletcher and P. Roberts, eds., *Religion, Culture and Society in Early Modern Britain: Essays in Honour of Patrick Collinson* (Cambridge, 1994).

Lamont, W., *Puritanism and Historical Controversy* (London, 1996).

Lane, A., 'The quest for the historical Calvin', *Evangelical Quarterly*, 55 (1983), 95–113.

Larner, C., Lee, C. H. and McLachan, H. V., *A Source-Book of Scottish Witchcraft* (Glasgow, 1977).

Lecler, J., *Toleration and the Reformation*, 2 vols. (London, 1960).

Lee, M., *The Road to Revolution: Scotland Under Charles I, 1625–37* (Chicago, 1985).

Leites, E., ed., *Conscience and Casuistry in Early Modern Europe* (Cambridge, 1988).

Leverenz, D., *The Language of Puritan Feeling: An Exploration in Literature, Psychology and Social History* (New Brunswick, 1980).

Lindsay, M., *Scotland: An Anthology* (London, 1974).

Lindsay, M., *History of Scottish Literature* (London, 1977).

Little, D., 'Reformed faith and religious liberty', in D. K. McKim, ed., *Major Themes in the Reformed Tradition* (Grand Rapids, Mich., 1992), pp. 196–213.

Lynch, M., 'Calvinism in Scotland, 1559–1638', in M. Prestwich, ed., *International Calvinism, 1541–1715* (Oxford, 1985), pp. 225–55.

Lynch, M., *Scotland: A New History* (London, 1991).

McConica, J., 'Humanism and Aristotle in Tudor Oxford', *English Historical Review*, 94 (1979), 291–317.

McCoy, F. N., *Robert Baillie and the Second Scots Reformation* (Berkeley, 1974).

McCrie, T., *The Life of Andrew Melville* (Edinburgh, 1899 edn).

MacDonald, A., 'David Calderwood: the not so hidden years, 1590–1604', *Scottish Historical Review*, 74 (1995), 69–74.

MacDougall, N., ed., *Church, Politics and Society: Scotland, 1408–1929* (Edinburgh, 1983).

MacFarlane, I., *Buchanan* (London, 1981).

McGiffert, M., 'God's controversy with Jacobean England', *American Historical Review*, 88 (1983), 1151–74.

McGrath, A. E., *The Intellectual Origins of the European Reformation* (Oxford, 1987).

McGrath, A. E., *Reformation Thought: An Introduction* (second edn: Oxford, 1993).

McGregor, J. F., and Reay, B., eds., *Radical Religion in the English Revolution* (Oxford, 1984).

MacInnes, A. I., *Charles I and the Making of the Covenanting Movement, 1625–41* (Edinburgh, 1991).

MacIntyre, A., *Whose Justice, Which Rationality?* (London, 1988).

Mack, P., 'Women as prophets during the English Civil War', *Feminist Studies*, 8 (1982).

Mackay, H., 'The reception given to the five articles of Perth', *Records of the Scottish Church History Society*, 19 (1977), 185–201.

Macleod, J., *Scottish Theology* (Edinburgh, 1843).

MacMillan, D., *The Aberdeen Doctors* (London, 1909).

MacPherson, J., *The Doctrine of the Church in Scottish Theology* (Edinburgh, 1903).

MacQueen, J., ed., *Humanism in Renaissance Scotland* (Edinburgh, 1990).

McWilliams, D., 'The covenant theology of the Westminster Confession of Faith and recent criticism', *Westminster Theological Journal*, 53 (1991), 109–24.

Makey, W. H., *The Church of the Covenant, 1637–51: Revolution and Social Change in Scotland* (Edinburgh, 1979).

Marsden, G., 'Perry Miller's rehabilitation of the Puritans: a critique', *Church History*, 39 (1970), 91–105.

Marsden, G., *Fundamentalism and American Culture: The Shaping of Twentieth Century Evangelicalism, 1870–1925* (Oxford, 1980).

Marsh, C., *The Family of Love in English Society, 1550–1630* (Cambridge, 1994).

Marshall, G., *Presbyteries and Profits: Calvinism and the Development of Capitalism in Scotland, 1560–1707* (Oxford, 1980).

Marshall, P. A., 'Quentin Skinner and the secularization of political thought', *Studies in Political Theory*, 1 (1992), 85–104.

Martin, H., *Great Christian Books* (London, 1945).

Marty, M and Appleby, R. S., eds., *Fundamentalisms Observed* (Chicago, 1991).

Marty, M and Appleby, R. S., eds., *Fundamentalisms and the State: Remaking Polities, Economies, and Militance* (Chicago, 1993).

Mason, R., 'Covenant and commonweal: the language of politics in Reformation Scotland', in N. MacDougall, ed., *Church, Politics and Society: Scotland, 1408–1929* (Edinburgh, 1983), pp. 97–126.

Mason, R., ed., *Scots and Britons: Scottish Political Thought and the Union of 1603* (Cambridge, 1994).

Masson, M. W., 'The typology of the female as a model for the regenerate: Puritan preaching, 1690–1730', *Signs*, 2 (1976), 304–15.

Matter, E. A., *The Voice of My Beloved: The Song of Songs in Western Medieval Christianity* (Philadelphia, 1990).

Maxwell, T., 'The Scotch Presbyterian Eloquence: a post-Revolution pamphlet', *Records of the Scottish Church History Society*, 8 (1944), 225–53.

Millar, J. H., *A Literary History of Scotland* (London, 1903).

Millar, J. H., *Scottish Prose of the Seventeenth and Eighteenth Centuries* (Glasgow, 1912).

Miller, J., *Popery and Politics in England, 1660–88* (Cambridge, 1973).

Miller, P., *The New England Mind: The Seventeenth Century* (New York, 1939).

Miller, P., *Errand into the Wilderness* (Cambridge, Mass., 1956).

Miller, P., *The New England Mind: From Colony to Province* (Cambridge, Mass., 1967 edn).

Milroy, A., 'The doctrine of the Church of Scotland', in R. H. Story, ed., *The Church of Scotland Past and Present*, IV (London, 1891).

Monk, R. C., *John Wesley: His Puritan Heritage* (London, 1966).

Morgan, E. S., *Visible Saints: The History of a Puritan Idea* (Ithaca, 1963).

Morrill, J., *Oliver Cromwell and the English Revolution* (London, 1993).

Morrill, J., *The Scottish National Covenant in its British Context, 1638–51* (Edinburgh, 1990).

Morrill, J., *The Nature of the English Revolution* (Harlow, 1993).

Morrill, J., 'A British patriarchy: ecclesiastical imperialism under the early Stuarts', in A. Fletcher and P. Roberts, eds., *Religion, Culture and Society in Early Modern Britain: Essays in Honour of Patrick Collinson* (Cambridge, 1994), pp. 209–37.

Morton, A. L., *The World of the Ranters* (London, 1970).

Mouw, R. J., *The God Who Commands* (Notre Dame, 1990).

Mullan, D., *Episcopacy in Scotland: The History of an Idea, 1560–1638* (Edinburgh, 1986).

Muller, R., *Christ and the Decree: Christology and Predestination in Reformed Theology from Calvin to Perkins* (Durham, NC, 1986).

Muller, R., *Post-Reformation Reformed Dogmatics, Volume I: Prolegomena to Theology* (Grand Rapids, Mich., 1987).

Muller, R., 'Arminius and the scholastic tradition', *Calvin Theological Journal*, 24 (1989), 263–77.

Muller, R., *God, Creation and Providence in the Thought of Jacob Arminius* (Grand Rapids, 1991).

Muller, R., *Post-Reformation Reformed Dogmatics, Volume II: Holy Scripture, the Cognitive Foundation of Theology* (Grand Rapids, Mich., 1993).

Muller, R., 'The myth of decretal theology', *Calvin Theological Journal*, 30 (1995), 159–67.

Muller, R., 'Calvin and the "Calvinists": assessing continuities and discontinuities between the Reformation and orthodoxy', *Calvin Theological Journal*, 30 (1995), 345–75.

Murray, I. H., *The Puritan Hope: Revival and the Interpretation of Prophecy* (Edinburgh, 1971).

Murray, I. H., 'The Scots at the Westminster Assembly', *The Banner of Truth* (August–September, 1994), 6–40.

Nicole, R., 'John Calvin's view of the extent of the atonement', *Westminster Theological Journal*, 47 (1985), 197–225.

Noll, M., Bebbington, D., and Rawlyk, G., eds., *Evangelicalism: Comparative Studies of Popular Protestantism in North America, the British Isles and Beyond, 1700–1990* (Oxford, 1994).

North, G., *Political Polytheism: The Myth of Pluralism* (Tyler, TX, 1989).

Nuttall, G. F., *The Holy Spirit in Puritan Faith and Experience* (Oxford, 1946).

Nuttall, G. F., 'A transcript of Richard Baxter's library catalogue', *Journal of Ecclesiastical History*, 3 (1952), 74–100.

Oakley, F., 'On the road from Constance to 1688: the political thought of John Major and George Buchanan', *Journal of British Studies*, 1 (1962), 1–31.

Oakley, F., *Omnipotence, Covenant and Order: An Excursion in the History of Ideas from Abelard to Leibniz* (Ithaca, 1984).

Ogilvie, J. D., 'The Kirkcudbright petition of 1637', *Transactions of the Edinburgh Bibliographical Society*, 14 (1926–30), 47–8.

Ogilvie, J. D., 'A bibliography of the Resolutioner–Protester controversy, 1650–59', *Transactions of the Edinburgh Bibliographical Society*, 14 (1930), 57–86.

Ong, W. J., *Ramus, Method, and the Decay of Dialogue: From the Art of Discourse to the Art of Reason* (Cambridge, Mass., 1958).

Packer, J. I., *Among God's Giants: The Puritan Vision of the Christian Life* (Eastbourne, 1991).

Parish, D. L., 'The power of female pietism: women as spiritual authorities and religious role models in seventeenth-century England', *Journal of Religious History*, 17 (1992), 33–45.

Paul, R. S., *The Assembly of the Lord: Politics and Religion in the Westminster Assembly and the 'Grand Debate'* (Edinburgh, 1985).

Pease, T. C., *The Leveller Movement: A Study in the History and Political Theory of the English Great Civil War* (London, 1916).

Pettit, N.,*The Heart Prepared: Grace and Conversion in Puritan Spiritual Life* (New Haven, 1966).

Pierard, R. V., 'Schaeffer on history', in R. Ruesegger, ed., *Reflections on Francis Schaeffer* (Grand Rapids, 1986), pp. 212–19.

Phillipson, N., Review of R. B. Sher and J. Smitten, eds., *Scotland and America in the Age of Enlightenment*, *Historical Journal*, 77 (1992), 433.

Plantinga, A., *The Nature of Necessity* (Oxford, 1974).

Pocock, J. G. A., 'The history of political thought: a methodological inquiry', in P. Laslett and W. G. Runciman, eds., *Philosophy, Politics and Society*, Second series (Oxford, 1962), pp. 183–202.

Pocock, J. G. A., 'Time, history and eschatology in the thought of Thomas Hobbes', in his *Politics, Language and Time* (London, 1972 edn), pp. 148–201.

Pocock, J. G. A., 'England', in O. Ranum, ed., *National Consciousness, History and Political Culture in Early Modern Europe* (London, 1975), pp. 98–117.

Pocock, J. G. A., 'British history: a plea for a new subject', *Journal of Modern History*, 47 (1975), 601–21.

Pocock, J. G. A., 'The limits and divisions of British history: in search of an unknown subject', *American Historical Review*, 87 (1982), 311–36.

Porter, H. C., 'The nose of wax: Scripture and the Spirit from Erasmus to Milton', *Transactions of the Royal Historical Society*, 14 (1964), 155–74.

Porterfield, A., *Female Piety in Puritan New England: The Emergence of Religious Humanism* (Oxford, 1992).

Prozesky, M. H., 'The emergence of Dutch pietism', *Journal of Ecclesiastical History*, 28 (1977), 29–37.

Rainbow, J., *The Will of God and the Cross: An Historical and Theological Study of John Calvin's Doctrine of Limited Redemption* (Allison Park, PN, 1990).

Reid, D., ed., *The Party Coloured Mind: Selected Prose relating to the Conflict between Church and State in Seventeenth-Century Scotland* (Edinburgh, 1982).

Reid, E., 'Prose after Knox', in R. D. S. Jack, ed., *The History of Scottish Literature, Volume I: Origins to 1660* (Aberdeen, 1988).

Rendall, J., *The Origins of Modern Feminism: Women in Britain, France and the United States, 1780–1860* (London, 1985).

Reventlow, H. G., *The Authority of the Bible and the Rise of the Modern World* (London, 1984).

Robertson, G., *Rural Recollections* (Irvine, 1829).

Robertson, J., *The Scottish Enlightenment and the Militia Issue* (Edinburgh, 1985).

Rogers, J. B. and McKim, D. K., *The Authority and Interpretation of the Bible: An Historical Approach* (New York, 1979).

Rolston III, H., *John Calvin versus the Westminster Confession* (Richmond, 1972).

Rose, C., 'Providence, protestant union and godly reformation in the 1690s', *Transactions of the Royal Historical Society*, 6th series, 3 (1993), 151–69.

Rupp, G., 'A devotion of rapture in English Puritanism', in R. B. Knox, ed., *Reformation, Conformity and Dissent: Essays in Honour of Geoffrey Nuttall* (London, 1977), pp. 115–31.

Russell, C., 'The British problem and the English civil war', *History*, 72 (1987), 395–415.

Russell, C., *The Causes of the English Civil War* (Oxford, 1990).

Russell, C., *The Fall of the British Monarchies, 1637–42* (Oxford, 1991).

Salmon, J. H. M., *The French Religious Wars in English Political Thought* (Oxford, 1959).

Sampson, M., 'Laxity and liberty in seventeenth century English political thought', in E. Leites, ed., *Conscience and Casuistry in Early Modern Europe* (Cambridge, 1988), ch. 2.

Sanderson, J., *'But the People's Creatures': The Philosophical Basis of the English Civil War* (Manchester, 1989).

Sanderson, J., 'Conrad Russell's ideas', *History of Political Thought,* 14 (1993), 85–102.

Schmidt, L. E., *Holy Fairs: Scottish Communions and American Revivals in the Early Modern Period* (Princeton, 1989).

Scott, P., *Andrew Fletcher and the Treaty of Union* (Edinburgh, 1992).

Sell, A. P., *The Great Debate: Calvinism, Arminianism and Salvation* (Worthing, 1982).

Sharpe, K., *Politics and Ideas in Early Stuart England: Essays and Studies* (London, 1987).

Sharpe, K., *The Personal Rule of Charles I* (New Haven, 1992).

Shaw, D., ed., *Reformation and Revolution: Essays Presented to Hugh Watt* (Edinburgh, 1967).

Sheils, W. J. and Wood, D., eds., *Voluntary Religion* (Oxford, 1986).

Shepherd, C., 'University life in the seventeenth century', in G. Donaldson, ed., *Four Centuries: Edinburgh University Life, 1583–1983* (Edinburgh, 1983), pp. 1–15.

Sher, R. B., *Church and University in the Scottish Enlightenment: The Moderate Literati of Edinburgh* (Princeton, 1985).

Sher, R. B., 'Witherspoon's "Dominion of Providence" and the Scottish jeremiad tradition', in R. B. Sher and J. R. Smitten, eds., *Scotland and America in the Age of Enlightenment* (Edinburgh, 1990), pp. 46–64.

Sinclair, J., ed., *Statistical Account of Scotland*, III (East Archley, 1979 edn).

Sizar, S., *Gospel Hymns and Social Religions* (Philadelphia, 1978).

Skinner, Q., *The Foundations of Modern Political Thought*, 2 vols. (Cambridge, 1978).

Smart, I. M., 'The political ideas of the Scottish Covenanters, 1638–88', *History of Political Thought*, 1 (1980), 167–93.

Smout, T. C., *A History of the Scottish People, 1560–1830* (London, 1969).

Sommerville, J. P., 'From Suarez to Filmer: a reappraisal', *Historical Journal*, 25 (1982), 525–40.

Sommerville, J. P., *Politics and Ideology in England, 1603–40* (London, 1986).

Sommerville, J. P., 'Oliver Cromwell and English political thought', in J. Morrill, ed., *Oliver Cromwell and the English Revolution* (London, 1990), ch. 9.

Steele, M., 'The "Politick Christian": the theological background to the National Covenant', in J. Morrill, ed., *The Scottish National Covenant in its British Context, 1618–51* (Edinburgh, 1990), pp. 31–67.

Stevenson, D., *The Scottish Revolution, 1637–44: The Triumph of the Covenanters* (Newton Abbott, 1973).

Stevenson, D., 'Conventicles in the kirk, 1619–37: the emergence of a radical party', *Records of the Scottish Church History Society* (1973), 99–114.

Stevenson, D., 'The radical party in the kirk, 1637–45', *Journal of Ecclesiastical History*, 25 (1974), 135–65.

Stevenson, D., 'The General Assembly and the Commission of the kirk, 1638–51', *Records of the Scottish Church History Society*, 19 (1975), 59–79.

Stevenson, D., 'The deposition of ministers in the Church of Scotland under the Covenanters, 1638–51', *Church History*, 44 (1975), 329–32.

Stevenson, D., *Revolution and Counter-Revolution in Scotland, 1644–51* (London, 1977).

Stevenson, D., 'Professor Trevor-Roper and the Scottish revolution', *History Today*, 30 (1980), 34–40.

Stevenson, D., 'The Western Association, 1648–50', *Ayrshire Collections*, 13 (1982), 145–87.

Stevenson, D., 'Scottish church history, 1600–60: a select bibliography', *Records of the Scottish Church History Society*, 21 (1982), 209–20.

Stevenson, D., *The Covenanters* (Edinburgh, 1988).

Stevenson, D., 'Cromwell, Scotland and Ireland', in J. Morrill, ed., *Oliver Cromwell and the English Revolution* (London, 1990), ch. 6.

Stevenson, D., *Kings College, Aberdeen, 1560–1641: From Protestant Reformation to Covenanting Revolution* (Aberdeen, 1990).

Stoever, W. K. B., *'A Faire and Easie Way to Heaven?: Covenant Theology and Antinomianism in Early Massachusetts* (Middletown, Conn., 1978).

Strehle, S., *Calvinism, Federalism, and Scholasticism: A Study in the Reformed Doctrine of the Covenant* (Bern, 1988).

Tamburello, D. E., *Union with Christ: John Calvin and the Mysticism of St Bernard* (Louisville, Ky, 1994).

Tawney, R. H., *Religion and the Rise of Capitalism* (Harmondsworth, 1964 edn).

Thomas, K., 'Women and the Civil War sects', *Past and Present*, 13 (1958), 42–62.

Thomas, K., *Religion and the Decline of Magic: Studies in Popular Beliefs in Sixteenth- and Seventeenth-Century England* (Harmondsworth, 1971).

Thomas, K., 'Cases of conscience in seventeenth-century England', in J. Morrill, P. Slack and D. Woolf, eds., *Public Duty and Private Conscience in Seventeenth-Century England: Essays Presented to G. E. Aylmer* (Oxford, 1993), pp. 29–56.

Todd, M., *Christian Humanism and the Puritan Social Order* (Cambridge, 1987).

Tolmie, M., *The Triumph of the Saints: The Separate Churches of London, 1616–49* (Cambridge, 1977).

Toon, P., ed., *The Emergence of Hyper-Calvinism in English Nonconformity* (London, 1967).

Toon, P., *Puritans, the Millennium and the Future of Israel: Puritan Eschatology, 1600–60* (Cambridge, 1970).

Torrance, J. B., 'Covenant or contract? A study of the theological background of worship in seventeenth-century Scotland', *Scottish Journal of Theology*, 23 (1970), 51–76.

Torrance, J. B., 'The covenant concept in Scottish theology and politics and its legacy', *Scottish Journal of Theology*, 34 (1981), 225–43.

Torrance, J. B., 'Strengths and weaknesses of Westminster theology', in A. Heron, ed., *The Westminster Confession in the Church Today* (Edinburgh, 1982).

Torrance, J. B. 'The incarnation and "limited atonement"', *Evangelical Quarterly*, 55 (1983), 83–94.

Torrance, J. B., 'Interpreting the Word by the light of Christ or the light of nature? Calvin, Calvinism and Barth', in R. V. Schnucker, ed., *Calviniana: Ideas and Influence of Jean Calvin* (Kirksville, Missouri, 1988), pp. 256–67.

Trevor-Roper, H., *Religion, the Reformation and Social Change* (London, 1967).

Trevor-Roper, H., *Catholics, Anglicans and Puritans* (London, 1987).

Tuck, R., 'Power and authority in seventeenth-century England', *Historical Journal*, 17 (1974), 43–61.

Tuck, R., *Natural Rights Theories: Their Origin and Development* (Cambridge, 1979).

Tuck, R., *Hobbes* (Oxford, 1989).

Tuck, R., *Philosophy and Government, 1572–1651* (Cambridge, 1993).

Tully, J., *Meaning and Context: Quentin Skinner and his Critics* (Cambridge, 1988).

Tyacke, N., 'Puritanism, Arminianism and counter-revolution', in C. Russell, ed., *The Origins of the English Civil War* (London, 1973), pp. 119–43.

Tyacke, N., 'Arminianism and English culture', in A. C. Duke and C. A. Tamse, eds., *Britain and the Netherlands, VII: Church and State since the Reformation* (The Hague, 1981).

Tyacke, N., *Anti-Calvinists: The Rise of English Arminianism, c. 1590–1640* (Oxford, 1987).

Tyacke, N., 'Archbishop Laud', in K. Fincham, ed., *The Early Stuart Church* (London, 1993).

Underdown, D., *Revel, Riot and Rebellion: Popular Politics and Culture in England, 1603–60* (Oxford, 1985).

van Ruler, J. A., 'New philosophy and old standards: Voetius' vindication of divine concurrence and secondary causality', *Nederlands Archief voor Kerkgeschiedenis*, 71 (1991), 61–6.

von Rohr, J., *The Covenant of Grace in Puritan Thought* (Atlanta, 1986).

Wakefield, G. S., *Puritan Devotion: Its Place in the Development of Christian Piety* (London, 1957).

Walker, E. C., *William Dell: Master Puritan* (Cambridge, 1970).

Walker, J., *The Theology and Theologians of Scotland, 1560–1750* (Edinburgh, 1985 edn).

Walker, P., *Six Saints of the Covenant* (London, 1901 edn).

Wallace, D., *Puritans and Predestination: Grace in English Protestant Theology, 1525–1695* (Chapel Hill, NC, 1982).

Walzer, M., *The Revolution of the Saints* (Cambridge, Mass., 1965).

Walzer, M., *Exodus and Revolution* (New York, 1985).

Ward, W. R., 'Orthodoxy, Enlightenment and religious revival', in K. Robbins, ed., *Religion and Humanism* (Oxford, 1981), pp. 275–96.

Watkin, E. I., *Poets and Mystics* (London, 1953).

Watt, R., *Bibliotheca Brittanica, or a General Index to British and Foreign Literature*, II (Edinburgh, 1824).

Watts, M., *The Dissenters: From the Reformation to the French Revolution* (Oxford, 1978).

Weber, A., *Teresa of Avila and the Rhetoric of Femininity* (Princeton, 1990).

Weir, D. A., *The Origins of Federal Theology in Sixteenth-Century Reformation Thought* (Oxford, 1990).

Wendel, F., *Calvin: The Origins and Development of his Religious Thought*, trans. P. Mairet (London, 1963).

Westerkamp, M., *Triumph of the Laity: Scots–Irish Piety and the Great Awakening, 1625–1760* (Oxford, 1988).

White, P., 'The rise of Arminianism reconsidered', *Past and Present*, 101 (1983), 34–54.

White, P., *Predestination, Policy and Polemic* (Cambridge, 1992).

Whitehead, J., *The Second American Revolution* (Eglin, IL, 1982).

Whitehead, J., *The Rights of Religious Persons in Public Education* (Wheaton, IL, 1991).

Willen, D., 'Godly women in early modern England: Puritanism and gender', *Journal of Ecclesiastical History*, 43 (1992), 561–80.

Williamson, A. H., *Scottish National Consciousness in the Age of James VI : The Apocalypse, the Union and the Shaping of Scotland's Public Culture* (Edinburgh, 1979).

Williamson, A. H., 'Latter day Judah, latter day Israel: the millennium, the Jews, and the British future', *Pietismus und Neuzeit*, 14 (1988), 149–65.

Williamson, A. H., 'The Jewish dimension of the Scottish apocalypse: climate, covenant and world renewal', in Y. Kaplan, H. Mechoulan and R. H. Popkin, eds., *Menasseh Ben Israel and his World* (Leiden, 1989), pp. 7–30.

Williamson, A. H., 'A patriot nobility? Calvinism, kin-ties, and civic humanism', *Scottish Historical Review*, 72 (1993), 1–21.

Wills, G., 'Evangels of abortion', *New York Review of Books* (15 June 1989), 15–21.

Wills, G., *Under God: Religion and American Politics* (New York, 1990).

Wilson, J. F., *Pulpit in Parliament: Puritanism during the English Civil Wars, 1640–48* (Princeton, 1969).

Woodbridge, J. D., *Biblical Authority: A Critique of the Rogers/McKim Proposal* (Grand Rapids, Mich., 1982).

Woodhouse, A. S. P., *Puritanism and Liberty* (3rd edition: London, 1986).

Wootton, D., 'The fear of God in early modern political theory', *Historical Papers* (1983), 56–80.

Wootton, D., ed., *Divine Right and Democracy: An Anthology of Political Writing in Stuart England* (London, 1986).

Worden, B. 'Toleration and the Cromwellian Protectorate', in W. J. Sheils, ed., *Persecution and Toleration* (Oxford, 1984).

Worden, B., 'Oliver Cromwell and the sin of Achan', in D. Beales and G. Best, eds., *History, Society and the Churches: Essays in Honour of Owen Chadwick* (Cambridge, 1985), pp. 125–45.

Worden, B., 'Providence and politics in Cromwellian England', *Past and Present*, 109 (1985), 55–99.

Wormald, J., *Court, Kirk and Community: Scotland, 1470–1625* (Edinburgh, 1981).

Wormald, J., 'The union of 1603', in R. Mason, ed., *Scots and Britons: Scottish Political Thought and the Union of 1603* (Cambridge, 1994), pp. 17–40.

Wrightson, K., *English Society, 1580–1680* (London, 1982).
Wrightson, K. and Levine, D., *Poverty and Piety in an English Village: Terling 1525–1700* (London, 1979).
Yule, G., *Puritans in Politics: The Religious Legislation of the Long Parliament, 1640–47* (Appleford, 1981).
Zagorin, P., *A History of Political Thought in the English Revolution* (London, 1954).
Zakai, A., *Exile and Kingdom: History and Apocalypse in the Puritan Migration to America* (Cambridge, 1992).
Zaret, D., *The Heavenly Contract: Ideology and Organisation in Pre-Revolutionary Puritanism* (London, 1985).

UNPUBLISHED DISSERTATIONS

Dissertations dealing specifically with Rutherford are listed above in the bibliography of Rutherford.
Dever, M. E., 'Richard Sibbes and "the truly evangelicall Church of England"', unpublished Ph.D. dissertation, University of Cambridge (1991).
Kitshoff, M. C., 'Aspects of Arminianism in Scotland', unpublished M.Th. dissertation, University of St Andrews (1967).
MacKay, W. D. J., 'The nature of church government in the writings of George Gillespie (1613–48)', unpublished Ph.D. dissertation, Queens University, Belfast (1992).
McMahon, G. I. R., 'The Scottish episcopate, 1600–38', unpublished Ph.D. dissertation, University of Birmingham (1972).
Malcolm, N., 'Thomas Hobbes and voluntarist theology', unpublished Ph.D. dissertation, University of Cambridge (1983).
Spear, W. R., 'Covenanted uniformity in religion: the influence of the Scottish commissioners upon the ecclesiology of the Westminster Assembly', unpublished Ph.D. dissertation, University of Pittsburgh (1976).
Yeoman, L. A., 'Heart-work: emotion, empowerment and authority in covenanting times', unpublished Ph.D. dissertation, University of St Andrews, (1991).

INDEX

Aberdeen 36, 43, 60, 87, 88, 200
  Doctors 43, 47, 76, 194, 196, 241
  Independents 58, 221–2
  Rutherford in 45–8
Achan 250
Act of Classes (1649) 55–6, 249, 251
Act of Revocation (1625) 41
Act of Union (1707) 21
Adamson, John 34, 37–8, 49, 66–7
adiapora 188, 194
Afflect, Andrew 51
Ahab, King 169
Allan, D. 24, 71
Allen, J. W. 16
Almain, Jacques 74, 158
Alsted, Johann 237, 238
Althusius, Johannes 180, 183, 218
Ambrose 73–4, 209
America 11–15, 257
  see also New England
Ames, William 95
Amyraut, Moise 121–3, 127, 141
An Apologeticall Narration 203
Anabaptists
  English sects compared to 72, 135, 206,
    212–13
  Scotland's radical Presbyterians compared
    to 192, 223
Antichrist 46, 90, 96, 150, 230–2, 237–47,
  255
antiformalism 70, 85, 188–9, 213–14, 218–19
anti-intellectualism, sectarian 70, 79, 217
Antinomianism 4, 53, 71–2, 79, 90, 131,
  134–9, 144, 212–13
Anwoth 1, 7, 39–45, 48, 49, 99, 112, 193, 197
apocalypticism 16, 20, 24, 88–9, 227, 230,
  236–47, 254–5
Aquinas, Thomas 74, 117, 124, 153, 154
Argyll, Earl of 3, 41, 60, 97–8, 149, 151,
  226, 235
aristocracy 173–4, 184

  see also nobility
Aristotelianism 63–71, 77–9, 117, 159, 174
Aristotle 34, 63–8, 70–1, 147, 152
Arminianism 7, 20, 168, 192, 228
  and the origins of the British troubles 140–2
  attacked by Rutherford 3, 34, 41–3, 47,
    119–21, 138–40
  attributed to ignorance of the power of
    grace 84
  used as a synonym for Laudianism 45, 193
Arminius, Jacob 119, 140
Armstrong, B. 71
Ashe, Simeon 59
assurance, the doctrine of 132, 136–8
Athanasius 74
atonement
  extent of 121–3, 136–7, 141
  not strictly necessary according to
    Rutherford 129–30
Augustine
  champion of grace 73
  critic of Donatists 206
  defender of persecution 218
  opponent of millenarianism 236–8
Augustinianism 73, 74, 83, 84, 96, 117, 126
  under attack in Catholic and Protestant
    Europe 117–19, 123–4

Bacon, Sir Francis 76, 131
Baillie, Robert 38, 43, 48, 49, 52, 53, 59, 60,
  69, 142, 197, 204, 238
  differs with Rutherford 200, 202, 204,
    223–4
Baker, J. W. 139
Balfour, Sir James 3, 38, 51
Balmerino, Lord 44, 46, 235
Báñez, Domingo 75, 124, 126
baptism
  infant 167, 206, 210
  private 35, 191
  Roman Catholic 206

295

Cambridge Studies in Early Modern British History

Titles in the series

Exile and Kingdom: History and Apocalypse in the Puritan Migration to America
AVIHU ZAKAI
The Pillars of Priestcraft Shaken: The Church of England and its Enemies, 1660–1730
J. A. I. CHAMPION
Stewards, Lords and People: The Estate Steward and his World in Later Stuart England
D. R. HAINSWORTH
Civil War and Restoration in the Three Stuart Kingdoms: The Career of Randal MacDonnell, Marquis of Antrim, 1609–1683
JANE H. OHLMEYER
The Family of Love in English Society, 1550–1630
CHRISTOPHER W. MARSH
The Bishops' Wars: Charles I's Campaigns against Scotland, 1638–1640*
MARK FISSEL
John Locke: Resistance, Religion and Responsibility*
JOHN MARSHALL
Constitutional Royalism and the Search for Settlement, c. 1640–1649
DAVID L. SMITH
Intelligence and Espionage in the Reign of Charles II, 1660–1685
ALAN MARSHALL
The Chief Governors: The Rise and Fall of Reform Government in Tudor Ireland, 1536–1588
CIARAN BRADY
Politics and Opinions in Crisis, 1678–1681
MARK KNIGHTS
Catholic and Reformed: The Roman and Protestant Churches in English Protestant Thought, 1604–1640
ANTHONY MILTON
Sir Matthew Hale, 1609–1676: Law, Religion and Natural Philosophy
ALAN CROMARTIE
Henry Parker and the English Civil War: The Political Thought of the Public's 'Privado'
MICHAEL MENDLE
Protestantism and Patriotism: Ideologies and the Making of English Foreign Policy, 1650–1668
STEVEN C. A. PINCUS
Gender in Mystical and Occult Thought: Behmenism and its Development in England
B. J. GIBBONS
William III and the Godly Revolution
TONY CLAYDON
Law-Making and Society in Late Elizabethan England: The Parliament of England, 1584–1601
DAVID DEAN

9 780521 893190